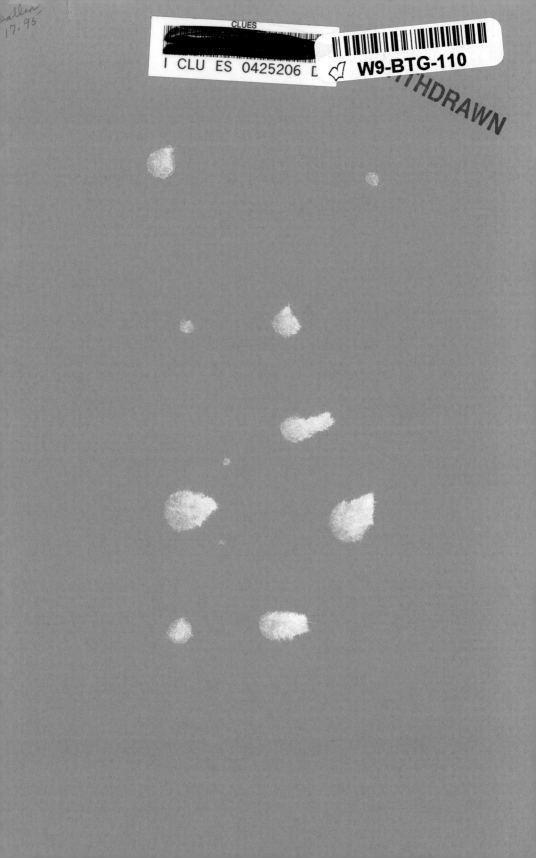

RENAISSANCE DRAMA

New Series VIII ❧ *1977*

Renaissance Drama

NEW SERIES VIII

The Celebratory Mode

Edited by Leonard Barkan

Northwestern University Press

EVANSTON 1977

THE ILLUSTRATION on the front cover is "H. E.," "Queen Elizabeth and the Three Goddesses" (1569). Reproduced by courtesy of H. M. the Queen.

THE ILLUSTRATION on the back cover is *Le Soir* by Michel van Lochon. Courtesy of the Bibliothèque Nationale, Cabinet des Estampes. Paris.

Publication of this volume was made possible by a grant from the College of Arts and Sciences, Northwestern University.

Editorial Note

The Italian festivals in their best form mark the point of transition from real life into the world of art.

JACOB BURCKHARDT,
The Civilization of the Renaissance in Italy

RENAISSANCE DRAMA, an annual publication, provides a forum for scholars in various parts of the globe: wherever the drama of the Renaissance is studied. Coverage, so far as subject matter is concerned, is not restricted to any single national theater. The chronological limits of the Renaissance are interpreted liberally, and space is available for essays on precursors, as well as on the use of Renaissance themes by later writers. Editorial policy favors articles of some scope. Essays that are exploratory in nature, that are concerned with critical or scholarly methodology, that raise new questions or embody fresh approaches to perennial problems are particularly appropriate for a publication that originated from the proceedings of the Modern Language Association Conference on Research Opportunities in Renaissance Drama.

It should come as no surprise that *Renaissance Drama* has often turned its attention to the celebratory mode. On the one hand, we have the testimony of no less an authority than Jacob Burckhardt that pageants, ceremonies, and celebrations were an essential, virtually a defining feature of the Italian Renaissance. On the other hand, we have the certain fact that mimetic drama as we know it evolved from rituals of celebration. So the celebratory mode becomes a nexus in which both *Renaissance* and *Drama* find their origins.

A closer look at the celebratory mode in the Renaissance reveals that it represents a nexus in other ways as well. Consider the word "celebratory": what is being celebrated in the dramatic mode? If we were looking at those beginnings of drama mentioned above (whether in ancient Greece or in Medieval Europe), it would be clear that the participants were all celebrating God. Indeed the very concept of celebrating a mass reminds us of this connection. The sixteenth and seventeenth centuries witness a decisive shift, for now it is most often the monarch who is celebrated. Celebration never completely loses sight of its religious origins, and yet it becomes a highly charged medium of political statement. And if we moderns tend to characterize political drama as direct, hard-hitting, and realistic, we must face the fact that the celebratory mode of the Renaissance embodies some of the most untrammeled flights of poetic fancy, some of the most purely aesthetic impulses to be observed in the whole period. Here, then, is a mode of drama that is religious in its heritage, political in its content, and fantastical in its techniques.

Finally—and here we betray our somewhat ethnocentric concentration on England—the celebratory mode is a nexus because in its variety of manifestations it appeals to and is written for a considerable range of social classes. What might delight King James in Westminster would in another form and a couple of miles to the east be offered up to please the burghers of the City and in yet another form be presented for the delectation of the gentry on their country estates. Indeed in some notable examples a single drama of celebration might combine all these appeals.

The essays that follow ought to speak for themselves. They are intended to represent a wide range of analytical and historical techniques and as wide a range of subjects. Taken individually or as a whole, they demonstrate how the celebratory mode bridges the gap between religion and monarchy, politics and aesthetics, high style and low style, and, as Burckhardt perceived, between life and art.

The Editor gratefully acknowledges many debts in the production of this volume. He is fortunate in riding on the coattails of three distinguished predecessors, who have all been enormously helpful: S. Schoenbaum, Alan Dessen, and Joel Kaplan. Without the help, both intellectual and practical, of Douglas Cole this book could not have appeared, and similar warm thanks are due to David Bevington, A. R. Braunmuller,

D. Allan Gray, Richard Peterson, and Frank Whigham. Finally, the award for being the most indispensable person of all goes to *RD's* administrative assistant, Tina T. Flanigan.

Volume IX of *Renaissance Drama* is concerned with "Renaissance Drama in the Theater," and it will include essays on such subjects as modern revivals of Renaissance dramas, Jonson's stagecraft, Hamlet's "O, o, o, o," Shakespeare's audience, performances of *Henry VI,* Elizabethan productions of Seneca, and stage violence.

The topic of Volume X is "The Theory and Practice of Comedy in the Renaissance." Manuscripts, for which the deadline is 28 February 1978, should be sent to Professor Leonard Barkan, Department of English, Northwestern University, Evanston, Illinois 60201. Prospective contributors are requested to follow the recommendations of the *MLA Style Sheet* (revised edition) in preparing manuscripts.

Contents

.

Louis Adrian Montrose *Celebration and Insinuation: Sir Philip Sidney and the Motives of Elizabethan Courtship* 3

Gordon Kipling *Triumphal Drama: Form in English Civic Pageantry* 37

Bruce R. Smith *Landscape with Figures: The Three Realms of Queen Elizabeth's Country-house Revels* 57

Judith Doolin Spikes *The Jacobean History Play and the Myth of the Elect Nation* 117

Paula Johnson *Jacobean Ephemera and the Immortal Word* 151

Alice S. Miskimin *Ben Jonson and Captain Cox: Elizabethan Gothic Reconsidered* 173

Michael McCanles *Festival in Jonsonian Comedy* 203

Mary C. Williams Merlin and the Prince: *The Speeches at Prince Henry's Barriers* 221

Jeffrey Fischer Love Restored: *A Defense of Masquing* 231

Cedric C. Brown *Milton's* Arcades: *Context, Form, and Function* 245

Timothy C. Murray *Richelieu's Theater: The Mirror of a Prince* 275

Notes on Contributors 299

ix

RENAISSANCE DRAMA

New Series VIII ❧ *1977*

Celebration and Insinuation: Sir Philip Sidney and the Motives of Elizabethan Courtship

LOUIS ADRIAN MONTROSE

R ENAISSANCE LITERARY THEORISTS customarily note an analogy between the sacred psalm or hymn of praise ("the first forme of Poesie and the highest & the stateliest") and poetic celebrations of earthly rulers ("a second degree of laude: shewing their high estates, their Princely genealogies and pedigrees, mariages, aliances, and such noble exploites, as they have done in th'affaires of peace & of warre to the benefit of their people and countries").[1] This analogy of sacred and secular encomia is strengthened when the incarnation of temporal authority and power happens to be a virgin queen who is head of both state and church, and whose personal mythology is contrived to be a national and Protestant substitute for a cult of the Blessed Virgin.[2] An imperial mythology, infused with the conventions of Petrarchism and enhanced by metaphysical sanctions

---

1. *The Arte of English Poesie* [1589], ed. Gladys Doidge Willcock and Alice Walker (Cambridge, 1936), pp. 30, 35. I accept the editors' ascription of this work to George Puttenham. Further references will be to this edition, cited as "Puttenham, *Arte.*" I have modernized Elizabethan typographic conventions.

2. On the policy and iconography of the Elizabeth cult, see Frances A. Yates, *Astraea: The Imperial Theme in the Sixteenth Century* (London, 1974).

3

deriving from Neo-Platonism, gives to celebrations of Queen Elizabeth a unique richness of allusion. The relationship between courtier-poets and queen is idealized as a love purified of physical desire; its erotic energy has been transformed into art and service. Because authority is incarnated in a woman, the mythological projection of the prevailing ideology can merge the idealization of a power relationship with an idealized relationship of love. The public ritualizations of intimate relationship manifested in pageants, processions, masques, tilts, orations, and other royal entertainments affirm and celebrate a strong and beautiful union between the ruler and her subjects. Royal pageantry serves as an instrument of internal and international policy, as a romantic mystification of the motives of the queen and her privy council. But royal celebrations can also function as idealizations of the motives of the queen's poet-courtiers: the grace that the faithful worshiper hopes from his goddess is preferment.

I. Persuasion and Manipulation

Of the younger generation of Elizabethan men who came to maturity in the 1580s and 1590s, those within the ambience of the court—aristocrats, lesser gentry, common-born but university educated writers and servant-bureaucrats—have been characterized as a generation "of high aspiration, revealed most commonly in intense personal ambition." [3] The generations of Burghley and Elizabeth had experienced directly and intensely the rigors, crises, and chaos of the mid-Tudor period; in later life, they came to enshrine the virtues of moderation and increasingly to inveigh against the inherent evil and self-destructiveness of overweening ambition. Men of the younger generation were raised in the relative tranquility of Elizabethan compromise politics, stirred by the currents of the continental Renaissance and by widening geographic horizons, comparatively well-educated in preparation for public careers, and exposed early to the new opulence of the English court. This "generation of 1560" came to revalue aspiration in all its endeavors.

3. Anthony Esler, *The aspiring mind of the Elizabethan younger generation* (Durham, N.C., 1966). The following two paragraphs are directly indebted to Esler's analysis.

Aspiration was focused on courtship of the queen in a reciprocal relationship of service and reward. Honors, power, and wealth were the personal goals that the younger Elizabethan aristocracy most ardently pursued; the baseborn writers who were their contemporaries pursued analogous goals within an appropriately narrowed and lowered range. These ambitions encountered various impediments: the hostility of a politically cautious and socially conservative older generation of power brokers; the ever-present possibilities of personal failure, of ungracious and even fatal performances, in the topsy-turvy worlds of military, political, financial, and amorous affairs; and, most critically, the severely limited resources of the crown for the bestowal of preferments, the queen's conservative fiscal policies, and her parsimonious character.

In a masterful essay on Elizabethan patronage, Wallace MacCaffrey concludes that, although "the successful distribution of patronage" was one of the conditions upon which "the imposing stability of the Elizabethan regime depended," it nevertheless "lacked adequate safeguards against a free-for-all scramble for spoils."

Yet, in judging the regime as a whole, high praise must be given for the transformation of English political habits which was accomplished during these years. By the end of the reign Englishmen were turning away from their bad old habits of conspiracy and treason—the resort to force as the final arbiter in politics. Under the tutelage of Burghley and his royal mistress they had learned the peaceful, if sometimes corrupt, habits of a new political order. They had mastered the subtler arts of persuasion and manipulation.[4]

Life within the Elizabethan court and on its margins was characterized by intrigue, backbiting, and bribery; by intense competition for personal and political influence, office, prestige, and income. This strife was

4. Wallace T. MacCaffrey, "Place and Patronage in Elizabethan Politics," in *Elizabethan Government and Society,* ed. S. T. Bindoff, J. Hurstfield, and C. H. Williams (London, 1961), pp. 95-126; I quote from pp. 125-126. See also the chapter on "Office and the Court" in Lawrence Stone's magisterial work, *The Crisis of the Aristocracy 1558-1641* (Oxford, 1965), pp. 385-504. On matters of literary patronage, see: John Buxton, *Sir Philip Sidney and the English Renaissance,* 2d ed. (London, 1964); Edwin Haviland Miller, *The Professional Writer in Elizabethan England* (Cambridge, Mass., 1959), pp. 94-135; Eleanor Rosenberg, *Leicester, Patron of Letters* (New York, 1955); J. W. Saunders, *The Profession of English Letters* (London, 1964), pp. 31-92.

partially controlled by the imposition of collective aesthetic forms on unruly personal energies.

Courtly cultural forms functioned to impose some order upon the forces of chaos within the court system at the same time that they facilitated manipulation of the system to personal advantage. Puttenham provides an unusually candid contemporary poetic and rhetorical analysis of these forms and their functions. Consider his englishing of the figure *Allegoria* as "the Courtier or figure of faire semblant." [5]

> The courtly figure *Allegoria* . . . is when we speake one thing and thinke another, and that our wordes and our meanings meete not. The use of this figure is so large, and his vertue of so great efficacie as it is supposed no man can pleasantly utter and perswade without it, but in effect is sure never or very seldome to thrive and prosper in the world, that cannot skilfully put in use, in so much as not onely every common Courtier, but also the gravest Counsellour, yea and the most noble and wisest Prince of them all are many times enforced to use it.
>
> (p. 186)

In Puttenham's "figure of faire semblant," Castiglione's Courtier masks Machiavelli's Fox. Puttenham's "Courtly figure *Allegoria*" operates as a synecdoche for his own text: a treatise on poetics masks an exemplary handbook on the conduct of relations among courtiers and between courtier and prince. Puttenham teaches vital strategies of persuasion and manipulation for survival and success in a complicated, dangerous, and highly competitive social world.

Symbolic pageantry, poetry, drama, music, dance, and visual iconography enhance a ritualistic system of rules for decorum and deference. They also proffer culturally refined media in which the queen's courtly celebrants can variously express, explore, prosecute, obfuscate, and sublimate both their idealistic personal aspirations and their material ambitions. Both as *texts* and as *events,* Elizabethan entertainments encourage us to explore the interaction of art with life, of cultural forms with social forces, of celebration with manipulation and persuasion. In what follows, I study how a uniquely gifted young gentleman-courtier-poet exploits the occasions of royal entertainment less to praise than to oppose, instruct,

5. Puttenham, *Arte,* p. 299.

and petition his queen. The extant *texts* of Philip Sidney's royal entertainments are distillates of the literary, biographical, and sociopolitical processes in which they were originally conceived, presented, and experienced; as historical *events,* these performed entertainments were integral elements in the dialectic of Elizabethan social reality. By analyzing what and how Sidney's entertainments signify, we may better understand the Elizabethan uses of celebration.

II. Life and Art

The Renaissance courtly style endeavored to obliterate the distinction between life and art. To many in the late Elizabethan and Jacobean periods, Philip Sidney incarnated this ideal. Well before his early death, he had already been mythologized by his family, friends, and political allies, and by the beneficiaries of his generous patronage. Sidney's few public addresses and public acts are full of a resolute and uncompromising idealism that Queen Elizabeth undoubtedly found willful and potentially dangerous. His substantial literary work, however, is not an unreflective and naïve projection of idealism but rather an interplay of ideals and actualities, reason and the infirmity of will, personal aspiration and the circumstantial impediments to its full expression. Sidney was a literary "amateur," whose great expectation was not to decorate the court but to profess arms and statecraft; he had been trained for a brilliant and central role in the pageant of English, and, indeed, European, affairs. In his life, as well as in his art, Sidney was in a position to actualize rhetorical and poetic *topoi;* to live out the ubiquitous humanist debate about the relative merits of action and contemplation, the major literary dialectic of heroic and pastoral kinds. As a poet and defender of poetry, Sidney was concerned to use the imaginative act of fiction-making as an intellectual instrument to clarify motives and options on the world's stage, where he was—or, at least, hoped to be—an actor. Lesser-born patronage poets were, for the most part, mere spectators at the living theater of the Elizabethan court.

The unsuccessful pursuit of influence, office, and income that characterizes Philip Sidney's brief career is epitomized in the slight but suggestive pastoral entertainment known as *The Lady of May*.[6] What we have is the transcribed text of a show performed before Queen Elizabeth in the garden of the earl of Leicester's estate at Wanstead (which had been a gift from the queen) in May of 1578 or, possibly, 1579.[7] Sidney created his royal show at a critical point in his own, his family's, and his

---

6. Like most Renaissance entertainments, *The Lady of May* (*LM*) is generically hybrid. Stephen Orgel, *The Jonsonian Masque* (Cambridge, Mass., 1965), writes that *LM* "is conceived in terms of the masque" (p. 45), and discusses it (pp. 44–55) in the context of the evolution of the Stuart masque. Robert Kimbrough and Philip Murphy, "The Helmingham Hall Manuscript of Sidney's *The Lady of May*: A Commentary and Transcription" (*RenD*, N.S. 1 [1968], pp. 103–119) identify *LM* as a mix of the "pseudo-dramatic pageants" Sidney probably witnessed at Kenilworth during the celebrated Progress of 1575, and the *commedia rusticale*, a "popular kind of farce" that he may have seen in Italy during his grand tour (p. 104). As Kimbrough and Murphy observe, this typology does not account for the pervasive pastoral themes and conventions in *LM*. Sidney's slight pastoral must, in fact, share primacy of place with Spenser's massive, contemporaneous effort (*The Shepheardes Calender*, 1579) in the history of English pastoral literature. William Ringler, Jr., in his edition of *The Poems of Sir Philip Sidney* (Oxford, 1962), calls *LM* "the earliest example in English of conventionalized pastoral drama" (p. 361) (to be cited as "Sidney, *Poems*"). I would add that we should credit Sidney with having developed the dramaturgical possibilities latent in the eclogue, the poetic kind that Puttenham classed with satire, comedy, and tragedy as morally reprehensible and educative *"drammatick* poems" (*Arte*, p. 38). In its presentation of shepherds and foresters, its rustic setting, its sophisticated treatment of the pastoral *topos* of contemplation and action (as well as in its structural exploitation of pastoral devices of song, contest, and dialogue), *LM* demonstrates its generic affinity to the eclogue.

7. *The Lady of May* received its title in the 1725 edition of Sidney's works. There are two extant substantive texts: the version printed with the 1598 edition of *Arcadia*, rpt. in *The Prose Works of Sir Philip Sidney*, ed. Albert Feuillerat, 4 vols. (1912; rpt. Cambridge, 1968), II, 208–217 (to be cited as "Sidney, *Prose Works*"); and a manuscript recently published in Kimbrough and Murphy, "The Helmingham Hall Manuscript," pp. 107–119. My citations of *LM* are from the modernized text in *Miscellaneous Prose of Sir Philip Sidney*, ed. Katherine Duncan-Jones and Jan van Dorsten (Oxford, 1973), pp. 21–32 (to be cited as "Sidney, *Miscellaneous Prose*"). This edition uses the 1598 version as copy text but incorporates readings from the Helmingham Hall manuscript, notably a final speech by Rombus for which this manuscript is the sole authority.

The queen visited Wanstead in May of both 1578 and 1579. Ringler (Sidney, *Poems*, p. 362) favors "the spring of 1578 as the date of composition and presentation" on stylistic grounds; Kimbrough and Murphy accept this dating. John Nichols, *The Progresses and Public Processions of Queen Elizabeth*, new ed., 3

faction's fortunes; analysis of its meaning must proceed in a historical context.

In June 1577, a year before the performance of *The Lady of May*, Philip Sidney returned from an embassy to the leaders of continental Protestant forces. Still in his mid-twenties, Sidney seemed to have made a brilliant start on the diplomatic and military career for which he had been so carefully groomed. He was to wait eight years for his next important commission, one that would take him to his death. A recent biographer of Sidney's early maturity has speculated that the dislike and distrust Elizabeth henceforth would show toward him began in the wake of his personal triumph among the Dutch: she was concerned that the desire of William of Orange to have Sidney as his son-in-law and military commander would not only jeopardize her delicately balanced foreign policy but might eventuate in her subject becoming ruler of a united, independent Netherlands and the Dudley faction's candidate to be her own successor.[8] Whether or not we wholly assent to this hypothesis, it does justly convey the irony that pervades the rest of Sidney's life: a nearly universal recognition of his enormous promise, and a royal distrust sufficient to keep that promise from opportunities for fulfillment.

In the months following Sidney's return, royal enthusiasm for a Protestant League faded away; no further preferments were forthcoming to advance Sidney's career and to relieve his financial embarrassment; Count Casimir's request for money, troops, and Sidney's services in the

---

vols. (1823; rpt. New York, 1966), reprints *LM* (II, 94–103) and assigns it to 1578. Duncan-Jones and van Dorsten maintain that "the evidence on neither side seems strong enough for one to make a firm decision between the two years" (Sidney, *Miscellaneous Prose*, p. 13). I accept the conclusion that 1578 is more likely, but my argument does not depend upon its certainty.

8. See James M. Osborn, *Young Philip Sidney 1572–1577* (New Haven, Conn., 1972), pp. 496–498. Fulke Greville's *Life of the Renowned Sir Philip Sidney* (written ca. 1610–1614; printed, 1652; rpt., with an introduction by Nowell Smith, Oxford, 1907) is the incomparable primary source of information and commentary on Sidney and his milieu. (References will be to the 1907 reprint, cited in my text as "Greville, *Life*.") In addition to the work of Osborn, the following modern biographical studies have been valuable sources of fact and interpretation: Roger Howell, *Sir Philip Sidney: The Shepherd Knight* (Boston, 1968); Malcolm William Wallace, *The Life of Sir Philip Sidney* (1915; rpt. New York, 1967); Richard A. Lanham, "Sidney: The Ornament of his Age," *SoRA*, II (1967), 319–340; F. J. Levy, "Philip Sidney Reconsidered," *ELR*, II (1972), 5–18.

Netherlands campaign got no affirmative response from the queen; Sir Henry Sidney, Philip's father and one of Elizabeth's longest and hardest-working but poorest-rewarded administrators, was recalled from his thankless task in Ireland. In addition to all these private and public sources of frustration and concern, the project of Elizabeth's marriage to the duke of Alençon, brother to the French king, now began to loom as a serious possibility. Negotiations reached a climax between 1578 and 1580; these years saw a decline in the prestige and influence of the Leicester-Walsingham faction, who most bitterly opposed the match within the councils of state.

The critical year 1579 saw the anonymous publication of John Stubbs's stridently anti-Catholic and patriotic *Gaping Gulf,* for which he lost his right hand in the marketplace at Westminster; the anonymous publication of Spenser's *Shepheardes Calender,* whose religiopolitical allegories seem to have earned Spenser the enmity of Lord Burghley; and the manuscript circulation of "A Letter written by Sir Philip Sidney to Queen Elizabeth, touching Her Marriage with Monsieur," which angered the queen and provoked Sidney's retirement from court. It has sometimes been suggested that Sidney's *Lady of May,* like Spenser's *Shepheardes Calendar,* uses a pastoral mask to express strong but dangerous opinions on the burning issue of the royal marriage and its religious and political implications. Arguments that *The Lady of May* is a topical allegory about the Alençon affair lack substantiation and fail to convince; nevertheless, the relationship of the crisis to Sidney's personal convictions and aspirations forms part of the context of meanings for *The Lady of May.* Sidney's royal entertainment attempts to define and advance his place in the Elizabethan body politic, and his relationship to the queen, in the light of those recent and ongoing developments and disappointments that I have been enumerating. In his "Letter to Queen Elizabeth," Sidney is bold—too bold—in claiming the courtier's right and duty to offer counsel to his prince; in *The Lady of May,* he dons the mask of pastoral entertainer in order, "under the vaile of homely persons, and in rude speeches to insinuate and glaunce at greater matters, and such as perchance had not bene safe to have beene disclosed in any other sort." [9]

Between 1577 and 1580, Sidney spent much of his time away from the

9. Puttenham, *Arte,* p. 38.

court, living a life of what his Protestant humanist friend and mentor, Hubert Languet, delicately called "dignified ease." Sidney's persistent attempts to gain patronage and to influence government policy were wholly unsuccessful. He appears to have heeded Languet's advice, if only reluctantly and sporadically: "Persevere as long as you can do anything that may benefit your country, but when you find that your opposition only draws on you dislike and aversion . . . give way to necessity and reserve yourself for better times." [10] In his partly sought, partly enforced, pastoral retirement at his sister's estate at Wilton, Sidney wrote analytical pastorals—*The Lady of May* and the original *Arcadia*—to cope imaginatively with necessities and to prepare for better times. He also maintained a personal correspondence, of which the following letter to Languet, written in March 1578, may have been contemporaneous with the composition of *The Lady of May*:

My mind itself, if it was ever active in any thing, is now beginning, by reason of my indolent ease, imperceptibly to lose its strength, and to relax without any reluctance. For to what purpose should our thoughts be directed to various kinds of knowledge, unless room be afforded for putting it into practice, so that public advantage may be the result, which in a corrupt age we cannot hope for? Who would learn music except for the sake of giving pleasure? or architecture except with a view to building? But the mind itself, you will say, that particle of the divine mind, is cultivated in this manner. This indeed, if we allow it to be the case, is a very great advantage: but let us see whether we are not giving a beautiful but false appearance to our splendid errors. For while the mind is thus, as it were, drawn out of itself, it cannot turn its powers inward for thorough self-examination; to which employment no labour that men can undertake, is any way to be compared. Do you not see that I am cleverly playing the stoic? yea and I shall be a cynic too, unless you reclaim me.[11]

Sidney writes in the *serio ludere* tone of Renaissance humanists; it is the attitude which, in another letter to Languet, Sidney calls "that seemly play of humour that is so natural . . . in the characters of some of the wisest men." [12] Sidney starts from his central commitment to the fruition

---

10. *The Correspondence of Sir Philip Sidney and Hubert Languet,* ed. Steuart A. Pears (London, 1845), p. 170. In further references, this text will be cited as "Sidney, *Correspondence.*"

11. *Ibid.,* p. 143.

12. *Ibid.,* p. 65.

in action of study, training, and self-cultivation; then he asks, what is the use of right knowing which is prevented from eventuating in right doing? He rejects the answer that knowledge has intrinsic value, that the readiness is all—such would be mere self-deception. His own response to these frustrations, so he writes, is to lapse into an *otium* of moral and intellectual vitiation. This pose of self-debasement he then maneuvers into an ethically tenable pose of inward-turning contemplation. Despite the personal, ethical preoccupations of Sidney's wit in this passage, there is no mistaking the sociopolitical source of his predicament: the difficulty of achieving a union of *gnosis* and *praxis* "in a corrupt age." [13] Sidney's mind moves lightly over precisely those issues which, within two months, will be dramatized in Wanstead garden before the queen.

In its mode of presentation, *The Lady of May* fuses life and art: as the queen walks in Wanstead garden, she is confronted by a group of rustics who ask her to judge between the suitors of the country maiden who is the May Lady. The queen has descended into the pastoral province of her domains; the rustic world of Leicester's country estate has been transmuted into courtly art. The May Lady is a character engaged in playing an elevated and temporary role in a folk rite; though only the daughter of "an honest man's wife of the country" (p. 20), she is able to tell the queen that "no estate can be compared to be the Lady of the whole month of May, as I am" (p. 24). She abases herself before the queen, however, because she knows instinctively that "you excel me in that wherein I desire most to excel" (p. 24). This pastoral fiction contains within it a rustic world with its own ritual observances and ideals; the living queen is the fictional May Lady's transcendent Idea. The opening supplication to the queen is followed by the entrance of "six shepherds, with as many fosters, haling and pulling to whether side they should draw the Lady of May, who seemed to incline neither to the one nor other side" (p. 22). The queen is witnessing a dramatized debate which, like any serious Renaissance art, demands interpretation and application by its audience: "In judging me," the May Lady tells the queen, "you judge more than me in it" (p. 30). Sidney's entertainment thus an-

13. This letter is interpreted with a different emphasis, as a context for the Arcadian poems, in Neil L. Rudenstine, *Sidney's Poetic Development* (Cambridge, Mass., 1967), pp. 7–8, 289–290.

nounces itself as an embodiment of the pastoral formula that William Empson calls "putting the complex into the simple." [14] An allegorical equation is made between the dynamics of fictive pastoral courtship and those of actual royal courtship. The active role of the royal spectator is to comprehend the relationship between simple and complex. By rendering judgment in the simplified courtship of the May Lady, Queen Elizabeth is led by analogy to a particular judgment about the conduct of her own complex and conflict-ridden courtier system.

Therion, a lively forester, and Espilus, a rich shepherd, contend for the May Lady's hand in marriage:

Therion doth me many pleasures, as stealing me venison out of these forests, and many other such like pretty and prettier services; but withal he grows to such rages, that sometimes he strikes me, sometimes he rails at me. This shepherd, Espilus, of a mild disposition, as his fortune hath not been to do me great service, so hath he never done me any wrong; but feeding his sheep, sitting under some sweet bush, sometimes, they say, he records my name in doleful verses. Now the question I am to ask you, fair lady, is whether the many deserts and many faults of Therion, or the very small deserts and no faults of Espilus be to be preferred.

(p. 25)

In the tradition of the eclogue, Therion challenges Espilus to a singing contest in which they demonstrate their natures: the "dialogue" consists of Therion's challenge and his undercutting of each successive stanza that Espilus sings. Espilus (whose sheep farming is on the scale of a major Elizabethan landholder) compares the lady to the two thousand sheep he owns; he courts her acquisitively: "Let me possess thy grace." Therion contrasts her to the two thousand deer he hunts but does not own: "Them I can take, but you I cannot hold" (p. 26). *The Lady of May* associates the forester figure with a freely given, though boldly self-reliant, love of service, and insinuates that the shepherd's life of pastoral *otium* is merely self-serving and small-minded. Espilus is a voluptuary masking as a contemplative; the role of the contemplative who seeks to guide the actions of others by his wisdom is parodied in the figure of Rhombus, a pedantic country schoolmaster whose attempts to arbitrate the debate are rendered absurdly ineffectual by his own obscurantism.

14. *Some Versions of Pastoral* (1935; rpt. New York, 1968), p. 22.

The decision must ultimately reside with the queen, whose own humanist education has prepared her for the judicious exercise of power.

The pastoral entertainment is an allegorical microcosm of the Elizabethan court; in a sense, it temporarily becomes the court, by virtue of the queen's presence and participation. It is in this context that Sidney presents to his royal mistress a choice of exemplary courtiers. His intention is not merely to entertain and compliment the queen. True to his conception of literature as a moral rhetoric, he attempts to manipulate her responses in such a way as to persuade her to choose his kind of courtier for her own. Politic Elizabethan poets spend their wit in praising their royal mistress, not in trying to educate her; ingenuous Sidney is unusually restrained in his courtly compliments and in the business of idolatry but downright audacious in the giving of unsolicited advice. An aspiring statesman and a potentially brilliant poet and defender of poetry, Sidney is doomed to endure a royal aesthetic which prescribes that courtly makers should strive to please but never presume to instruct. Although both *The Lady of May* and the nearly contemporaneous "Letter . . . to Queen Elizabeth, touching her marriage with Monsieur" are written at the behest of the earl of Leicester, Sidney is not writing merely as his elders' tool but in service of his own ideological commitments and personal ambitions. In judging between the May Lady's alternatives, the queen has to judge what mode of courtship is truly in her own and her state's best interests. As in the court masque, here the royal personage is much more than the chief auditor and spectator of the work; she is the leading player, who must perfect the entertainment's open form. When the May Lady tells Elizabeth, "In judging me, you judge more than me in it," the implication is that the queen's judgment will be a judgment upon her own wisdom. From one perspective, the queen infolds the pageant; from another perspective, the pageant encompasses the queen.

The judgment asked of the queen requires a transformation of the traditional values inherent in the conventions that the entertainment employs. Elizabeth is being presented with a variant of the Judgment of Paris, a device often used to turn compliments to Tudor royalty. Goddesslike, the queen is an ultimate arbiter of the choice that the May Lady cannot make; at the conclusion of the judgment, Elizabeth will have proved herself (as Rhombus puts it), "Juno, Venus, Pallas *et profecto plus*" (p. 31). Thus, Sidney's entertainment utilizes the strategy of praise that will shortly become the *coup de théâtre* of George Peele's courtly pastoral, *The Araygnement of Paris* (performed at court, ca. 1582; printed, 1584). Sidney and Peele are of the same generation but of very different family background and social status. They make their literary debuts with courtly pastoral entertainments that employ the same mythological conceit, which is directed to the same audience of one. In Peele's play, Diana rejudges the contest between the three goddesses that Paris has mismanaged. Diana awards the prize to the nymph Eliza, whose kingdom is Elizium; play culminates in ritual as the goddess presents the golden apple to her incarnation, Queen Elizabeth herself. Because the queen infolds their separate perfections, the goddesses gladly resign to her; because her virtues are "more than may belong. / By natures lawe to any earthly wight," the Fates lay their instruments at her feet.[15] When compared to Peele's fulsome and spectacular exploitation of the device as a vehicle for flattery of the queen, the encomiastic restraint and the intellectualism of Sidney's treatment are all the more notable. Peele entertains and celebrates; Sidney instructs and tests.

It is my suggestion that Sidney's initial opposition of unbalanced and objectionable extremes—innocuous shepherd and savage forester—are allegorical caricatures of courtier types: roughly speaking, they caricature the pliable placeman and the impetuous free spirit. This confrontation is continued in the dialogue of Rixus, a bold young forester, and Dorcas, an old shepherd of the pastoral philosopher type that includes Spenser's Meliboe and Shakespeare's Corin. It is important to emphasize that the debate between Dorcas and Rixus does not merely repeat or elaborate the initial opposition of Espilus and Therion. (The May Lady has said that she likes them both and loves neither; the queen has little reason to like either of them.) Instead, it moves the debate to a higher level of analysis. Sidney's rhetorical strategy is to unfold the implications of the objectionable initial appearances.[16]

15. *The Araygnement of Paris,* ed. R. Mark Benbow, in *The Dramatic Works of George Peele,* C. T. Prouty, gen. ed. (New Haven, Conn., 1970); I quote lines 1221–1222. For the convention, see: J. D. Reeves, "The Judgment of Paris as a Device of Tudor Flattery," *N&Q,* N.S. II (1955), 7–11; I.-S. Ekeblad, "On the Background of Peele's *Araygnement,*" *N&Q,* N.S. III (1956), 246–249.

16. That the Espilus/Therion opposition reflects Sidney's support of the aggressive foreign policy advocates in the privy council has been suggested by Ringler

Dorcas's praise of the unaspiring, otiose pastoral life brings the work to the center of its concerns:

How many courtiers, think you, I have heard under our field in bushes make their woeful complaints, some of the greatness of their mistress' estate, which dazzled their eyes and yet burned their hearts; some of the extremity of her beauty mixed with extreme cruelty; some of her too much wit, which made all their loving labours folly? O how often have I heard one name sound in many mouths, making our vales witnesses of their doleful agonies!

(p. 28)

The conventions of pastoral provide an imaginary landscape into which to project the problems encountered in courting the great mistress whose name sounds in many mouths. The courtier suffers rejection and frustration in his struggle for advancement in the favors of a grudging and capricious monarch; this suffering provides a social referent for the impulse to flee, for the attraction of the mean degree, and for the ironic praise of a shepherd-courtier who is "as quiet as a lamb that new came from sucking" (p. 27).

As David Kalstone has pointed out, the explicit terms of Sidney's pastoral debate are the traditional ones of Contemplation and Action.[17] But poets as subtle as Sidney work complicating variations on these simplistic categories. Sidney harmonizes action and contemplation in the forester's life, while he transforms the traditionally contemplative shepherd into a personified conflation of the contemplative and voluptuary lives. At its worst, the shepherd's life is one of intellectual and moral sloth, of sly courting for material gain. At its best, the shepherd's life is merely an element in a life of active virtue that absorbs and transcends pastoral *otium*:

(Sidney, *Poems*, p. 362), and supported by Howell (*Sir Philip Sidney*, pp. 155–156). William Gray, Sidney's early nineteenth-century editor, suggested that Therion was an Aleçon figure; Kimbrough and Murphy assert that "the active Therion is clearly a Leicester-figure" ("The Helmingham Hall Manuscript," p. 105). Previous studies have paid insufficient attention to the shift from Espilus / Therion to Dorcus / Rixus, and to the interpenetration of politics and autobiography within the text.

17. *Sidney's Poetry: Contexts and Interpretations* (1965; rpt. New York, 1970), pp. 42–47. Kalstone finds the conventional active / contemplative, pastoral / heroic, duality; he stresses Sidney's synthesizing impulse. I find a triadic pattern, and stress Sidney's discriminating impulse.

The shepherd's life had some goodness in it, because it borrowed of the country quietness something like ours. But . . . ours, besides that quiet part, doth both strengthen the body, and raise up the mind with this gallant sort of activity. O sweet contentation, to see the long life of the hurtless trees; to see how in straight growing up, though never so high, they hinder not their fellows; they only enviously trouble, which are crookedly bent. What life is to be compared to ours, where the very growing things are ensamples of goodness?

(p. 29)

Rixus interprets the forester-courtier as a man of heroic action and virtuous aspiration; his impetuosity and occasional bluntness are the manifestations of his essential honesty and dedication to the best interests of his lady. Ideally, this relationship is one based on respect and love; it is a reciprocal relationship in which the courtier can expect to be justly rewarded for his devotion. Oppositions of young forester to old shepherd and of young trees that grow straight to those that are crookedly bent insinuate the intergenerational conflict of temperaments and policies that continues to keep Sidney, as well as Greville and other like-minded friends, from places of real power and sources of substantial income under the regime of Burghley and his queen.

Languet, Sidney's Protestant-humanist mentor, is in England from late 1578 to early 1579—about the time that *The Lady of May* is performed. Soon after, he writes to Sidney that,

To speak plainly, the habits of your court seemed to me somewhat less manly than I could have wished, and most of your noblemen appeared to me to seek for a reputation more by a kind of affected courtesy than by those virtues which are wholesome to the state, and which are most becoming to generous spirits and men of high birth. I was sorry . . . to see you wasting the flower of your life on such things, and I feared . . . lest from habit you should be brought to take pleasure in pursuits which only enervate the mind.[18]

Languet's observations and judgment help us to reconstruct the social basis of the shepherd and forester models, to put back the simple into the complex. Furthermore, Languet's letter suggests that, in *The Lady of May*, Sidney is as deeply engaged in clarifying issues for himself as in clarifying them for the queen. Sidney conducts a dialectical examination of the role of the courtier—Castiglione's theme—through the

18. Sidney, *Correspondence*, p. 167.

manipulation of pastoral *topoi*. Self-reflexively examining his own role as courtier-poet, Sidney simultaneously uses and judges both pastoral literary conventions and their analogous courtly social forms. He champions the legitimacy of virtuously directed personal aspiration which serves queen, country, and Protestant-humanist ideals while it satisfies the freeborn English gentleman's right to perfect his self. *The Lady of May* exemplifies, relatively simply but with considerable specificity, a mutual mirroring between art and life, between cultural form and historical moment; it gives substance and definition to Renaissance defenses of poetry's efficacy and to ideologies that claimed the courtier's self to be a work of art.

Sidney inclined to that mode of life which in the decorum of pastoral is exemplified by the forester type: his quick temper and ideological zeal are testified both by his actions and by the words of his friends.[19] Sidney's partiality is also clear from the internal structure of *The Lady of May*. Its debate structure is not a simple set of stated and restated oppositions but a dialectical unfolding and revision of oppositions; its rhetorical intention is to move the audience from a situation of indecision between two antithetical extremes to a realignment that shows one term to incorporate, revise, and transcend the other. That the mediation arrived at by Rixus was conceived by Sidney as the superior position is confirmed by the songs intended as an epilogue to the queen's judgment. In the songs, Silvanus the forest god wins his love, while Pan the shepherd god loses his love to Hercules. In Renaissance iconography, Hercules is preeminently a moral hero. The crucial decision in his life is to choose, on the threshold between youth and maturity, to follow the arduous path of virtue rather than the easy path of pleasure.[20] This sig-

19. Languet, for example, advises Sidney "to reflect that young men who rush into danger incautiously almost always meet an inglorious end. . . . Let not therefore an excessive desire for fame hurry you out of your course" (*ibid.*, p. 137).

20. Erwin Panofsky, *Hercules am Scheidewege* (Leipzig and Berlin, 1930) is the definitive iconographic study; Hallett Smith, *Elizabethan Poetry* (1952; rpt. Ann Arbor, Mich., 1968), pp. 291–303, discusses the theme's prevalence in English Renaissance literature. In September 1580, Languet writes to Sidney of European friends who "fear that those who do not so well know your constancy may suspect that you are tired of that toilsome path which leads to virtue, which you formerly pursued with so much earnestness. They are fearful too, that the sweetness of your lengthened retirements may somewhat relax the vigorous energy with which you

nificant variation on the judgment of Paris can be an iconological demonstration that virtuous life on earth is ideally a union of contemplation and action. No Renaissance humanist puts it better than Sidney himself, in his *Defence of Poetry:* "The highest end of the mistress-knowledge . . . stands . . . in the knowledge of a man's self, in the ethic and politic considerations, with the end of well-doing and not of well-knowing only." [21] In Greville's biography, Sidney becomes the fulfillment of an ideal that Rixus merely shadows. Greville consistently describes Sidney in terms that recall the forester ideal of *The Lady of May:*

His very waies in the world, did generally adde reputation to his Prince, and Country, by restoring amongst us the ancient Majestie of noble, and true dealing: As a manly wisdome, that can no more be weighed down, by any effeminate craft, than *Hercules* could be overcome by that contemptible Army of Dwarfs. . . . His heart and tongue went both one way, and so with every one that went with the Truth.[22]

In Sidney's songs, the victory of Herculean hero over Panic shepherd and the successful courtship of the Sylvan forester leave no doubt as to his own inclinations. In Wanstead garden, however, the queen chose to smile upon Espilus. The extant texts invoke the limitations of pastoral decorum: they only note, with a certain cryptic brevity, that "it pleased her Majesty to judge that Espilus did the better deserve [the May Lady]; but what words, what reasons she used for it, this paper, which carrieth so base names, is not worthy to contain" (p. 30).

David Kalstone suggests that "perhaps Sidney's unorthodox treatment of pastoral convention went unnoticed, and the queen chose the shepherd as the usual representative of the contemplative life; royalty has been known to nod before and since." [23] If this were the case, the

used to rise to noble undertakings, and a love of ease . . . creep by degrees over your spirit" (Sidney, *Correspondence,* pp. 182–183). Here Hercules' Choice between Virtue and Pleasure is not cited as an exemplum; it occurs as an internalized conceptual category, through which a Renaissance humanist mind constructs and interprets experience.

21. Sidney, *Miscellaneous Prose,* pp. 82–83.

22. Greville, *Life,* pp. 34–35.

23. Kalstone, *Sidney's Poetry,* p. 46; Kalstone cites and seconds the opinion of Orgel, *Jonsonian Masque,* p. 54. My sense of Elizabeth's response is in basic agreement with that of Kimbrough and Murphy, "The Helmingham Hall Manuscript," p. 106.

entertainment's debacle would testify to the difficulty of communicating novel ideas in traditional literary forms; it would also preserve a rare moment of obtuseness in the public life of an exceptionally well-tutored and sharp-witted prince. But Sidney, like Dorcas's courtiers, might rather have had reason to complain of his mistress's too much wit. If we grant that the lady knew very well what she and Sidney were about, we are unlikely to suppose that her choice was merely a mistake. It was, surely, a conscious and pointed rejection of Sidney's pastoral paradigm for the just and temperate relationship that should obtain between freeborn English gentlemen and their sovereign; it was a repudiation of the relationship which Sidney wanted to establish between himself and his queen. Sidney, too, seems to have known what they were both about: in the texts that we have, Silvanus's song is given to Espilus, and Pan's song is given to Therion. Sidney must have been prepared for either choice. He can hardly have had much expectation that Elizabeth would be easily persuaded by his lively images. But it was characteristic of him to speak his mind (however obliquely) on an issue of obsessive personal concern which he believed to be of critical significance for the destiny of the English nation.

The *text* that we call *The Lady of May* is the surviving trace of one small constituent *event* in the dialectical process of Elizabethan history. An act of historical imagination, restoring *The Lady of May* to its living context, reveals that a slight pastoral entertainment can mediate a major distemperature of the body politic within its own symbolic form. When its immediate contexts in literary history and authorial biography are sufficiently enlarged, *The Lady of May* can be recognized as a crystallization in cultural form of an incipient social conflict. That conflict grows in intensity and complexity at the end of Elizabeth's reign and under the Stuarts; within seventy years, it culminates in open warfare and regicide.

III. Cultural Forms and Social Forces

Queen Elizabeth's conservatism in fiscal, social, and religious policy was the hard-won lesson of a youth that had witnessed the destructive effects of ambition, innovation, and faction at firsthand. The consensus of modern historians validates Elizabeth's cautious and temporizing foreign policy; it was the most realistic response to the European and intercontinental configuration of power, wealth, and resources. Had not the Elizabethan *via media* proved itself by keeping the Commonwealth of England relatively healthy and peaceful for two decades? Elizabeth's distrust of Sidney and his friends is understandable, but not above criticism.[24] Her choice of Espilus reflects a concern to promote the innocuous conventions of erotic pastoralism that helped to maintain a stable, elegant, and adoring courtly ethos. I am not suggesting that Elizabeth wanted to surround herself with advisers, administrators, and soldiers who were just so many silly sheep. For the most part, the men whom she entrusted with government were mature in years, in professional experience, and in the arts of political manipulation and accommodation. However, one of her most pressing domestic problems was effectively to check, control, and channel the talents and energies, the thirst for self-aggrandizement and the ideological zeal, of men in the upper strata of a mobile, disequilibrious, and intensely competitive society. It was a problem that began to intensify during the last two decades of the century and the reign, as the younger generation of gentlemen and university graduates grew to their majority in a socioeconomic order unable to supply the preferments and offices that they desired and had been led to expect.

By many means, ranging from the manipulation of sacred images to acts of physical mutilation and execution, the Crown sought to establish and maintain control over the various socioeconomic strata and religiopolitical factions of an unruly and changeful society. The institution of the court provided a resplendent aura of majesty and authority to the monarch; at the same time, it monitored and defused the independent

24. For a balanced assessment of Elizabethan foreign policy, see R. B. Wernham, "Elizabethan War Aims and Strategy," in *Elizabethan Government and Society,* pp. 340–368. Recently, in *The Causes of the English Revolution 1529–1642* (New York, 1972), Lawrence Stone has placed Elizabeth's achievements in a long and critical perspective. He concludes that, in matters of civil order, religion, parliamentary tactics, finance, and trade, "the very success of the Elizabethan policy of cautious compromise and artful procrastination was an important source of trouble for the Stuarts." " 'Love-tricks' were all very well in the short run, but they were no substitute for a consistent policy. . . . The tactical successes of Elizabeth, and her studied avoidance of dealing with underlying problems," are to be reckoned among the fundamental preconditions of the Revolution (see Stone, *Causes of the English Revolution,* pp. 115–116).

initiatives of the aristocracy and men from other socioeconomic statuses or occupational groups who bound their fortunes to the court system. Courtly poetry and pageantry were designed to create illusions of royal power; and the illusion of power helped to create the reality of power. Efficacious illusions would be well received by the Crown, and could advance their creators, performers, and promoters to a share in the fruits of the real power that they were helping to sustain. Sidney was as covetous of material advancement—and as desperately in need of it—as any prodigal young Elizabethan courtier committed to the code of ostentation and largesse.[25] But he was trapped within a patronage system that was reluctant to promote him despite—in part, because of—his accomplishments and promise. Puttenham reminded his courtly readers that it was the decorum of "a Courtly Gentleman to be loftie and curious in countenaunce, yet sometimes a creeper, and a curry favell with his superiours." [26] Sidney did not adjust himself to his situation by using his highly valued skills as a verbal maker to celebrate and energize the illusions of royal power. On the contrary, he went about to explore the foundations and limits of royal power, and to promote the rights and interests of men of his own status vis-à-vis the Crown and the peerage.

The commitments ineffectually insinuated through the pastoral mask of *The Lady of May* were more forcefully expressed in the following months. The second half of 1579 was a period of crisis for the political aims and personal fortunes of the Leicester-Walsingham-Sidney faction. The queen was intensifying her marriage negotiations with the duke of Alençon's representative, Simier, who revealed to her the secret marriage of Leicester to Lettice Knollys, the dowager countess of Essex. The queen's intense displeasure severely compromised the Dudley and Knollys families, and reached out to include Sidney's mother (Leicester's sister) and himself. During those tense weeks, there occurred Sidney's notorious public altercation with the earl of Oxford, Burghley's son-in-law. This flap drew from the queen a personal lecture to Sidney on "the difference in degree between Earls, and Gentlemen; the respect inferiors ought to their superiors; and the necessity in Princes to maintain their

25. See Wallace, *Life of Sir Philip Sidney*, pp. 169–173, 392–393. Estimates of the debts that Walsingham assumed after his son-in-law's death range from £6,000 to £17,000.

26. *Arte*, p. 293.

own creations, as degrees descending between the peoples licentiousness, and the anoynted Soveraignty of Crowns"; in response, Sidney "besought her Majesty to consider," among other things, "that although [the Earl of Oxford] were a great Lord by birth, alliance, and grace; yet hee was no Lord over him: and therefore the difference of degrees between free men, could not challenge any other homage than precedency."[27] When the loyal opposition mobilized against the royal marriage, Sidney was prevailed upon to act as spokesman. The active role taken by a private gentleman in this whole affair can hardly have endeared him to his anointed sovereign.

Sidney spent most of 1580 in retirement at Wilton, finishing the first version of his *Arcadia*. In August 1580, he wrote to Leicester: "For my selfe I assure yowr Lordeshippe uppon my trothe, so full of the colde as one can not heere me speake: which is the cawse keepes me yet frome the cowrte since my only service is speeche and that is stopped."[28] Using "The Courtier, or figure of faire semblant," Sidney insinuates that he is sick with a politic illness caught of the queen's displeasure.[29] In writing poetry and prose fiction, and in writing a defense of such imaginative writing, Sidney is not merely utilizing enforced idleness; he is transforming it into the environment for mental action. Sidney's *Defence of Poetry* is a witty, impassioned, and eloquent defense of literary writing as a fit occupation for gentlemen, as an instigation to virtuous action, and as an intellectual form of virtuous action in and of itself. Sidney's *Defence* constructs a universal, systematic moral and rhetorical theory of poetry that precisely addresses his personal predicament: writing is almost the only avenue of action available to him. His *Defence of Poetry* is also a self-defense, and a self-consolation.

In May 1581, three years after the performance of *The Lady of May*,

27. Greville, *Life*, pp. 67–68.

28. Sidney, *Prose Works*, III, 129.

29. Compare Puttenham, *Arte*, pp. 299–300: "Is it not perchance more requisite our courtly Poet do dissemble not onely his countenances & conceits, but also all his ordinary actions of behaviour, or the most part of them, whereby the better to winne his purposes & good advantages, as . . . when a man is whole to faine himselfe sicke to shunne the businesse in Court . . . & when any publique affaire or other attempt & counsaile of theirs hath not receaved good successe, to avoid therby the Princes present reproofe, to coole their chollers by absence, to winne remorse by lamentable reports, and reconciliation by friends intreatie[?]"

a sumptuous pageant was performed before the queen in the tiltyard at Whitehall; Sidney played a major role in its performance and, almost certainly, in its creation. The French commissioners in the protracted royal marriage negotiations were conspicuously present, and the pageant must have been partially directed to them. In the only substantive analysis of this work, Norman Council writes that,

> to the degree that the allegory of the tilt has a political purpose, it describes the queen as being beyond the reach of Anjou's suit for marriage, and thereby displays the queen's apparent decision against the match. But the tilters also take this opportunity to add another hyperbolic chapter to the myth of the Virgin Queen, distinguishing between her identity as the goddess of merely natural beauty and her more proper and exalted identity as the goddess of heavenly beauty.[30]

These intentions are indeed conspicuously present. But I would suggest that the political purpose—or, rather, the psychosocial function—of the pageant involves much more than another factional slap at the French and another Platonizing compliment to Elizabeth. Like *The Lady of May,* the *Triumph of The Fortress of Perfect Beauty* is both an offering of praise and a symbolic vehicle expressing the immediate personal and collective concerns of its promoters and participants. Although it was probably not yet clear that Elizabethan had decided against the French marriage, it was already clear that any final decision would be hers alone. Elizabethan courtiers and councilors had now to think of repairing and ensuring the continuity of their personal ties to the queen, whatever shape the future might take.

The basic scenario of the entertainment consists of a challenge to the

---

30. Norman Council, *"O Dea Certe:* The Allegory of *The Fortress of Perfect Beauty," HLQ,* XXXIX (1976), 329–342; I quote from p. 330. The extant record of the triumph is Henry Goldwell's composite text of songs, speeches, and descriptions, printed in 1581; I have used the reprint in Nichols, *Progresses and Public Processions of Queen Elizabeth,* II, 312–329. (Parenthetical citations in my text will be to vol. II of Nichols's work.) Although the authorship of the triumph is uncertain, it has often and plausibly been maintained that Sidney had a large share in its conception and its composition: Ringler (Sidney, *Poems,* pp. 518–519) accepts the attribution to Sidney of the two sonnets in the triumph; the scenario has been attributed to Sidney by Wallace (*Life of Sir Philip Sidney,* p. 264), Howell (*Sir Philip Sidney,* p. 87), Council (*"O Dea Certe,"* p. 336), and Ronald A. Rebholz (*The Life of Fulke Greville* [Oxford, 1971], p. 36).

queen by the Foster Children of Desire; an attack upon the Fortress of Perfect Beauty, which allegorizes the queen's person and state; a defense of the Fortress by a contingent of gentlemen-courtiers; and the final capitulation of the challengers after two days of speeches, songs, heraldry, and tilting. What is intriguing about this pageant is that two of the "four Foster Children of Desire" whose challenge generated and governed the entire action were "Master Philip Sidney, and Master Fulke Grevill." [31] Their challenge had been delivered to the queen some days earlier: "A martial messenger of Desire's fostered children, without making any precise reverence at all, uttered these speeches of defiance, to the Queen's Majestie":

Know ye . . . all onely Princesse, that hereby (for far of they are never) there lyes encamped the foure long haples, now hopeful fostered children of Desire; who having bin a great while nourished up with that infective milke, and to too much care of their fiery fosterer, (though full oft that dry nurse Dispaier indevered to wainne them from it) being nowe as strong in that nurture, as they are weake in fortune, incouraged with the valiaunt counsaile of never fainting Desire, and by the same assured, that by right of inheritaunce even from ever, the Fortresse of Beautie doth belong to her fostered children. These foure I say . . . doe will you by me, even in the name of

31. Nichols, *Progresses and Public Processions of Queen Elizabeth*, II, 313. "The Earl of Arundel" and "Lord Windsor" are named as the other two "Children." With the help of *The Complete Peerage* (ed. G.E.C., rev. ed. Vicary Gibbs et al., 13 vols. [London, 1910–1959]), I have identified these artistocratic companions of Sidney and Greville as Philip Howard, Earl of Arundel, and Frederick Windsor, Baron Windsor of Stanwell. All four were of the same generation, only four years separating the oldest from the youngest. Windsor, like Sidney and Greville, was in the elaborate train with which the Earl of Leicester escorted Alençon to the Netherlands a few months before the tilt; he died in 1585, at twenty-six. (See *Complete Peerage*, XII, pt. 2, 798–799.) Arundel, like Sidney, was the godson and namesake of King Philip of Spain. Three years after the pageant, he was imprisoned in the Tower for converting to Catholicism and secretly attempting to leave England. He was heavily fined and attainted for high treason; he died (in 1595, at thirty-eight) in the Tower, after eleven years of imprisonment. Among the family papers is a manuscript biography of the earl which describes him as wild, undutiful, profligate, and deeply in debt before his religious conversion. (See *Complete Peerage*, I, 252–255.) Neither young aristocrat seems to have had a literary bent. On the shape of Greville's life, see Rebholz, *The Life of Fulke Greville*; and F. J. Levy, "Fulke Greville: The Courtier as Philosophical Poet," *MLQ*, XXXIII (1972), 433–448.

Justice, that you will no longer exclude vertuous Desire from perfect Beautie.
. . . But if . . . Beautie be accompanied with disdainful pride, and pride
waighted on by refusing crueltie . . . they will beseige that fatal Fortresse,
vowing not to spare (if this obstinacie continue) the swoorde of faithfulnesse,
and the fire of affection.

(pp. 313–314)

This "plaine proclaimation of warre" (p. 314) will not be adequately
explained if interpreted merely in terms of the Neo-Platonic metaphysics
gracefully suggested by its erotic imagery. The allegory is transparently
political; the politics are internal as well as international, concerned with
the queen's relationship to her courtiers as well as with her relationship
to Alençon.

It is likely that much of the ubiquitous amorous literature of the period
enabled a transformed expression of desires for socioeconomic advancement. In an ideological system dominated by hostility to personal ambition and social change, desires for wealth, status, and power might be
intentionally disguised or unconsciously displaced in metaphors of erotic
and spiritual desire. Loss of specific historical and biographical contexts
for most of these works has left them with the illusory appearance of
being merely conventional, impersonally manipulated poetic ornaments.
Transformations of erotic imagery make possible a management of carnal-
spiritual tensions. The enactment by Sidney and Greville of the public,
ritual roles of Foster Children who desire to possess Elizabeth's Fortress
of Perfect Beauty suggests the possibility that these cultural conventions
can become vehicles for the sublimation of urgent *social* tensions, as well
as carnal-spiritual ones. This sort of amateur performance by vitally
interested social actors has the status of a *lived* topical allegory. It gives
added conviction to the hypothesis that Elizabethan courtly literature is
pervasively topical; at the same time, it suggests how much more affect
must have been generated by topical allegory in an actual performance
situation than by topical allegory occuring within the more heavily
mediated experiences of writing and reading.

Other knights come in to defend the Fortress; among them are the
"foure legitimate sonnes of Despaire, brethren to harde mishap . . .
long time fostered with favourable countenance, and fed with sweet
fansies, but now of late (alas) wholie given over to griefe and disgraced
by disdaine" (p. 325). These were, in fact, "the foure sonnes of Sir

Francis Knolles" (p. 324), a privy councilor squarely in the Leicester-Walsingham camp on the issue of the French marriage. Because of his policy positions and his daughter's marriage to Leicester, Knollys had been suffering the force of much of Elizabeth's irritation and spite of late. The quartet of young gentleman-courtiers who were Sir Francis's sons and Lettice's brothers had an urgent need to impress the queen with a romantic display of their own adoration, obedience, and utility. This they did by offering to defend her against the challengers, whom they explicitly associated with the Titans and with Phaeton, archetypes of illegitimate and doomed ambition.

At the end of the second day of tilting and pageantry,

the foster children of Desire (but heires onelie to misfortune) . . . deliver . . . their most humble-hearted submission. They acknowledge this fortresse to be reserved for the eie of the whole world, farre lifted up from the compasse of their destinie. They acknowledge the blindnesse of their error, in that they did not know Desire (how strong soever it be) within itselfe to be stronger without itselfe than it pleased the desired. They acknowledge they have degenerated from their fosterer in making Violence accompanie Desire. They acknowledge that Desire received his beginning and nourishment of this fortresse, and therefore to commit ungratefulnesse in bearing armes (though desirous armes) against it. They acknowledge noble Desire should have desired nothing so much, as the flourishing of that fortresse, which was to be esteemed according to itselfes liking. . . . Therefore they doo acknowledge themselves overcome, as to be slaves to this Fortresse for ever.

(pp. 328–329)

Put among Sidney's other personal and literary performances, the *Triumph* assumes a significant position in the dialectic of his life and art. *The Lady of May* dramatizes the eclogue; *The Triumph of the Fortress of Perfect Beauty* dramatizes the chivalric romance. The two entertainments are generically interrelated as enacted versions of the pastoral and heroic kinds. Furthermore, the later, larger, and more spectacular work has as its predominant theme the opposition of the two fundamental modes of royal courtship upon which *The Lady of May* was constructed. Decorum of kinds demands a change in the allegorical vehicle: a singing contest and debate between shepherds and foresters becomes a series of armed encounters between opposed groups of knights. The fundamental difference between the two entertainments is that the outcome of the later contest is made to reflect the queen's choice in the earlier dispute.

Wild foresters have become attackers of the Lady; docile shepherds have become her defenders. In the audacious challenge, the repudiation, and the eventual submission of the Foster Children of Desire, we can see Sidney imaginatively identifying himself with the Therion-Rixus model, symbolically testing it, and finally abandoning the illusion that it can be effective within the constraining ideological system successfully manipulated by the queen. When we recall that "foster" is an Elizabethan variant of "forester" (one that occurs in both of the extant substantive texts of *The Lady of May*), the possibility begins to suggest itself that the conceit of "Foster Children of Desire" may contain a pun alluding to the strong-willed, impetuous, ambitious, even insolent stance toward the role of courtier that Sidney had so firmly associated with the forester type only three years before.

Among the "Juelles given to her Majestie at Newyer's tyde, 1580–81," is listed "a juell of goulde, being a whippe, garnished with small diamondes in foure rowes and cordes of small seede pearle. Geven by Mr. *Philippe Sydneye.*" [32] Like that recent gift, this current performance was Sidney's symbolic offering of submission to the great goddess who had blessed Espilus. But we can also detect Sidney's persistent audacity in his choice of New Year's gift: the gesture is sufficiently ambiguous to allow the symbol of Sidney's contrition and obedience to insinuate its own antithesis, an aesthetic sublimation of the giver's antipathy to the recipient. Puttenham writes suggestively that "devices" (a generic term including "liveries, cognizances, emblemes, enseigns and impreses"), "insinuat some secret, wittie, morall and brave purpose presented to the beholder, either to recreate his eye, or please his phantasie, or examine his judgment, or occupie his braine or to manage his will either by hope or by dread." [33] I would add that "devices" (and symbolic forms, generally) have emotive as well as conative and cognitive functions; their effect is to express the maker as well as to affect the beholder. Offerings of devoted submission may be functionally ambiguous. They may allow an oblique and limited expression of the aggression or independence that is being denied, and a purgation of the resentment that the submission en-

---

32. Nichols, *Progresses and Public Processions of Queen Elizabeth*, II, 300–301.
33. *Arte,* p. 108.

tails. The bejeweled icon that Sidney presents to the queen and the sumptuous pageant in which he performs before her are homologous cultural forms.

If we attend to the speech and action of the pageant, if we imaginatively experience it as a cultural event enmeshed in the process of Elizabethan social life, then its meaning emerges as something more complex than the sycophancy of its surface: it is a socially sanctioned cultural medium for the raising and casting out of discontent and hostility that would otherwise eventuate in overt dissent and civil disorder. *The Lady of May* is an aristocratic appropriation of May games; *The Pageant of the Fortress of Perfect Beauty* contains an aristocratic analogue of the Saturnalian rites of misrule. Men from within the ranks of the ruling elite are constrained by the highest levels of social and artistic decorum. Working through the allegorized oxymoron of erotic warfare, they can play out the flouting, threatening, and necessary reaffirmation of the royal personage who in fact has the power of life and death over them.[34] On the first day of the pageant, after the magnificent entry of the four challengers and their retinues, the bearer of their original challenge again addresses the queen on their behalf:

Your eies, which till now have beene onelie woont to discerne the bowed knees of kneeling hearts, and inwardlie turned, found alwaies the heavenlie peace of a sweet mind, should not now have their faire beames reflected with

34. The stifled and restless energy of the young, ambitious Protestant warhawks, and their resentments against the queen, are well testified in the actions and writings of Sidney and Greville. Sidney also had cause to resent the poor treatment of his dear parents at Elizabeth's hands: the lack of recompense or apparent gratitude for his father's long and devoted public service, and for his mother's selfless personal nursing of the queen. Council ("*O Dea Certe*," p. 342) plausibly suggests that Arundel's presence in this anti-Alençon pageant was intended as a conspicuous display of loyalty to the Elizabethan Settlement and its incarnation by the heir of a family with noted Catholic sympathies. It is not unreasonable to surmise that this political necessity must have aroused ambivalent feelings in a young peer who had been made to wait unduly long for the Crown's confirmation of his title; whose father, Thomas Howard, duke of Norfolk, the greatest peer of the realm, had been beheaded in 1572 for continually conspiring against Elizabeth; who would himself, within three years, embrace Catholicism and, as a result, spend the rest of his life in the Tower.

the shining of armour, should not now be driven to see the furie of Desire, nor the fierie force of Furie. . . . You see them, readie in hart as you know, and able with hands as they hope, not onelie to assailing, but to prevailing.

(p. 317)

The erotic metaphor can accommodate the expression of desires for disinterested service and self-interested gain; and, at the same time, it can insinuate that stifled desire leads to hostility and aggression.[35] Performing in a ceremonial tilt and masking in a pageant are forms of action modified and controlled by their ludic context; their status is mediatory between the imaginative reality fictions and the tangible reality of overt political acts.

The sociopolitical circumstances of 1581 made possible the successful containment of potential violence in the play-forms of aristocratic culture. Exactly twenty years later, in the deep social discontent and political turmoil of Elizabeth's last years, her most brilliant courtier led a short-lived revolt of desperate losers in the deadly game of courtship:

The Essex rebellion derived from the impossible situation in which Essex found himself in the last years before 1601. Denied access to the source of patronage and influence, he must either see his power sterilized and his following shrink . . . or he must break through to gain access to—if necessary, control over—that source. . . . Essex in the end was caught in the ineluctable dilemma of power inherent in the existing political structure.[36]

That most observant of ornamental courtiers, Sir John Harington, wrote "that ambition thwarted in its career, dothe speedilie leade on to madnesse; herein I am strengthened by what I learned in my Lord of Essex, who shyftethe from sorrowe and repentaunce to rage and rebellion so suddenlie, as well provethe him devoide of goode reason or righte mynde." [37] Essex was, of course, the son of Lettice and grandson of Sir Francis Knollys; a protégé of Leicester, and his stepson; Sidney's companion-in-arms in the Netherlands; the second husband of Sidney's widow, Frances, daughter of Sir Francis Walsingham. Sidney, on his

35. Compare *LM:* "Therion doth me many pleasures . . . but withal he grows to such rages, that sometimes he strikes me, sometimes he rails at me" (Sidney, *Miscellaneous Prose,* p. 25).

36. Joel Hurstfield, "The Succession Struggle in Late Elizabethan England," in *Elizabethan Government and Society,* pp. 369–396; I quote from p. 390.

37. *Nugae Antiquae,* ed. Henry Harington (1779; rpt. 3 vols., 1968), II, 225.

deathbed, recorded in a codicil to his will: "Item, I give to my beloved and much honoured lord the Earl of Essex, my best sword."[38] It was a bequest of great symbolic significance for the impetuous young royal favorite, and for all those gentleman-courtiers who came to share in the idealization of Sidney and in Essex's discontent.

As a public incitement on the eve of their rebellion, Essex's supporters commissioned a performance of a play of Richard II—it was presumably Shakespeare's, and contained a deposition pageant and fictional enactment of regicide. They failed to raise the citizens of London. But that they even considered such a strategy remains an oblique testimonial to the potential power of the public theater. Another dimension is added to the complex dialectic between Elizabethan cultural forms and social forces by the awareness that play might be not only an effective way to contain violent action but might also effectively catalyze it. The Essex rebellion evidences a dysfunction in the process of cultural containment.[39] Harington's meditation on Essex closes with an image of frustration that has been twisted out of the amorous discourse of sonnet-courtships: "The Queene well knowethe how to humble the haughtie spirit, the haughtie spirit knoweth not how to yield, and the mans soule seemeth tossede to and fro, like the waves of a troubled sea."[40] The source of Sidney's relief was to play at aggression and submission—and to look in his heart, and write.

IV. Knight and Shepherd

I have sought to contextualize *The Lady of May* as a specific cultural mediation of a large and complex range of problems besetting Philip

38. Sidney, *Miscellaneous Prose*, p. 152.

39. Stone writes that "in the early and middle years of the reign of Elizabeth the Court successfully contained within a single political system of checks and balances the representatives of a series of conflicting ideas and interests. . . . After the rebellion and execution of the Earl of Essex . . . this central political switchboard broke down, and many of these diverse and increasingly hostile groups began to organize locally and to band together, independent of the national political process at Court and even in open opposition to it" (*Causes of the English Revolution*, pp. 85–86).

40. *Nugae Antiquae*, II, 226.

Sidney and other men of his social status, ideological persuasion, financial obligations, temperament, and generation in the late sixteenth century
in England. Fulke Greville, Sidney's intimate friend, fellow ideologue,
and brother in desire, wrote his justifying and idealizing *Life* of Sidney
during the first decade of the new reign, when he himself was out of
favor and out of office; his analysis of Sidney's situation by the mid-
1580s harks back to the paradigmatic scenario of *The Lady of May:*

Sir Philip found . . . his large, and sincere resolutions imprisoned within
the pleights of their fortunes, that mixed good, and evill together unequally;
and withall discerned, how the idle-censuring faction at home had won
ground of the active adventures abroad. . . . [In] his Native Country, he
found greatness of worth, and place, counterpoysed there by the arts of
power, and favor. The stiring spirits sent abroad as fewell, to keep the flame
far off: and the effeminate made judges of danger which they fear, and honor
which they understand not.[41]

Frustrated in his attempts to unite knowledge and action in life, Sidney
sublimated his predicament into the imaginative interplay of pastoral
and heroic literary modes. "His active spirit . . . that had no delight to
rest idle at home" (p. 78) had long been ready when his commission
finally arrived. Sidney's life of frustrated action found an ironic consummation in the fatal, chance wound he received on his first military
campaign.

The fusion of pastoral and heroic modes, contemplation and action,
was only attainable through death and apotheosis: in pastoral elegies,
Sidney could be venerated as a heroic shepherd; as *"Scipio, Cicero,* and
Petrarch of our time"; as a blessed soul in that syncretic heaven where
"Venus on thee smiles, *Apollo* gives thee place, / And *Mars* in reverent
wise doth to thy vertue bow."[42] Elizabethan pastoral literature was
largely created in the enforced idleness of a courtier who sought the role
of an Elizabethan hero in his life; after his death, he was internalized
within the pastoral literary tradition that he had shaped. Sidney himself
became the subject of celebration. We can see this process of his trans-

41. Greville, *Life,* pp. 77–78.

42. See the pastoral elegies by Spenser and others, printed with Spenser's own
pastoral court satire, *Colin Clouts Come Home Againe,* in 1595. I quote from the
often reprinted *Oxford Standard Authors* edition of Spenser's *Poetical Works,* ed.
J. C. Smith and E. de Selincourt, pp. 559, 553, respectively.

formation taking place before us in *Astrophel,* Spenser's pastoral elegy
for Sidney. In narrating Astrophel's destruction and his transformation
into a flower, Spenser's poem verbally enacts the metamorphosis it purports to recount:

> But thou where ever thou doest finde the same,
> From this day forth do call it *Astrophel.*
> And when so ever thou it up doest take,
> Do pluck it softly for that shepheards sake.
>
> (ll. 195–198)

Sidney is made perpetually available as a pastoral subject, enabling the
inner tensions, contradictions, and ironies of courtship to be articulated,
allowing the desires and ambitions frustrated in experience to be sublimated and gratified.

It remains dubious that Sidney's stifled career had really begun to
flower just before his death. In a letter written to Walsingham from
Utrecht only a few months before his death, Sidney complained of "how
apt the Queen is to interpret every thing to my disadvantage. . . . I
understand I am called very ambitious and prowd at home, but certainly
if thei knew my ha[rt] thei woold not altogether so judg me." [43] In adversity, his self-resolve remained firm: "I think a wyse and constant man
ought never to greev whyle he doth plai as a man mai sai his own part
truly though others be out but if him self leav his hold becaws other
marrin[ers] will be ydle he will hardli forgive him self his own fault"
(p. 166). Wisdom, constancy, virtuous action, personal integrity—although the themes remain fundamentally unaltered from their first
articulation by Rixus, they have been deepened and confirmed by time;
they are now reaffirmed directly and intimately, rather than through the
mediations of a dramatic eclogue. What is fundamentally different is the
openness with which Sidney expresses the distinction and priority of his
allegiances: "Her Majesty . . . is but a means whom God useth and I
am faithfully persuaded that if she shold withdraw her self other springes
woold ryse to help this action. . . . I can not promis of my own cource
. . . becaws I know there is a hyer power that must uphold me or els I
shall fall, but certainly I trust, I shall not by other mens wantes be drawn
from my self" (pp. 166–167). Sidney's role as Protestant hero is dissociated

43. Sidney, *Prose Works,* III, 167.

from his role as Renaissance courtier; the affirmation of the inviolability of personal conscience and personal faith is opposed to unconditional obedience to temporal authority. These trends are inseparable from the concern of Sidney and some of his friends and associates with relatively advanced political theories of limited monarchy and constitutional government.[44]

Sidney was no revolutionary. But he did play his part in the articulation of what Lawrence Stone calls "the preconditions" of the English Revolution:

Dissatisfaction with Elizabeth's refusal to modify her religious policy in a more Puritan direction, her refusal to marry or to settle the succession, her cautious and ambiguous foreign policy, and finally her obstinate defence of a morally untenable position about economic monoplies, slowly drove the more active members of the House of Commons to make wholly new constitutional claims. They moved from a position of asking to speak their minds on issues put before them without fear of punishment, to a position of demanding the right to initiate discussion and influence policy on any issue they chose.[45]

The sociopolitical transformations of the half-century following Sidney's death, fed by economic change and the incompetence of the reactionary Stuart monarchs, lead circuitously but surely from Sidney to Milton. Milton resonantly declared that "He who would not be frustrate of his hope to write well hereafter in laudable things, ought himself to be a true poem, that is, a composition and pattern of the best and honorablest things."[46] This was an apotheosis of the Renaissance courtly ideal, the moral dialectic of self and work that Sidney strove to exemplify. Critical and analytic functions of the kind that Sidney had attempted to insinuate into royal celebrations were purged as the romantically medieval pageants of the Elizabethan entertainment were transformed into the brilliant

44. See Howell, *Sir Philip Sidney*, pp. 212–218; Levy, "Philip Sidney Reconsidered"; James E. Phillips, "George Buchanan and the Sidney Circle," *HLQ*, XII (1948), 23–55; Ernest William Talbert, *The Problem of Order* (Chapel Hill, N.C., 1962), pp. 89–117.

45. *Causes of the English Revolution*, pp. 92–93. On Sidney's brief career in the House of Commons (which began in the Parliament of 1581), see Howell, *Sir Philip Sidney*, pp. 75–80.

46. "Apology for Smectymnuus" (1642), rpt. in John Milton, *Complete Poems and Major Prose*, ed. Merritt Y. Hughes (New York, 1957), p. 694.

High Renaissance illusions of the Stuart masque. For those outside the Stuart court system, the court masque came to epitomize the cultural isolation, political tyranny, and spiritual corruption of the monarch and the aristocracy.[47] For Milton, the task of the inspired Christian poet was to destroy the spurious Renaissance analogy of royal encomium and sacred hymn, to reveal that the celebration of kings was a demonic parody of the celebration of God.

47. See Stephen Orgel, *The Illusion of Power* (Berkeley and Los Angeles, 1975).

Triumphal Drama: Form in English Civic Pageantry

GORDON KIPLING

I N LONDON during the sixteenth century, the art of the civic triumph
enjoyed a popularity unparalleled elsewhere in England.[1] In its early
history, the development of the triumph in London had closely paralleled
the development of the great Corpus Christi cycles in the provinces;
while the citizens of York, Chester, and Coventry continued to expand
and perfect their traditional religious pageants, London concentrated
upon civic triumphs, devising increasingly elaborate pageants to honor
their sovereigns, welcome foreign princes, and celebrate military victories.

1. In the Renaissance the art of the triumph was a European—not just a London
—phenomenon. Thus, much of what I shall have to say here is applicable to Paris,
Bruges, or even Rome, and I shall use examples from outside London where
necessary to illuminate my argument. Nevertheless, there are some different approaches: in Italy and throughout Southern Europe, the procession tended to be
more important than the pageant structures, and the dramatists' efforts were spent
more in devising emblematic chariots and floats than in the arches. In Northern
Europe, however, the pageant arches became more important, and the dramatist
spent most of his effort in devising them. In London, we see both types at the
same time: "Royal Entries" tended to emphasize stationary pageant structures;
"Lord Mayors' Shows" tended to emphasize chariots and floats.

37

But with the suppression of the Corpus Christi cycles in the provinces during the sixteenth century, the civic triumph enjoyed an efflorescence in the capital. From mid-century on, in addition to frequent pageant shows to celebrate a coronation or royal marriage, Londoners staged annual triumphs to mark the inauguration each 29 October of the Lord Mayor of London. By the end of the century, these shows had become so popular and influential that the most illustrious of Shakespeare's fellow dramatists eagerly sought commissions to devise them: Jonson, Peele, Middleton, Marston, Dekker, Heywood, Webster, and Munday either designed civic triumphs in their entirety or at least wrote speeches for the actors in these shows. Nor did the poets regard such efforts as mere hackwork; most published accounts of their pageantry, counting these effusions among their best works. Undoubtedly, most would have agreed with Dekker that

Tryumphes, are the most choice and daintiest fruit that spring from *Peace* and *Abundance;* Loue begets them; and Much Cost brings them forth. *Expectation* feeds upon them but seldome to a surfeite, for when she is most full, her longing wants something to be satisfied. So inticing a shape they carry, that *Princes* themselves take pleasure to behold them; they with delight; common people with admiration.

Compared to the honor of designing a London triumph, the fame of a common playwright must have seemed paltry indeed.[2]

As Dekker's language makes clear, Renaissance poets thought of these shows primarily as "triumphs"; our modern terms—"royal entries," "*tableaux vivants,*" or even "Lord Mayors' Shows"—decidedly miss the point. When kings, visiting princes, or mayors entered the city and traveled through streets decorated with tapestries and punctuated by elaborate pageant structures, Londoners saw these shows as continuing a

2. *The Dramatic Works of Thomas Dekker,* ed. Fredson Bowers (Cambridge, 1953-1961), III, 230. Since neither Shakespeare nor any of his successors as "ordinary poet" to the King's Company (Fletcher, Massinger, Shirley) devised triumphs during their tenure of office, we may suspect that contractual obligations to the playhouse may have prohibited any such activities. For this, see G. E. Bentley, *The Profession of Dramatist in Shakespeare's Time, 1590–1642* (Princeton, N.J. 1971), pp. 111–144. Shakespeare, however, as one of the King's Servants, apparently marched in James I's coronation procession. E. K. Chambers, *William Shakespeare* (Oxford, 1930), II, 73.

form of celebration begun by the Caesars. William Lilly's comparison between Charles V's triumphant entry into London (1522) and the triumphs of Pompey and Scipio is merely typical:

> What ioye eke was / the tryumphe of Scipion
> And of hym Pompey / to the romayns echone
> Lyke ioye to vs Charles / prince of Clemency
> Is at thy comyng / with pusaunt kyng Henry.[3]

The conscious classical parallel becomes even more obvious when we consider the structure of the English royal triumph. Just as the Roman procession moved from the Campus Martius, outside the walls of the city, to the Capitol, where an offering of thanksgiving was made in the Temple of Jupiter, so the London procession followed one of two similar routes. Foreign princes and native kings returning from abroad usually began their triumphs in Southwark and proceeded over the Bridge and through the streets to St. Paul's, where a *Te Deum* service of thanksgiving was held. Most coronation processions, however, conventionally entered the City from the Tower, proceeded through the City to Westminster, and often celebrated a *Te Deum* in the Abbey. In Roman and English processions alike, crowds lined the streets, and triumphal arches or similar structures appeared at various stations along the route.[4] Even the elaborate triumphal chariots of the Roman celebration found their English counterparts in the "Chares" routinely provided for the noble visitor and his retinue. "Diversly appareilled" to "accorde wyth thestatis of them that shalbe in them," the most "richely garnysshed" was reserved for the *triumphator,* and it might be emblematically decorated. In 1588, for example, Queen Elizabeth triumphantly rode through London in a symbolic "chariot-throne made with foure pillars behind to have a

3. *Of the tryūphe / . . . that Charles themperour / & the most myghty redouted kyng of England . . . were saluted with / passyng through London* (London, 1522), fol. a iv[r].

4. For recent books on the London triumph, see Sydney Anglo, *Spectacle, Pageantry, and Early Tudor Policy* (Oxford, 1969); David M. Bergeron, *English Civic Pageantry, 1558–1642* (Columbia, S.C., 1971); Glynne Wickham, *Early English Stages, 1300–1660,* 2 vols. (London, 1959–1972). For the Roman triumph, see Robert Payne, *The Roman Triumph* (London, 1962); H. Versnel, *Triumphus; an Inquiry into the Origin, Development and Meaning of the Roman Triumph* (Leiden, 1970).

canopie, on the toppe whereof was made a crowne imperiall, and two lower pillars before, whereon stood a lyon and a dragon, supporters of the armes of England, drawne by two white horses."[5] Similar chariots, such as the *"Chariot Triumphant"* drawn by two "luzernes" and containing "a *Russian Prince* and *Princesse*," were common sights in seventeenth-century Lord Mayors' triumphs.[6]

Throughout the history of the form, civic triumphs in London were almost always accompanied by allusions to their Roman originals, whether in speech, dramatic action, or pageant structures. Upon the occasion of important military victories, for example, English sovereigns riding through London tended to repeat the Roman pattern with literal fidelity. After his victory at Agincourt, Henry V led his prisoners through London in a triumph worthy of a Caesar.[7] In a similar fashion, Henry VII's triumph after Bosworth Field included a display of the spoils of the vanquished and an offering of his victorious battle standards in St. Paul's, just as Roman *triumphators* had dedicated theirs in the Temple of Jupiter.[8] To commemorate her victory over the Spanish Armada, Queen Elizabeth, "imitating the ancient Romans, rode into London in triumph":

She was carried thorow her sayd City of London in a tryumphant chariot, and in robes of triumph, from her Palace unto the Cathedrall Church of Saint Paul, out of the which the ensignes and colours of the vanquished Spaniards hung displayed.[9]

Celebrations of political and social occasions—the arrival of a foreign prince, a coronation, or a Lord Mayor's installation—were similarly

---

5. *The traduction & mariage of the princesse* (London, 1500), fol. 3ᵛ; John Nichols, *The Progresses and Public Processions of Queen Elizabeth* (London, 1823), II, 538–539.

6. Dekker, "Britannia's Honor," *Dramatic Works*, IV, 89.

7. James Hamilton Wylie, *The Reign of Henry the Fifth* (Cambridge, 1919), II, 257–269.

8. *The Great Chronicle of London*, ed. A. H. Thomas and I. D. Thornley (London, 1938), pp. 238–239; *The Anglica Historia of Polydore Vergil, 1485–1537*, ed. Denys Hay, Camden Soc., 3d. Ser. (London, 1950), LXXIV, 4–5.

9. Richard Hakluyt, *The Principal Navigations, Voyages, Traffiques & Discoveries of the English Nation* (London, 1907), II, 400.

triumphal.[10] We have already seen how Charles V, entering the city upon a state visit in 1522, seemed as orthodox a *triumphator* as Caesar to the Londoners. So Henry VI's entry into London in 1432 was said to surpass the triumphs of Julius Caesar and Scipio; King James passed to his coronation in 1603 beneath Stephen Harrison's "Arches of Triumph"; and even the mayors of London found themselves transformed into Roman *triumphators,* for "The *Praetorian* Dignity is therefore come from the ancient Roman, to inuest with Robes of Honor, our *Lord Maior* of *London:* Their *Consuls* are our *Sheriefes:* their *Senators* our *Aldermen."* [11]

Because Renaissance Englishmen thought that "the triumphs of the Romans excelled all their other shews," [12] they tended to regard their own triumphs as one of the most important forms of their national drama, "the most choice and daintiest fruit that spring from Peace and Abundance." Because we see them as a succession of *tableaux vivants,* however, we tend to regard them as mere nondramatic spectacles. Thus, modern criticism often robs the civic triumph of any sense of dramatic coherence by equating the separate pageant structures with theaters and reducing the *triumphators* to a moving audience of one:

Normally, in northern countries, the processional element was incidental. The one audience was the noble visitor—a moving audience that advanced from outer gate to city hall or palace. . . . As he approached each new place, music from a special gallery or scenic device, or perhaps hidden, must welcome him. Addresses and allegorical shows must impress on him the loyalty of the subjects, their special compliments, and at times their needs. Hence both the dramatic conventions and the scenic forms of the *tableaux vivants* were determined by their origin as street decoration; they were never drama.

10. As Sir William Segar, a learned participant in many of these spectacles, points out: "Triumphs haue bene commonly vsed at the Inauguration and Coronation of Emperors, Kings, and Princes: at their Mariages, Entry of cities, Enterviewes, Progresses and Funerals. Those pompous shewes, were first inuented and practised by the Romanes whom diuers other Princes haue imitated" (*Honor military, and ciuill, contained in foure bookes* [London, 1602], p. 138).

11. Dekker, IV, 82; *Great Chronicle,* pp. 169–170 (verses by Lydgate); Stephen Harrison, *Arches of Triumph* (London, 1604).

12. Raphael Holinshed, *Chronicles* (London, 1808), IV, 466.

They were showpieces, looking like picture or architectural structure or heraldic device—showpieces that by means of living actors were able to move, to speak, or to sing; showpieces that took their places beside the tapestries, the painted "histories," and the ornamented gates and fountains as part of the decorations for a festival.[13]

To an age familiar with the proscenium theater, this may well make a lot of sense. The noble visitor, the "one audience," watches passively "down here" while the actors—if they can be called that—perform "up there" in the pageant. But because the shows in each "theater" are brief, and because the noble visitor moves on to a new show, the sense of drama remains very limited. Speeches are usually monologues; only tenuous thematic comparisons link the pageants to one another. There is no conflict, no action, merely a series of three-dimensional pictures fleshed out with live performers.

But to a Tudor spectator, this description would seem very strange, for his eyes were trained upon the *triumphator's* splendid procession while it encountered the city's pageants. As a Londoner watched this spectacle of procession and pageantry from his "standing" along the street, who could blame him for thinking himself the true audience for whom this show was designed? As Dekker complains, "the multitude" —that is, the humble Londoners who line the streets—are "our Audience, whose heads would miserably runne a wooll-gathering, if we doo but offer to breake them with hard words." [14] For such an audience, the *triumphator,* far from a passive viewer of a series of playlets, would seem the protagonist of a drama which takes all London as its stage. In fact, Richard Mulcaster makes this very point about Elizabeth I's coronation triumph: "If a man shoulde say well," he writes, "he could not better tearme the citie of London that time, than a stage wherein was shewed the wonderfull spectacle, of a noble hearted princesse toward her most louing people." [15]

13. George R. Kernodle, *From Art to Theatre: Form and Convention in the Renaissance* (Chicago, 1944), p. 62. But on the same page Kernodle also observes, "in Northern Europe the royal procession kept some aspects of the triumphal parade."

14. Dekker, II, 255.

15. *The Passage of our most drad Soueraigne Lady Quene Elyzabeth through the citie of London to westminster the daye before her coronacion* (London, 1558), fol. Aii[v].

Such theatrical characterizations of London triumphs are far from idle metaphors. By carefully exploiting the dramatic possibilities inherent in the encounter of *triumphator* and pageant, the designers of these "wonderfull spectacles" obliged their "noble hearted" protagonists to play roles, not merely attend performances. Thus, the approach of Katharine of Aragon in 1501 miraculously causes the gates of the Castle of Policy to swing open. "Who openyd these gatis?" inquires the captain of the castle, "what, opened they alone?" Then, searching the skies as the triumphant princess approaches, he discovers the reason:

> The bright sterre of Spayne, Hesperus, on them shone,
> Whoes goodly beames hath persid mightily
> Through this castell, to bring this good lady,
> Whoes prosperous comyng shall right joyefull be.[16]

Not all such encounters produced such spectacular results, of course, but the "miracle" wrought by an approaching *triumphator* did become one of the most popular scenes in the history of these shows. The Blessed Virgin might descend from a cloud to bless the king, the illustrious dead might awaken to greet their successors, or the approach of the prince might breathe life into mere pageantry:

Also att the Stockys ther dyd stand a pageaunte off an ylonde betokenyng the Ile off englonde compassede all abowte with water made in silver and byce lyke to waves off the see and rockys ionyng therto. . . . And att the comyng off the emprowr the bestys dyd move and goo, the fisshes dyd sprynge, the byrdes dyd synge reioysing the comyng off the ij princes the emprowr and the kynges grace.[17]

Even if the *triumphator* were determined to do no more than watch the show, such carefully contrived incidents as these would have made him appear to interact with the pageant actors. But many did willingly perform roles in these triumphal dramas, and particularly skillful performers—Elizabeth I for example—greatly impressed their subjects with an astonishingly varied performance, sober and humble at one pageant,

16. London, College of Arms, MS. 1st M. 13, fol. 35ᵛ.

17. Anglo, p. 197. We still find the "miracle" wrought by the approaching *triumphator* the central device in Anthony Munday's Lord Mayors' Shows in the early seventeenth century. In 1611 and again in 1616, the approach of the newly installed Lord Mayor had power to resurrect his revered predecessors from their tombs (Bergeron, pp. 149–151, 156–157).

extravagantly rhetorical at the next. Thus, early in her 1559 coronation triumph, Elizabeth paused before a pageant representing "The vniting of the two howses of Lancastre and Yorke," and listened with care as the child actor advised her to seek concord among the contending factions in her realm as her grandparents had. Then, "after that her grace had vnderstode ye meaning thereof, she thanked the citie, praised ye fairenes of the worke, and promised that she woulde doe her whole endeuour for the continuall preseruacion of concorde, as the pageant did emport." At another station, however, this solemn and respectful demeanor explodes into a histrionic display that might have done credit to the Globe. As she pauses before a pageant which contrasts a "decayed commonweale" with a "florishyng commonweale," an expositor explains to the queen that the cause of the decay of the first commonwealth is the neglect of the book which one of the pageant characters, Truth, holds in her hand. The book, he declares, is an English Bible, and only by embracing it can Elizabeth show that she "vnderstandste the good estate and nought" necessary to plant Wealth in her kingdom "and barrennes displace." At this point, Elizabeth's performance becomes politically as well as dramatically crucial; acceptance or rejection of the book which Truth now offers the queen becomes a test of the *triumphator's* intentions with respect to the Protestant faith. Melodramatically, Elizabeth not only accepts the *Verbum veritatis,* but

when her grace had learned that the Byble in Englishe should there be offered, she thanked the citie therefore, promysed the reading therof most diligentlye, and incontinent commaunded, that it should be brought. At the receit wherof, how reuerently did she with both her handes take it, kisse it, & lay it vpon her breast to the great comfort of the lookers on.

Certainly her performance delighted a staunch Protestant like Richard Mulcaster, who concluded upon seeing it that "God will undoubtedly preserue so worthy a prince, which at his honor so reuerently taketh her beginning." [18]

Even the henchmen marching with the *triumphator* in procession often donned costumes and performed crucial mimetic actions. In most coronation triumphs, for example, actors representing the king's illustrious ancestors, the dukes of Normandy and Aquitaine, would walk just before

18. *The Passage of our most drad Soueraigne,* fols. Bi[r]-Bi[v], Ciiii[v], Eiiii[v].

the chariot costumed in "old fashioned hats, powdered on their heads, disguised."[19] Whifflers, usually dressed as "devells and wyldmen," were conventionally pressed into service as actors. Thus, in the 1617 mayoral triumph, the crowd was kept back by "men masked as wild giants who by means of fireballs and wheels hurled sparks in the faces of the mob and over their persons." [20] And certainly "those twelve that rode armed" in Sir John Swinnerton's mayoral procession came prepared to play their scene in Dekker's *Troia-Nova Triumphans,* for just at the climactic moment they fired their pistols in volley, frightening away Envy and assuring Sir John's achievement of Honor.[21]

Such encounters as these provided the pageant artist with the raw materials for a fully developed dramatic plot. As the *triumphator* moves from pageant to pageant through the streets of London, he can be made to perform a mimetic action predetermined by the dramatic craft of the civic dramatist. The anonymous dramatist who designed Katharine of Aragon's triumph, for example, cast her as the heroine of a medieval dream vision. By carefully structuring the princess's pageant encounters, he makes Katharine travel from earth, through the spheres of the cosmos, to an apotheosis upon the Throne of Honor above the firmament. At the first pageant, on London Bridge, Saints Katharine and Ursula descend from the "Court Celestial" to announce that the princess will be "conveyed . . . to honor" in the heavens, where she will become the star Hesperus set among the "stars bright." Thereafter, Katharine begins her ascension, climbing from the earthly Castle Policy (pageant two), to the

19. The appearance of these traditional figures was already "an old custom" when they marched in the coronation procession of Anne Boleyn (*Tudor Tracts, 1532–1588,* introduction by A. F. Pollard [Westminster, 1903], p. 14). Cf. Edward VI's coronation procession in John Leland, *Collectanea,* 2d ed. (London, 1774), IV, 311. They were still marching in coronation processions during the Restoration; see John Ogilby, *The King's Coronation* (London, 1685), p. 1.

20. "But all proved unavailing to make a free and ample thoroughfare" (*Calendar of State Papers, Venetian, 1617–1619* [London, 1909], XV, 61). "Devells and wyldmen" were traditional by 1575 (E. K. Chambers, *The Elizabethan Stage* [London, 1923], I, 136). Cf. the young men of Edinburgh, who would traditionally dress as Moors to serve as whifflers in the "convoy before the cairt triumphant" (Anna Jean Mill, *Mediaeval Plays in Scotland* [Edinburgh, 1927], pp. 188–191, 202–203).

21. Dekker, III, 245. See discussion of this triumph below.

sphere of the moon (pageant three), to the sphere of the sun (pageant four), to the throne of God the Father (pageant five). At each station she acquires the virtues she will need for the next stage in her ascent. Finally, she is invited to take a throne beside Honor himself, a throne fixed upon the eternal foundation of the seven virtues and set above the cosmos (pageant six).[22] By the time she reaches St. Paul's, Katharine has performed in the same sort of narrative plot that might characterize a more conventional drama.

By means of a similar structuring of pageant encounters, Thomas Dekker's *Troia-Nova Triumphans* (1612) contrives to make Sir John Swinnerton serve as the hero of a morality plot in which the new Lord Mayor acquires the virtues he will need to conquer Envy. In this case, Dekker skillfully employs mobile pageants to represent Sir John's successive mastery of the necessary virtues.[23] Thus, as the mayor rides in triumph, he first encounters the triumphal chariot of Neptune, who proclaims that he has come "thus farre-vp into th'Land . . . Beyond his Bownds" that he might "with his Sea-troops wait" his "wish't arriuall to congratulate." By having Neptune join Sir John's triumphal procession, Dekker thus represents London's mastery of the seas in dramatic action: the *triumphator* of the seas yields to triumphant London and becomes a mere henchman in the Lord Mayor's procession. In this same pattern, the mayor next encounters the triumphal chariot of Virtue, who likewise yields to join his lordship's more triumphal procession, for London's success is based upon virtue, not just merchant seamanship. Now armed with Neptune's strength and the assurance of Virtue, Sir John is prepared to encounter the Castle of Envy, which blocks his passage to Guildhall. Because Envy cannot stand up to Virtue, the *triumphator* passes safely on to the Temple of Fame, where the goddess assures the mayor that he and London are enrolled in her eternal book. Having achieved fame, Sir John now adds the goddess's temple to his procession and turns about for a final attack upon Envy. This time, Envy is not merely avoided, but defeated. "On, on," shouts Virtue from Sir John's

22. College of Arms, MS. 1st M. 13, fols. 33ᵛ–43ᵛ.

23. In London Lord Mayors' triumphs, the civic pageants were designed to be carried in procession. As soon as the mayor had encountered a pageant in the streets and heard the explanatory speeches, it joined his procession and traveled immediately before him.

procession, "The beames of *Virtue* are so bright, / They dazzle *Enuy:* On, the *Hag's* put to flight." On this cue, "those twelue that ride armed" in the mayor's procession "discharge their *Pistols,* at which *Enuy,* and the rest, vanish, and are seene no more." Finally, the new Lord Mayor and his by-now splendid procession arrive before Justice, who welcomes him and explains his duties.[24]

Not all triumph plots are narratively structured of course; some may more properly be described as conceptual or typological expositions. Thus, barely a year after Henry VII overthrew the House of York upon Bosworth Field, he was literally crowned—pageant by pageant—in the streets of York. The plot is a clearly defined one, but it is based upon the coronation ceremony instead of a narrative fable. At the first station, Ebraucus gives Henry the keys to the city and a crown descends from heaven to cover a Union Rose. In the next, a council of past English kings awards him with the Scepter of Wisdom, while at a third station, a pageant-David invests the king with the Sword of Victory. Now that Henry has received all of the coronation regalia, the Virgin Mary descends from Heaven in a final pageant to present him with God's blessings.[25] By contrast, Anne Boleyn's triumphal plot is typological in structure. In pageant after pageant, she receives a series of golden gifts— gold coins, Paris's golden apple, a gift of "golden" verses, the golden crown of a queen. As the pageant speakers make clear, these are all emblems of the golden age that can be renewed upon her coronation. But the Golden Age requires its Saturn, and in return for these gifts, London asks a golden gift from Anne: a new son of the king's blood who shall bring that golden world to his people.[26]

The decided homiletic emphasis in most of these plots may tempt us to draw parallels between the art of the triumph and the art of the morality play. In fact, however, this didactic function of the civic triumph derives more directly from medieval and Renaissance conceptions of the Roman triumph. Petrarch's *Trionfi,* for example, exemplifies one of the chief

24. Dekker, III, 231–247.

25. H. A. Smith, "A York Pageant, 1486," *London Mediaeval Studies* (1939), 382–398; John C. Meagher, The First Progress of Henry VII," *RenD,* N.S. I (1968), 49–59.

26. *Tudor Tracts,* pp. 12–19.

organizing principles in the plot of a civic triumph, a principle which
demands that the *triumphator* must acquire certain virtues at one station
before he may pass on to the next. Thus the *Trionfi* takes the form of a
series of six pageantlike allegorical triumphs arranged in a homiletic
series. As Petrarch describes these triumphs, each allegorical *triumphator*
conquers his predecessor and falls victim to his successor; beginning with
the Triumph of Love, Chastity overthrows Love, Death overthrows
Chastity, Fame overthrows Death, Time overthrows Fame, and Eternity
overthrows Time. In England, the illustrations for this poem—tapestries,
pictures, and manuscript illuminations—far outstripped the influence of
the poem itself. In one illustration, for example, Death would be riding
her ox-drawn triumphal chariot with Chastity bound and lying at her
feet. In the next, the Lady Fame would triumphantly ride her triumphal
chariot, drawn by four winged horses, while Death lay chained and
helpless at her feet.[27] At times, the *Trionfi* were even translated from
illustrations to pageantry. In 1579, for example, Queen Elizabeth witnessed a pageant performance based upon Petrarch's Triumph of Chastity. First, Cupid entered the queen's presence in his triumphal chariot.
Next, Dame Chastity with her four maids—Modesty, Temperance, Good
Exercise, and Shamefastness—entered, threw Cupid from his chariot,
despoiled him of his cloak, and took away his bow and arrows. Chastity
then mounted the chariot, rode to the queen, and presented her with
the spoils of conquest: the cloak, bow, and arrows.[28]

As they traveled through the streets of the city, many a London
triumphator also found himself obeying the familiar homiletic logic of
this Petrarchan classic. Katharine of Aragon was obliged to understand
Noblesse and Virtue before she might ascend to the sphere of the moon.
She then gained philosophical wisdom upon the moon before she could
ascend further to the sun, and so on. In similar fashion, Mulcaster takes

27. Cf. Sir Thomas More's "Tapestry Poem," *The English Works of Sir Thomas
More,* ed. W. E. Campbell and A. W. Reed (London, 1927), I, 332–335. See also
D. D. Carnicelli's introduction to his edition of Lord Morley's *"Tryumphes of
Fraunces Petrarcke": The First English Translation of the "Trionfi"* (Oxford,
1972).

28. Edwin Greenlaw, Charles Grosvenor Osgood, Frederick M. Padelford, eds.,
The Works of Edmund Spenser: A Various Edition (Baltimore, Md., 1934), III,
355. See also III, 301, 354–355, 359, 398.

particular care to point out the dependence of each new pageant upon its successor during Queen Elizabeth's coronation triumph:

The mater of this pageāt depēdeth of them yt went before. For as the first declared her grace to cōe out of ye house of vnitie, ye second yt she is placed in ye seat of gouernement staied with vertue to the suppressiō of vice, and therefore in the third the eight blessinges of almighty god might well be applyed vnto her: so this fourth now is, to put her grace in remembrāce of the state of the common weale, which Time with Truth his doughter dooth reuele, which Truth also her grace hath receiued, and therfore cannot but be mercifull and carefull for ye good gouernemēt therof.[29]

Perhaps Dekker's 1612 triumph for Sir John Swinnerton even more clearly approximates Petrarch's idea. When Sir John encounters Neptune in his triumphal chariot, Neptune yields and becomes a henchman to Sir John's triumph. Next come encounters with Virtue (who also rides a triumphal chariot) and Fame, each repeating this initial pattern. In a variation upon the Petrarchan pattern, the triumph of Virtue succeeds the triumph of Neptune; the triumph of Fame succeeds that of Virtue. Together, these three moral triumphs now make possible Sir John's destruction of Envy. Significantly, each of the pageants which Sir John conquers takes a place in the mayor's procession just proceeding him; in both the Roman procession and the *Trionfi* illustrations, that position is reserved for the conquered.

In addition to the Petrarchan Trionfi, pageant designers also drew from another traditional formula in designing their plots. According to an extremely popular description of the Roman triumph that appears in many moral and allegorical works of the late Middle Ages, the victorious *triumphator* was paid a triple honor.[30] First, all people, whether of high or low estate, should meet him "with grete Ioye & reuerence, in þer beste and richeste aray." Second, all his captives, "fetrid and manaclid," should "rownde abowte environ his chare" and go through the streets with him in procession. Third, the *triumphator* should ride in a chariot like a god, wearing the mantle of Jupiter and crowned with laurel. But along with

29. *The Passage of our most drad Soueraigne*, fol. Di^v.

30. Bromyard, *Summa Praedicantium*, T.v.36; *Gesta Romanorum*, chap. xxx; John Gower, *Confessio Amantis*, VI.2328–2490; John Lydgate, *The Serpent of Division*, ed. H. N. MacCracken (London, 1911), pp. 53–54.

this "triple honor" goes a dose of humility. In order "to schewe clerely þat all worldely glorie is transitori and not abidynge and evidently to declare þat in hiʒe estate is none assurance," a "Ribald" sat uppermost in the triumphal chariot, where he might "smyte þe conqverroure euer in þe necke and uppon þe hed." "Know thyself," he would shout at the *triumphator,* reminding him that despite the purple cloak of Jupiter he was merely mortal.[31] Furthermore, upon the day of a triumph any man might heap what scorn he would upon the conqueror, without fear of punishment. Where honor is freely given, vanity must be sternly suppressed.

The widespread popularity of this moral emblem undoubtedly explains why the plots of so many English triumphs describe the protagonist's achievement of fame or his discovery of a true honor based upon virtue instead of lineage. Thus Katharine of Aragon travels through the streets of London in search of the Throne of Honor, only to find that

> Honour, ye wott well, the rewarde of vertue is,
> And thoughe that vertuelesse many a man or this
> Hath semyd honourable, yet was he not so;
> Such honour is counterfaite and is lightly goo.

Over a century later, Sir John Swinnerton must similarly go to the House of Fame and learn that *"in this* Court *of* Fame / *None else but* Vertue *can enrole thy* Name" before he can defeat Envy.[32] Indeed, the achievement of Honor became the single most important theme of the London mayoral triumph as the titles of so many of them suggest: *The Triumphs of Honor and Industry, The Triumphs of Honor and Virtue, Monuments of Honor, Britannia's Honor,* and even *The Triumphs of Fame and Honor.*[33] Very few London *triumphators* took the stage without encountering some representative of Honor—whether a temple, a chariot, a globe, or even a character named Honor. In each case, the purpose of the *triumphator*'s encounter with these structures and characters is the

31. Lydgate, *Serpent of Division,* pp. 53–54.

32. College of Arms, MS. 1st M. 13, fol. 43ᵛ; Dekker, III, 240.

33. Devisers and dates as follows: Thomas Middleton, *Triumphs of Honor and Industry* (1617) and *Triumphs of Honor and Virtue* (1622); John Webster, *Monuments of Honor* (1624); Thomas Dekker, *Britannia's Honor* (1628); John Taylor, *Triumphs of Fame and Honor* (1634).

same: he must learn that however great the glory of his name and office, true honor depends upon his selfless service to the commonwealth.

In order to enforce this distinction between mundane glory and honorable duty, some dramatists provide their *triumphators* with uncomfortable "Ribalds," even while setting them in chariots and surrounding them with obsequious nobles. The entry of Mary Queen of Scots into Edinburgh in 1561 shows how far the dramatist's license to humble his protagonist might extend. At the first pageant station, an angel presents Mary with the keys to the city, an English Bible, and a Protestant Psalm book—pointed enough gifts, perhaps, for a Catholic queen. Next, she witnesses a scene designed to show her what papist idolators like herself might expect if they cling to their Catholic ways. In the "Venegance of God upon Idolatry," she sees the fire of the Lord consume Korah, Dathan, and Abiram because of their rebellion against the congregation of Moses. Perhaps she does not need to be told that Moses in Scotland is John Knox, but lest she miss the point, a priest is also burned in the very act of elevating the Host at the altar. In John Knox's Scotland, the idolatry of the Host will not be tolerated. But Mary is still not through with witnessing the fiery vengeance of the Lord: at a final pageant, the Beast of the Apocalypse burns before her eyes. If Moses had represented John Knox in the previous pageant, there can be little doubt whom the Beast of the Apocalypse is meant to figure in this one.[34]

In London triumphs, the admonition of the "Ribald" is usually not this bold, but it does occur—occasionally with devasting results. The creator of Katharine of Aragon's triumph of 1501, for example, is particularly adept at administering the licensed dose of humility. As the princess ascends the heavens where she will become the star Hesperus, she pauses upon the sphere of the sun where she sees an image of her husband, represented as King Arthur riding a stellar chariot. The stellar chariot is her husband's seven-starred constellation, Arcturus, which Englishmen then knew as "Arthur's constellation." Thus, as the princess rides the streets of London in her own triumph, she suddenly confronts her own husband riding through the heavens in a magnificent star-chariot. While she pauses before this vision, she becomes a part of the grand design to

---

34. Mill, 188–191; in the context of the antipapal imagery, I assume that the reference to "the dragon" must mean the Beast of the Apocalypse.

the London audience. No longer a *triumphator* riding in her own earthly triumph, she now takes her place as a henchman in Arthur's grander celestial one. The Petrarchan logic of the pageant diminishes her while exalting Arthur; just as the Chariot of Fame replaces the Chariot of Death in successive illustrations to the *Trionfi,* so Arthur's stellar chariot supercedes Katharine's earthly one. In the pageant as in life, forces beyond her control doom her to ride as a mere henchman in the triumphal procession of the Tudor dynasty. Only after she learns her subordinate place in this English dynasty can she complete her journey to the Throne of Honor. A place has been made ready for her there, she discovers, not because of her own intrinsic worth, but because she is the wife of a Tudor prince.

In most cases, however, triumph dramatists admonished their protagonists to "know themselves" in a less devastating way. Typically, a triumph plot equips the *triumphator* with the virtues and knowledge that he will need to succeed as king or mayor, thus winning glory for himself, his city, and his country. The particular virtues necessary to his success will, of course, depend upon the occasion, Thus, when Henry VI entered London in 1432, the pageant designer understandably focused upon the boy-king's necessary education. First, Nature, Grace, and Fortune shower him with their gifts: strength and fairness of body, the seven Gifts of the Holy Ghost and the seven matching Gifts of Grace, and Prosperity and Wealth. These are the gifts that are his by right of birth into the royal house of England. But to be successful as a king, Henry discovers at the next pageant, he must improve these gifts by means of Dame Sapience and the Seven Liberal Arts; he must, in short, go to school. In the two succeeding pageants, he finds that his throne depends upon law and that he must become a Well of Mercy to his subjects; presumably his scholastic education will prepare him to distinguish between Justice and Mercy in ruling his subjects. If he succeeds in ruling properly, as the final two pageants make clear, he will be worthy of the two crowns of England and France that he has inherited, and the Heavenly Trinity will keep him from "all damage" during his reign.[36]

35. See my book, *The Triumph of Honor* (Leiden, 1977), chap. IV, for a complete discussion of this triumph.
36. *Great Chronicle,* pp. 156–170.

When Elizabeth I performed her coronation triumph over a century and
a quarter later, however, the pageant designer emphasized the virtues
of concord and adherence to religious truth that the queen would find
necessary in an England divided by the Reformation. Thus, in order that
she might know her duties more clearly, the dramatist posted a summary
statement of all that she had learned in her triumphal passage through
the city:

> The first arch as true heyre vnto thy father deere,
> Did set thee in the throne where thy graund father satte,
> The second did confirme thy seat as princesse here,
> Vertues now bearing swaye, and vyces bet down flatte.
>
> The third, if that thou wouldst goe on as thou began,
> Declared thee to be blessed on euery syde,
> The fourth did open Trueth, and also taught thee whan
> The commōweale stoode well, & when it did thence slide.
>
> The fifth, as Debora declared thee to be sent
> From heauen, a long comfort to vs thy subiects all,
> Therefore goe on, O Queene, on whom our hope is bent,
> And take with thee this wishe of thy towne as finall.[37]

Although hereditary right and personal virtue qualify her to occupy the
English throne, Elizabeth discovers, they will not in themselves guarantee
the successful continuance of her reign. If she hopes to "go on as she began," she must play the role of a Deborah, delivering her nation from the
oppression of its Jabin (Philip of Spain), thereby upholding true religion
and restoring the commonwealth to its previous flourishing estate. By
enthusiastically clasping the English Bible to her breast, she signifies her
willingness to perform this difficult role that her subjects have thrust
upon her.

Mayors' triumphs are particularly characterized by such dramatic reve-
lations of the *triumphator*'s future duties. In 1585, just before the Armada,
Peele saw Wolstan Dixi's chief duty as the defense of queen and country.
Only in this way might he "adde to Londons dignity, / And Londons
dignity . . . adde" to his.[38] Thirty-two years later, however, Thomas

---

37. *The Passage of our most drad Soueraigne,* fol. Ej[v].
38. *The Life and Minor Works of George Peele,* ed. David H. Horne (New
Haven, Conn., 1952), p. 210.

Middleton was preparing his mayor to enter the "Castle of Fame or Honour" by schooling him in the arts of peace. Accordingly, at the beginning of his triumph, Dame Industry reminds him that she is "the life-blood of praise: / To rise without me, is to steal to glory." As one of Industry's "sons," a place is reserved for him in the Castle of Honor, but in order to claim that place

> Great works of grace must be requir'd and done
> Before the honour of this seat be won.
> A whole year's reverend care in righting wrongs,
> And guarding innocence from malicious tongues,
> Must be employ'd in virtue's sacred right
> Before this place be fill'd.[39]

Just as the "Ribald" warns the *triumphator* not to "wex prowde" in the "worldly glorie" of his triumph, so the Lord Mayor finds that the glory and adulation of his fine triumph have only brought him "a whole year's reverend care." His lesson parallels the one that Henry V learns on the eve of Agincourt: "What infinite heart's-ease must kings neglect that private men enjoy."

The protagonists of these triumphal dramas, of course, might react to these moral exhortations and doses of humility in different ways. As we have seen, Elizabeth I was able to transform Lady Truth's gift of a Bible into a melodramatic statement of support for the Protestant faith, a performance that evidently won her great favor in the eyes of her subjects. Two years later, however, Mary Queen of Scots found herself performing the same scene, but with quite the opposite results. As she approached one of the triumphal arches in her coronation procession, a "cloude opynnit" and a child "discendit doun as it had bene ane angell, and deliuerit to hir hienes . . . ane bybill and ane psalme buik." The angel declared these gifts "to be emblems of her defending the Reformed religion." But instead of kissing the Bible and clasping it to her breast, as Elizabeth had done, Mary "began to frown. For schame sche could not refuise it, but she did no better, for immediatelie sche gave it to the most pestilent Papist within the Realme." Such a refusal to "play the role" assigned to her could not be expected to win her any support among the

39. *The Works of Thomas Middleton,* ed. A. H. Bullen (London, 1886), VII, 303.

followers of Knox.[40] A few other similar instances suggest that *triumphators* did not always play their roles gladly,[41] but Henry VII's reaction to the role he assumed during his triumphal entry into Bristol in 1486 more nearly illustrates the ideal. Saluted in pageant after pageant as a king sent by God "to reforme thyngs that be contrarious / Unto the Comen Wele," Henry responds by seeking to restore Bristol's shipbuilding and clothmaking industries, which had lately fallen into decay:

After Evensonge the Kinge sent for the Mayre and Shrife, and Parte of the best Burges of the Towne, and demaunded theym of the Cause of ther Povertie; and they shewde his grace for the great Losse of Shippes and Goodes that they had loost within 5 yeres. The King comforted theym, that they shulde sett on and make new Shippes, and to exercise ther Marchandise as they wer wonte for to doon. And his Grace shulde so helpe theym by dyvers Means like as he shewde unto theym, that the Meyre of the Towne towlde me they harde not this hundred Yeres of noo King so good a Comfort.[42]

Such a response is dramatically as well as politically appropriate. It shows that the king is willing to perform in earnest the role that his subjects have thrust upon him in the triumphal drama.

For Londoners in the Renaissance, the Roman celebration of military victory had been transformed into a civic drama of moral triumph. The king or mayor who rode through the streets of London did not merely witness a series of pageant shows; he also played the lead in the "wonderfull spectacle" that the London multitude witnessed. The plots for these triumphal dramas were based upon the *triumphator*'s encounters with the series of pageants that awaited him in the streets. By cleverly defining and arranging the pageant encounters, the dramatist made his protagonist perform any number of actions: ascend the heavens, fulfill a knightly quest, conquer envy, travel to the House of Fame, become a

40. Mill, p. 190; Knox's report here is probably extremely prejudiced.

41. Compare Anne Boleyn's supposed anger at the Easterlings, who "set the Imperial eagle over the royal arms and her own" upon one of her coronation pageants, and the Bishop of Winchester's intimidation of a painter who had dared to portray Henry VIII holding "a booke, whereon was wrytten *Verbum Dei*" during Philip of Spain's London triumph (Anglo, pp. 250 n. 2, 329).

42. Leland, IV, 202; Meagher, p. 72.

king, or—more simply—accept a series of symbolic gifts and give one in
return. The possibilities are as endless as the dramatist's imagination. But
because the Roman triumph had itself become a moral emblem to
Renaissance Londoners, these encounters became moral as well. As the
Petrarchan moral pattern would have it, the *triumphator* often ac-
complishes a series of moral triumphs in his passage through London,
each one dependent upon its predecessor. The dramatist, of course, arranges these moral encounters because he finds them significant; the
virtues that the protagonist masters in his drama are the virtues that the
dramatist and his audience hope their governors will master in performing the duties of their offices. The "general end" of this drama, as
Spenser might have explained it, is "to fashion a magistrate." But where
the writer of an epic hopes to teach by example rather than rule, the
deviser of a triumph teaches by mimesis. After performing his role in
the triumphal drama, perhaps the magistrate is now fit to perform it
again in "real life."

Landscape with Figures: The Three Realms of Queen Elizabeth's Country-house Revels

BRUCE R. SMITH

A MONG OTHER THINGS, she had tamed a Savage Man with her presence; she had freed the Lady of the Lake, imprisoned in the castle's waters since the days of King Arthur; and now, after nearly three weeks, Queen Elizabeth was leaving Kenilworth Castle and taking her summer progress elsewhere. She had given very short notice. To George Gascoigne came the Earl of Leicester's command "to devise some Farewel worth the presenting." As the queen was riding over Kenilworth one last time, then, she turned to discover trotting along on foot behind her no less a personage than Sylvanus, god of the woods. Behind the disguise was Gascoigne himself, and as the queen rode along he spun a continuous thread of what he later claimed was extempore speechmaking. Taking up objects in the actual landscape—"this old Oke," "yonder Popler," "this Ashtree," "this bramble Bryer," "this braunch of Ivy," "yonder same *Lawrell* tree"—Sylvanus discovered beneath their leaves the trembling presences of metamorphosed lovers. Under Gascoigne's Midas touch the landscape of Kenilworth Castle became an enchanted landscape, alive with ideas, growing with human feeling. His golden poesy was measured not in syllabic feet but land miles:

Here her majestie stayed her horse to favour *Sylvanus,* fearing least he should
be driven out of breath by following her horse so fast. But *Sylvanus* humbly
besought her Highnesse to goe on, declaring that if hys rude speech did not
offend her, he coulde continue this tale to be twenty miles long.

(*PP,* C4)

Coming finally to "this *Holy bush,*" Sylvanus introduced from among the
prickly leaves the voice of Deep Desire, a not very dark disguise for the
Earl of Leicester himself. To soft instrumental accompaniment the voice
in the holly bush—speaking in Leicester's persona, doubtfully in his
person—pleaded that Elizabeth would metamorphose him from a languishing plant back into a dutiful courtier.[1] Tongues in trees indeed.

   In few other places in English Renaissance literature do we find the
Elizabethan dramatic impulse given such extravagant and spontaneous
expression. The Kenilworth shows of 1575 are, of course, the most
famous of the outdoor sports that engaged the Virgin Queen's vanity
and fancy on her annual summer progresses over her realm. But the
custom goes back to the very first summer of her reign. From Henry
Machyn's diary we know a good deal about the entertainments that

---

   1. Two documents allow us to reconstruct the Kenilworth sports in some detail. Verses and speeches by Gascoigne, William Hunnis, Edward Ferrers, one
"Muncaster" (=Richard Mulcaster?), and others appeared the next year as *The
Princelye pleasures, at the Courte at Kenelwoorth,* an octavo pamphlet that was
fortunately reprinted in *Kenilworth Illustrated* (Chiswick, 1821) before the unique
copy was destroyed in the Birmingham Free Library fire of 1879. Minus the
printer's address to "studious and well disposed yong Gentlemen" and some
marginal notes, all these verses and speeches by sundry hands found their way
into *The Whole woorkes of George Gascoigne Esquyre* (1587). My quotations
from this reprinting of *The Princelye pleasures* are indicated *PP* in the text and
include page references. In these and all other quotations I have retained original
spelling but have expanded scribal abbreviations and have made *u* and *v* and *i* and
j accord with modern orthography. The second document takes the form of *A
LETTER: Whearin, part of the entertainment untoo the Queenz Majesty, at
Killingworth Castl, in Warwik Sheer in this Soomers Progress 1575. iz signified:
from a freend officer attendant in the Coourt, unto hiz freend a Citizen, and
Merchaunt of London.* Printed with no printer's name and no date, this narrative
account by one "R. L." is dated at Worcester on 20 August, about a month after
the event. From F. J. Furnivall's edition of the text as *Robert Laneham's Letter*
(New York and London, 1907) come my quotations, indicated *LL* and including
page references to the original, which Furnivall gives marginally.

greeted the new queen on her 1559 progress through Surrey and Middle-sex.[2] Even across this great expanse of years, however, the Kenilworth shows loom as a landmark. The enterprising news- and ballad-printer Richard Jones joined forces with the enterprising news- and ballad-makers Leicester had hired to devise the shows and published a ha'penny pamphlet of the text. From this occasion in 1575 down to the last summer of Elizabeth's reign we possess not just diary accounts or financial records but full texts for no fewer than fifteen country-house devices. About half this number were printed soon after they were played; the other half survive in manuscript.[3]

The historical and antiquarian interest of the texts prompted John Nichols to collect and print as many of them as he could lay hands on in *The Progresses and Public Processions of Queen Elizabeth* (first edition in four volumes, 1788–1821); but it was Sir Walter Scott who first introduced a wide public to the curiosities of the court's country sports. The splendor of the Kenilworth shows fired Scott's historical imagination, and

2. *The Diary of Henry Machyn,* ed. J. G. Nichols, Camden Society no. 42 (London, 1848), pp. 202 ff.

3. On Richard Jones's specialties as a news and ballad printer see R. B. McKerrow, ed., *A Dictionary of Printers and Booksellers in England, Scotland and Ireland . . . 1557–1640* (London, 1910), p. 159. The cheap price of pamphlets like *The Princelye pleasures* is indicated in Raphael Holinshed's apology for including an account of the 1578 East Anglian progress in his *Chronicles,* 2d ed. (1587): "Here though somewhat out of place (for it should have beene entered in 1578) it were better to record the receiving of the queenes majestie into Suffolke and Norffolke, than making no commemoration therof at all, to let it perish in three halfepenie pamphlets, and so die in oblivion" (*Chronicles of England, Scotland and Ireland* [London, 1808], IV, 375). As the literary quality of the devices improved, so did the respectability of the printers. Thomas Cadman published the Woodstock sports of 1575 ten years after the event but only one year after he had secured rights to John Lyly's modish court comedies *Alexander and Campaspe* and *Sapho and Phao.* Apologetic though he is in the preface, the printer of the devices at Bisham, Sudeley, and Rycote in 1592 was no less a personage than Joseph Barnes, official printer to Oxford University. As an appendix to this essay I have assembled a catalog of the fifteen surviving country-house entertainments, indicating for each (1) the occasion, (2) sources of the text, (3) motives and themes, (4) extant musical settings and parts anthologized, and (5) the modern edition. A glance at the fourth column will show how many poems and songs from the later devices were good enough to stand alone and so found their way into anthologies of verse and collections of lute songs.

he includes a full account of them in *Kenilworth, a Romance* (1821). Studying the texts with a historical imagination rather less flammable than Scott's, twentieth-century historians and critics have found Elizabeth's progress entertainments interesting for several different reasons. Only David M. Bergeron has attempted a full account of them, and it is to his *English Civic Pageantry 1558–1642* (1971) that a reader should turn for a chronological narrative of the fifteen surviving texts. Royal entries into cities and towns, receptions of the queen at the universities, and Lord Mayors' Shows figure along with country-house revels in the pageantry that Bergeron analyzes as a series of experiments at joining the "body" of spectacle, speeches, music, and dancing to the "soul" of allegorical ideas.[4] Taking her cue from the numerous occasions when a ceremony of gift-giving provides dramatic structure for country-house welcomes, M. C. Bradbrook has discussed the Kenilworth shows in their social and seasonal context, styling them "drama as offering." Country-house sports are strictly an occasional art, she argues, contained within a very particular social situation. Spectacle, speeches, and music were as much a gift to Elizabeth as the jewels and gowns she usually took home as souvenirs.[5] Rather less sociable motives sometimes lurk in these ceremonies of giving. Though none of Elizabeth's progress entertainments comes under sharp political scrutiny in *Splendor at Court: Renaissance Spectacle and the Theater of Power* (1973), Roy Strong would teach us always to listen for the propagandist's firm voice in the lyric accents of gods and goddesses.[6] Certainly Elizabeth undertook her progresses as much for the realm to see the state of the queen as for the queen to see the state of the realm. Frances Yates, finally, has connected the Woodstock sports of 1575 and 1592 with the Accession Day tilts held every November at Westminster and has discovered in the chivalric myth acted out on those occasions "the continuity of its ceremonial and mystique with pre-Reformation times." The golden Arthurian fiction that Elizabeth and her courtiers so clearly liked to live gave a legitimate out-

4. David M. Bergeron, *English Civic Pageantry 1557–1642* (London and Columbia S.C., 1971).

5. M. C. Bradbrook, "Drama as Offering: *The Princely Pleasures at Kenilworth,*" in *The Rise of the Common Player* (London, 1962), pp. 243–264.

6. Roy Strong, *Splendor at Court: Renaissance Spectacle and the Theater of Power* (London and Boston, 1973).

let for "modes of thought and feeling" that otherwise found little place in the new religious order.[7]

The figure of George Gascoigne, jogging and fabling behind Elizabeth's horse, reminds us, however, that in two respects at least Queen Elizabeth's country-house sports are as distinct from civic entries, tournaments, and masques as they are from conventional plays. Those respects are time and place. No formal occasion contains these devices: they spill over into days and weeks, interweaving golden threads of artifice into the green fabric of Elizabeth's entire stay at a country estate. Where could the queen be caught off guard? The plotters delight in catching her as she rides back from hunting or as she walks in the garden. Suddenly characters pop out of hedges and groves; music starts up from players hidden in the bushes. Surprise, spontaneity count for all. Elizabeth's impromptu response one day might become part of tomorrow's design. At Kenilworth one afternoon Gascoigne—this time in the guise of a club-wielding "Hombre Salvagio"—leaped out from behind a tree as she was riding home from the chase. Her presence civilized him on the spot. When the soothed Savage split his oak club and flung it away, Elizabeth's horse, perceiving no fiction, reared up and very nearly spilled the queen. "No hurt! no hurt!" she cried—"which words," one bystander reports, the audience took as "the best part of the play" (*LL*, 20–21). But that was not all she said. A marginal note in the original printed account declares that Elizabeth recovered from the scare to comment tartly that "the Actor was blind." Taken aback but not abashed, Gascoigne worked her remark into a playlet planned for several days later. Into a little debate among Diana and her nymphs the Savage's son was to come in, reporting that his father "(uppon such wordes as hyr highnesse dyd then use unto him) lay languishing like a blind man, untill it might please hyr highnesse to take the filme from his eyes" (B2ᵛ). Elizabeth herself found just the right word for such familiar banter when she took her leave of one of the Kenilworth characters, promising she would "common" with her again later (*LL*, 11).

As no formal occasion delimits Queen Elizabeth's country-house revels, so, too, no place constricts them. The stage for these sports is no platform

---

7. Frances A. Yates, "Elizabethan Chivalry: The Romance of the Accession Day Tilts," *JWCI*, X (1957), 4–25.

of boards, nor the long streets of a city, nor even the broad spaces of a tournament ring, but the whole wide landscape of a country-house estate. When the queen and her scores of courtiers, their hundreds of retainers, and their three to four hundred baggage carts entered an estate, the road through the park to the house became a ceremonial parade course. Just as when she entered a city, Elizabeth might stop along the way to receive welcoming speeches and welcoming gifts. In towns her official greeters were actual inhabitants of the place; in the country, more often than not, they were gods and goddesses from faraway Greece and Rome. Later in her stay witty disputants might waylay her in the garden and ask her to settle their debate; breathless shepherdesses might run up to her in the meadows, seeking refuge from lusty young gods; questing knights might cross her path in the wooded chase. Elizabeth's entertainers may have borrowed their motifs from Roman verse and medieval romance, their motives from Machiavelli, their give-and-take mode from medieval drama, and their festive mood from native folk customs, but the dramatic event that sprang up in country-house landscapes is an exotic hybrid, different from any of the strains that produced it. Above all else, it is the interplay between art and life, so outrageous and yet so subtle, that makes Elizabeth's country-house revels fascinating for us to reconstruct and imagine. How did characters of Roman mythology and medieval romance come to find refuge in sixteenth-century country-house parks? What happened when such personages suddenly found themselves face and face with real people in garden, meadow, or woods? In just what spirit did denizens of the political world "common" with denizens of myth and romance? Answers to these questions lie in the peculiarities of time and place that make Queen Elizabeth's country-house revels distinct from anything else in English Renaissance drama.

I. Landscape as Stage

Special conditions of time gave Elizabeth's country-house revels pace and mood; special conditions of place gave them plot. Gascoigne in his Sylvanus disguise is typical of the mostly anonymous devisers of these sports, not only in the second-rate quality of his verse-making (who, after all, could do better on such short notice and for such an ephemeral occasion?) but in the way his fiction-making springs up naturally from the setting. The fictions acted out on these country-house landscapes bring to dramatic life the same fictions that Elizabethans planted there in landscape design. If we look for physical survivals of those fictions today, we are almost everywhere disappointed. The eighteenth-century turn in the tides of taste so thoroughly innundated England's countryside that Andrew Marvell was uncannily prophetic in pouring Noah's flood over the gardens of Appleton House. When we as postdiluvian readers imagine Elizabeth's country revels in action, we must inevitably picture them against a backdrop by Capability Brown, against that parklike expanse of grass and groves, that studied naturalness that the Continent to this day calls the *jardin anglais*. With the small exception of the enclosed Old Pond Garden at Hampton Court, very little remains to show us firsthand what an Elizabethan country-house landscape was like. What we lack in firsthand information, however, we can partly make up from the second-hand information in the texts of country-house entertainments themselves, from accounts by sixteenth-century travelers in England like Paul Hentzner (1598), Thomas Platter (1599), and Baron Offenbach (1609), and, in one case at least, from what we can read in a surviving garden plan.[8]

As grand in scale as it is, John Smythson's "Platforme" of the gardens of Thomas Cecil, Earl of Exeter's house at Wimbledon, Surrey, may give us an unrealistic picture of how *extensive* English country-house gardens were in 1609; but it corroborates what we know from other sources about how those gardens were *organized* (see Figure 1). What we dis-

---

8. Paul Hentzner, *Itinerarium Germaniae, Galliae, Angliae, Italiae* (1612), portion on England trans. Richard Bentley as *Travels in England during the Reign of Queen Elizabeth* (1797), ed. Henry Morley (London, 1901); Thomas Platter the Younger, MS diary (1605-1606), portion on England trans. Clare Williams as *Thomas Platter's Travels in England 1599* (London, 1937) (hereafter cited as *Platter*); Georg von Schwartzstät, baron of Offenbach, MS diary (Folger MS. 1837.1), parts trans. G. P. V. Akrigg as "England in 1609," *HLQ*, XIV (1950), 75-94. For information on landscape design in the sixteenth century I am indebted to Marie Louise Gothein, *A History of Garden Art*, trans. Laura Archer-Hind, 2 vols. (London, Toronto, and New York, 1928); Miles Hadfield, *Gardening in Britain* (London, 1960); Derek Clifford, *A History of Garden Design* (London, 1962); and Terry Comito, "Renaissance Gardens and the Discovery of Paradise," *JHI*, XXXII (1971), 483-506.

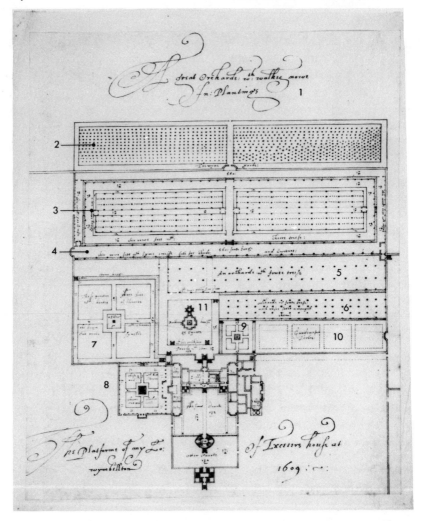

FIGURE I. John Smythson's "Platforme" of the Gardens of Wimbledon House, Surrey (1609). Reproduced by courtesy of the Royal Institute of British Architects, London.

cover in Smythson's plan is not at all the uninterrupted vista, the single sweep of parkland we see in English country-house parks today but a series of discrete spaces, walled off and separate from one another. Farthermost from the house, outside the garden walls, stretches a "great Orcharde wth walkes" (labeled area 1). Walking within the walls, directing ourselves toward the house, we enter, first, a vineyard (area 2), then two large "plantations" laid out in a more regular pattern (area 3). Crossing a long walk planted with lime trees "both for shade and swetnes" (area 4), we find ourselves in two smaller orchards, the first with fruit trees bordered by quickset hedges (area 5), the second with "fruite trees and roses set amongst them" (area 6). Closest to the house itself, then, we discover three severely geometric pleasure gardens (areas 7, 8, and 9) and an herb garden (area 10). Among all these, finally, there is a large open space, paved with stones and surmounted by a banqueting house (area 11). Remarkably regular within each enclosed space but remarkably irregular in the way those spaces are fitted together, Smythson's plan seems calculated to appeal to just the relish for variety that Sir Henry Wotton describes in *The Elements of Architecture* (1624):

> . . . I have seene a *Garden* (for the maner perchance incomparable) into which the first Accesse was a high walke like a *Tarrace,* from whence might bee taken a generall view of the whole *Plott* below; but rather in a delightfull confusion, then with any plaine distinction of the pieces. From this the *Beholder* descending many steps, was afterwards conveyed againe, by severall *mountings* and *valings,* to various entertainements of his *sent,* and *sight:* which I shall not neede to describe (for that were poeticall) let me onely note this, that every one of these diversities, was as if hee had beene *Magically* transported into a new Garden.[9]

Like Wotton's "mountings and valings," only small gateways link together the spaces in Smythson's plan. The walls serve not only to set these spaces off from each other but to set the whole garden off from the surrounding countryside with an abruptness unimaginable in the eighteenth century.

The spaces in Smythson's "Platforme" and the "delightfull confusion" in Wotton's incomparable garden are not quite the random patchwork they may first appear. For the principle that gives them order we should

9. Sir Henry Wotton, *The Elements of Architecture,* ed. F. Hard (Washington, 1968), p. 110.

take a second look at the landscape—this time following Ben Jonson's perceptive eye. When Jonson sets out to celebrate the Sidneys' "Penshurst Place" (printed 1616) he moves toward the manor house from the estate's outer reaches. Starting from the wooded Mount, haunt of Dryads and of game for hunting (ll. 10–21), Jonson escorts us through the pastoral "lower land" and "middle grounds" with their grazing sheep and cattle, their horses, pheasants and partridge, rabbits, and well-stocked ponds (ll. 21–38), through the orchard and flower garden (ll. 39–44), and into the walls of the house itself, where he sits us down to feast and commends at length the Sidneys' hospitality (ll. 45–88), not stopping until he has turned our attention finally to the private lives of the inhabitants (ll. 89–102).[10] From woods, through fields, then through orchard and garden into the house itself, Jonson's leisurely stroll is a progression from public to private, from nature to human art. At the first extreme, at the verge of the estate, are the wilds of the forest; at the other extreme, at the center of the estate, the civility of the manor house. In between lie, first, pastoral fields, then orchard and garden. Each of these middle realms strikes a distinctive balance between art and nature: nature only begins to give way to art in the pastoral fields nearer the woods; art's powers are stronger in the cultivated spaces of orchard and garden nearer the house. With its wide vineyard and orchards at the edge of the plot, its smaller, severely geometric gardens closest to the house, Smythson's Wimbledon "Platforme" shows in graphic form the same progress Jonson describes in verse.

Though they were laid out by Le Nôtre's pupil Beaumont more than seventy-five years after Jonson's poem and Smythson's plan, the famous topiary gardens at Levens Hall, Cumbria, remain to show us the relationship between gardens and countryside that Smythson, Wotton, and Jonson could see (see Figure 2). Between art and nature the demarcation could hardly be sharper. The imaginative distance between the pollarded prodigies in the foreground and the free-growing groves on the horizon is much farther than the physical distance across the open fields between them. Wyngaerde's bird's-eye views of Greenwich Palace

10. Ben Jonson, *Works,* ed. C. H. Herford and Percy and Evelyn Simpson, 11 vols. (Oxford, 1925–1952), VIII, 93–96.

FIGURE 2. Beaumont's Topiary Gardens, Levens Hall, Cumbria (laid out 1689).

in 1558 confirm what we can see at Levens Hall today (see Figure 6). Viewed from the hill, the rectangular geometry of the Greenwich gardens figures Turkish carpets; walled off from each other as well as from the outside world, these gardens seem more like grand extensions of the palace itself than part of the fields and woods that lie beyond.

It was a progress like Jonson's from nature toward art that Elizabeth traced when her entourage entered Lady Russell's park at Bisham Abbey, Berkshire, in 1592.[11] Her approach to the house was down the side of a hill, and at three points on her descent creatures of the land paid their

11. *Speeches Delivered to Her Majestie This Last Progresse at the Right Honorable the Lady Russels, at Bissam, the Right Honorable the Lorde Chandos, at Sudley, at the Right Honorable the Lord Norris, at Ricorte* (Oxford, 1592), rpt. in R. W. Bond, ed., *The Complete Works of John Lyly* (Oxford, 1902), I, 471–477.

homage. Out of the wild woods on the hilltop bounded a wild man who, like his predecessor at Kenilworth, was instantly tamed by Elizabeth's presence. Unlike his predecessor, however, he did not cast off his club but kept it, "not as a Salvage," he explained, "but to beate downe those that are." In a field at the middle of the hill Elizabeth came upon Pan and two virgins keeping sheep. The lusty young god's persuasions to love moved these maids only to some pretty arguments for chastity, and in the end Pan, too, yielded himself willingly to Elizabeth's power. Like Spenser's Colin Clout, he broke his pipe. He did so not, like Colin, to dispel the pastoral peace that lay over the fields, he told Elizabeth, but to "followe the sounde which followes you." At the bottom of the hill, finally, "entring into the hous," Ceres offered the queen her bounty, "a Crowne of wheat-ears with a Jewell"—a token of human art and industry.

Lady Russell's Savage Man is reminiscent of Gascoigne at Kenilworth, not only in *what* happened to him but in *where* it happened. Taking his bearing from the castle, our informant at Kenilworth is careful to specify that the taming of the savage took place "at the hither part of the Chase"—that is, at the verge of the chase nearest the house, where woods verged into open meadow. Taming the distracted creature was no instantaneous act: he charmed himself into civility through an elaborate dialogue with Echo. "Enforme me some good man," he cried as he rushed toward Elizabeth's hunting party,

> speake, speake some courteous knight,
> They all cry mumme, what shall I do,
>   what sunne shal lend me light?
> Wel Eccho, where art thou
>   could I but Eccho finde,
> Shee would returne me answere yet
>   by blast of every winde.
> Ho *Eccho: Eccho,* ho,
>   where art thou *Eccho,* where?
> Why *Eccho* friend, where dwellest thou now,
>   thou woontst to harbour here.
>
> (*PP,* A4ᵛ)

"Here!" obliged Echo, setting off an antiphonal dialogue that is one of the earliest appearances in English of a poetical tour de force made famous in the pastoral landscape of Sannazaro's *Arcadia.*

> But wherefore doe [t]hey so rejoyce?
>   is it for King or Queene?
>   *Eccho.*   Queene
> Queene? what the Queene of heaven?
>   they knewe hir long agone?
> No sure some Queene on earth,
>   whose like was never none.
>   *Eccho.*   None
> O then, it seemes the Queene,
>   of England for to be:
> Whose graces make the Gods to grudge,
>   me thinkes it should be shee.
>   *Eccho.*   Shee
>
>   (*PP*, A4ᵛ–A5)

The play of sound must have been all the more marvelous for turning into harmony the cacaphony that had been thrilling our observers in the woods—"the earning of the hoounds in continuauns of their crie, . . . the galloping of horsez, the blasting of hornz, the halloing and hewing of the huntsmen, with the excellent Echoz between whilez from the woods and waters in valleiz resounding . . ." (*LL*, 17). This cacaphony yielded to musical harmony, to the interplay of verse and echo arising from the land itself that combined magically with Elizabeth's civilizing presence to bring the raging moss-and-ivy-covered savage down on adoring knees.

It was just such powers of art that Elizabethans liked to celebrate when they designed their gardens. Sir Nicholas Bacon's garden at Gorhambury, Hertfordshire, for instance, was not quite the triumph of nature over art that we would expect from his son's famous essay "Of Gardens." Part of the garden, roving John Weever reports, had been laid out by Lord Keeper Bacon as an orchard, part as a tract of trees and shrubs in orderly patterns. It was the woodland plants, not the orderly pattern of planting, that prompted Renaissance Englishmen to call this tract a "wilderness." Presiding over orchard and "wilderness" was a statue of Orpheus. On a portal above the master of the lyre were inscribed verses spoken in unison by the plants themselves, just as effigies are wont to speak on Renaissance tombs:

> Not long ago I was rough in appearance,
>   a hiding place for beasts and rustic gods.
> By lucky chance I was tamed when Orpheus came here,

who does not allow me to revert to my uncultivated state.
He calls together the pruned branches
   to make an abode that would please the gods.
Like a husbandman to me are Orpheus and his tilling.
O long may our love together flourish![12]

In a single vista, then, one might see both unfruitful "wilderness" and the pruned, productive plants of Orpheus's musical "tilling." From Orpheus's lyre, as from the echo song at Kenilworth, radiated a civilizing power.

John Smythson's plan of the gardens at Wimbledon House, Ben Jonson's panoramic view of Penshurst Place, Elizabeth's taming of savages at Kenilworth and Bisham Abbey, Lord Keeper Bacon's statue of Orpheus at Gorhambury: the testimony of all these invites us to see in Elizabethan country-house estates not a single sweep of landscape but an ordered vista of *three* landscapes—garden, meadow, and woods—each of which reflects a different balance between art and nature. If with our observer at Kenilworth we take the country house itself as our point of reference, the vista before us resolves into a foreground of house and garden, a middle distance of pastoral meadowland, and a far horizon of woods. The view outward from the topiary gardens of Levens Hall shows us these three landscapes in the sharp juxtaposition that was characteristic of Renaissance country estates. When we take a closer look at these three tracts, we discover striking differences not only in the flora but in the fictions that take root and flourish there. Each of the three landscapes is haunt to characters with distinctly different literary origins; each demands a different imaginative and emotional response

---

12. My translation. John Weever describes the layout and transcribes the verses in his *Ancient Funerall Monuments within the United Monarchie of Great Britaine, Ireland, and the Islands adjacent* (London, 1631), pp. 583–584: "Horrida nuper eram aspectu latebraeque ferarum, / Ruricolis tantum numinibusque locus. / Edomitor fausto huc dum forte supervenit Orpheus / Ulterius qui me non sinit esse rudem; / Convocat, avulsis virgulta virentia truncis / Et sedem quae vel Diis placuisse potest. / Sique mei cultor, sic est mihi cultus & Orpheus: / Floreat o noster cultus amorque diu." The closest thing in Renaissance landscape design to what *we* would call a "wilderness" would be the "heath" Sir Francis Bacon describes in his essay "Of Gardens," but of Bacon's thickets of wild plants growing randomly on molehills there are no known examples in Renaissance England.

from the courtly visitors who pass through. We can map not only the geography of the country-house stage but its mythography as well. By moving from garden foreground through pastoral middleground to the woods on the far horizon we can observe in its full variety the flirtation with myth and romance that engrossed the court in the country.

II. Foreground

To a twentieth-century observer it is surprising how few of Queen Elizabeth's country-house revels did *not* involve extravagant make-believe. Inviting the locals to come in and put on some characteristic entertainment for the queen strikes us as a great deal more obvious and politic than it seems to have struck Elizabeth's hosts. But there are some signal occasions when real English countrymen elbowed their way in among nymphs, shepherds, and questing knights to capture the court's fancy. Surprisingly, the occasion about which we know the most occurs amid the costliest, most recherché spectacle of them all. Of all the princely pleasures at Kenilworth our observer R. L. devotes most space in his descriptive letter to a country bridale and to a special performance of the traditional Hock Tuesday play from nearby Coventry.

R. L.'s initial reference to the wedding feast as "a *solem* brydeale" is our first hint that the whole affair was certainly *not* staged to appeal to the court's antiquarian curiosity or sentiments about quaint folkways. Trussed up in his holiday best, the bridegroom, for instance, cut an irresistibly funny figure:

. . . but the bridegroom formost, in hiz fatherz tawny worsted jacket, (for his freends wear fayn that he shoold be a brydegroom before the Queen) a fayr strawn hat, with a capitall crooun steepl wyze on hiz hed: a payr of harvest glovez on hiz hands, az a sign of good husbandry: a pen & inkorn at his bak, for he woold be knowen to be bookish; lame of a leg, that in his yooth was broken at football: wellbeloved yet of hiz mother, that lent him a nu mufflar for a napkin, that was tyed too hiz gyrdl for lozyng: It was no small sport too marke this minion in hiz full apointment, that throogh good scoolation becam az formall in his action az he had been a bride groom indeed: with this speciall grace by the wey, that ever az he woold have framed him the better countenauns, with the woors face he lookt.

(*LL,* 27–28)

This bumpkin was all the funnier because he took himself so seriously. "A brydegroom before the *Queen*"—imagine! The bride herself, on the other hand, was like nothing so much as a lumbering old horse:

Then follœd the worshipfull Bride, led (after the cuntrie maner) between too auncient parishionerz, honest toounsmen. But a stale stallion and a wel spred, (hot as the weather waz,) God wot, and an il smelling, waz she: a thirtie yeer old, of colour brounbay, not very beautifull in deed, but ugly, fooul, ill favord: yet marveyloous fain of the offis, because shee hard say shee shoold dauns before the Queen, in which feat shee thought shee woold foote it az finely az the best: Well, after this bride cam thear, by too and too, a dozen damzels for the bridesmaides: that for favor, attyre, for facion and cleanlines, were az meete for such a bride, as a treen ladl for a porige pot. . . .

                                                              (*LL,* 29)

She, too, only increased her ridiculousness by not seeing the irony so obvious to an urbane gentleman like R. L.: she was so "merveyloous fain of the offis." Touchstone finds just such amusement in William and Audrey, near-neighbors, in fact, of Leicester's Warwickshire countrymen in the Forest of Arden.

Chief among the revels that this rustic crew put on for their court visitors was a quintain, a mounted charge at barriers with wooden poles, but the barriers in this case were no grand theatrical prop, as in jousts at court, but simply a plank dropped across the road. Such parody of court spectacle roused R. L. to derisive laughter and to some genuinely funny description. The bridegroom broke his spear *"tres hardiment"* but he did have trouble staying on his horse. The bridale festivities included also a morris dance "according too the auncient manner, six daunserz, Mawdmarion, and the fool" (*LL,* 28). Vigorous reenactment of legendary history in the Coventry Hock Tuesday play struck R. L. as every bit "az good a sport" (*LL,* 32). Particularly was he thrilled with one of the performers, a certain Captain Cox, mason of Coventry and a renowned teller of tales.

Crinkle-eyed irony, then, was one of the ways a courtier liked to look at the country. But when the country looked at him, he expected wide-eyed wonder. Touchstone puts it to Audrey just so: "I am here with thee and thy goats, as the most capricious poet, honest Ovid, was among the Goths" (*As You Like It,* III.ii). The Italians, as we might expect, had been more affectedly literary about this state of affairs and even had a generic name to describe it: *commedia rusticale*.[13] Bumptious country farce delighted the same courtly audience who, from the very different perspective of Sannazaro's displaced city-man Sincero, looked wistfully on the landscape of *Arcadia*. The humor of *commedia rusticale* lies to a great extent in just this matter of perspective. The poignancy of Sincero's position in the *Arcadia* consists in his being a city man *in* a green world who would be *of* it; in *commedia rusticale*, on the other hand, the city man never forgets himself, never forgets his place. He stands back from the spectacle before him, only his wit engaged by rustics who are so enthralled at performing before nobility that they see no irony, no glimpse of the larger, more complicated world beyond their fields.

At Cowdray in 1591 and at Sudeley in 1592 golden fictions one day gave way to homely sports the next. Although Elizabeth's welcomer to Cowdray was a porter who hailed her as a latter-day Amphion whose presence steadies walls and roof in musical harmony, it was country dancing that awaited her later in her stay. Sussex countrymen were invited into the park to dance for her, and in a high-spirited breach of decorum Lord and Lady Montecute themselves joined in.[14] At Sudeley, Gloucestershire, the next summer, Elizabeth's progress took her not only into the pastoral landscape of Apollo and Daphne but into a very distinctive English landscape inhabited by Englishmen on whom that landscape had imprinted its character. Her greeter at Lord Chandos's castle was no prophecy-propounding Porter but "an olde Shepheard" from the craggy Cotswold hills:

Your Highnes is come into Cotshold, an uneven country, but a people that carry their thoughts, levell with their fortunes; lowe spirites, but true harts; using plaine dealinge, once counted a jewell, nowe beggery. These hills afoorde nothing but cottages, and nothing can we present to your Highnes but shephards. The country healthy and harmeles; a fresh aier, where there are noe dampes, and where a black sheepe is a perilous beast; no monsters; we carry our harts at our tongues ends, being as far from dissembling as our

13. Ireneo Sanesi, *La Commedia,* 2d ed. (Milan, 1954), I, 438 ff. On *commedia rusticale* as farce see Marvin T. Herrick, *Italian Comedy in the Renaissance* (Urbana, Ill., 1960), pp. 26 ff.

14. *The Speeches and Honorable Entertainment given to the Queens Majestie in Progresse, at Cowdrey in Sussex* (London, 1591), rpt. in Bond, *Lyly,* I, 421–430.

sheepe from fiercenesse; and if in any thing we shall chance to discover our lewdnes, it will be in over boldnesse, in gazinge at you, who fils our harts with joye, and our eies with wonder.[15]

On the next day, however, that rocky "uneven country" was transformed into the smooth landscape of Ovid's *Metamorphoses,* as queen and court saw a dramatization of the story of Apollo and Daphne. Had bad weather not prevented, Elizabeth would later have witnessed a metamorphosis in reverse and seen, not an episode from Ovid, but a Cotswold shepherds' holiday, revels of the sort we see in Shakespeare's Bohemia.

Keeping company with Lord Chandos's Cotswold shepherd and with Leicester's Warwickshire wedding party are several other earthy figures who welcomed Elizabeth to their masters' demesnes. When the old queen came calling at his Thames-side house at Chiswick in July 1602, Sir William Russell stationed at the gates a garrulous and engaging Angler, just up from fishing on the riverbank.[16] During the last surviving entertainment of her reign a few days later Elizabeth rode into Sir Thomas Egerton's park at Harefield, Middlesex, to find herself confronted by a bluff bailiff and a pert dairymaid. They pretended not to recognize her and handed her a bejeweled rake and fork, along with their mistress's instructions: any lodger at Harefield would have to earn his entertainment by working in the fields! Nearer to the house two starkly allegorical figures, Time with an hourglass that had stopped running and "little pretie privat *Place"* in a parti-colored robe, gave Elizabeth on behalf of their master and mistress a deer wrought in crystal, "a pledge and mirror of their harts that owe thee." [17] Place and Time were not too rarified to enjoy a good pun.

Commedia rusticale at its most sophisticated, with its most subtle play of irony, we find not amid the craggy Cotswold hills, where queen and courtiers were sojourners only, but in the Earl of Leicester's garden at Wanstead. There, close enough to London for short retreats, the cour-

15. *Speeches Delivered . . . at Sudley,* rpt. in Bond, *Lyly,* I, 471–477.

16. MS. Finch Hatton 2414, Northamptonshire Records Office, ed. Leslie Hotson with *Queen Elizabeth's Entertainment at Mitcham* (New Haven, Conn., 1953), pp. 35–36.

17. Conway MSS, printed in Bond, *Lyly,* I, 491–504.

tier's impulse to lead a life of committed action and his impulse to lead
a life of retired quiet were held in a balance as precarious as the balance
of art and nature in the garden itself. But it was Elizabeth's displeasure,
not precariously balanced desires, that had rusticated Leicester there
when Elizabeth came calling in May 1578. One day during her stay,
". . . her most excellente Majestie walkinge in Wanstead garden[,] as
she passed owne into the grove there came sodenly amonge the trayne
one apparelled Like an honeste mans wyf of the Countrie. . . ." [18] In
pert importunity Sir Thomas Egerton's bailiff and dairymaid seem
reticent beside this huswife. Two suitors, she explained to Elizabeth, a
shepherd and a woodsman, were seeking the hand of her daughter.
Would the queen choose between them? There on the spot, on the
verge between garden and grove, Elizabeth obliged. Or rather she did
not oblige. The choice seemed clear-cut enough: would it be the vigorous
forester Therion or the mild shepherd Espilus, "the manie Desertes and
manie faultes of *Therion* or the smale Desertes and no faults [of]
Espilus"? Dialogue and singing match alike play on the contrast of the
suitors' habitats as well as habits. Young Philip Sidney had contrived
this little drama with tact, instructing the May Lady who finally poses
the question to remind Elizabeth discreetly "that in Judinge me you
Judge more then me in yt." Vigorous Therion was a fetching disguise for
out-of-favor Leicester, as the epilogue to the Helmingham Hall manuscript makes clear. But Elizabeth needed no epilogue to see through the
disguise: she chose the mild Espilus and threw off the whole ending
Sidney had planned. Her headstrong decision on this occasion may be
what John Dowland alludes to nearly a quarter-century later in his
adaptation and lute setting of Sidney's "O Sweet woods the delight of
solitarinesse." Dowland's final stanza laments:

> You woods in you the fairest Nimphs have walked,
> Nimphes at whose sight all harts did yeeld to Love,
> You woods in whom deere lovers oft have talked,
> How doe you now a place of mourning prove,

18. Robert Kimbrough and Philip Murphy, "The Helmingham Hall Manuscript
of Sidney's *The Lady of May:* A Commentary and a Transcription," *RenD*, N.S. 1
(1968), 103–119. See also Stephen Orgel, "Sidney's Experiment in Pastoral: The
Lady of May," *JWCI*, XXVI (1963), 198–204.

Wansted my Mistres saith this is the doome,
Thou art loves Childbed, Nursery, and Tombe.[19]

With his "Lady of May" device Sidney is quite clearly pointing us in
a new direction. *Commedia rusticale,* with its ironic laughter at country
simplicity, may *begin* his little drama, but by the end the queen's mind
has been directed to those complicated court concerns that *commedia
rusticale* pleases by excluding. No longer can the onlooker be comfortable with simple ironic detachment. Sidney's two suitors, the one
vigorous and committed to action, the other mild and retired, engage
the queen's judgment and compel her to make a choice. The choice
she must make here is peculiarly appropriate to the retired garden setting:
will it be commitment or retreat, a life of activity or a life of contemplation?

For a well-read courtier like Sidney, the notion that a garden is a
place not simply for relaxation but for debate comes probably from
Cicero, who delights in removing the interlocutors in his philosophical
dialogues from the stresses of Rome and setting them down in a country
villa to sort things out. The *Tusculan Disputations,* for instance, take
their name from Cicero's villa at Tusculum—his "manor," as John
Dolman englishes it in 1561. It is not only the country setting that
Sidney has appropriated at Wanstead but Cicero's method of argument
as well. Before any proposition is published in writing, Cicero says in
Book II of the *Tusculan Disputations,* it ought to be put to the test of
learned readers.

And for that cause, the auncient custome [of] Peripatetikes and academikes,
to reason on eyther parte of every question, doth marvaylously well like me:
not onely for that by no other meanes the truthe of everye doubtefull question might be tryed, but also because there is in it a greate exercyse and
practyse of Rhetorique: whych Aristotle chiefly used, and all they that folowed
him.[20]

---

19. No. 10 in John Dowland, *The Second Booke of Songs or Ayres* (1600). Text
quoted from *Lyrics from English Airs 1596–1622,* ed. Edward Doughtie (Cambridge, Mass., 1970), p. 104.

20. *Those fyve Questions, which Marke Tullye Cicero, disputed in his Manor of
Tusculanum,* trans. John Dolman (London, 1561), sigs. J4ᵛ–J5, incorporating cor-
rections of printer's errors noted at end of volume.

And in that following none were ever more enthusiastic than the Elizabethans, who learned to debate from their earliest years in school and
loved to deploy the arts of language, no matter how trivial the question
at hand. Philo of Larissa, Cicero goes on to say, divided his students'
time between study of rhetoric and study of philosophy.

To the whyche order I[,] beynge lykewyse moved of my familyar fryendes,
spente there in suche leasure as I had in my maner of Tusculanum. Wherfore when I had spent the morninge in the studye of Rhetoryke, after noone
we came downe to our scoole: in the which such reasoninge as we had I do
nowe expresse: not as if I tolde it, but even in maner wyth the selfe same
wordes, as it was done. Therfore, whyles we walked, we fell into this talke.

And so begins his dramatic account of his friends' debate on the proposition "Pain is the greatest of evils." (Not so, they finally decide.) This
"scoole" in which Cicero and his friends walked and talked was the
Academia of his villa, an open-air space laid out to recall the groves
where Plato taught. However much England may have lacked the warm
Mediterranean sunshine that encouraged such alfresco cerebration, hardy
humanists like Sidney found a garden a decorous place for debate.

The topics at issue before Elizabeth were almost never, however, the
fatiguing sort posed by Sidney's honest wife of the country. At Woodstock in 1592 Constancie and Inconstancie carried on a debate with such
style that the compiler of *The Phoenix Nest* (1593) anthologized their
arguments. They debated a moot question, of course, with Elizabeth,
semper eadem, standing by.[21] Again, at Dr. Julius Caesar's house at
Mitcham in 1598, an answerless question inspired a good quarter-hour of
rapid-fire wit worthy of John Lyly even if he didn't write the script
himself. Poet, Painter, and Musician reach absolutely no agreement on
who practices the worthiest craft, and we begin to suspect that no answer
was ever expected in the first place. Elizabeth's presence solves the debate
neatly: she transcends all three contenders.[22]

The wit and polish of the Mitcham debate, like Sidney's "Lady of
May" device, delight us even now, when the issues no longer seem like

21. BL MS. 41499 ("Ditchley MSS"), printed in Sir E. K. Chambers, *Sir Henry
Lee: An Elizabethan Portrait* (Oxford, 1936), pp. 276–297.
22. BL MS. Add. 12497, printed in Leslie Hotson, *Queen Elizabeth's Entertainment at Mitcham,* pp. 16–30.

issues at all. We cannot say the same about the debate on royal marriage that was to have struck a didactic note amid the delights of Kenilworth in 1575. Gascoigne's artless verses and even more artless arguments for marriage could hardly have persuaded Elizabeth to change her mind about this touchy matter, even if weather and occasion had permitted Diana and her nymphs to declaim the speeches they had memorized. Serious subjects, we must conclude, did not inspire the best debating: the more trivial the issue, the more brilliant was the display of wit. What proved true in Renaissance gardens has often proved true in the halls of Westminster. It was how the debate was carried on, not what it solved, that delighted the queen.[23] Delight she relished; instruction, no.

One other of the debates Elizabeth heard is like Sidney's "Lady of May" device in making thematic use of the garden setting. No private country house for the queen's reception was grander than Lord Burghley's house, Theobalds. He had built it, he said, especially for entertaining her. A fountain with flowing water plashed in the queen's own chamber, and the trees painted on the walls looked so realistic, said a German traveler, that birds flying in from the garden mistook the boughs for real. When Elizabeth came calling in May 1591 she happened upon two quarreling servants; boldly they asked her to settle their dispute. While laying out a garden nearby for Burghley's youngest son Sir Robert, they have discovered a casket containing a precious jewel. Which of them should have it? The mole catcher declaims wonderful euphuistic prose, outrageous puns and all, when he asks the queen to settle the dispute in his favor: "I cannot discourse of knots and mazes: sure I am that the ground was so knotty that the gardener was amazed to see it; and as easy had it been, if I had not been, to make a shaft of a cammock as a garden of that croft." [24] He clinches his appeal with a deft

23. On the pleasures of debate see John Stevens, *Music and Poetry in the Early Tudor Court* (London, 1961), pp. 159-167, and G. K. Hunter, *John Lyly: The Humanist as Courtier* (London and Cambridge, Mass., 1962), pp. 118-123.

24. Rpt. in Bond, *Lyly,* I, 417-419, from Alexander Dyce's edition of George Peele's *Works,* 2d ed., III (London, 1839), 165-169, who had copied the Gardener's and Molecatcher's speeches "from a MS. in Peele's handwriting, which has been obligingly lent to me by Mr. Collier, who was not possessed of it when he gave his excellent *History [of English Dramatic Poetry* (1831)] to the public" (III, 160). Since obliging "Mr. Collier" is none other than the infamous forger John Payne

comparison of kingdom-at-large and garden-in-small. In the "garden" she rules, he tells her, he seeks out troublemaking moles, "heavers at your state." However such watchfulness deserves reward, verses on the casket make it clear to whom the jewel rightly belongs:

> I was a giant's daughter of this isle,
> Turn'd to a mole by the Queen of Corn:
> My jewel I did bury by a wile,
> Again never from the earth to be torn,
> Till a virgin had reigned thirty-three years,
> Which shall be but the fourth part of her years.

Mole catcher and gardener are only too happy, of course, to give over their claims.

The political meaning that the mole catcher spaded up in Burghley's garden was calculated to appeal to a ruler who had once cast herself as a gardener in her own verses. In the garden conceit that lurks fitfully among the other images in her poem "The Doubt of Future Foes" (ca. 1568), young Elizabeth places herself as a prudent husbandman who will see to it that the "top" of suppositious hope will end up as "the root up-reared," that "grafted guile" will not bear fruit, that seditious sects will have their "tops" cut back.

> My rusty sword through rest shall first his edge employ
> To poll their tops that seek such change or gape for future joy.[25]

It took a great deal of polling to keep a Renaissance garden, no less than a Renaissance kingdom, in order. When Thomas Platter and his companion strolled through the enclosed "earthly paradise" at Hampton Court in 1599, they discovered there not the open expanse of grass and flowers we would expect but just the knotted and mazed affair the mole catcher describes—a landscape as crowded with men and animals as the streets of London:

Collier and since I have not been able to trace the present location of his MS, it is possible that the Gardener's and Molecatcher's speeches are forgeries. For a thorough survey of what we know about Lord Burghley's magnificent house see Sir John Summerson, "The Building of Theobalds, 1564–1585," *Archaeologia*, XCVII (1959), 107–126. The travelers' accounts are quoted at length in Ian Dunlop, *Palaces and Progresses of Elizabeth I* (London, 1962), pp. 166–179.

25. *The Poems of Queen Elizabeth I*, ed. Leicester Bradner (Providence, R.I., 1964), p. 4.

On descent and exit from the church the gardener presented himself, and after we had offered a gratuity to our first guide, the gardener conducted us into the royal pleasaunce.

By the entrance I noticed numerous patches where square cavities had been scooped, as for paving stones; some of these were filled with red brick-dust, some with white sand, and some with green lawn, very much resembling a chess-board. The hedges and surrounds were of hawthorn, bush firs, ivy, roses, juniper, holly, English or common elm, box and other shrubs, very gay and attractive.

There were all manner of shapes, men and women, half men and half horse, sirens, serving-maids with baskets, French lilies and delicate crenellations all round made from the dry twigs bound together and the aforesaid evergreen quick-set shrubs, or entirely of rosemary, all true to the life, and so cleverly and amusingly interwoven, mingled and grown together, trimmed and arranged picture-wise that their equal would be difficult to find.

Indeed. Platter's description makes the shrubs of Levens Hall (Figure 2) seem quite tame. A well-weeded-out vestige of this madcap display survives today in the Old Pond Garden at Hampton Court, one of very few Elizabethan gardens or even parts of gardens to survive eighteenth-century improvements. Exceeding even John Lyly's far-fetched similes, such prodigies of nature as Platter describes have prompted Derek Clifford to label these displays of Tudor magnificence "gardens of Euphues." [26] At Theobalds in 1591 and at Mitcham in 1598 we not only *see* the triumphs of euphuistic wit in the gardens' knots and mazes; we *hear* it in the voices that debate there.

When we position ourselves with Elizabeth and her courtiers in the foreground of the country-house stage, in the grounds closest to the house itself, we find ourselves confronted with two rather different prospects. On the one hand, the landscape before us is a lively, lived-in place, a farm that is home to English countrymen who offer us frank, hearty welcome and keep us entertained with wedding games, country dancing, and shepherds' holidays. Sophisticated courtiers that we are, we take in such simple pleasures with amused irony. On the other hand,

26. Clifford, *Garden Design,* pp. 87–110. Commenting on the lack of a rational over-all design in any of the great sixteenth-century gardens of England, Clifford concludes, "The flavour of these gardens despite their considerable size seems to have been carefree and frivolous; they pleased the fancy rather than the imagination" (p. 89).

we see before us the mazes, knots, and topiary marvels of an enclosed garden. Like the gardens of Cicero's villas, this is a place not just for retreat and refreshment but for argument and debate. Of the topics that might engage us there, one above all seems to spring naturally from the setting: which is better, a vigorous life of action or a mild life of repose? Withdrawn from the court though we are, that world of action is never far behind us. Indeed, it takes little prompting to see in the garden itself a metaphor for the realm at large.

III. The Middle Distance

Beyond the garden wall on one side, not far behind us, is the crowded world of the court. Beyond the garden wall on the other side, is an open, less crowded landscape. The figures we meet in those green meadows are neither laboring countrymen nor lolling courtiers but luxuriating creatures of classical mythology. At Bisham Abbey in 1592 it was Pan, we have seen, who greeted Elizabeth as she passed through that middle landscape. The two nymphs to whom the goatish piper was plying his passion silenced him with their praises of the Virgin Queen, prompting him, too, to break his pipe and join the paean. ". . . heare I breake my pipe," he declares to Elizabeth, almost breaking into verse, "which *Apollo* could never make me doe; and follow that sounde which followes you."

Apollo himself was destined, in fact, to see proof of Elizabeth's powers just a few days later. Several days after her welcome to Sudeley by the Cotswold shepherd, the queen chanced to cross the path of a maid breathlessly pursued by two shepherds. A marvel! The maid changed shape into a tree. (The published text neglects to explain how.) Beneath the tree the first shepherd sat down to grieve, while the second stepped forward to tell the queen their story. Daphne was the maid, Apollo her close pursuer, he Daphne's forsaken suitor. Grief was not so pressing, however, as to hold back a superb display of euphuistic wit in the shepherd's speech, nor was Apollo too choked with surprise and sorrow to favor the queen with these elegantly turned verses, possibly underscored by John Dowland's heavenly touch upon the lute:

My hart and tongue were twinnes, at once conceaved;
　The eldest was my hart, borne dumbe by destenie,
The last my tongue, of all sweete thoughts bereaved,
　Yet strung and tunde, to play harts harmonie.
Both knit in one, and yet asunder placed,
　What hart would speake, the tongue doeth still discover;
What tongue doth speake, is of the hart embraced,
　And both are one to make a new found lover:
New founde, and onely founde in Gods and Kings,
　Whose words are deedes, but deedes nor words regarded:
Chaste thoughts doe mount, and she with swiftest wings,
　My love with paine, my paine with losse rewarded:
Engrave upon this tree, *Daphnes* perfection,
　That neither men nor gods, can force affection.[27]

Of a sudden "the tree rived," out bounded Daphne, after her flew Apollo. Taking refuge with Elizabeth, Daphne thanked Her Majesty for preserving her from Apollo's advances. It was Elizabeth's chaste and chastising power that had worked the metamorphosis.

For all its pastoral charms, then, the middle landscape is not quite the place of peace and repose it would first appear. On the far horizon loom the wooded haunts of Savage Men, and from time to time their forces of lust and aggression erupt here, too. Into this unsettled landscape the

---

27. *Speeches Delivered . . . at Sudley,* rpt. in Bond, *Lyly,* I, 471–477. Apollo's conceited sonnet understandably struck the fancy of the anthologizer of *Englands Helicon* (1600). Dowland's setting, which treats the quatrains as three repeated stanzas and the couplet as a coda, appears as no. 18 in Dowland's last collection, *A Pilgrimes Solace* (1612), long enough after the Sudeley revels and the poem's publication in *Englands Helicon* to cast some doubt on Dowland's involvement in the original event. His setting alters the final couplet to remove the topical reference to "this tree": "Then this be sure, since it is true perfection, / That neyther men nor Gods can force affection" (Doughtie, *English Airs,* p. 410). Despite the late publication of Dowland's setting, Diana Poulton seizes on a speaker abbreviated "Do." in the shepherds' holiday script to connect Dowland with the original performance (*John Dowland: His Life and Works* [London, Berkeley, and Los Angeles, 1972], pp. 29–30). However likely or unlikely that Dowland would have played a Cotswold shepherd, Poulton is certainly wrong in implying that the scenes in the entertainment were acted continuously, not on successive days, and that the shepherds' holiday was in fact performed, when the rubric makes it clear that unfit weather prevented.

queen enters as a calming, civilizing force. Her powers can work sudden metamorphoses, compelling a Savage Man to cast off his club, Pan to break his pipes, Daphne to change into a laurel. With just such grace and wisdom compassionate Rosalind soothes passionate Silvius and Phebe.

The metamorphoses acted out in the meadows of Kenilworth, Bisham, and Sudeley were not isolated events: the same drama could be seen anytime, frozen in stone in the royal park at Nonsuch. There strolling visitors like Paul Hentzner, Thomas Platter, and Baron Offenbach could wander out of the house, through the gardens and orchards, among the trees and shrubs of the artfully artless "wilderness" and find themselves confronted suddenly with three naked nymphs bathing in a pool, watched over by an astonished young man from whose forehead sprouted a stag's antlers. Three dogs barked at his feet. Framing this three-dimensional emblem—so incredibly lifelike, it seemed to Platter, who prized that quality at Hampton Court, too—was a gate with gold letters identifying the place as "The Grove of Diana." Latin verses on the gate's inner side brought the silent drama to life. Poised precariously betwixt man and stag, Actaeon demanded back his proper head:

> It would cause resentment if the painter should choose to join
> A horse's neck or a dog's face to a human head.
> Diana added a stag's head to these shoulders.
> Against her who is unjust I demand my proper flesh.

But Diana would hear no excuses:

> There is need of intelligence lest a beastly nature in human form
> Parrhasius should paint and Praxiteles carve.
> Actaeon, yours is a stag's heart: why should there not be horns?
> With insight I complain that your heart is that of a beast.

Beyond the fountain and its disputatious denizens was a little retreat— Platter calls it "a small vaulted temple"—that offered a stroller shade and rest at the same time that it prompted him to moral reflection. On the front of the structure a wanderer found this terse epigram:

> The Goddess of virtue calls for nothing impure;
> The punishment of crime calls for nothing disgraceful;
> But an evil mind, an evil spirit do.

Sitting in the shelter's shade and looking out on the fountain and its tableau of characters, a visitor looked up to find on one wall a moralization of his present situation:

> Shade for the person who is hot,
> A seat for the one who faints;
> Do not in the shade
> Be quiescent;
> Nor let there be to the one who is sitting
> The eyes of the serpent.

In Latin "shade" (*umbra*) and contemplative retirement, being "quiescent" (*umbratilis*), are more than imaginatively allied. An inscription on the shelter's other wall, finally, drew a more general moral for a visitor to take away and ponder:

> The streams of the impure fountain
> Are unwelcome.
> The eyes of the ungrateful mind
> Are impure.[28]

Sermons in stones, clearly enough, were not peculiar to Duke Senior's Forest of Arden. Reveling in the densely planted trees, the rough stones, the flowing water, Baron Offenbach ventures to affirm a beholder "would swear that this is indeed the grove of Diana of old." [29]

Baron Offenbach has read his Ovid. The devisers of this "Grove of Diana" inside Nonsuch park have done nothing else but translate into stone, water, and growing plants the description of Gargaphie in Book Three of the *Metamorphoses:*

> There was a valley thicke
> With Pinaple and Cipresse trees that armed be with pricke.
> *Gargaphie* hight this shadie plot, it was a sacred place
> To chast *Diana* and the Nymphes that wayted on hir grace.
> Within the furthest end thereof there was a pleasant Bowre
> So vaulted with the leavie trees, the Sunne had there no powre:
> Not made by hand nor mans devise, and yet no man alive,

28. *Platter,* pp. 195–196, with a few changes in word choice and punctuation from Clare Williams's translation. The original Latin inscriptions are transcribed in the German original of Platter's *Beschreibung,* ed. R. Keiser (Basel and Stuttgart, 1968), II, 830–831.

29. Offenbach, "England in 1609," p. 88.

A trimmer piece of worke than that could for his life contrive.
With flint and Pommy was it wallde by nature halfe about,
And on the right side of the same full freshly flowed out
A lively spring with Christall streame: whereof the upper brim
Was greene with grasse and matted herbes that smelled verie trim.[30]

All the details have materialized in Nonsuch Park: the lofty trees, the craggy stones, the shaded "pleasant Bowre . . . vaulted with the leavie trees" at the far end.

More remarkable still is the moral meaning that has materialized along with the physical details. Actaeon's metamorphosis, claims Diana, only does visual justice to his true beastly nature: a stag's heart deserves a stag's horns. Before this spectacle of pruriency punished, the verses on the wall will not let an observer rest innocent and content. Enjoy the shade, the epigram invites, but be not "quiescent," look not with "the eyes of the serpent." The eyes of an "ungrateful" observer are as "impure," the verses imply, as muddy water in a fountain. Lust and disloyalty are intertwined in a way that Renaissance readers of Ovid would find not at all curious. The commentary that George Sandys appends to each book of his *Ovid's Metamorphosis Englished, Mythologiz'd, And Represented in figures* summarizes centuries of exegesis and gives a distinctly political reading of Actaeon's metamorphosis:

. . . this fable was invented to shew us how dangerous a curiosity it is to search into the secrets of Princes, or by chance to discover their nakednesse: who thereby incurring their hatred, ever after live the life of a Hart, full of feare and suspicion. . . .[31]

Even more than they pleased Elizabeth, such sentiments must have pleased King Charles, seven years into his catastrophic reign when Sandys dedicated the volume to him in 1632.

It was political significance, then, as well as the lesson in unlawful lust, that made Diana and Actaeon appropriate subjects to stand silent but sententious in a grove in Nonsuch park. If the political meaning seems oblique there, it was pointedly direct in verses on the gate through

30. *Shakespeare's Ovid, being Arthur Golding's Translation of the* Metamorphoses [1567], ed. W.H.D. Rouse (Carbondale, Ill., 1961), p. 66.

31. *Ovid's Metamorphosis Englished, Mythologiz'd, And Represented in figures*, trans. George Sandys, ed. Karl K. Hulley and Stanley T. Vandersall (Lincoln, Neb., 1970), p. 151.

which Elizabeth and her entourage rode into the park of Whitehall
Palace:

> The fisherman who has been wounded, learns, though late, to beware;
> But the unfortunate Actaeon always presses on.
> The chaste virgin naturally pitied:
> But the powerful goddess revenged the wrong.
> Let Actaeon fall a prey to his dogs,
>   An example to youth,
> A disgrace to those that belong to him!
>   May Diana live the care of Heaven;
>   The delight of mortals;
> The security of those that belong to her!

Richard Bentley's suggestion that this inscription refers to Philip II, his
unsuccessful suits to Elizabeth, and the destruction of his Armada may
be forcing too topical a meaning on what Elizabeth's subjects saw as a
more general similarity between Diana and the Virgin Queen.[32]

At Bisham and Sudeley, as at Nonsuch and Whitehall, the *genius
loci* of the middle landscape is Ovid. From the lines of his *Metamorphoses* spring almost all the characters we encounter there—Pan, Apollo,
Daphne, Actaeon, Diana—and they invite us to look at them with just
that poise of abandon and austerity that Renaissance readers brought to
Ovid. The landscape in which these characters are at home is a shadowy
place not only because sudden metamorphoses make us wary of what we
see but because Elizabeth almost always entered that landscape in late
afternoon. At Sudeley the swain tells us it was "by the sunne, a Shepheardes diall . . . four of the clocke" when his Daphne was turned into
a laurel—by mid-September a time of long shadows in England. Exigencies of travel meant that almost always the royal party arrived at a
country house in the waning light of early evening. At Kenilworth in
July 1575 our observer R. L. specifies Elizabeth's arrival time as eight
o'clock in the evening—still daylight so soon after the summer solstice at
that northern latitude—and notes that by the third pageant in the
welcoming procession blazing torches were necessary to light the Lady
of the Lake as she floated across the castle moat on her movable island.
When the Savage Man came out of hiding a few days later, it was nine
o'clock and Elizabeth was attended by torchlight as she rode home from

32. Hentzner, *Travels, pp.* 33–34, with translator's note.

hunting. So at Bisham Abbey in August 1592 we can imagine Elizabeth encountering first the Savage, then Pan and the two nymphs in the golden light of late afternoon.

Thanks to R. L., we know precisely the time and the quality of light when Elizabeth worked her most spectacular magic at Kenilworth. The metamorphosis she touched off on this occasion was not from the pages of Ovid—she liberated the Lady of the Lake, imprisoned in Kenilworth Castle's waters since the days of King Arthur, a fugitive from the lust of Sir Bruse sans Pity—but niceties of chronology failed to make several Ovidian characters feel out of place there. It was Triton, in fact, who stage-managed the whole affair. After he had successfully sued Elizabeth to free the Lady of the Lake, after the lady had offered humble thanks, the queen's eyes were greeted with a marvelous dolphin floating across the water with Arion on his back; her ears were greeted first with the sounds of instrumental music issuing from the fish's belly, then with a song from Arion, identifying himself as one of the "heardmen of the seas" and hoping that his song would settle a "calm consent" upon the queen [*PP*, Bl^v]. Whether this dramatic "piscatorial" worked its spell on Elizabeth we do not know, but the combination of music, echoes upon the calm water, and golden late evening light wafted R. L. into a state of absolute ecstasy. "Noow syr," he tells his correspondent back in London,

the ditty in miter so aptly endighted to the matter, and after by voys so delicioously delivered: the song by a skilful artist intoo hiz parts so sweetly sorted: each part in hiz instrument so clean & sharpely toouched, every in-strument again in hiz kind so excellently tunabl: and this in the eev[en]ing of the day, resoounding from the callm waters: whear prezens of her Majesty, & longing too listen, had utterly damped all noyz & dyn; the hole armony conveyd in tyme, tune, & temper, thus incomparably melodious: with what pleazure (Master Martin), with what sharpnes of conceyt, with what lyvely delighte, this moought pears into the heerers harts, I pray ye imagin yoor self az ye may; for, so God judge me, by all the wit & cunning I have, I cannot express, I promis yoo.

(*LL,* 43)

For all his apology, R. L. speaks pretty well for himself. What for us are words on a page (and William Hunnis's verses for Arion remain de-cidedly earthbound) were to R. L. a kinesthetic melody heard in sound, seen in the landscape, felt in the air. "As for me," R. L. concludes, "surely I was lulld in such a liking, & so loth too leave of, that mooch a doo, a good while after, had I, to fynde we whear I waz" (*LL,* 44).

R. L.'s expansive response is all the more remarkable if another witness can be believed. One of the humorous anecdotes recorded in British Library MS. Harleian 6395 claims that the actor playing Arion was hoarse, so he gave over the pretense, ripped off his disguise, declared that "he was none of Arion not he, but eene honest Harry Goldingham," and ended by giving Elizabeth his personal welcome—all to her great delight.[33]

If the foreground landscape of Elizabeth's country-house revels belongs to Bruegel, this Ovidian middle landscape, shadowy and calm in the late afternoon light, belongs to Poussin. Even closer to Kenilworth in time and space is the famous picture called "Elizabeth and the Three Goddesses" at Hampton Court, signed by one H. E. (= Hans Eworth?) and dated 1569. Out of a shadowy interior space Elizabeth, already holding her golden orb as prize, is beckoned by Juno into an open landscape where Pallas and Venus with Cupid await her in a complimentary revision of the Judgment of Paris (see Figure 3).

The still moment that R. L. describes at Kenilworth became elsewhere the ground for the whole revels. In their bluff, straightforward way Place and Time at Harefield in 1602 attempt, as we have seen, to articulate the same harmony of place and time that R. L. felt at Kenilworth. Elizabeth's presence generates a harmonious idyll, set apart from the rest of the world. The sports sponsored by Edward Seymour, Earl of Hertford, at Elvetham, Hampshire, in 1591 gave this graceful fiction its grandest enactment of Elizabeth's reign. The printed text and description of these entertainments, complete with a woodcut overview of the landscape stage, are the fullest we possess apart from the Kenilworth *Princelye Pleasures* (see Figure 4). A "Proem" provides an elaborate setting-of-scene and plenty of glances behind the scenes to the feverish activity that anticipated the queen's coming. A crescent-shaped pond was constructed for a burlesque water battle on the second day. Among the scores of temporary structures that were erected was "a withdrawing place for her majestie," a veritable Bower of Bliss with an interweaving

33. BL MS. Harleian 6395, quoted in Bergeron, *English Civic Pageantry,* p. 34.

FIGURE 3. "H.E.," "Queen Elizabeth and the Three Goddesses" (1569). Reproduced by courtesy of: H. M. the Queen.

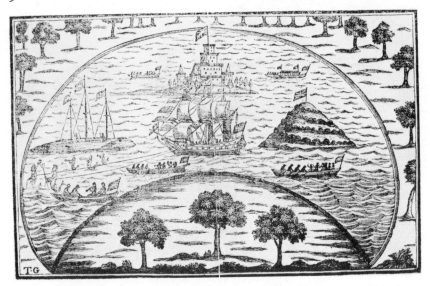

FIGURE 4. Overview of the Naumachia, Elvetham, Hampshire, 1591, from *The Honorable Entertainement gieven to the Queenes Majestie in Progresse, at Elvetham in Hampshire* (London, 1591). Reproduced by courtesy of the Folger Shakespeare Library, Washington, D.C.

of art and nature. Hung with boughs and nuts outside, this bower observed decorum of place; hung with rich tapestries inside, it observed decorum of persons. The thematic ground for the four days' devices was mapped out in the speech of a green-clad poet who welcomed Elizabeth to Elvetham:

> Behold, on thee how each thing sweetly smiles,
> To see thy brightnes glad our hemispheare:
> Night only envies: whome faire stars doe crosse:
> All other creatures strive to shew their joyes.[34]

The queen-as-sun inspires a sympathetic landscape where animals romp in pleasure, where trees show their happiness with quivering leaves, meadows with new grass, vines with grapes, streams with silver music. Heaven, earth, and floods join in a grand concord:

34. *The Honorable Entertainement gieven to the Queenes Majestie in Progresse, at Elvetham in Hampshire* (London, 1591), rpt. in Bond, *Lyly,* I, 431–452.

Thee, thee (*Sweet Princes*), heav'n, & earth, & fluds,
And plants, and beasts, salute with one accord:
And while they gaze on thy perfections,
Their eyes desire is never satisfied.

In this landscape, alive with music, the queen's solar power illumines a golden idyll free from storms, doubt, and fear. That idyll, hopes the green-clad poet, will be drawn out from "these dayes to yeares, / Yeares to an age, ages to an aeternitie." Singing a song that was reprinted both in *England's Helicon* and with a musical setting in Francis Pilkington's *First Booke of Songs or Ayres* (1605), the Graces and the Hours conducted Elizabeth to the house, removing on their way the blocks that Envy had set in the path.

The substance of the next three days' entertainment was just that salutation of "heav'n, & earth, & fluds, And plants, and beasts" that the green-clad poet had mentioned. On the second day the gods of woods and waters offered their homage and carried on a slapstick mock-battle on— and *in*—the crescent-shaped pond. In one very original episode during this entertainment the queen was asked by Naerea to christen a ship that would sail the seas in Her Majesty's name and "attempt a golden fleece." Elizabeth named the vessel "the Bonadventure." The queen of the little cosmos of land and sea inside Elvetham park inspired not only the pastoral peace of a golden age but the heroic action of an age of adventure. On the third day a plowman "in auncient countrey attire" offered Elizabeth a delicately crafted May-Day-greenwood ditty that, like the Graces' and Hours' song, found its way into the pastoral preserve of *England's Helicon*. It is attributed there to "Nicholas Breton." On the fourth day, finally, the usually invisible creatures of the underground came out into the garden to offer Elizabeth *their* homage, just as the gods of wood and water had done. The song with which the Fairy Queen and her nymphs favored Elizabeth hails her as the *genius loci* of the land, and by its end landscape and queen have become one body:

Elisa is the fairest Queene
That ever trod upon this greene.
Elisaes eyes are blessed starres,
Inducing peace, subduing warres.
Her wordes are balme, her lookes are light.
Elisaes brest is that faire hill,

> Where vertue dwels, and sacred skill,
> O blessed bee each day and houre,
> Where sweete *Elisa* builds her bowre.

Elizabeth's departure is the dispelling of the idyll and the cursing of the land. "For how can Sommer stay, when Sunne departs?," asks the refrain of the green-clad poet's farewell verses. Illumined with the queen's golden presence, softened with music, favored by gods, the landscape of pastoral poetry is evoked more brilliantly in no other country-house entertainment of Elizabeth's reign.

However thorough Elizabeth and her hosts were in turning metaphors into dramatic realities, reality could sometimes prove recalcitrant. No factors that the devisers of these shows had to contend with were more recalcitrantly real than British rain, and on one occasion at least during Elizabeth's stay at Elvetham the metaphor of sun-blest idyll had to remain a metaphor. But Elizabeth's hosts and their poets were not to be put off by trifles like weather. For weeks before the queen's late summer visit to Beddington, Surrey, Sir Francis Carew covered a cherry tree with canvas to shade it from the sun and sprayed it with water to offset the summer heat. When the mistress of Time entered Beddington in late summer she could command the fruits of spring a full month after their disappearance from the rest of England.[35]

The pastoral fiction sustained at Elvetham is more than a place: it is also a time. Two precocious Wiltshire shepherds turn this decorous fiction of eternal spring and summer into a historical fact with mythical power. Elizabeth's progress of 1602 was planned to extend into Wiltshire, and it was possibly for an intended visit by the queen to Wilton House that Mary Sidney, countess of Pembroke, devised her "Dialogue between Two Shepherds," printed in *A Poetical Rhapsodie* that same year. This dialogue is one of only two surviving original works by Sir Philip Sidney's sister, whose versifying of the Psalms is one of the masterpieces of Elizabethan translation. Dramatizations of pastoral eclogues were staple fare at the courts of Italy, but the countess of Pembroke's exercise in *egloga rappresentativa* stands as the signal example, if not the only one,

---

35. Sir Hugh Plat, *Floraes Paradise* (London, 1608), pp. 173–175.

in English Renaissance literature.[36] The countess's English shepherds have carefully studied their Virgil. In that most famous of his eclogues, the fourth, Virgil's shepherd-persona lauds the birth of a miracle-working boy whose growth to manhood will mark the return of a golden age to the iron world. With his birth, sings Virgil's persona, the goddess Astraea will return to earth, bringing with her the justice that deserted men with their fall from golden-age innocence. In just these terms the countess of Pembroke's shepherds celebrate Elizabeth: she is Astraea descended; her coming is the founding of a new golden age.

Though it was Virgil who gave the return of the golden age its political turn, it was Ovid whom Elizabethans looked to for a full description of what that age was like. It was a time of natural law, a time when men knew no other countries but their own, a time of no wars. But above all it was a time when men were in perfect harmony with the land, when earth produced her bounty spontaneously and spring lasted all the year:

The fertile earth as yet was free, untoucht of spade or plough,
And yet it yeelded of it selfe of every things inough.
And men themselves contented well with plaine and simple foode,
That on the earth by natures gift without their travell stoode,
Did live by Raspis, heppes and hawes, by cornelles, plummes and cherries,
By sloes and apples, nuttes and peares, and lothsome bramble berries,
And by the acornes dropt on ground from *Joves* brode tree in fielde.
The Springtime lasted all the yeare, and *Zephyr* with his milde
And gentle blast did cherish things that grew of owne accorde.
The ground untilde, all kinde of fruits did plenteously avorde.
No mucke nor tillage was bestowde on leane and barren land,
To make the corne of better head and ranker for too stand.
Then streames rank milke, then, streames ran wine, and yellow honny flowde
From ech greene tree wherone the rayes of firie *Phebus* glowde.[37]

Despite the incongruities of rain and summer heat, this was the landscape spread before Elizabeth at Elvetham, Beddington, and Wilton. Though

---

36. *A Poetical Rhapsody, 1602–1621,* ed. H. E. Rollins (Cambridge, Mass., 1931–1932), I, 15–17. On Italian *egloghe rappresentative* see W. W. Greg, *Pastoral Poetry and Pastoral Drama,* new ed. (London, 1959), pp. 169–176, and Appendix I, pp. 423–443.

37. *Shakespeare's Ovid,* p. 36.

hosts and their poets liked to celebrate Elizabeth as the generatrix of this golden-age vision of man at ease in nature, the true *genius loci* was Ovid.

Bounded by the garden's knots and mazes on the one side and by the woods' dark depths on the other, the middle landscape of Elizabeth's country-house revels is thus Ovid's creation in both its aspects: as a shadowy place of sudden metamorphoses and as the uncultivated fields of mankind's lost golden age. With untamed nature encroaching on the one side and man's civilizing art on the other, the landscape of metamorphosis is an unsettled and unsettling place. Beneath its surface throb forces of lust and aggression that only the civilizing power of the queen can subdue. As Astraea, as divine justice returned to the earth, she wields power strong enough not only to subdue passion but to put men back into harmony with the land and with time, to restore them to the golden age they once knew. Our response to this middle landscape is a curious blend of sensuous revel and sententious reflection. With R. L. at Kenilworth we may give ourselves up to "the hole armony" and find ourselves saying with him, ". . . mooch a doo, a good while after, had I, to fynde me whear I waz"; but with Thomas Platter at Nonsuch we are called back to ourselves at once. Here is shade for the hot and a seat for the faint, but in that shady repose we must not be "quiescent." We may be *in* the shade (*umbra*), but we may not be *of* it (*umbratilis*). There is moral and political profit to temper our pleasure in the prospect before us. Especially in moments like R. L. describes at Kenilworth or like those celebrated for four days at Elvetham, we can see how very far we have come from the landscape of rustic comedy where we began. There we never lost our comfortable sense of irony; here we must strike a balance. Before us, however, lies a landscape that even more insistently invites us to lose ourselves.

IV. The Far Horizon

The wooded landscape of the far horizon is, above all else, a place for hunting. Elizabeth was returning from a day's sport in the chase of Kenilworth, we recall, when she encountered the Hombre Salvagio near its edge. Though from a distance the chase looks wild enough to be the haunt of such a creature, we must not imagine it quite so forbidding at

FIGURE 5. The Queen in a Forest Landscape, from George Tuberville, *The Noble Arte of Venerie or Hunting* (London, 1575). Reproduced by courtesy of the Folger Shakespeare Library, Washington, D.C.

closer range. As R. L. describes it for us, the chase at Kenilworth was, to
be sure, "wast, wyde, large, and full of red Deer and oother statelie
gamez for hunting." But it was also "beautified with manie delectabl,
fresh & umbargioous Boow[r]z, Arberz, Seatz, and walks, that with
great art, cost, & diligens, wear very pleazauntly appointed . . ."
(*LL*, 4). So provided with amenities, its "tall and fresh fragrant treez &
soil" might have suited Diana herself, R. L. concludes. The comforts of
"Seatz, and walks" did not, apparently, keep riders through these woods
from reflecting on the natural beauty of the place. In the very year of the
Kenilworth shows George Turberville—or was it indeed George
Gascoigne himself?—published his treatise on *The Noble Arte of
Venerie or Hunting* and included in it a discourse and woodcut depicting "the place where and howe and assembly should be made, in the
presence of a Prince, or some honorable person" (see Figure 5). His
prescriptions fit R. L.'s descriptions exactly. Any wanderer through
classical Greek and Latin verse will be certain he has seen this place before, for Turberville's woodland glade shares many features of the
locus amoenus:

> The place should first be pight, on pleasant gladsome greene,
> Yet under shade of stately trees, where little sunne is seene:
> And neare some fountaine spring, whose chrystall running streames,
> May helpe to coole the parching heate, ycaught by *Phoebus* beames.
> The place appoynted thus, it neyther shall be clad,
> With Arras nor with Tapystry, such paltrie were too bad:
> Ne yet those hote perfumes, whereof proude Courtes do smell,
> May once presume in such a place, or Paradise to dwell.[38]

38. *The Noble Arte of Venerie or Hunting* (London, 1575), pp. 91–92. Arguing
from George Whetstone's reference to a book of hunting among Gascoigne's works,
Charles T. and Ruth Prouty give Gascoigne credit for translating and paraphras-
ing the French *La Vénerie* (1561 and later eds.) to produce *The Noble Arte of
Venerie*. Since the verses describing "howe an assembly should be made" are
among the few places where the English departs from the French original and
since the accompanying woodcut is one of only 5 out of 32 in the book that are
not copied from woodcuts in *La Vénerie,* the Proutys propose that this whole sequence, especially the long speech a huntsman makes to the queen, was originally
devised for dramatic performance in the Kenilworth revels ("George Gascoigne,
The Noble Arte of Venerie, and Queen Elizabeth at Kenilworth," in James G.
McManaway et al., eds., *Joseph Quincy Adams Memorial Studies* [Washington,
1948], pp. 639–664).

We may well wonder which is more soporific, Turberville's poulterer's measure or the scene he describes, but nowhere could we find a better evocation of the art that nature makes. On one point Turberville is insistent: his shaded "gladsome greene" is worlds away from the tapestries and "hote perfumes" of the court.

Into what fictions did Elizabeth ride when she passed from Ovid's meadows into this greenwood glade? At Woodstock a few weeks after the Kenilworth shows we find her seated her first afternoon "in a fine Bower made of purpose covered with greene Ivie, and seates made of earthe with sweete smelling hearbes"—just the kind of spot Tuberville would choose.[39] She has retired there with a hermit, Hemetes (her host, Sir Henry Lee, in disguise), with two knights who moments before have been struggling to the death, and with a distraught young princess. It is well the queen is seated, for she has ridden straight into the *medias res* of a medieval romance, and it takes Hemetes some time to explain the plot. The two knights and the lady, it turns out, are all lovers on quests. The princess Gaudina is heir apparent to her father's throne, but she has fled king, kingdom, and kingly responsibility to seek her lover Contarenus, a subject of low degree whom her father, with only her own good in mind, has banished from the kingdom. One of these knights is in fact the long-sought Contarenus; the other is the lady's befriender Loricus; and the quarrel has arisen through mistaken identities. And Hemetes the hermit was once blinded by amorous passion but has now this very moment recovered his sight, fulfilling a prophecy by the Delphic oracle that "when thy eyes shal beholde what thy heart delighteth in, even a Lady in whom inhabiteth the most vertue, Learning, and beauty, that ever yet was in creature, then shal they be opened, and that shall be thy warrant." In the meantime Hemetes has been given marvelous powers of *occult* vision to make up for physical vision. Elizabeth, of course, is the Lady of the Oracle's prophecy.

Partly, no doubt, to recover from the fatigue involved in sorting out such complicated affairs, Elizabeth and Hemetes proceeded farther into Woodstock park to a banqueting house atop an artificial mount forty feet high where they sat down to an elegant picnic that sounds rather

---

39. *The Queenes Majesties Entertainment at Woodstocke* (London, 1585), ed. A. W. Pollard (Oxford, 1903, 1910).

like the one pictured in Turberville's woodcut. Boughs of an oak tree shaded this hilltop banqueting house—Hemetes calls it his "hermitage" —and once beyond its portal woven of "Ivy & spanges of gold plate" Elizabeth could sit down in "a chayre costly made of Crymson velvet, imbrodred with branches & pictures of wild beasts & trees, as it had beene a peece of woorke made in the desartes." Ranged about the walls were "Pictures with posies of the Noble or men of great credite," all of them figuring "Allegories" that unfortunately eluded our informant.

No sooner was dinner over than Elizabeth looked down from her hill to see rolling toward her, as if from a Petrarchan triumph, a "waggon of state" drawn by six children. The queen atop that wagon was destined to become of the queen of England's own alter ego. She greeted Elizabeth as one monarch to another:

> As I did roame abroade in wooddy range,
> In shade to shun the heate of Sunny day:
> I met a sorrowing knight in passion strange.
> by whom I learned, that coasting on this way
> I should ere long your highnesse here espie,
> to whom who beares a greater love than I?

> Which then tooke roote still mounting up on height
> When I behelde you last nigh to this place,
> With gratious speech appeasing cruell fighte.
> This love hath caused me to come before your eyne,
> now white, then blacke, your frend the fayery Queene.

Here for the first time the Queen of Fairy and the Queen of England met face to face. The "wooddy range" over which the Fairy Queen reigns is the landscape of medieval romance, the haunt of hermits, questing knights, and princesses who would give up their kingdoms for love.

Just how Elizabeth looked at this world was made dramatically clear the next day. The intrigues of the day before were resolved in a play. Crisis comes when Gaudina's father comes looking for her: which will it be, love or duty? At last Contarenus nobly gives up his private passion for the good of the country and for Gaudina's public responsibility. Prompted by the Fairy Queen's wise advice, Gaudina has no choice but nobly to do the same:

> Wel, *Contarenus* wel, what shal ensue?
> You are the cause whose yeelding makes me yeeld,

> Yet of my word for ever hold this true,
> wheron you may assured comfort build:
> Til death my soule and body shal depart,
> your love shal lodge in some part of my heart.

Real-life reflections of the Fairy Queen's verdict must have overcome what reads like a very long hour's worth of arguments pro and con:

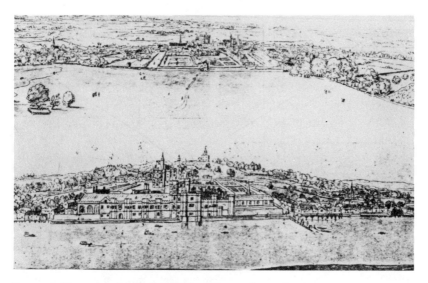

FIGURE 6. Two views of Greenwich by Wyngaerde, 1558
Lower: view from river with Duke Humphrey's Tower ("Mirefleur") at top of hill
Upper: view from Duke Humphrey's Tower toward river

Elizabeth and her ladies were so moved, our informant reports, "that her Graces passions, and other Ladies could not but shew it selfe in open place more then every hath beene seene." He goes on to confide that the whole affair had an allegorical relationship "with this present world," but just what that relationship was neither he nor anyone since has been able to determine for sure. One fact, however, is clear enough: when the distant world of medieval romance was set side by side "with this present world" of political exigencies, the irony moved one to longing and regret. We may comfortably stand aloof from the world of *commedia rusticale,* but the world of medieval romance compels us to enter.

Where exactly Hemetes' "hermitage" was situated at Woodstock the printed account does not specify. In Smythson's plan of Wimbledon the banqueting house crowns a pebble-strewn court near the main house, but at Nonsuch, we know, the banqueting-house on its artificial mount was more than a quarter mile from the castle, well beyond garden, orchard, "wilderness," and the Grove of Diana.⁴⁰ Though they lack banqueting houses, relics of the artificial mounts that were a standard feature of Renaissance country-house landscapes survive today at Rockingham Castle, Northamptonshire, and Boscobel House, Shropshire. Wherever the Woodstock banqueting-house "hermitage" was in fact, *imaginatively* it belonged on the "wooddy range" of the far horizon, away from the mundane realities of the house, with its bad memories of Elizabeth's imprisonment there during her sister Mary's reign. It was on the horizon, on the hill above the tournament field at Greenwich, that Elizabeth had her own "hermitage." Duke Humphrey's century-old tower there—so Elizabeth and her courtiers agreed to pretend—was Mirefleur, favorite retreat of the heroine Gloriana in *Amadis de Gaule* (see Figure 6). Certainly the location was right. "Now you must understand," explains the narrator in Chapter 11 of Book II,

that this place *Mirefleur,* was a little Castle most pleasantly seated two leagues from *London,* built upon the side of a hill, and compassed upon the one side with the Forrest, and upon the other with many Orchards, full of all sorts of trees and pleasant flowers: moreover it was invironed with many great Fountaines, which watered it on all parts. And because that once the King [Lisuart] (being there on hunting with the Queene) seeing that his daughter tooke great pleasure in the place, hee bestowed it upon her, and afterwards she caused a Nunnerie to bee builded within a bow shot thereof, whereunto she sometimes went to recreate her selfe.

Gloriana—it was a role in which poets liked to cast Elizabeth and a role she liked to play.⁴¹ In neomedieval romance, no less than in Ovidian my-

40. John Dent, *The Quest for Nonsuch* (London, 1962), pp. 127–130.

41. Hentzner, *Travels,* pp. 51–52, is not the only visitor who was told about the identification of Duke Humphrey's tower with Mirefleur. No changes in the French whatever were necessary to secure the coincidence of these two places when Anthony Munday translated Book II of *Amadis de Gaule* (London, 1619), p. 64. On Elizabeth as Gloriana see E. C. Wilson, *England's Eliza* (Cambridge, Mass., 1939), pp. 321–369.

thology, Elizabeth and her courtiers delighted in turning literary fictions into literal realities.

Imaginatively if not literally "compassed upon the one side with the Forrest, and upon the other with many Orchards," Mirefleur was one romantic spot in a wide and varied landscape at Greenwich, but the whole of Kenilworth Castle was conceived in the spirit of medieval romance. Two symmetrically placed masses dominated the countryside: a craggy Norman keep called "Caesar's Tower"—"rather . . . for that it iz square and hye foormed, after the maner of Cezarz Fortz, then that ever he bylt it," R. L. concedes—and a *new* ancient tower just built by Leicester himself (*LL*, 4–5). This properly was the house for a man who numbered himself, the revels writers tell us, among *"Arthurs* heires and their servants" (*PP*, Al^r)[42] R. L. devotes several pages at the beginning of his account to filling us in on the great antiquity of Kenilworth Castle. Its founder, he declares in a piece of thoroughly bogus history, was one Kenulph, a Saxon lord of eighth-century Mercia. Leicester's welcoming pageants, not to mention the "plot" involving the Lady of the Lake, were designed to evoke just these romantic associations. A white-robed Sybil, six eight-foot giants "much exceeding the common stature of men in this age" (*PP*, Al^r), and Hercules himself preceded the Lady of the Lake in emerging from the dusky afternoon shadows of antiquity to welcome Elizabeth as she rode into Kenilworth park. Whether "by chauns, by constellation of starz, or by fatal appoyntment," R. L. tells us, the clock on Caesar's Tower had stopped (*LL*, 76). More than a time *when*, the Kenilworth shows were a time *where*.

In space Kenilworth may have been the broadest landscape on the far horizon, but in time nothing can rival the grand chivalric fiction that Elizabeth's Woodstock host Sir Henry Lee sustained for thirty-five years. Just where he left off in 1575 he took up again when Elizabeth returned

42. Leicester was hailed as Arthur of Britain when he made his triumphal entry into The Hague ten years later. See Roy Strong and Jan Van Dorsten, *Leicester's Triumph* (Leiden and London, 1964), pp. 47–48. Leicester's Kenilworth was not the only English Renaissance country house to be conceived in the image of medieval romance. In *Robert Smythson and the Architecture of the Elizabethan Era* (London, 1966), Mark Girouard describes a shift during the century from incipient classicism in houses like Longleat (begun 1559) to romantic fantasy in dream castles like Wollaton Hall (begun 1580).

to Woodstock in 1592.[43] Elizabeth's reentry into the fiction was through an enchanted grove. A knight who had keeping of the grove warned her not to enter: the trees of this grove were transformed lovers, yielding up "nothinge els but syghes & mornful songes." Not to be daunted by such things at age fifty-nine, Elizabeth went ahead and heard the complaints of the knights who were the trunks of the trees and the ladies who were the leaves. "Unconstancie" ruled the grove as the seasons rule plants. But Elizabeth, *semper eadem,* was subject to no such power, and, walking through the grove unharmed (and so liberating the metamorphosed lovers, it was later reported to her), she was escorted out of that bower's "darkness" and "deadness" and into "the openes of a fresh ayer." In that open landscape, free from the inconstancy outside, she remained for the rest of her visit to Woodstock.

After an echo song had sounded the harmony of man in nature—more profound, surely, than the Savage's speech at Kenilworth, since this song was in Latin—Elizabeth came upon an entranced knight. It was Loricus, the befriender of Gaudina seventeen years before. The Fairy Queen had given him the allegorical pictures from the hermitage for safekeeping from the eyes of the "over curious," but his attentions had been diverted by "a stranger ladies thrall"—a coy reference to Lee's dalliance with Mistress Anne Vavasour?—and the Fairy Queen had cast him into this "deadlie sleepe" as punishment. A page bade Elizabeth to look on these pictures that had baffled our informant in 1575: her penetration through to the allegory would be a liberating penetration into Loricus's enchantment. Of course her powers sufficed. As if the theme of constancy had not quite been liberated from the artifice yet, Constancie and Inconstancie came out themselves for a bit of debate. Faithfulness, not to changing external objects, but to a treasured *inner* image, was Constancie's main argument. Confronted with Elizabeth's silent example, Inconstancie had finally to submit "to be my selfe as she is, *Semper eadem."* They took their leave with verses invoking Elizabeth's *impresa* of crown and column: "Constant Piller, constant Crowne, / Is the aged Knightes renowne."

In a final episode some days later Elizabeth penetrated through the en-

---

43. BL MS. Add. 41499, Hamper MS, Petyt MS, printed in Chambers, *Lee,* pp. 276–297.

chanted grove, through the artifice, through the allegory, through the portal of Loricus's hermitage to the very center of this landscape. There she found "the aged Knight," dying yet still keeping vigil by an image of the "Constant Piller, constant Crowne." A hermit received Elizabeth outside and told her Loricus's story—how, cut off from the active life of a courtier by Envy and Age, Loricus had come to him here in the country and had talked with him about the inconstancy of the world, how Loricus had decided to become a hermit also, and how together they had decided to erect a shrine to constancy, the very "Crowne Oratory" before which the queen now stood. Inside this "monument for his minde" Elizabeth would find Loricus, dying with his eye fixed on the constant crown. Her entry into the oratory brought life, for no sooner had she come out than a page brought tidings of Loricus's recovery and presented the queen a copy of Loricus's legacy. He left her nothing less than his country estate, a landscape of real plants that shadowed a state of mind:

Item. I bequethe (to your Highnes) THE WHOLE MANOR OF LOVE, & the appurtenaunces thereunto belonging:
(Viz.) Woodes of hie attemptes,
 Groves of humble service,
 Meddowes of greene thoughtes,
 Pastures of feeding fancies,
 Arrable Lande of large promisses,
 Rivers of ebbing & flowing favors,
 Gardens hedged about with private, for succorie,
  & bordered with tyme: of greene nothing but
  hartesease, drawen in the perfect forme of a true
  lovers knott.
 Orchards stored with the best fruit:
  Queene Apples, Pome Royalls, &
  Soveraigne Peares.

And so on. The country landscape that Elizabeth entered at Woodstock was, more certainly than anywhere else, a landscape of the mind. In the center of that landscape, as in the mind of its tenant Sir Henry Lee, there was constancy, a timeless dream of medieval romance, shut off from the vicissitudes of the world outside by an enchanted grove.

The origins of his role as hermit in the pages of medieval romance did not prevent Lee from posing as the *beatus vir* of Horace's second epode. Among the items in Lee's manuscripts are some verses addressed to him as *"Layius"* and dated "this 3 Kallendel [read "Kalends"] of October 1575." They praise his state of being, "ever constant in a settled place":

> And if I might according to my will
> devise a lyfe that wold content me best
> No mase for pompe nor riches seed of ill
> wold I desier, nor be tryumphant drest
>
> On gennets whit to draw the captyves band
> but I my home in place unknowne wold chuse
> and saffe possest, in gardens & my ground
> in noyse of springes & muses studies use.
>
> .   .   .   .
>
> As Layius heare my friend I gladly wold
> die well to god, a great man & old; finis.[44]

By some years these verses anticipate the Horatian compliments to gentlemen in their country seats that Ben Jonson directed to Sir Robert Wroth, Robert Herrick to Thomas Herrick and Endymion Porter, and John Dryden to the cousin who shared his name.

In her study of Elizabeth's Accession Day tilts Frances Yates has masterfully laid out the chapters that intervene in Sir Henry Lee's romantic fiction between the Woodstock revels of 1575 and their sequel in 1592.[45] Several of the speeches and challenges devised for the annual tournaments at Westminster seem indebted to the plot and characters we first meet in the groves of Woodstock in 1575. In one of these devices a hermit takes on a storytelling role like Hemetes' and introduces a company of country folk led by a clownishly clad knight. A fugitive from the court after he gazed there on an incomparable but unobtainable jewel, this knight has sojourned in the country and reflected on the instability of life at court. Now he begs a part in this festival. In another device a Black Knight appears who tilted the year before, has since sojourned with a hermit, and now returns "in new habite." But in the most famous of all the Accession Day tilts Lee himself took on the hermit's role for good. When he retired

---

44. In printing these verses Chambers, *Lee,* pp. 272–273, notes an echo of Seneca's *Thyestes,* ll. 336 ff. On Horace's *beatus vir* in Renaissance guise see Maren Sofie Røstvig, *The Happy Man: Studies in the Metamorphoses of a Classical Ideal 1600–1700* (Oslo, 1954).

45. Yates, "Elizabethan Chivalry," pp. 27–28. The devices she discusses are printed in Chambers, *Lee,* pp. 276–297.

as the queen's official champion in 1590, Lee took vows to become Elizabeth's "Beadsman." In a temple of Vestal Virgins Lee enshrined his "saint": before the temple's door there stood "a crowned Pillar, embraced by an Eglantine tree"—the very image before which Loricus was keeping vigil at Woodstock two years later. Lee took his leave of the court in verses that John Dowland's setting has made one of the most famous songs of the English Renaissance. Sung on this occasion by the royal lutenist Robert Hales, "My golden locks time hath to silver turnd" sets in its final stanza the scenario in which we find Lee at Woodstock in 1592:

> And when I sadly sit in homely Cell,
> I'le teach my Swaines this Carrol for a song,
> Blest be the hearts that thinke my Sovereigne well,
> Curs'd be the soules that thinke to doe her wrong.
> Goddesse, vouchsafe this aged man his right,
> To be your Beadsman now, that was your knight.[46]

For the epilogue to Sir Henry Lee's neomedieval romance—a story as extended in time as *Amadis de Gaule* in pages—we can turn to another song set by John Dowland. As Dowland perhaps glanced at Elizabeth's Wanstead visit in his adaptation of Sidney's "O Sweet Woods," so to Sir Henry Lee's own words he fashioned a musical monument to the fiction that the queen and Lee had sustained for thirty-five years. The occasion for Lee's verses, and quite possibly for Dowland's setting too, was a visit that the new queen, James's wife Anne, made to Lee and Mistress Anne Vavasour in 1608:

> Farre from triumphing Court and wonted glory,
> He dwelt in shadie unfrequented places,
> Times prisoner now he made his pastime story,
> Gladly forgets Courts erst afforded graces,
> That Goddesse whom hee servde to heav'n is gone,
> And hee on earth, In darknesse left to moane.

But now "a glorious light . . . from the place where erst this Goddesse dwelt," a new star, has risen to command his devotion and to prompt

46. Quoted from William Segar's transcription in first person in his account of the event in his *Honor, Military and Civill* (London, 1602). Other texts of the poem and other accounts of the event are surveyed in Thomas Clayton, " 'Sir Henry Lee's Farewell to the Court': The Texts and Authorship of 'His Golden Locks Time Hath to Silver Turned,' " *ELR*, IV (1974), 268–275.

him to enshrine in his heart a new saint's image. Dowland's splendid
setting exploits the new recitative style to accentuate the tensions in Sir
Henry Lee's dramatic pose: quick, syncopated repetitions of a single note
beg that the first phrase, "Farre from triumphing Court," be sung like a
brass fanfare with a final high-pitched burst on "glory"; a sustained, low-
pitched melodic phrase then darkens "shadie unfrequented places." [47]

The dramatic contrast that quickens the musical pulse of Dowland's
song is the same dramatic contrast that quickens the pulse of life in the
fictions of the far horizon. Far more than the classical fictions of the
middle landscape, the medieval romance that awaited Elizabeth in the
woods of Woodstock had a quality we might call "livability": the roles
of knight and lady suited Elizabeth and her courtiers as the personages
of classical mythology could not. Human content, above all, fleshed out
these roles from medieval romance. For an hour one might play Astraea,
but for thirty-five years . . . ? For that one needed a role with emotional
depth. Changing Daphne into a laurel tree to preserve her chastity might
have flattered Elizabeth, but it could not move "her Graces passions" like
the amorous plight of Gaudina. Partly these heroes and heroines of medieval romance captivated Elizabeth and her courtiers because they were
so immediate: they shared with their audience the same adventurous
and amorous impulses. But partly, too, these figures appealed because,
paradoxically, they were so distant: they belonged to a dream world
where passions were huge, where abstract ideas like Constancie and Inconstancie walked about in splendid dress, where time and the vicissitudes
of politics had no dulling power. It was a world *semper eadem,* and Elizabeth and her courtiers passionately liked to imagine themselves in it.

Entering triumphantly in her "waggon of state," the monarch who pre-
sides over the fictional realm of Woodstock is the Fairy Queen. The fact
that this same figure, though in a more remote and shadowy guise, pre-
sides over Spenser's visionary realm makes it tempting to see in *The
Faerie Queene* the consummate achievement of the impulse we feel at
Kenilworth and Woodstock: the impulse to reduce the blur and flux of

---

47. John Dowland's setting appeared with two other of his songs in the musical
anthology *A Musicall Banquet* (1610) assembled by his son Robert. Text quoted
from Doughtie, *English Airs*, p. 350. Poulton, *John Dowland*, pp. 315-316, quotes
John Chamberlaine's letter describing Queen Anne's visit with Lee.

everyday experience to clarity and fixity in the trammels of a golden net. In several of the introductory sonnets to the enlarged 1596 edition of *The Faerie Queene* Spenser indicates that some of the clear, fixed images in his multifaceted mirror are flattering reflections of actual persons at court. His sonnet to Essex is particularly revealing in its promise to "make . . . memory" of Essex's "Heroicke parts" in books of the poem still to be written:

> Yet doe not sdeigne, to let thy name be writt
> In this base Poeme, for thee far unfitt.
> Nought is thy worth disparaged thereby,
> But when my Muse, whose fethers nothing flitt
> Doe yet but flagg, and lowly learne to fly
> With bolder wing shall dare alofte to sty
> To the last praises of this Faery Queene,
> Then shall it make more famous memory
> Of thine Heroicke parts, such as they beene
> . . . .[48]

Fused with ideal images in other facets of Spenser's mirror, such studies from the life make up the composite image of "vertuous and gentle discipline" he claims in his letter to Raleigh.

When we compare ideal images and "Heroicke parts, such as they beene," we can see in the hermit who takes in Arthur, Timias, and Serena in Book VI of *The Faerie Queene* some curious similarities in character and situation to the hermit who received Elizabeth at Woodstock in 1575, who succored knights between Accession Day tilts, who retired from an active life at court and received the queen in his hermitage in 1592. In setting and outward show the hermitage that Arthur, Timias, and Serena discover, "like a little cage, / . . . / Deckt with greene boughes, and flowers gay beseene" (VI.v.38), recalls that oak-shaded Woodstock hermitage before which the Fairy Queen made her first appearance in England. But it is the inner reality, not the outward show, that makes the similarity suggestive. Like Loricus in 1592, Spenser's hermit is a man who has made a "religious vow," and the "Chappell" in which he carries out his devotions shares with Lee's "Crown Oratory" not only its appearance but its purpose:

48. *Spenser's Faerie Queene*, ed. J. C. Smith (Oxford, 1909), II, 494. Other quotations from *The Faerie Queene* are from this edition.

> . . . towards night they came unto a plaine,
>   By which a little Hermitage there lay,
> Far from all neighborhood, the which annoy it may.
>
> And nigh thereto a little Chappell stoode,
>   Which being all with Ivy overspred,
>   Dekt all the roofe, and shadowing the roode,
>   Seem'd like a grove faire braunched over hed:
>   Therein the Hermite, which his life here led
>   In streight observaunce of religious vow,
> Was wont his howres and holy things to bed;
> . . . .
>
> (VI.v.34–35)

On the subject of these "holy things" Spenser is vague—strategically so,
one suspects—but one doubts that Fairy Land is papist. Like Loricus,
Spenser's hermit has been forced by age to give up a career of chivalrous
action and take up his solitary devotions:

> And soothly it was sayd by common fame,
>   So long as age enabled him thereto,
>   That he had bene a man of mickle derring doe:
>   But being aged now and weary to
>   Of warres delight, and worlds contentious toyle,
>   The name of knighthood he did disavow,
>   And hanging up his armes and warlike spoyle,
> From all this worlds incombraunce did himselfe assoyle.
>
> (VI.v.37)

Marvelous powers of occult vision bless Spenser's hermit no less than
they blessed the hermit Hemetes at Woodstock in 1575. Like that hermit
who succored the fugitive knight, stunned by his gaze on an incomparable but unobtainable jewel, and who then sent him into action on the next
Accession Day, Spenser's hermit heals the wounds that Serena and Timias
have suffered from the Blatant Beast: he warns them against the infec-
tions of passion and sends them, cured, back on their quests. Even if they
are independent reflections of the same grand fiction—hermits, after all,
play as essential a part in medieval romances as knights, ladies, and
dragons—Spenser's hermit and Sir Henry Lee's sustained performance
in that role show us how sublimely preoccupied Elizabeth and her courtiers were when they drew near the border between fact and fiction.

The prospect before us is tempting, but to pass on farther would be to enter another kind of landscape. Beyond the far horizon lie reaches of imaginary experience that merge imperceptibly with the real greenwood where we stand. Between these two places our own more self-conscious age would insist on a wall; for Elizabeth and her courtiers and poets the borderline between life and art was not so easy to mark. Though we cannot enter it here, that imaginary realm in the distance is, after all, a place we are familiar with from reading Spenser's great poem and other poets' verses. It is the shadowy borderland between the imagined landscape and the actual landscape that seems strange to our twentieth-century perspective.

When we turn around to take in the view behind us, to take stock of where we have been, we look back on a landscape that falls away from us in three quite distinct phases. Closest to the house we see the geometric rigidities of garden and orchard, from this vantage point so clearly extensions of the architecture of the house. Within these artful spaces we have savored the irony of *commedia rusticale* and embroiled ourselves in debate. In the middle distance, between the garden walls and the woods where we stand, range broad open meadows. The pastoral peace that from a distance seems to reign there is discovered closer up to be the product of an uneasy balance between art and nature, the result of civilizing power quelling the forces of lust and aggression that pulse beneath the surface. The denizens of this demesne are the sensually sensuous but cerebrally sententious creatures of Ovid's *Metamorphoses*. When swayed by Astraea's justice, this middle realm shows us an image of the golden age Ovid celebrates in his account of creation. In the shadowy woods around us, finally, we hear echoes not only of Savage Men waiting for us to deliver them to civilization but of questing knights and passionate princesses waiting to deliver *us from* civilization. Geographically, the journey from the house toward the far horizon is a journey from art toward nature, but mythographically it seems just the reverse: as the visible signs of art grow fainter, our impulse to live life in imitation of art grows stronger. That is the impulse that turns reality into revel.

APPENDIX

Queen Elizabeth's Country-House Revels:
A Catalog of Surviving Texts

Date, Place, Host	Source	Motives & Themes
July 1575 Kenilworth Castle, Warwicks. Robert Dudley, Earl of Leicester	George Gascoigne, William Hunnis, Edward Ferrers, & others, *The Princelye pleasures at the Courte at Kenelwoorth* (London: Richard Jones, 1576) "R. L.," *A LETTER: Whearin part of the entertainment . . . . at Killingwoorth Castl . . . iz signified* (no imprint, no date) [description] BL MS. Harleian 6395 [description]	1. gift ceremony at entry: gifts of gods at last of 4 portals 2. Queen as liberator: Savage Man Lady of the Lake Deep Desire 3. debate advising marriage: Diana overruled by Juno [planned but not performed] 4. rustic bridale & Coventry Hock Tuesday play
September 1575 Woodstock, Oxon. Sir Henry Lee	*The Queenes Majesties Entertainment at Woodstocke* (London: "for Thomas Cadman," 1585)	1. Queen as liberator: restores sight of hermit Hemetes 2. debate advising against marriage: Gaudina, Contarenus, Loricus; presided over by Fairy Queen
May 1578 Wanstead, Essex Robert Dudley, Earl of Leicester	Sir Philip Sidney, "The Lady of May," printed in 1598 folio of *Arcadia* MS at Helmingham Hall, Suffolk, with additional speech at end	debate: Queen as judge between shepherd ("smale Desertes and no faults") & forester ("manie Desertes and manie faultes")
May 1591 Theobalds, Herts. William Cecil, Lord Burghley, or Sir Robert Cecil	MS once owned by J. P. Collier; present location untraced	debate & gift ceremony: Queen as judge between Gardener and Molecatcher

110

	Ed. J. W. Cunliffe in *The Complete Works of George Gascoigne* (Cambridge, Eng., 1910), II, 91–131
—	Ed. F. J. Furnivall as *Robert Laneham's Letter* (London, 1907)
—	Ed. A. W. Pollard as *The Queen's Majesty's Entertainment at Woodstock in 1575* (Oxford, 1903, 1910)
—	MS printed by R. Kimbrough & P. Murphy, "The Helmingham Hall Manuscript of Sidney's *The Lady of May:* A Commentary and a Transcription," *RenD,* N.S. 1 (1968), 103–119
	Rpt. of nineteenth-century printing in R. W. Bond, ed., *The Complete Works of John Lyly* (Oxford, 1902), I, 417–419

Date, Place, Host	Source	Motives & Themes
August 1591 Cowdray, Sussex Anthony Browne, Lord Montecute	*The Speeches and Honorable Entertainment given to the Queenes Majestie in Progresse, at Cowdrey in Sussex* (London: Thomas Scarlet, 1591)	1. landscape as political emblem: house's walls (Porter) tree hung with noble arms (Pilgrim & Wild Man) fishpond (Angler) 2. gift ceremony: nymph gives Queen crossbow 3. country dancing
September 1591 Elvetham, Hants. Edward Seymour, Earl of Hertford	*The Honorable Entertainement gieven to the Queenes Majestie in Progresse, at Elvetham in Hampshire* (London: John Wolfe, 1591)	Queen as *genius loci* of golden-age landscape: salutation of "heav'n, & earth, & fluds" (Fairy Queen appears with creatures of underground)
August 1592 Bisham Abbey, Berks. Elizabeth, Lady Russell	*Speeches Delivered to Her Majestie This Last Progresse at the Right Honorable the Lady Russels, at Bissam, the Right Honorable the Lorde Chandos, at Sudley, at the Right Honorable the Lord Norris, at Ricorte* (Oxford: Joseph Barnes, 1592)	gift ceremony at entry: Queen as liberator of Savage Man and Pan
7–13 September 1592 Sudeley Castle, Glos. Giles Brydges, Lord Chandos	*Speeches Delivered . . . at Sudley* (1592)	1. Queen as liberator: saves Daphne from Apollo 2. Cotswold shepherds' holiday [planned but not performed]
18–23 September 1592 Woodstock, Oxon. Sir Henry Lee	BL MS. Add. 41499 ("Ditchley MSS") Hamper MS Petyt MS	Queen as liberator: metamorphosed lovers in grove dying Loricus Constancie over Inconstancie
28–30 September 1592 Rycote, Oxon. Sir Henry Norris	*Speeches Delivered . . . at Ricorte* (1592)	gift ceremony: host's absent children send gifts by messengers on successive days

—	Ed. Bond, *Lyly,* I, 421–430

"With fragrant flowers we strew the way," rpt. *Englands Helicon* (1600) as by "Thos. Watson"; musical setting in Francis Pilkington, *First Booke of Songs or Ayres* (1605)

"In the merrie moneth of May," rpt. *Englands Helicon* (1600) as by "N. Breton"

"Eliza is the fairest Quene" & "O Come againe faire Natures treasure," musical settings by Edward Johnson in BL MS. Add. 30,480–484

Ed. Bond, *Lyly,* I, 431–452

"Swel *Ceres* now, for other Gods are shrinking," rpt. *Englands Helicon* (1600)

Ed. Bond, *Lyly,* I, 471–477

"My hart and tongue were twinnes, at once conceaved," rpt. *Englands Helicon* (1600); musical setting by John Dowland, *A Pilrimes Solace* (1612)

"Hearbes, wordes, and stones, all maladies have cured," rpt. *Englands Helicon* (1600)

Ed. Bond, *Lyly,* I, 477–484

debate between Constancie & Inconstancie printed in *The Phoenix Nest* (1593)

Ed. Sir E. K. Chambers in *Sir Henry Lee: An Elizabethan Portrait* (Oxford, 1936), pp. 376–397

Ed. Bond, *Lyly,* I, 485–490

DATE, PLACE, HOST	SOURCE	MOTIVES & THEMES

1593 (?)
Theobalds, Herts.
William Cecil,
  Lord Burghley, or
Sir Robert Cecil
	Bodleian MS. Rawlinson 1340	gift ceremony: Hermit offers
		  devotion

September 1598
Mitcham, Surrey
Dr. Julius Caesar
	BL MS. Add. 12497	debate & gift ceremony: Queen
		  as judge among Poet,
		  Painter, Musician

1601 (?)
Wilton, Wilts. (?)
Mary Sidney Herbert,
  Countess of Pem-
  broke
[perhaps planned; no
  record of perform-
  ance]
	Mary Sidney Herbert, Countess
	of Pembroke, "A dialogue
	between two shepheards,"
	printed as no. 4 in *A Poetical
	Rapsodie* (1602)
		Queen as Astraea, restorer of
		  golden age

July 1602 Chiswick, M'sex. Sir William Russell	MS. Finch Hatton 2414, Northamptonshire Records Office	welcome & farewell by Angler

31 July–3 August
  1602
Harefield, M'sex.
Sir Thomas Egerton
	Conway MSS
	1803 copy, now untraced, of
	  lost sixteenth-century MS
		1. gift ceremonies: dairymaid
		   & bailiff
		   Place & Time
		   St. Swithin
		   mariner (Queen as Cynthia)
		2. complaint of satyrs against
		   disdainful nymphs

—	Printed in John Nichols, *The Progresses and Public Processions of Queen Elizabeth* (London, 1823), III, 241–245
—	Ed. Leslie Hotson as *Queen Elizabeth's Entertainment at Mitcham: Poet, Painter, and Musician* (New Haven, Conn., 1953)
—	*A Poetical Rhapsody, 1602–1621*, ed. H. E. Rollins (Cambridge, Mass., 1931–1932), I, 15–17
—	Ed. L. Hotson in *Queen Elizabeth's Entertainment at Mitcham* (1953)
"A Lottery," printed in *A Poetical Rapsodie* (3d ed., 1611), misdated to 1601 & attributed to "I.D." (=Sir John Davies?) "Cynthia Queene of Seas and lands" (from "A Lottery"), musical setting in Robert Jones, *Ultimum Vale* (1608) and in BL MS. Add. 24665 ("Giles Earle's Book," 1615)	Ed. Bond, *Lyly*, I, 491–504

The Jacobean History Play and the Myth of the Elect Nation

JUDITH DOOLIN SPIKES

W HEREAS MOST OF THE history plays of the 1590s treat events of the
fifteenth century—largely, the period covered by "the Tudor
myth"[1]—all of the Jacobean plays dramatize Tudor history itself.
Whereas the earlier plays take for their subjects battles and other broadly
significant affairs of state, the Jacobean plays treat peacetime diplomacy
and clashes between individuals at court. The central characters of the
nineties plays are kings and warriors, those of the Jacobean plays saints
and martyrs. In their concentration on moral dilemmas and acts of choice,
the Elizabethan history plays are most nearly related to humanist historiography, while the Jacobean plays rest squarely within the Christian

1. Although Tillyard's Tudor-myth interpretation of the historical drama of the
nineties is currently undergoing revision, it provided the framework within which
much of the most important and influential work on the history play was written
for almost a quarter of a century. As such, it still provides the best background
against which to highlight such other trends as the one described here. Thus I
make several references to the Tudor myth and the criticism which incorporates
it, although I do not accept it as a complete interpretation of the historical drama
of the nineties.

tradition descended from Eusebius and Augustine. These and many other similarities among the Jacobean plays may be traced directly to a common source, John Foxe's *Acts and Monuments of these Latter and Perilous Days,* and to the climate of belief and historical interpretation summed up by and promulgated through Foxe's book.[2]

The critics who have read the Jacobean plays at all sympathetically have focused on the "play" and blinked the "history," for there has been a consensus that the history-play genre is defined by the plays of the nineties, a significant number of which lend themselves, as the later plays do not, to a reading in terms of the Tudor myth. The later plays, it has been held, lack a "considered philosophy of history" such as constitutes a major center of interest in the Elizabethan plays.[3] Yet, in the light of expectations provided by the *Acts,* what has been called the "flatness" of characterization in these plays—utter depravity versus spotless purity—appears to be occasioned far less by lack of thoughtfulness on the part of the playwrights than by a philosophy which viewed world history as the temporal manifestation of the cosmic warfare, of God's Elect sanctified from all eternity against the irremediably damned followers of Antichrist. Further, the action is seen to consist not of a series of imperfectly integrated episodes, but of a closely connected sequence of attacks upon a purely good character by a wholly evil one. It ends when the good char-

---

2. As William Haller has thoroughly acquainted us with the sources and purpose of Foxe's philosophy of history and its impact on the thought and action of its time, I shall merely recall that philosophy in general outline and cite specific passages from the *Acts* as they relate to the history plays. Readers of Haller's *The Elect Nation: The Meaning and Relevance of Foxe's Book of Martyrs* (New York, 1963) and *The Rise of Puritanism. Or, The Way to the New Jerusalem as Set Forth in Pulpit and Press from Thomas Cartwright to John Milton, 1570–1643* (New York, 1957) will recognize their influence on my understanding of Foxe's historiography and its role in English culture. These two works offer an exhaustive account of this mode of thought as it was both lived and promulgated.

3. The quotation is from Irving Ribner's summation of prevailing opinion in *The English History Play in the Age of Shakespeare* (New York 1965), p. 223. R. A. Foakes may be taken as representative of the more sympathetic critics: "The plays written after 1600 on themes taken from English history tend to be of a different kind, not so much glorifying England or presenting an idea of history with lessons for the present, as making use of stories from the past for effective theatre" (The Arden *Henry VIII,* 3d ed. [Cambridge, Mass., 1964], p. xliv).

acter or his cause triumphs, not a victim of fate but its instrument, in an action not tragic but tragicomic, as is the action of the Christian drama itself. The juxtaposition of the plays and their source most strongly suggests that they were never intended as expositions of the minds and hearts of individuals, nor as timely lessons in practical politics, but rather as representations of segments of temporal history which find their context and their meaning—as did the mystery and miracle plays whose form they resemble—in an apocalyptic drama ultimately contained in the mind of God. They may profitably be viewed as late-Reformation versions of the religious drama which the early Reformation had suppressed in England.

Foxe's charge from his patron Edmund Grindal was to produce a mere "Book of Martyrs," a sort of Protestant calendar of saints. As word reached Foxe on the Continent of Philip's departure, Mary's severe illness, and the forces presaging the accession of Elizabeth, he conceived the idea of turning a simple farrago of pathetic tales into a great demonstration of the proposition that the Elect had always suffered persecution under the agents of Antichrist, that the trials currently afflicting England and the sufferings of the Marian martyrs constituted clear and evident signs that God had called the English people to a redemptive role in universal history, and that Elizabeth was to be both symbol and instrument of England's mission of deliverance. Foxe's outstanding achievement was to set Grindal's collection of tales of the Marian martyrs in a scriptural-historical context woven out of the revolutionary millinarianism, Protestant propaganda, and incipient nationalism which so strongly and so variously agitated the minds and lives of his contemporaries. As these forces remained current and urgent right up to the Civil War, Foxe's book provided a version of English history and a definition of English destiny which remained contemporary throughout three reigns. This paper will show how turn-of-the-century playwrights mining Foxe for dramatizable material carried away not only his stories but also his patterning of action both human and cosmic, his view of historical personalities, and his conception of the privileges and responsibilities of being English. Read in the context of Foxe's apocalyptic scheme, these later history plays emerge as coherent expressions of a national—as opposed to a merely dynastic— myth. Appearing first in early Tudor plays based on or otherwise closely related to Foxe, it was eclipsed by the great vogue in the nineties of plays based primarily on Hall, Holinshed, and other dynastic-oriented chroniclers, and reappeared to dominate the historical genre in Jacobean drama.

Foxe's great synthesis owed much to his mentor John Bale, in whose *Kynge Johan* a similar perspective on English history had already been staged in the 1530s. Several times revised and surviving in the version presented before Elizabeth in 1591, *Kynge Johan* is an adaptation and partial translation of the Antichrist play *Pammachius* of Thomas Kirchmayer, a mystery play the central figure of which is the king.[4] Widowe Ingelonde is far closer to the damsel-in-distress of chivalric tradition than to the central Psychomachia figure of the morality to whom she is most commonly compared; she is a hapless victim defended by her champion John against the agents of the pope, who is frankly identified with the Antichrist. Although John dies, his cause is shown to be gloriously triumphant in the prophesied accession of Elizabeth.[5]

Bale's characters are simultaneously abstractions and historical personages, and the level of abstraction as it affects both action and characterization is taken from Revelation. Bale also follows the practice of the apocalyptic writer in adopting as his time base a point in the distant past, so that although the events he relates are wholly past he appears to be describing past, present, and future, thus giving an air of revelation to his account by "foretelling" things that have already occurred and lending credibility to that part of his scheme of history which does in fact project itself into the future.

4. Jesse W. Harris, *John Bale, A Study in the Minor Literature of the Reformation* (Urbana, Ill., 1940), pp. 96–98; Hardin Craig, *English Religious Drama* (Oxford, 1964), pp. 368, 370–371.

5. To the English reformers John was, as the first English sovereign to oppose the papacy, both national hero and martyr-king, and, of course, one of God's Elect. William Tyndale had alluded to him in these terms in his *Doctrinal Treatises,* and Bale deliberately set out to rescue him from the hostile pages of the Catholic chronicler Polydore Vergil. Bale's vindication was wholly accepted by Foxe, and also influenced Holinshed's account of John's reign. See Ribner, p. 35; David Bevington, *Tudor Drama and Politics* (Cambridge, Mass., 1968), p. 104; Honor McCuskor, *John Bale, Dramatist and Antiquary* (Bryn Mawr, Pa., 1942), pp. 90–93; Rainer Pineas, "William Tyndale's Influence on John Bale's Polemical Use of History," *Archiv für Reformations-geschichte,* LIII (1962), 79–96.

Kynge Johan foreshadows the history play of the nineties in its glorification of England, its interpretation of history to support doctrine, and its use of a historical event as an analogy to a contemporary problem.[6] Other elements, neglected for the most part by earlier dramatists, reappear in *The Troublesome Reign of King John* as well as in the seventeenth-century history plays. Among these are kinship to the mystery and miracle plays rather than to the morality; the identification of the "mere English" with the Elect, and the foreign-born and foreign-influenced with the Antichrist; the role of the monarch as religious leader of his people; the transformation of complex historical personages into Protestant types of vice and virtue; the centering of the dramatic action in the contention between Good and Evil for the fate of England, with the Good at last triumphant in fact or in prophecy; and the use of apocalyptic devices, chivalric allegory, and the imagery of Revelation.

Following Bale, Foxe conceived of human history as the temporal reflection of the cosmic warfare between Christ and Antichrist described in Revelation, narrowed down to an age-long battle of English rulers and people, God's Elect, against the alien, corrupting influence centered in Rome.[7] Throughout universal history Foxe traced God's great plan to make of the English His Chosen People, the Elect Nation whose destiny it was to lead all mankind out of popish superstition into the clear light of the New Jerusalem. It is this philosophy of history which shapes and informs the English history plays performed for the most part during the reign of James Stuart. Their subject is Tudor history itself.

The *Acts* begins with the martyrdoms of the Apostles and continues through the Ten General Persecutions of the Faithful, which came to end under the "British-born" Constantine the Great. The Peace of Constantine is presented as the reflection in human history of the imprisonment of the Antichrist and the beginning of the millennium. Foxe then makes note of the various traditions alleging the establishment of the

6. These aspects are thoroughly discussed by Ribner, pp. 35–36.

7. Bale's most rigorous exposition of the theme is found in his *Image of Both Churches*. Bale was, of course, writing in the tradition of Eusebius and Augustine, who had established the opposition-of-two-orders structure and the analogical relationships among Christ and Antichrist, the true Church and the corrupted church, the City of God and the city of the world, the Elect and the reprobate.

primitive Church of Britain, setting the stage for his presentation of English history as the age-long march toward the New Jerusalem.

The encroachments of the "bishop of Rome" upon the English Church are dated from the arrival of Augustine, and the first concerted effort to throw off Roman influence is located in the Wycliffite movement which began in the reign of Edward III and was suppressed under Richard II. In the comparatively humanistic Tudor myth, the deposition of Richard is a free act which sets off a providentially directed train of events culminating in the accession of the Tudors. For Foxe, the initiating episode is not the deposition of Richard, but Richard's yielding to the pope in the suppression of Wyclif and the Gospel, which Foxe views as the first act of Antichrist upon being released from his thousand-year imprisonment. In the *Acts,* then, the ensuing century of civil war is neither a curse upon a sinful people, as the Tudor-myth formulation would have it, nor a period of suffering which men have inflicted upon themselves, as recent anti-Tillyardian critics have argued that it is in the pages of Hall, Holinshed, and other sixteenth-century chroniclers. Rather, in the Wars of the Roses Foxe locates the beginning of the final period of trial and proof of the Elect which is to culminate in the Second Coming.

Foxe pauses over the reign of Henry V to detail the persecution of Wyclif's Lollard followers, giving particular attention to the "martyrdom" of Sir John Oldcastle, then passes quickly to the reign of Henry VIII, when "Britain began as a body to cast from herself the errors of Rome." He rejoices in the careers of Cromwell, Cranmer, and Tyndale, singling out three great advances in the Reformation during this reign: the throwing off of papal supremacy, the suppression of the monasteries, and the circulation of the Scriptures in English. He laments, however, that religious opinion was still in a "transition state" which occasioned a number of martyrdoms of the Elect. The "latter and perilous days" themselves are located in the reign of Mary Tudor; and the dedication to the first English edition (1563), likening Elizabeth to Constantine and Foxe himself to Eusebius, embodies the apocalyptical expectancy with which the exiles and their party greeted Elizabeth's accession, while the dedication to the 1570 edition promises a display of the mercy and justice of God in the "loosing and tying up again of Satan the disturber of commonweals."

Although the influence of Foxe's work was felt in such early Elizabethan plays as Nathaniel Woodes's *Conflict of Conscience* and the anonymous *New Custom*,[8] the Elect Nation myth had its greatest impact in drama during the first decade of the seventeenth century, a period which brought once more to the foreground the burning issue that had informed Foxe's treatment of English history: would Protestantism or Catholicism triumph in England? At the turn of the century, Elizabeth was sixty-seven, without issue or other direct heir. James Stuart was the logical successor, and at that time there was no reason to doubt that he would maintain the reform establishment of religion. But there were rival claimants, both domestic and foreign: upon one of these, Lady Arabella Stuart, the Catholics placed their hopes, and two treasonous intrigues formed around her in the opening years of the seventeenth century. Contemporaneous with the reemergence of the religious question at the end of the reign of Elizabeth came the plays of *Oldcastle* and *Cromwell,* drawn from the history that had addressed that question at the beginning of her reign.

These, the earliest of the history plays drawn directly from Foxe's pages, embody the essential elements of the myth of the Elect Nation which were to be fully developed in the Jacobean historical drama. Each has a central character modeled on Foxe's interpretation of a historical personage occupying a pivotal position in the Elect Nation scheme of history. Oldcastle, whose execution as a traitor and heretic in 1417 marked the end of Lollard influence in English affairs, was taken up in the sixteenth century as a protomartyr by the reformers; and he was elevated, as was King John, to the status of Protestant saint through the offices of Tyndale, Bale, and Foxe.[9] Also, in Foxe's view it was Cromwell who "alone, through the dexterity of his wit and counsel," set England free from the tyranny of Rome [V, 366–401].)[10] The behavior of the saintly hero, in private life and at court, provides the focus of the dramatic action when he comes into conflict on a religious issue with a Catholic antagonist whose repeated

8. Leslie M. Oliver, "John Foxe and *The Conflict of Conscience," RES,* XXV (1949), 1–9; Bevington, *Tudor Drama,* p. 130.

9. The development of the Oldcastle legend is traced by Rudolph Fiehler, "How Oldcastle Became Falstaff," *MLQ,* XVI (1955), 16–28; other pertinent aspects are discussed by Mary G. M. Adkins, "Sixteenth-Century Religious and Political Implications in *Sir John Oldcastle," University of Texas Studies in English,* XX (1942), 86–104.

10. All references to the *Acts* are to the Stephen Reed Cattley edition, 8 vols. (London, 1837–1841).

attacks seriously threaten the hero's life as well as the quiet enjoyment of his religious practices. The action is resolved when the hero or his cause finds favor with the English monarch, who up to that point has stood apart from the conflict, hearing impartially the persuasions of both parties.

The persuasion scenes imitate Foxe's practice of focusing a tale upon a theological debate between the martyr and the bishops or other papal examiners, a debate in which the "Believer in the Word" bases himself upon Scripture while the "Believer in the Mass" counters with papal decrees and prescribed interpretations. In the *Acts* these debates function primarily to place the Reformers' position before the readers, the first among whom was Elizabeth. That is, while the initial impetus to the composition of the *Acts* was the desire to drum up Continental sympathy and support for the Marian exiles, a primary aim of the first English edition was to instruct Elizabeth in the role the reformers deemed appropriate to the English monarch. This Foxe accomplished partly by praising Elizabeth for already having adopted attitudes and courses of action which he wished her to adopt,[11] and partly by highlighting the deeds of earlier English monarchs who had (he said) so acted. The pedagogical and declamatory aspects of this procedure are much less prominent in the plays, in which the debate scenes are manipulated to produce dramatic excitement rather than conversion in the audience, the vast majority of whom were already converted.

A major center of interest in the first of the Elect Nation plays is found in following the conversion of the king by means of the heroes' exhortations recalling England to her destiny as God's temporal agent in the cosmic warfare. The exiles and their party had made just such an accommodation between the doctrine of predestination and the proselytizing they found necessary to their own survival: since every English soul

---

11. This practice is most apparent in Foxe's introduction to Elizabeth's own story, where he hails her as "so good, godly, and virtuous a queen; such a chosen instrument of his clemency . . . so godly disposed, so merciful . . . so humble . . . so moderate . . . so maidenly without pomp, through whom we cannot deny, as amends and recompense, now to be made to England, for the cruel days that were before," and he provides a very litany of virtues: Elizabeth "reformeth religion, quencheth persecution, redresseth the dross . . . cometh in like a mother, not like a step-dame . . . she rusheth not in to hang and draw; her majesty beheadeth none, burneth none, spoileth none, forgiveth all" (VI, 601–602).

was elected to grace, the preachers were not about the business of saving souls, but merely of rooting out the corrupt and superstitious beliefs and practices which centuries of popish rule had planted.

Thus we find both in Foxe and in the plays drawn directly from his pages much expounding of Scripture and exhortation to all and sundry to submit themselves to the "true" will of God. In the midst of all this the English monarch plays an oddly passive role, attending first to one party, then to the other. In the plays he rises in stature as the action progresses and the reform party gains the ascendancy. Both *Oldcastle* and *Cromwell,* with differing degrees of vehemence, bring to the early seventeenth-century stage the religious controversy of the 1560s, the issues and polemics of which had become once again alarmingly pertinent. Mouthing the again-relevant sentiments and sophistries of their historical counterparts, adherents of both parties engage in a battle to the death which revolves around the monarch without touching him, and which is resolved when he at last inclines to the reform party.[12]

The peaceful accession of James appeared to lay the ghosts from the past; yet Protestant enthusiasm for James scarcely survived his arrival on English soil. His Catholic queen pointedly refused the Anglican Communion at her coronation, sought offices for English Catholics, corresponded warmly with the Spanish Infanta. James himself—born of a Catholic martyr and raised in the church of John Knox—became more enigmatic every day. At the Hampton Court Conference of 1604 he entertained the Puritan ministers' petitions and proposals, engaged in earnest

12. Such a fortunate issue is, of course, contrary to modern historians' understanding of both the Oldcastle and Cromwell stories. Henry's tardy pardon of Cromwell in the play parallels Foxe's account of the deep regret Henry suffered at the end of his life over Cromwell's death and his attempt to make amends by protecting Cranmer from Gardiner and proposing to eradicate all Romish practices (V, 691–692). Both aspects are dramatized in later Elect Nation plays: the protection of Cranmer provides the climax in *Henry VIII*, and in *When You See Me* Henry vows "an I live / But seven years longer, we'll take order thoroughly." *Oldcastle* ends with the title character triumphantly secure in the good favor of Henry V, who, attending to the voice of God as uttered by Oldcastle, a believer in the Word, purposes to lead the nation into the fulfillment of His divine purpose. The extant "first part" is true to its source's vision of the pattern ordering universal history, the position of England in that pattern, and the role befitting the English monarch.

but good-natured debate with their leaders, then turned them away and confirmed the authority of the bishops.[13] August of the same year brought James's unpopular peace treaty with Spain, and the first suggestion of the detested "Spanish match" for the heir to the English throne. His Protestant subjects' direst fears were aroused, fears which soon found confirmation in the Gunpowder Plot. On all sides men heard the sound of Antichrist rattling his chains.

The Tudor-oriented historiography which had previously presided over the English historical drama could not be made to serve under the new dynasty. The old and familiar *Acts,* however, offered a marvelously adaptable pattern and a view of history wholly compatible with the new Stuart regime. Whereas the other existing versions of English history were dynastic, insular, and circumscribed in time, Foxe's was universal, beginning with Creation and looking forward to the Last Judgment, designed not only to explain past and present but also to predict the future, passing beyond the experience, ambitions, and destiny of a dynasty to those of the nation and beyond providential causation to the apocalyptic. The message of the *Acts* remained particularly appropriate as the Elizabethan order passed away and the Jacobean uneasily took its place. Foxe's scheme of history, conceived at a time when English Protestants of all persuasions made common cause against the Roman Catholic Church, embodied traditions from which all sides in the developing crisis could find support. It lent itself with almost equal facility to the Puritan-High Church controversy as to the Protestant-papist one, and many of the plays here discussed as participants in the Elect Nation mythos have been considered by other writers as "last-ditch" efforts at reconciliation between the Puritans and the stage.[14]

13. This issue is discussed in detail by David Harris Willson, *King James VI and I* (New York, 1967), pp. 201–209.

14. Even the Puritans generally exempted historical subjects from their condemnation of imaginative literature, and plays like these in which brave and loyal shopkeepers and artisans consort with kings were especially popular with the middle-class audiences, as Louis Wright among others has pointed out (*Middle Class Culture in Elizabethan England* [Ithaca, N.Y., 1958], pp. 621–627). The list of Elect Nation playwrights reads like a roll call of the bourgeois dramatists of the day—Heywood, Dekker, Munday, Rowley, Chettle—and all except the prototype *Kynge Johan* were performed by the Admiral's Men, the Chamberlain's Men, or their successors (Prince Henry's and the Palsgrave's, and the King's Men, re-

Foxe himself had recognized the effectiveness of the drama as a medium of religious propaganda: "players, printers, and preachers," he wrote, "be set up of God, as a triple bulwark against the triple crown of the Pope, to bring him down, as, God be praised, they have done meetly well already" (VI, 57). And when the accession of James Stuart cast doubt upon the direction the state was to take in the future, the popular playwrights turned to the well-known and revered *Acts* and set its stories and its philosophy upon the stage.

In his Address to *The Whore of Babylon*, Thomas Dekker refers to the distinct "laws" binding the poet and the historian, and mentions the alteration of chronology of historical events permitted to the poet as the sole specific point on which those laws differ. Samuel Rowley's startling rearrangement of the events of the reign of Henry VIII in the first Jacobean history play, *When You See Me You Know Me,* creates a faithful dramatic reflection of Foxe's historical interpretation of the reign, and also suggests a parallel with the court of James in 1604, the year the play was most probably performed.[15]

When You See Me is concerned with the history of a reign rather than with the biography of a king, and the character who does most to hold the historical episodes together is Wolsey, whom Foxe had described as "this glorious cardinal . . . more like a prince than a priest" (IV, 589). The play opens with a disquisition on Wolsey's "labors in th' affairs of kings" (p. 5).[16] He proposes to form a triple alliance among England,

---

spectively), save *Wyat* and *If You Know Not Me* whose stage history is obscure (*Wyat*, and possibly *If You Know Not Me*, was performed by Queen Anne's Men but originally bought in whole or part by Henslowe for Worcester's Men). Commercial plays, they were written by popular playwrights for the general public, an audience broadly enough conceived to include all patriotic, God-fearing Londoners, offensive in their sentiments only to the extremes of Catholic or Puritan feeling, and appealing to tastes in theater more conservative or plebian than those of the courtly audiences for whom Beaumont and Fletcher were writing.

15. *When You* was entered in the Stationers' Register in February 1605. F. P. Wilson, editor of the Malone Society edition, makes a strong argument for performance after 9 April 1604. The play is based primarily upon Foxe, with some material drawn also from Holinshed, as shown by Leslie Mahon Oliver, "Rowley, Foxe, and the *Faustus* Additions," *MLN*, LX (1945), 391–394.

16. References are to *When You See Me You Know Me: A Chronicle-History by Samuel Rowley*, ed. Karl Elze (Dessau, 1874).

the Empire, and France—a purpose that justifies the anachronistic intrusion of the marriage of Henry's sister Mary to Louis XII, which was one component of the alliance. The price he sets on his labors is support of his candidacy for the papacy:

> If Wolsey to the Pope's high state attain,
> The league is kept, or else he'll break't again.
>
> (p. 4)

The prompt death of Louis, however, shatters Wolsey's plan, for Henry is delighted at the opportunity it affords him to send Anne of Cleve back to France so as to be free to wed Katherine Parr (p. 37). In the following scene Wolsey reflects that with Louis dead and the emperor cold to his proposal, the only way to gain the papacy is to outbid the other candidates, one of whom he has learned has offered "three score thousand pound" (p. 38). The news that Henry has married Katherine Parr threatens Wolsey's plans even more sharply:

> Holy Saint Peter shield his majesty!
> She is the hope of Luther's heresy;
> If she be queen, the protestants will swell,
> And Cranmer, tutor to the prince of Wales,
> Will boldly speak 'gainst Rome's religion.
> But, bishops, we'll to court immediately,
> And plot the downfall of these Lutherans.
>
> (p. 39)

Thus the conspiracies against Queen Katherine and Cranmer are linked to the failure of the English-French alliance, all three episodes to Wolsey's aspirations, and a motive—the purchase of the papal tiara—for the extortion and hoarding of treasure which contributes to Wolsey's fall and to Henry's turning away from Catholicism is associated with the whole congeries. In this way Rowley rearranges the historical material into a closely interconnected train of events all of which have their origin in the opening scenes of the play.

The point at issue is the fate of England, not the fate of any individual. The action is played out between the godly Cranmer, Queen Katherine, and Prince Edward on the one side, and the evil bishops Wolsey, Bonner, and Gardiner on the other. King Henry stands between the two parties, as in *Oldcastle,* simply because he *is* the king: Rowley presents Foxe's view of the monarch as head of the national Church, through whom all reform must be accomplished and, consequently, the necessary and sufficient target of godly persuasion.

Rowley, like the author of *Oldcastle,* charts his course between extremes. Anti-Catholic sentiment is pronounced, but radicalism in reform is also condemned. Henry refers to Luther as a "damn'd schismatic" and a "dangerous knave" (p. 60), and his decrying of Luther's "haughty insolence" provokes the confrontation scene between Gardiner and Katherine, the almost formal debate in which the issues are clearly defined.

The Catholic Gardiner calls attention to the "bloodshed there is now in Germany / About this difference in religion" (p. 56), and asserts:

> To smooth the face of false rebellion
> Proud traitors will pretend religion;
> For under color of reformation,
> The upstart followers of Wicklif's doctrine,
> In the fifth Henry's days arose in arms,
> And had not diligent care prevented them,
> Their powers had suddenly surprised the king.
> And, good my liege, who knows their proud intent,
> That thus rebel against your government?
>
> (pp. 58–59)

The Protestant Katherine counters this and carries the day by raising the issue of the pope's presumed authority over kings and subjects alike:

> But you that are sworn servants unto Rome,
> How are ye faithful subjects to the King,
> When first ye serve the Pope then after him?
>
> (pp. 59–60)

Anti-Catholic though it be, the primary emphasis of the play is on the larger issue of the vital community of interest among monarch, nation, and the reformed Church, with the most pointed criticism aimed at those who would allow doctrinal differences to foment civil and international discord. This is in perfect alignment with the political orientation of Foxe, upon whom the millinarian influence did not extend to the mystical anarchism that drove Melchior Hoffmann to prophesy that Christ would found the Kingdom at Strasbourg in 1533 and John of Leyden to declare himself king of the New Zion in Münster in that same year. Foxe and the people for whom the *Acts* was originally written and from whom the threads of this philosophical fabric were drawn were not the illiterate oppressed among whom millinarianism had flourished during the Middle Ages; they were people much like Rowley's Katherine and Cranmer, educated members of the governing class who longed not to abolish the power structure but to defend or reclaim their positions in it. By bringing together the themes of apocalypse and national destiny, Foxe pointed dramatists the way to securing the advantages of a magnificently moving rhetoric without at the same time promoting the political disorder and violence which had so often accompanied the apocalyptic theme on the Continent.

Rowley's portrayal of Henry's wavering between the persuasions of Katherine and Gardiner, so excessive that the king appears ready to believe whoever succeeds in getting the last interview, derives largely from Foxe and somewhat, perhaps, from James. Foxe had presented Henry as a king "so inclinable and forward in all things virtuous" when good counsel prevailed, but during whose reign "religion and all good things . . . revolted backward again" the moment evil counselors intruded (V, 605). On the other hand, already in the first year of his reign James had shown that an unflinching constancy was not to be expected of him. The honeymoon between James and his new subjects was over almost before it had fairly begun, and Prince Henry became ever more the hope of the majority of Londoners, if not of all England. Rowley portrays a king and a court far from the ideal, and Prince Edward is looked to as the chief hope for order, peace, and justice in the realm (pp. 41, 54). Edward is nothing if not a Protestant, but the play is most eloquent on the civil dangers inherent in religious faction and appears to favor something very much like a continuation of the Elizabethan settlement, a middle way between extremes, with a strong and resolute monarch at the head of Church and State. Rowley's glorification of Prince Edward appears to mirror a hopeful expectation that the waverings of James and the uncertainties of his government might be peacefully resolved under his successor.

Whether or not, however, we are justified in finding such narrowly topical meaning in the play, it is evident that Rowley's alteration of the chronology of Henry's reign was neither thoughtless nor inept, but provided a context for the reexamination of the again-urgent religious question and for a study of the interpenetration of religious and temporal issues in the motivation of individuals.

In Dekker and Webster's *Famous History of Sir Thomas Wyat* (ca.

1604), the reflections in the dramatized history of events contemporaneous with the play's performance are so numerous and so strong—Wyat's rebellion / Essex's rebellion; Queen Mary's Spanish marriage / the Spanish marriage proposed for Prince Henry; Lady Jane / Lady Arabella Stuart —that deliberate parallelism cannot be doubted.[17] *Wyat* brings together two historical episodes, covering the months between the death of Edward VI (6 July 1553) and the execution of Lady Jane Grey (12 February 1554).[18] The first part of the play deals with Northumberland's attempt to wrest the line of succession from Henry VIII's issue to that of his sister Mary. The second part treats the national crisis arising out of the decision of Queen Mary (daughter of Henry VIII) to marry Philip of Spain. Some alterations of fact and emphasis allow the playwrights to unify the two episodes around the title character, centering the dramatic action in Wyat's two revolts against *de facto* rulers and creating a parallelism between the two parts of the dramatic action which causes them to reflect and comment upon each other.

While the play's delineation of the issue of rebellion against a lawful sovereign appears confused when *Wyat* is read within the framework of expectations provided by the Tudor myth, the issue becomes much clearer

17. The *a quo* date is fixed by Henslowe's 21 October 1602 entry of what appears to be the final payment for the first part of the lost "playe called Lady Jane," of which *Wyat* is held to be an adaptation. On 19 March 1603 stage plays were prohibited until further notice, and playing was not resumed until after James's accession (G. B. Harrison, *Elizabethan Plays and Players* [London, 1940], p. 295). Thus, in order to ascribe the first performance of *Wyat* to the Elizabethan period it is necessary to argue that an "old" play, *Lady Jane* (with or without its second part), was turned into a "new" one, *Wyat,* within a period of less than five months. It is far more plausible to assume that the text (1607) represents a Jacobean play, and the title page itself assures us that it represents a play actually performed (although not necessarily for the first time, of course) during the reign of James (the title page reads, "As it was lately acted by the Queen's Majesty's Servants"—that is, by Queen Anne's Company, the successor of Worcester's Men, for whom Henslowe bought *Lady Jane,* reorganized in the queen's name probably by Christmas of 1603 and certainly before 19 February 1603/4 [Edmund K. Chambers, *The Elizabethan Stage* (Oxford, 1923), II, 229]).

18. The sources are Foxe and Stowe and possibly also Grafton and Holinshed, as shown by Philip Shaw, "*Sir Thomas Wyat* and the Scenario of *Lady Jane,*" *MLQ*, XIII (1952), 227–238; and Mary Foster Martin, "Stow's *Annals* and *The Famous Historie of Sir Thomas Wyat,*" *MLR*, LIII (1958), 75–77.

when referred to expectations derived from the play's primary source. Foxe had somewhat tortuously brought his expression of the nature of kingship and of the subject's duty of obedience into apparent alignment with orthodox Tudor doctrine, which explained ungodly reigns as God's punishment upon a sinful people and held that the subject was, consequently, bound to obey the tyrant, who would be removed by the hand of God Himself as soon as the sin had been expiated. The largely Calvinistic view with which Foxe began, however, was rather different. Holding the throne by divine right, the monarch was expected to govern in accord with the law of God. Difficulty arose, however, from differing conceptions of God's law, and of the duty of a subject to a monarch who appeared to contradict it. John Ponet and John Knox, for example, certain that God made His will known through the utterances of the preachers and in the still voice of conscience rather than in the decrees of the Roman hierarchy, had disavowed the subject's duty of obedience to the "ungodly" monarchs Mary Stuart and Mary Tudor. Foxe's apocalyptic framework suggested a way of condoning resistance to monarchs like the Marys without actually supporting rebellion: since periodic persecutions of the faithful were allowed by God as a trial of the Elect, it was the clear duty of the latter to remain firm in the Faith, whatever the cost. If they perished, no matter; by their death they purchased a martyr's crown.[19]

Although a careful reading of *Wyat,* unlike *Oldcastle* and *Cromwell,* will not support an interpretation of the title character as a Protestant saint, that fact is more a testimony to the artistic complexity of this play than it is to the confusion of its authors. They examine, through the dramatization of parallel historical episodes, the burning issues of the hour: the religious settlement, succession, and the subject's duty of obedience. Wyat is glorified as a loyal Englishman pursuing the national interest in ways sanctioned by popular Protestant doctrine—yet, unlike the stage Oldcastle, he fails; and unlike the stage Cromwell, he is given neither gallows speech nor choral commentary to identify him as saint and martyr. That position is here allotted to Lady Jane.

Presented in the Mary Tudor-Lady Jane conflict are the issues of claim to succession through royal blood and through royal will, of innocence

19. Haller reviews the Protestant controversy on the relationship among God, state, monarch, church, and the individual in *Elect Nation,* pp. 75–79.

victimized by self-seeking nobles, of the claims of *de facto* government in the face of popular disfavor, and of the role of the virtuous man in such a crisis. The three latter issues continue to be explored in the context of the Spanish marriage; they are modified and complicated by the changed historical realities, and with variation in the roles assigned to the parties in the new conflict.

The subplot concerning the fates of Lady Jane and young Guilford, which may be a recasting of the lost *Play of Lady Jane,* shows Foxe's influence, in structure and in interpretation. Jane was apotheosized by Foxe, who could not, however, give any semblance of credibility to her claim to the throne without casting a shadow on that of Mary's sister, Elizabeth. The playwrights depict Jane and Guilford as the hapless victims of their fathers' treasonable ambition, who would have escaped their sad fate had it not been for the enmity of Stephen Gardiner, bishop of Winchester.[20]

Gardiner, "that seemingly ever-present villain of the biographical drama,"[21] made his first stage appearance in the play of *Cromwell.* Foxe's excoriation of Gardiner, a conscientious albeit arch-conservative statesman, grew out of Foxe's conviction that Gardiner was chief among the Marian ministers who sought the destruction of Elizabeth as a matter of state and church policy. When he came to write of the Tudor era, Foxe cast Gardiner in the role of the prime adversary of the Lord's Elect, as the very pattern of the meddlesome, worldly prelate, "in his own opinion and conceit flattering himself too much, in wit crafty and subtle" (VII, 585), who becomes on the stage a snarling, high-stepping, self-consciously evil

20. Wyat argues before the council and pleads with Mary herself on their behalf (I.vi.89–92; III.i.45–50), but Gardiner succeeds in carrying the day against them, and the "poor innocent souls," though "both from guilt are free" (II.ii.43) are condemned to die. References are to the edition of Fredson Bowers (Cambridge, 1953).

Gardiner is similarly, and again contrahistorically, cast in the role of villain in the treatment of the marriage of Queen Mary to Philip of Spain. He and Wyat again take the parts of the Evil and the Good Counselor in the council at which the match is decided. In fact, Gardiner was strongly opposed to Philip's suit, but in the play it is on his advice and under his influence that Mary decides in favor of the Spanish marriage. See H.F.M. Prescott, *Mary Tudor* (New York, 1962), pp. 219–228; Albert J. Loomie, S.J., *The Spanish Elizabethans* (New York, 1963), p. 16.

21. Ribner, p. 220.

figure but slightly removed from the morality Vice. It is fitting, then, that Gardiner's first appearance as stage villain should be found in the play of *Cromwell,* and that he plays this role in Heywood's play on the troubles of Elizabeth; and when he was made the (contrahistorical) antagonist of Lady Jane and other Protestant saints, the playwrights did no more than extend the principle found in their source.[22]

The playwrights center their treatment of Mary's success against the forces of Suffolk and Northumberland in the petition presented to Mary, soon after her accession, on behalf of the Suffolk men. This incident concerns Mary's alleged promise to those who joined her cause at Framlingham to make no alteration in the religious establishment of Edward's reign. The reference is to the story put in circulation by Foxe that when the Suffolk men offered her their aid against Northumberland, they made it a condition "that she would not attempt the alteration of the religion which her brother King Edward had before established." "Unto this condition," Foxe continues, "she eftsoons agreed, with such promise made unto them that no innovation would be made of religion . . . Thus Mary, being guarded with the power of the Gospellers, did vanquish the Duke" (VI, 387).

H.M.F. Prescott, Mary's modern biographer, regards the story as incredible,[23] but there can be little doubt that it was widely credited by the playwrights' contemporaries. Its appearance in Foxe's pages assured it a large and sympathetic audience, and it is there no mere detail, but a pivotal point in Foxe's interpretation of recent history. He had, for one thing, to explain away what looked like the hand of God in Mary's success against a Protestant partisan and seemingly insuperable odds—hence the oath which brought the "power of the Gospellers" to Mary's side. In the subsequent violation of the oath Foxe located the act by which the undeniably legitimate heir evinced her opposition to the divine purpose—a

22. Only the comparative obscurity of Stephen Gardiner renders this less jarring to our expectations today than Felix Schelling found the transformation of Cromwell from the "Machiavellian instrument of Henry's tyrannical exactions into the type of that honorable thrift, capacity in trade, frugality, piety, and stanch Protestantism which constituted the ideal of London merchant citizenship" (*Elizabethan Drama* [Boston, 1908], I, 286).

23. Prescott, p. 193.

neat resolution of the problem of which Heywood, too, made full use in *If You Know Not Me You Know Nobody*.

Foxe's pattern of history demonstrated that the Elect of the Lord had always suffered persecution under the agents of Antichrist; it followed that martyrdom was the surest sign of election to God's grace. Ideologically useful as this scheme was to the surviving coreligionists of the Marian victims, it left some doubt as to the destination of their own souls. To resolve this difficulty, they evolved the doctrine that their preservation and that of their sovereign were the result of the direct intervention of God: they and their nation had been spared and singled out as the Chosen People to lead all nations into the fulfillment of His divine purpose. "The Miraculous Preservation of the Lady Elizabeth, now Queen of England, from Extreme Calamity and Danger of Life, in the Time of Queen Mary, her Sister" is the crowning episode in Foxe's great pattern. Through an astounding feat of imagination and synthesis of Protestant propaganda Foxe makes of Elizabeth's accession the grand historical climax of the cosmic warfare.

If You Know Not Me (1605), identified with Thomas Heywood's otherwise lost *Play of Queen Elizabeth*,[24] gives full and coherent expression to the Elect Nation version of English history. The Catholic party, whose figurehead is Mary Tudor but whose agent in the action is Stephen Gardiner, bishop of Winchester, seeks the downfall of the Princess Elizabeth, hope and symbol of the Protestant party, whose fortunes go from bad to worse until the king-consort Philip of Spain intervenes in her behalf and eventually reverses the stream of affairs by exposing and disgracing her enemies. The falling movement of the fate of Mary and her party is then hurried to its end, with Winchester's illness and death, Philip's departure, and Mary's illness and death coming in rapid succession. The major action of Elizabeth's ascendance continues with her dream of her nuptials, a prophecy of the mystical union of the

24. Mary F. Martin, "*If You Know Not Me You Know Nobody* and *The Famous History of Sir Thomas Wyat*," *The Library*, ser. 4, XIII (1932), 272–281; Madeleine Doran, ed., *MSR*, 1935, pp. xi–xvii (line references are to this edition). Based primarily on the *Acts*, the play also draws on Holinshed and Fabyan, as shown by Arthur M. Clark, *Thomas Heywood: Playwright and Miscellanist* (Oxford, 1931), p. 102.

sovereign and her people. The ceremonial ritual symbolizing the union is represented in the final coronation scene, which is climaxed by Elizabeth's receipt of the gift of an English Bible from the Lord Mayor, and concluded by Elizabeth's speech in praise of the book.[25]

As Foxe tells the tale, the forces of darkness, of which Gardiner is both symbol and instrument, concentrate their nefarious might upon the destruction of the saintly virgin princess, Elizabeth, bereft of human succor; the powers of evil are, however, combated by God's providence, which settles upon a variety of human agents until at last Gardiner, like his infernal prototype, overreaches himself and brings about his own undoing:

> We declared before how that the lady Elizabeth being in the Tower, a writ came down, subscribed with certain hands of the council, for her execution; which, if it were certain, as it is reported, Winchester (no doubt) was deviser of that mischievous drift. And, doubtless, the same Ahithophel had brought his impious purpose that day to pass, had not the fatherly providence of Almighty God (who is always stronger than the devil) stirred up master Bridges, lieutenant the same time of the Tower, to come in haste to the queen . . . to know further her consent, touching her sister's death. Whereupon it followed, that all that device was disappointed, and Winchester's devilish platform. . . . through the Lord's great goodness came to no effect.
>
> (VI, 618–619)

But, such was the gracious and favourable providence of the Lord, to the preservation not only of her royal majesty, but also of the miserable and woeful state of this whole island, and poor subjects of the same, whereby the proud platforms and peevish practices of this wretched Ahithophel prevailed not; but, contrariwise, both he, and all the snares and traps of his pernicious

25. The body of the play details a crescendo of threats to Elizabeth's position as heir apparent, which range from attempts to send her abroad as wife to some private gentleman or German princeling, through efforts to secure her legal execution by implicating her in Wyat's conspiracy against Queen Mary, to, finally, an attempt on her life by private assassins. Each of these dramatic episodes, many of which lack historical authority, closely parallels Foxe's account. The playwright was not moved to depart from this source even in the interest of providing the obligatory comic-relief scene. This scene, involving Elizabeth, her "jailer" Sir Henry Bedingfield, and a goat, is taken directly from Foxe's lengthy digression presented "by the way [of] refreshing the reader, if it be lawful in so serious a story to recite a matter incident, and yet not impertinent, to the same" (VI, 616).

counsel laid against another, were turned to a net to catch himself, according to the proverb, "Malum consilium consultori pessimum."

(VI, 622)

Following Foxe, Heywood selects events, real or apocryphal, which cast Elizabeth in the role of God's chosen instrument. Foxe sees "no cause why the communion of her grace's afflictions also, among the other saints of Christ, ought to be suppressed in silence, especially seeing that the great and marvellous working of God's glory, chiefly in this story, appeareth above all the rest" (VI, 604). Heywood's heroine expresses her willingness to suffer whatever trials God may visit upon her (ll. 333, 1418-1420), refers to herself as an analogue of Christ in the "Tanquam ovis" scene, taken from Foxe, and informs her servants: "If I miscarry in this enterprise, and [they] ask you why, / [Say] a Virgin and a Martyr both I die" (ll. 341-342). *If You Know Not Me* Part I is clearly related to the miracle play, and Grivelet, in fact, refers to it without hesitation as a dramatic hagiography.[26] This is a Protestant saints-play, as the source from which it was taken is a Protestant *Legenda Aurea;* but, like so many of Foxe's hagiographies, it is a story of martyrdom avoided —or rather of sainthood postponed, for Elizabeth is assured that "With Heaven's King / One day in choirs of angels I shall sing" (ll. 417-418).

The sympathetic role assigned to the Spanish king has been the occasion of considerable surprise. It has been conjecturally explained as evidence of Heywood's tolerance, or as superogatory evidence that the play was written after the accession of James, because of "the implicit support which it gives to James I's new policy of reconciliation with Spain."[27] It has not been noted that the use of Philip as the pivot of the dramatic action corresponds to the pivotal position in history accorded him in the *Acts.* There were sound political reasons for Philip's support of Elizabeth, of course; but to Foxe, the preservation of "the Gospellers'" queen by

26. Michel Grivelet, *Thomas Heywood et le drame domestique Élizabéthain* (Paris, 1957), p. 133. Cf. Anne Lancashire's discussion of other Jacobean saints' plays, some of them based on Foxe, in *"The Second Maiden's Tragedy:* A Jacobean Saints' Life," *RES,* XXV (1974), 267-279.

27. *Eg.,* Fredrick M. Velte, *The Bourgeois Elements in the Dramas of Thomas Heywood* (Mysore City, India, 1924), p. 33; Frederick S. Boas, *Thomas Heywood* (London, 1924), pp. 21-22; Boas, *An Introduction to Stuart Drama* (Oxford, 1946), p. 175; the quote is from Ribner, p. 221.

the hand of the arch-enemy of Protestantism was a clear and evident sign of God's special care for Elizabeth and for the national religion of which she was made symbol and head. In the play, Gardiner himself is made to express this view, apropos of Philip's having foiled his last desperate plot against Elizabeth: "Her life is garded by the hand of heauen, / And we in vaine pursue it" (ll. 1150–1151).

It is clear that Heywood has taken from Foxe not only the raw material of his play, as is generally acknowledged, but also Foxe's conception of the pattern of history and of the significance of Elizabeth's accession within that pattern, as well as the plotting of the action as a series of attacks upon Elizabeth instigated by Gardiner, leader of the Catholic party, with disaster averted time and again until at last evil is defeated and the just triumph.

The real Elizabeth was none too pleased with the role of Puritan saint and new Moses leading her people into the Promised Land which the radical reformers sought to impose upon her, but she often found it useful. As William Haller has shown, in the English mind God's will and the good of England and the English Church, of which Elizabeth was the symbol and head, became completely identified, and Foxe's *Acts* both crystallized that belief and popularized it.

The continued attacks of the nation's and the Church's adversaries served not only to fortify the godly in their sense of election, but also to persuade many besides . . . that there must be something special about being English, that the English were being subjected to the unusual trials now afflicting them because they were nothing less than an elect people called to play a particular part in the designs of providence. This conviction, which received something like official support with the official recognition of Foxe's book in 1571, grew with every one of the queen's narrow escapes from the attacks of her enemies, and when Antichrist finally came sailing up the Channel in 1588 and the wind, as Milton reminded the Long Parliament in 1641, scattered him over the northern ocean even to the frozen Thule, it was natural to conclude that, as as Aylmer had said in 1559, God was indeed English.[28]

Part I ends with the virtual apotheosis of Elizabeth, a saint whom God has temporarily exiled from Heaven as a special favor and blessing on the English people. This was only the beginning of the march to the New Jerusalem, a destination the Puritans confidently expected to reach in

28. Haller, p. 245.

their lifetimes. The interpolated incidents of national life found in *If You Know Not Me* Part II—Dr. Parry's treason and the defeat of the Armada—are significant episodes in the evolving form of the myth as Elizabeth's reign progressed. Possibly they once belonged, as is frequently suggested, to a lost second part of Heywood's *Play of Queen Elizabeth*. Such a play would naturally find its appropriate ending in the final scene of Part II of *If You Know Not Me*, for the defeat of the Armada was the high-water mark of the scheme of history which the *Acts* made a part of the English national consciousness. It is the point at which Thomas Dekker ends his allegorical treatment of Elizabeth's reign in another play conceived in the same apocalyptical framework, *The Whore of Babylon*.

The Whore of Babylon is a historical allegory of the reign of Elizabeth, with the "tropical and shadowed colours" taken from chivalric literature and the Book of Revelation, with the *Faery Queen* as probable intermediary. The play survives in a reading edition prepared by Dekker and printed in 1607. In his introductory address to the reader he refers to his work as a "dramatical poem," the purpose of which is "to set forth . . . the incomparable heroical virtues" of Elizabeth and "(on the contrary part) the inveterate malice, treasons, machinations, underminings, and continual bloody stratagems, of that purple whore of Rome, to the taking away of our Princes' lives, and utter extirpations of their kingdoms." [29]

The first scene represents the slumber of Truth and her awakening upon the death of Queen Mary to "pull . . . the veils from the Councillors eyes," and to present Queen Elizabeth with an English Bible, thus taking up the history at the precise point at which Heywood leaves it in *If You Know Not Me* Part I.[30] Titania (Elizabeth), the Empress of Babylon (the papacy), and their respective satellites engage in no activities which would strain credulity were they presented as the historical figures they so transparently represent rather than as Fairies and Hurtful Spirits. Even the patently allegorical characters find analogues among

---

29. References to Dekker's *The Whore of Babylon* are to *The Dramatic Works,* ed. Fredson Bowers, 4 vols. (Cambridge, Eng., 1953–61), II, 496–584.

30. Dekker repeats several of the apocryphal episodes embodied in *If You,* but the proliferation of precise and ephemeral detail suggests that he consulted a number of minor tracts as well as Foxe and the other standard chronicles for the historical matter.

the stock types of the conventional history play: Plain-Dealing performs the function of the clown or fool, Truth that of the good counselor, and Time resembles the prophetic Cranmer of *Henry VIII*. The only divergence from the strict truth of historical fact occurs in the interest of plot construction, so that the action consists solely in a series of Babylonian attacks repeatedly repelled by Titania and her Fairies—that is, Dekker subordinates the truth of historical fact to what he takes to be the truth of historical meaning.

Although the use of fairies and abstractions rather than human characters has little effect on the action of the play, Dekker's allegorical mode permits an explicit identification of Elizabeth as the symbol of England, and of England's role and destiny in temporal history as a manifestation of the working of providence, and he takes full advantage of the opportunity. The Babylonian (Roman Catholic) designs on the life of Titania are secondary to the larger purpose of conquering Fairyland (England), and Fairyland itself is the object of Babylonian concern solely as the home of Fairies (Protestants) and hence the champion of "Fairyism." This is made explicit at the end of Act II, scene i, where Titania receives the embassy from "the nation [the Netherlands] With whom our Fairies interchange commerce, / And by negotiation grown so like us, / That half of them are Fairies: the other half / Are hurtful Spirits [Catholics]" (ll. 233–237);[31] and again in Act III, scene i, where First Cardinal (Cardinal Como) points out that even though Titania die, "out of her ashes may / A second Phoenix rise . . . Of stronger talent . . . so bonie and so large of gripe / That it may shake all Babylon . . . Thus, to fell down their Queen is but one stroke; / Our axe must cleave the kingdom, that's the oak" (ll. 234–248).[32]

The play ends with a vision of the future in the apocalyptic mode, as

31. The English reformers considered the English Church to be the true primitive Church, founded long before the emissaries of Rome arrived with their "corrupting" doctrine; thus Dekker sees England and not the Continent as the home of "the true faith," although most Englishmen admitted that the most recent impulse to reform came from Luther and Calvin.

32. Cf. "Of Gardiner it is reported, that in his often discoursing about punishing heretics (as he called them), he would say, 'We strip the leaves and lop the bows; but unless we strike at the *root*, that hope of heretics (meaning the lady Elizabeth), we do nothing'" (*Acts*, VI, 619, n. 1).

Time conjures up the Empress's reception of the news of the defeat of the Armada. Titania comments upon the vision: "Mark: those that most adore her [the papacy], most are slaved; / She never does grow base but when she's braved" (V.iv.133–134). It was a pertinent warning for the new reign which was having its own difficulties with Rome, and it points the way out of the drama and back into the actual life of the audience for whom it was written.

Dekker has returned Foxe's view of English history to its source. As Bale had phrased it in his *Image of Both Churches*, "after the true opinion of St. Austin, either we are citizens in the New Jerusalem with Jesus Christ, or else in the old superstitious Babylon with Antichrist the vicar of Satan."[33] The "whore of Babylon," a Reformation commonplace for reference to the pope is, of course, the purple-clothed woman seated upon the scarlet Beast of Revelation, whose name was Babylon the Great, the Mother of Harlots and Abominations of the Earth, "drunken with the blood of the saints and . . . of the martyrs of Jesus" (Rev. 17). Dekker has taken the characteristic devices of apocalyptic literature—"prophetic" visions, symbolism, deliberate obscurity, interpreting angel (Truth)— and adapted them to the machinery of the history play, creating a historical allegory in which England, the champion of Protestantism, is overtly cast in the role of the Angel of Light and Catholicism in that of the Fiend of Darkness in the timeless cosmic warfare.

If You Know Not Me and *Whore* take as their subject what was in Foxe's apocalyptic scheme the culminating episode of universal history, the tale among all those he recounts in which "the marvellous working of God's glory . . . chiefly appeareth above all the rest." Yet, as William Haller remarks, "after the Armada the great redemptive climax towards which history was supposed to have been moving since Wyclif had not come off,"[34] and after an initial period of disillusionment the reformers were forced to admit once more that the national myth had been brought to rest on the wrong reign. Just as the reigns of Henry V and of Henry VIII had come to be seen not as culminations but as respites, so did the reign of Elizabeth. Just as medieval millinarian chroniclers had tried to see the Last Emperor in each new monarch and, that

33. Quoted by Haller, p. 68.
34. *Ibid.*, p. 236.

expectation defeated, had imagined the consummation postponed to the following reign, so did the gospelers who had expected Kingdom Come during the reign of Elizabeth continue to project that expectation into the future. Disillusionment with James, the death of Prince Henry, and the catholicizing of Charles were successively incorporated into the myth as minor setbacks, until with the convening of the Westminster Assembly the Puritans once again believed their dream of heaven-on-earth to be on the threshold of fulfillment.

In the meantime, crises in James's reign periodically revived interest in the history play. In 1612 and 1613, years surrounding the death of Prince Henry, a number of old plays were reissued, and probably revived on stage (among them *Wyat, Cromwell, When You See Me,* and *If You Know Not Me*), and one new play marked by the Elect Nation myth appeared: *Henry VIII.* The last of the Elect Nation plays—*The Duchess of Suffolk* and *A Game at Chess*—appeared in 1623–1624, years which again saw a national crisis and renewed interest in the history play.[35]

The many elements of the Elect Nation myth which find expression in *Henry VIII* suggest that the myth goes far toward providing an "over-all consistent philosophical scheme such as makes cohesive unities out of all of Shakespeare's earlier histories," the apparent absence of which has been deplored in *Henry VIII.*[36] We find here the almost obligatory appearance of Gardiner as villain, now the persecutor of the righteous Cranmer; the portrayal of the king, who rises in authority and gains in stature as he throws off the influence of the evil papist Wolsey; the structuring of the episodes as a series of contrasts and opposition scenes centering in the four trials which, in their pitting of lies and sophistries against the plain unvarnished truth, bear a striking similarity to the pattern common to all of Foxe's many examinations of the faithful by papal representatives; the proliferation of choruslike characters who keep the nation and national feeling in the forefront; the greatly quali-

---

35. Space does not permit a thorough discussion of these late plays; here I merely suggest the main points of interest in relation to the Elect Nation myth.

36. The quotation is from Ribner, p. 289, who is relating prevailing opinion. Shakespeare's exceedingly careful attention to his sources for this play—Foxe and Holinshed primarily, and also perhaps Halle and Speed—has frequently been remarked.

fied approval of Henry with his primary claim to praise located in the accident of having fathered Elizabeth; the optimistic, ever forward-looking pattern focused on the nation rather than on a dynasty, which saw English history not as a series of sins and curses but as one of trials and triumphs; and also "patience in adversity" and "the contrast between heavenly and earthly justice," the two major themes of the play,[37] which are also the major themes of Foxe's historical view. Shakespeare dramatizes a period of national trial, which led to triumph—not the ultimate triumph, as Foxe had prophesied, but a triumph nonetheless. He writes during a subsequent period of trial, and looks forward, in Cranmer's closing prophecy, to another triumph which truly lies in the future, beyond the reign of James, to "Wherever the bright sun of heaven shall shine, / His honour and the greatness of his name / Shall be, and make new nations" (V.iv.50–52). Like so many of the history plays based on the *Acts, Henry VIII* ends with a prophetic vision in the style of the apocalyptist, lending credibility to the actual prophecy through the spurious "foretelling" of accomplished events.

The Duchess of Suffolk epitomizes the story of English Protestantism from Edward VI through the reign of Mary to the accession of Elizabeth.[38] Katherine Willoughby's high birth and rank made her the natural focus of any treatment of the English fugitives; her story is accorded disproportionate space in Foxe's account of "Divers who escaped the fire in Queen Mary's Reign," and it is one of the two stories from Foxe included in Holinshed's brief treatment of the period. Around this salient figure the playwright groups some 125 minor characters, representing among them every shade and nuance of English Protestantism

37. R. A. Foakes, in *Henry VIII*, p. lviii. References are to this edition.

38. *Duchess* was licensed in 1623 for the Palsgrave's Company (successors of the Admiral's Men), under the patronage of Frederick (elector palatine of the Rhine and husband of James's daughter Elizabeth) from 1612 to 1631. A predecessor of Frederick figures prominently in the last act of the play. A strong argument, too lengthy for presentation in this place, can be made for topical reference in the play to one of the hottest issues of 1623: Frederick had assumed the crown of Bohemia and had almost as quickly been expelled not only from Bohemia but also from his own Rhenish palatinate by the Hapsburg Emperor Ferdinand. The play is drawn from the *Acts*, possibly Timothy Bright's 1589 abridgment; it is likely that the playwright had also seen Thomas Deloney's ballad on the subject in his *Strange Histories*.

of the time, from the tilers of the comic scene, representative of the dozens of nameless little people of Foxe's pages who escaped the fire by pardon or oversight, through the recanting recanter Cranmer, to the steadfast martyrs Ridley and Latimer—the three central figures of the English Reformation. Ranged against them are the bishops, Bonner and Gardiner, and their allies. The action is structured as a series of attempts on the freedom and safety of the Duchess, who narrowly escapes disaster time and again until at last the accession of Elizabeth permits her to return to England in triumph, in time to see her enemies cast into prison.

Upon receipt of the news of Elizabeth's accession, the Duchess exclaims:

> I render thanks unto the gratious heavens,
> Thou that send'st Balme of comfort to the wounded,
> Ioy to the brused heart, opprest for truth,
> Lengthen her dayes as long as heaven hath starres,
> Or this faire frame foundation for a world.
> Or if it be Thy gratious providence
> For to remoove her to a happier place,
> Let in her stead arise, and from her ashes come,
> A Phenix may enlighten Christendome.
>
> (I.1^r)

It has been assumed that the phoenix reference is a politic Jacobean addition to a revamped Elizabethan play; yet there is no evidence for dating *Duchess* earlier than 1623, and such prophecies, real or spurious, are among the salient characteristics of the Jacobean history play.[39]

Thomas Middleton's *A Game at Chess* dramatizes the final episode in the train of events known to historians as "the Spanish match." A marriage between the heirs apparent of England and Spain, first proposed in

---

39. Leslie Oliver has suggested an identification of the comic servant Thomas Fox, whose wily machinations as double agent secure the Duchess's safety more than once, with the martyrologist John Foxe, who was (according to some not altogether reliable reports) at one time a tutor in Katherine Willoughby's household: "That the sober, studious, godly Foxe should be shown as worshipping his Protestant heroine, foiling the villainous prelates, and smoothing the path of Protestant exile might be taken . . . as an allegory of the effect of his book upon the Protestant world" ("Thomas Drue's *Duchess of Suffolk:* A Protestant Drama," *SB*, III [1950], 243).

1604, was a pawn in Spanish-English negotiations until 1623. In that year Prince Charles and Buckingham made a surprise visit to Madrid to fetch the illusive bride; this romantic experiment resulted in the humiliation of the two adventurers and, subsequently, in England's declaration of war on Spain and the Empire.[40]

The ground of the political allegory in the play is the confrontation between Protestant England and Catholic Spain during the reign of James, just as the allegorized history of *Whore* is the same confrontation during the reign of Elizabeth. As in *Whore*, many points in the allegory defy precise identification, and, again as in *Whore*, it is likely that the obscurity is intentional, in the manner of the apocalyptist. Nevertheless, the central theme of the defeat by England of the Spanish-Catholic plot for world domination is clearly established (I.i.49–52, 243–245, 292–293; II.i.101, 127, 166–167; III.i.80–84; V.iii.80–100), as is the casting of that conflict in apocalyptic terms.[41] Here, for example, are the White Knight (Prince Charles) and White Duke (Buckingham) discussing their motives for the journey to Madrid:

WHITE KNIGHT

True noble duke, fair virtue's most endeared one,
Let us prevent their rank insinuation
With truth of cause and courage, meet their plots
With confident goodness that shall strike 'em grovelling.

WHITE DUKE

Sir, all the gins, traps, and alluring snares
The devil has been at work since '88 on
Are laid for the great hope of this game only.

40. There is, of course, no direct contact between *Game* and the *Acts*. By the time *Game* was written, the Elect Nation myth had become one of the received ideas of the churchgoing *and* playgoing public. *Game* was staged only weeks after the events it dramatizes occurred; Middleton fitted those events into a pattern already at hand.

41. References are to the edition of J. W. Harper (New York, 1966). Seen by at least one-sixth of the population of London during its nine-days' run at the Globe in August of 1624, the play was "followed by all sorts of people old and young, rich and poor, masters and servants, papists and puritans, wise men, etc., churchmen and statesmen . . . and a world beside" (*The Chamberlain Letters*, ed. with notes by Elizabeth Thomson [n.p., 1966], pp. 299, 306).

WHITE KNIGHT

Why, the more noble will truth's triumph be;
When they have wound about our constant courages
The glittering'st serpent that e'er falsehood fashioned
And glorying most in his resplendest poisons,
Just heaven can find a bolt to bruise his head.

(IV.iv.1–12)

In the concluding speech the White King (James) calls attention to the connection between the universal and the political levels of the allegory:

So, now let the bag close, the fittest womb
For treachery, pride, and malice, whilst we, winner-like,
Destroying, through heaven's power, what would destroy,
Welcome our White Knight with loud peals of joy.

(V.iii.216–19)

That is, England's role is the, by now, familiar one in Jacobean history plays, that of the instrument of God in the cosmic warfare, embodying the vision of England's role in universal history which John Foxe impressed upon the English national consciousness The Black Knight (a complex allegorical figure at once representing Spain, Catholicism, the spirit of "gamesmanship," and Count Gondomar, Spanish ambassador to the court of James until 1622) is not merely a deceiver but the Deceiver ("He'll peck a hole in the bag and get out shortly"—V.iii.206), who, until the end of history itself, may lose an engagement but not the battle, *a* game but not *the* game. Thus it is necessary for the White Queen's Pawn (Protestantism besieged at home and abroad) to step forward at the end to exhort the audience to take warning from this revelation of treachery.

None of the "biographical" plays here studied fits the currently accepted pattern, a pattern defined by Richard Simpson on the basis of what he imagined to be the form of the lost play he supposed to lie behind *The Life and Death of Captain Thomas Stukley*. The lost play, Simpson believed, treated the adventures of its title character from youth to death, in five different countries, one country to an act; the action was unified by the constant presence of the title character, but was essentially episodic in that the content of the scenes and the order of their sequence were not determined by cause and effect.[42] It is everywhere admitted that none of the biographical plays, not even the extant version of *Stukley* itself, corresponds to this pattern: yet it is everywhere assumed that such is the "formula" of the biographical play, a formula obscured by corrupt texts or particularly inept playwrights.

A formulation of the pattern of these plays based on extant texts would include the following points: the use of the *Acts* as primary source; a single, unified dramatic action centering in the mortal conflict between the Protestant protagonist and a Catholic antagonist; adjunct episodic material designed to locate the protagonist's story in the context of universal history; and an appeal to the audience, often direct, to behold this exemplum of God's great plan for the English people, and to carry it forward with all dispatch. Such a formulation would comfortably embrace most of the extant examples of the type—*Oldcastle, Cromwell, If You Know Not Me,* and *Duchess. Wyat* is a more complex play; it matches such a pattern in part but is not subsumed by it.

The suggested formulation helps, as well, to account for the often remarked differences between the plays just mentioned and the two remaining extant examples of biographical drama, *Stukley* and *Sir Thomas More.* Significantly, the two last-named are, alone among biographical-play heroes, Catholics: Stukley, a soldier of fortune and notorious traitor embarked at the time of his death upon an invasion of England financed by the pope; More, a Catholic martyr sanctified in this century. *More* is based closely on William Roper's biography, and owes nothing to the *Acts* but a short comic scene drawn from Foxe's apocryphal biography of Cromwell. The sources of *Stukley* are diverse and mostly ephemeral; in its extant form it deals less with English than with Afro-Portuguese history, and is closer to Peele's *Battle of Alcazar* than to any of the English history plays.[43] The larger issues raised by the *Stukley* play concern legitimacy of rule and intervention in foreign affairs. The theme of the

42. Richard Simpson, ed., *School of Shakespeare* (New York, 1878), Introduction to *Stukley.* Cf. Arthur F. Hopkinson on Simpson and "the biographical class of plays" in the Introduction to *Sir Thomas More (Harleian MS. 7368)* (New York, 1915), pp. xxxv–xxxvi.

43. The central characters of the Stukley play are Ab-el-melec, rightful king of Barbary, and his ally, Sebastian of Portugal, and the dramatic action centers in their conflict with the usurping king of Barbary.

More play, embodied more or less perfectly in each and every one of its "episodes," is *conscience;* the action and the dramatic conflict are for the most part contained in the mind of the protagonist, and in its constant emphasis upon the character of the title figure, its steady concern with depicting the kind of man he was, it is nearer to modern ideas of the nature of biography than are any of the more biographical plays.[44]

Thus, the *Stukley* and *More* plays differ on every one of the points—source, dramatic structure, philosophy, and theme—which serve to unite *Oldcastle, Cromwell, If You Know Not Me, Duchess,* and *Wyat,* and which these last named, the main body of biographical drama, share with *Whore, When You See Me, Henry VIII,* and *A Game at Chess,* the remaining extant English history plays of the Jacobean period. These points also differentiate the seventeenth-century history plays from those of the great vogue of the 1590s, which treat earlier reigns, are based for the most part upon Hall and Holinshed, resemble the morality in structure, attend to political problems of practical statecraft, and embody a pattern of English history and a philosophy of politics and history more dynastic than national.

Thus it appears that we have to do not so much with one considered philosophy of history which permeates the *true* English history play, and with a number of variants of the type written by less historically thoughtful playwrights; but rather with one group of history plays written more or less in accord with the Tudor-myth view of history, and a second, for the most part later, group written in accord with the equally thoughtful, coherent, and enduring concept of the Elect Nation. The myth of the Elect Nation is an important element the neglect of which has fragmented and dislocated the history of the genre.

Although Trevelyan identified Foxe as one of the two most influential authors of Shakespeare's age, Leslie Oliver stated in 1949, with all propriety, that the influence of his book "upon the thought and action of the time has never been fully assessed."[45] If William Haller's study remedied this defect in the field of the history of ideas, the influence of the work has remained neglected, or improperly assessed, by literary

---

44. This reading is set forth in detail in my *"The Book of Sir Thomas More: Structure and Meaning," Moreana,* XI (1974), 25–39.

45. Oliver, "John Foxe," p. 1.

critics and historians, who confine their attention to the *Acts* to the notation that it served as source of such and such a play. But the *Acts* served a function far more important than that of mere repository of odd biographical lore: it provided also an interpretation of English history and of historical personalities and a pattern of structuring action and event of which the playwrights took full advantage as they transposed the material from the realm of history to that of the imagination.

Jacobean Ephemera and the Immortal Word

PAULA JOHNSON

Out of the slightest labours and employments there may that
virtue sometimes arise that may enlighten the best part of man.
Nor have these kind of triumphs an idle relish, especially if
they be artfully accomplished: under such an esteemed slight-
ness may often lurk that fire that may shame the best perfection.
Thomas Middleton, *The Triumphs of Honor and
Industry,* 1617[1]

W HEN JAMES I was to make his ceremonial entry into London on
the Ides of March, 1604, the citizens, their hopes still high for this
welcome "man-ruler," outdid themselves in celebration. Stephen Harrison, the chief artificer of the five triumphal arches set up by the city
along the king's route of progress, published his account of these icono-
graphically complex structures; Gilbert Dugdale printed a spectator's
report of the great day, as *The Time Triumphant.* And the two

---

1. Middleton, *Works,* ed. A. H. Bullen (London, 1886), VII, 295. For the sake
of consistency, the spelling of all quotations has been modernized.

playwrights commissioned to invent the "devices," Ben Jonson and Thomas Dekker, published their own versions.[2] Harrison's booklet is even graced with pictures,

for, albeit those monuments of your loves were erected up to the clouds, and were built never so strongly, yet now their lastingness should live but in the tongues and memories of men, but that the hand of Art gives them here a second more perfect being, advanceth them higher than they were before, and warrants them that they shall do honor to this City, so long as the City shall bear a name.

The impulse to preserve a very special occasion was not Harrison's alone; Jonson and Dekker, too, are commentators, whose differing methods of preserving the moment have radiating implications.

At Fenchurch

The scene presented itself in a square and flat upright, like to the side of a city: the top thereof, above the vent and crest adorned with houses, towers, and steeples, set off in prospective. Upon the battlements in a great capital letter was inscribed,

LONDINIUM:

According to Tacitus: *At Suetonius mira constantia, medios inter hosteis Londinium perrexit, cognomento quidem Coloniae non insigne, sed copia Negotiatorum, & commeatu maxime celebre.* Beneath that, in a less and different character, was written,

. . . [the king's] passage along that Court offering itself, for more state, through seven gates, of which the first was erected at Fenchurch; thus presenting itself: It was an upright flat square, for it contained fifty foot in the perpendicular, and fifty foot in the ground line, the upper roof thereof, one distinct gate, bore up the true models of all the notable houses, turrets, and steeples, within the City. The gate under which his Majesty did pass was twelve foot wide, and eighteen foot high; a postern likewise at one side of it, being four foot wide, and eight foot in

2. There were also arches erected by the Dutch and by the Italians, and a "rainbow" by the city of Westminster and the duchy of Lancaster. Stephen Harrison, *The Arches of Triumph* (1604): I quote from J. G. Nichols, *The Progresses, Processions, and Magnificent Festivities, of King James the First* (London, 1828), I, *331. Dugdale cited by David M. Bergeron, *English Civic Pageantry, 1558–1642* (London, 1971), p. 88 n; Jonson, *His Part of King James his Royall and Magnificent Entertainment . . .* , ed. C. H. Herford and Percy and Evelyn Simpson, 11 vols. (Oxford, 1925–1952), VII, 75–109; Dekker, *The Magnificent Entertainment . . .* , in Nichols, I, 337–376.

CAMERA REGIA,

Which title immediately after the
Norman conquest it began to have
. . .

Jonson, *His Part of King James
his Royall and Magnificent Entertainment,* p. 83

heighth. . . . I could shoot more arrows at this mark, and teach you
without rule how to measure all the
proportions belonging to this fabric.
But . . .

Dekker, *The Magnificent Entertainment,* pp. 343–344

Dekker does not, in the end, make a longer business of describing the first
arch. He goes on to list, summarily, the personages who appeared on it,
and to compliment "Mr. Allin's" delivery of the welcoming speech. He
mentions the main inscription (that explained by Jonson, above), then remarks that his majesty didn't stay long—and Dekker moves on, too.
Jonson is understandably more particular about what was, after all, his
own device. He gives us a whole series of inscriptions, beginning with
those quoted, each with a commentary drawn from history or an explanatory note of his own, complete with footnotes. The figure of Monarchia
Britannica is justified by a Latin quotation out of Camden, and her
clothing and properties are detailed; so, too, for Theosophia; and, with
yet more particularity, the key speaking personage, Genius Urbis. Jonson
further quotes in its entirety a Latin elegy written "in the center, or
midst of the pegme," and includes a dramatic moment:

This, and the whole frame, was covered with a curtain of silk, painted like
a thick cloud, and at the approach of the King was instantly to be drawn.
The allegory being, that those clouds were gathered upon the face of the
City, through their long want of his most wished sight: but now, as at the
rising of the sun, all mists were dispersed and fled. When suddenly, upon
silence made to the musics, a voice was heard to utter this verse;
     Totus adest oculis, aderat qui mentibus olim,
Signifying, that he now was really objected to their eyes, who before had
been only, but still, present in their minds.

(p. 90)

At this point, Jonson takes time out to comment on the symbols, which

are not, neither ought to be, simply hieroglyphics, emblems, or impreses,
but a mixed character, partaking somewhat of all, and peculiarly apted to
these more magnificent inventions: wherein, the garments and ensigns deliver the nature of the person, and the word the present office. Neither was it
becoming, or could it stand with the dignity of these shows (after the most
miserable and desperate shift of the puppets) to require a truchman, or

(with the ignorant painter) one to write, *This is a dog;* or, *This is a Hare;* but so to be presented, as upon the view, they might, without cloud, or obscurity, declare themselves to the sharp and learned: And for the multitude, no doubt but their grounded judgments did gaze, said it was fine, and were satisfied.

(p. 91)

Genius's speech follows; "which banquet being taken away," continues Dekker after a one-sentence summary of Jonson's hundred lines of verse,

with sound of music there ready for the purpose, his majesty made his entrance into this his court royal . . . Too short a time (in their opinions that were glued there together so many hours to behold him) did his majesty dwell upon this first place; yet too long it seemed to other happy spirits, that higher up in these Elysian fields awaited for his presence. He sets on therefore . . .

(p. 344)

That Jonson, as author of the device, has a vast advantage of information, is obvious; but it does not account for the difference in rhetorical approach. Dekker in describing his own device, *Nova felix Arabia,* is similarly particular, but he is far less interested than Jonson in learned references or in interpretations. His emblematic figures are relatively transparent and commonplace: Fame, the Five Senses, the Three Graces, Detractio, Oblivio, and so on. Dekker has an eye constantly on the live occasion:

[The procession] was gotten so far as St. Mildred's Church in the Poultry; close to the side of which a scaffold was erected, where, at the City's cost, to delight the queen with her own-country music, nine trumpets and a kettle-drum, did very spritely and actively sound the Danish march; whose cunning and quick stops by that time they had touched the last lady's ear in the train, behold, the king was advanced up so high as to Cheapside . . .

(p. 354)

Dekker looks through the eyes of the ideal and perfectly situated beholder, often King James himself, and invites us, too, not only to contemplate but to participate. If we were to consider whole corpora, Jonson is far and away the finer artist; but in the choice of a rhetoric for describing ephemera, Dekker is perhaps the more appealing. He is a retailer of experience, bringing the common or provincial (or for that matter, the modern) reader in momentary touch with magnificence. His technique includes not only the participant's-eye view and a dwelling on appropriate feelings of expectation and joy; Dekker is also constantly aware of what's backstage, of the fact that just under the festive surface is ordinary humanity. Genius's speech, he tells us, "was delivered with excellent action, and a well-tuned *audible* voice" (italics mine)—no small accomplishment in a noisy crowd (Jonson's "silence made to the musics" takes on vividness in this context). In *Nova felix Arabia* "The presenter was a boy, one of the Choristers belonging to Paul's"; later, "one of Mr. Mulcaster's scholars" delivers a Latin oration; at the Conduit in Fleet Street James is addressed by Zeal, "whose personage was put on by W. Bourne, one of the servants to the young prince." As part of his introduction to the whole description, Dekker tells us about the "carpenters, joiners, carvers, and other artificers, sweating at their chisels" in preparation for the day, and about how "the streets are surveyed; heights, breadths, and distances taken, as it were to make fortifications for the solemnities." The practicalities never fade out for long. As a basis for this rhetoric of presence, Dekker chooses to report not just his own inventions, as Jonson does, but the entire progress from beginning to end, from the setting up to the dismantling of the triumphal arches.

These two kinds of descriptive procedure—Jonson's learned, logical, reflective; Dekker's concrete, conversational, participatory—are alternative ways of responding to the same cultural need. Both were published as what today we might call souvenir programs, designed to salvage something of an extraordinary, unrepeatable celebration. Jonson's more exalted technique proclaims a faith in high tradition, in values perduring beyond the fleeting event.[3] Even his occasional use of past tense does not affirm the temporal "body." As proof that intellectual invention, not scenery, is the thing that counts, Jonson scarcely more than mentions the rainbow in the Strand, "to which body (being framed before) we were to apt our soul." The note of contempt is unmistakable: devices should be drawn up beforehand for a performance that is thereby absolved from taking place. The soul, that is, the learned references and the "apted" speech, he gives in full: visual event melts into verbal Truth.

Not so for Dekker—or, not in the same way. We should not suppose

3. See D. J. Gordon, "The Intellectual Setting of the Quarrel between Ben Jonson and Inigo Jones," *JWCI*, XII (1949), 152–178.

that the chattier rhetoric of presence is any less serious an attempt to conquer time than is Jonson's universalizing. Dekker is explicit:

Behold how glorious a flower happiness is, but how fading! The minutes, that lackey at the heels of Time, run not faster away than do our joys. What tongue could have expressed the raptures on which the soul of the City was carried beyond itself for the space of many hours? . . . And yet see, her bridgegroom is but stepped from her, and in a minute, nay, in shorter time than a thought can be born, is she made a widow. All her consolation being now to repeat over by rote those honors, which lately she had perfectly by heart. And to tell of those joys, which but even now she really beheld . . .

(PP. 374–375)

If this passage were the end of Dekker's description, we might well class him with medieval lamenters of transient glory, a Jacobean Last Survivor. But Dekker's attack of nostalgia is not the end; he goes on to mention the rainbow and Jonson's speech (spoken by Electra, the invisible member of the Pleiades, "in the figure of a comet"); then to give a "credits" list of committees and officers, and the numbers of workmen employed in this vast effort. Dekker's way of overcoming temporality is not transcendence but anamnesis. He returns us in memory to the lost moment, transforms unrecoverable history into present story. Where Jonson cites classical and Renaissance historians as guarantors of permanent meaning, Dekker adapts the same historians' presentational techniques.[4] The Jonson-Dekker opposition in the "war of the theaters" is not surprising— the base newsmonger versus the stuffy pedant—but fortunately, we are not obliged to choose sides.

Students of civic pageantry regularly observe that, after 1600, spectacular public celebration (if royally centered) moved indoors; where it remained in the city streets, it centered on the magistrate.[5] Not, of course,

4. Dekker's rhetoric may also be compared to the "composition of place": see Louis L. Martz, *The Poetry of Meditation*, rev. ed. (New Haven, Conn., 1962), pp. 27–32.

5. The standard contemporary reference is Arthur Wilson: e.g., Bergeron, p. 75; Nichols, I, 339 n. Concerning the Lord Mayors' Shows, see Jean Robertson and D. J. Gordon, eds., *A Calendar of Dramatic Records in the Books of the Livery Companies of London, 1485–1640*, Malone Society Collections, III (Oxford, 1954) (hereafter cited as *MSC* III); W. W. Greg, *A List of Masques, Pageants, etc. Supplementary to a List of English Plays* (London, 1902); Robert Withington, *English Pageantry: An Historical Outline* (Cambridge, Mass., 1920), vol. II; Sheila

that the Lord Mayors' Shows were a new development—far from it. But it is a simple fact that the most interesting documents of public celebration from Elizabeth I's reign are those of her progresses; the most interesting such documents from James I's reign are those of the mayoral inaugurations. Some thirty of the souvenir booklets for these processions survive from the earlier seventeenth century (1585–1639, to be exact). The three "devices of the pageant" dating from before 1600, two by George Peele and one by Thomas Nelson, are texts of verse speeches only; though Peele's 1591 *Descensus Astraeae* and Nelson's pamphlet do contain a few scanty stage directions. Only two booklets from the first decade of the seventeenth century remain, one of which is fragmentary; the 1604 pageant, by Ben Jonson, is unfortunately lost.[6] But from 1611 the extant series is almost unbroken. Their annual regularity and the similar general form make these little texts as near to a controlled demonstration of change as the literary historian is likely to encounter. Dekker's and Jonson's contrasting rhetorics for the 1604 royal entry will provide us with a rule for recognition of this aspect in the different pageant writers of the ensuing decades; but a few other rules apply as well.

These seem the most salient: first, from about the date of James's accession, the printed booklet becomes an invariable part of the mayoral festivities. This in itself is a new phenomenon; though we cannot perhaps explain it, a few modest speculations are in order. Certainly, there comes to be a heightening of civic ritual during the reigns of the early Stuarts, parallel to the increasing costliness and visual elaboration of the court masques. These, however, are parallel, not combined developments. James's dislike of crowds is the usual reason given for the shift of outdoor London entertainments from royal to civic; whatever the cause, as the enclosed court denies access to its magnificence, the street comes to display a ("rival," one is tempted to say) magnificence of its own. Such a

---

Williams, "The Lord Mayor's Show in Tudor and Stuart Times," *The Guildhall Miscellany*, X (1959), 3–18.

6. See Greg, *List of Masques;* also David H. Horne, ed., *The Life and Minor Works of George Peele* (New Haven, Conn., 1952), pp. 155–160, 209–219. For Nelson, see Bergeron, pp. 132–134; Withington, "The Lord Mayor's Show for 1590," *MLN*, XXXIII (1918), 8–13; and John C. Meagher, "The London Lord Mayor's Show of 1590," *ELR*, III (1973), 94–104. The evidence for Jonson's authorship of the 1604 show is reprinted in *MSC* III, 63.

division seems in retrospect a kind of emblem, itself, for the contest for power of prince and citizen, prerogative and law.

As the court masques are commemorated in print, so too are the shows. The relative literary merits of masque and pageant books are from this perspective less striking, as a cultural development, than the common impulse to turn ephemeral entertainment into enduring text. The poet's claim to give immortal renown to mortal worthies is an ancient one; but the pageant authors rarely repeat it explicitly, as writers of the preceding century might have done. Yet the booklets share with another new phenomenon, the earliest "newspapers," an implicit assumption that a printed report somehow validates the event. A similar assumption may motivate the subgenre of place poems: the *word* is required, to give permanence even to buildings, hills, rivers, woods. Drayton thus translates all of England into chorographical alexandrines; Jonson, always judiciously selective, commemorates Penshurst; Stow (and the pageant-writer Anthony Munday after him) "surveys" London. And Munday, Dekker, Middleton, Webster, Thomas Heywood—even John Taylor the water poet and the otherwise unknown John Squire—see to the printing of their devices for the pageants.

Which brings us to the second general rule. Not a single one of the Lord Mayors' Shows is anonymous; and only one is not by an established professional writer. The livery companies were not hiring just anybody to invent their displays—though some evidence does suggest that the job might be awarded to whichever poet submitted the lowest bid, like town building contracts today. That the name of a recognized poet should appear on the booklet's title page was, I suspect, part of the conspicuous consumption reflected in the titles themselves.[7] Conversely and obviously,

---

7. For haggling over price, see *MSC* III, 99, 115, 122–123. A sample title (from Greg): *"Monuments of Honor.* Derived from remarkable Antiquity and Celebrated in the Honorable City of London, at the sole Munificent charge and expences of the Right Worthy and Worshipfull Fraternity of the Eminent Merchant Taylors. Directed in their most affectionate Loue at the Confirmation of their right Worthy Brother Iohn Gore in the High Office of His Maiesties Lieutenant over this Royall Chamber. Expressing in a Magnificent Tryumph, all the Pageants, Chariots of Glory, Temples of Honor, besides a specious and goodly Sea Tryumph, as well particularly to the Honor of the City, as generally to the Glory of this our Kingdome. Invented and written by Iohn Webster Merchant-Taylor. *Nicholas Okes.* 1624."

the naming of the deviser represents the author's own claim to fame (silver trumpets and all); and, more practically perhaps, an advertisement of competence: "poet available for civic employment; specimen of work in following pages." No doubt it helped to have connections, as Peele, Munday, and Webster certainly had;[8] but a glance at parallel lists of dates, authors, and companies suggests also that success might breed future contracts.

The companies' pride in their displays and the fact that printed records of past shows were at hand probably acted together to help on the increasing elaboration and cost to which both the records and the booklets bear witness. The same records, though, prove that certain features of the shows were invariant. The pageants themselves multiplied from one or two in 1605 to six by 1634;[9] but the city waits were paid about fifty-three shillings year in and year out. Where greater numbers might add to the impression of magnificence, more performers in traditional categories came to be employed: whifflers, trumpeters, fencers, "greenmen." These standard kinds of participants, however, are almost never mentioned in the printed texts; we know of them from spectators' letters and from the account books. We need to bear in mind when Dekker, say, convinces the reader that "you are there," that the printed description is a carefully selected, formalized, even fictionalized report. It is a literary work, however slight its poetical merits, not a complete or perhaps even an accurate factual record.

Keeping the long-past event and the still-extant description from collapsing together is not always easy, even for the expert.[10] The booklets may have had the effect of making the processions themselves more literary as well as more expansive. But the poets' claim to give the only

8. *Peele,* ed. Horne, pp. 71–73. Munday was free of the drapers' company; Webster, of the merchant-taylors. See also Sheila Williams, "A Lord Mayor's Show by John Taylor, the Water-Poet," *Bulletin of the John Rylands Library,* XLI (1958–1959), 501–531.

9. John Taylor, *The Triumphs of Fame and Honour* (London, 1634).

10. Bergeron, *passim;* J.H.P. Pafford, ed., *Chruso-thriambos* (London, 1962), introduction; Withington, *passim.* None of the authorities I have been able to consult consistently distinguishes description from event; Jean Robertson comes the nearest to doing so, in "Rapports du poete et de l'artiste dans la preparation des cortèges du lord maire (Londres 1553–1640)," in *Les Fêtes de la Renaissance,* ed. Jean Jacquot (Paris, 1960), I, 265–278.

possible kind of permanence was of course perfectly valid. Only the slender pamphlets, with their old-fashioned spelling and typefaces, survive; the wonderful constructions of lath and plaster and painted canvas (some of which the companies did keep for a while) can only be rebuilt in fancy. The divergence of text from event in its own time, let alone now, makes evaluations of a given show's "dramatic unity" radically fallacious.[11] We might try to judge a *text's* dramatic unity—though such a criterion virtually ensures disappointment; but the texts, as the other evidence proves, are far more independent of the actual performances than are the scripts of plays, or even of masques. They are a combination of script, schema, and report, written according to developing customs and in changing styles. It is with these, and with the ways in which the writers station themselves and their readers with regard to the passing wonders—with their rhetoric, in short—that this survey has to do.

The first extant pageant booklet after the momentous *Entertainment* of 1604 is Anthony Munday's 1605 *Triumphs of Re-united Britain*. From anyone's point of view except Munday's, it's a pity that he succeeded so well in getting the livery companies to hire him. Jonson took a satirical shot at Munday in *The Case is Altered,* as the pageant-poet Antonio Balladino, who is employed, he himself admits, "when a worse cannot be had." No less than seven of the thirty surviving texts are Munday's work, and some of the lost ones were his, too. Munday, though not much of a rhetorician in any direction, leans in 1605 toward Jonson's way of emphasizing the permanent:

Because our present conceit reacheth unto the antiquity of Britain, which (in many minds) hath carried as many and variable opinions, I thought it not unnecessary (being thereto earnestly solicited) to speak somewhat concerning the estate of this our country, even from the very first original, until her honorable attaining the name of Britannia, and then lastly how she became to be called England. Most writers do agree, that after the deluge Noah was the sole monarch of all the world . . .[12]

History is a branch of the high tradition of ancient learning that Jonson called upon to justify his iconography. Jonson, however, used his authori-

11. Glynne Wickham, *Early English Stages, 1300–1600* (London and New York, 1959), I, 81, observes that processional stations must settle for thematic rather than dramatic unity. On this and other relevant matters, see the whole of chap. 3, pp. 51–111.

12. Nichols, I, 564.

ties to support a dimension of eternal meaning for the temporarily visible figures he describes; Munday sets his entire discourse in the context of origins and continuity. He ends his introduction with a transition: ". . . now come we to discourse the whole frame and body of our device, in this solemn triumph of re-united Britannia." Remembering that the "body" of the show meant, for both Jonson and Dekker, its physical constructions, we reasonably expect Munday to continue by describing one of these. But no. Under the title, "The Ship Called the Royal Exchange," is a verse dialogue between master, mate, and boy, which reaches a climax with a pun on the new Lord Mayor's name—not an uncommon trick when it could be worked, and this year Munday was lucky enough to have for his honoree, Leonard Holliday. Next is another title, "The Lion and the Camel" (symbolic animals for the merchant-taylors), with a defense of method rather like Daniel's preface to *The Vision of the Twelve Goddesses*.[13] On these animals, "we do figuratively personate Neptune and his Queen Amphitrita, who first seated their son Albion in this land." Since times and manners have changed, these persons may "speak according to the nature of the present business in hand, without any imputation of grossness or error, considering the laws of poesy grants such allowance and liberty." Munday has at last come to the event he is commemorating:

THE PAGEANT.

On a mount, triangular as the island of Britain itself is described to be, we seat in the supreme place, under the shape of a fair and beautiful nymph, Britannia herself, accosted with Brute's divided kingdoms, in the like female representations, Leogria, Cambria, and Albania.[14]

This is as close as Munday comes to a visualizable description of the pageant. We do not know how any of the personages was attired, or what the "mount" looked like, besides its being triangular. Earlier on, we have no hint about how the "ship of the Royal Exchange" was decorated, or even, with certainty, whether it was presented on water or land. The new Lord Mayor, the presumptive person addressed, is nowhere mentioned.

Clearly Munday is not trying to recreate a moment—at least, not for those of us who weren't there. The question of intended audience is im-

13. Ed. Joan Rees, in *A Book of Masques, in Honour of Allardyce Nicholl* (London, 1967); see esp. pp. 25–30.
14. Nichols, I, 568.

portant. Munday was paid £6 by the merchant-taylors for having the book printed;[15] we know that in some instances the books were not for public sale, but for the members of the company to distribute or keep. Munday is perhaps relying on the memories of readers who had also been participating witnesses to fill out his verbal account. He is far less thorough than Jonson in assimilating visual details to his symbolic scheme; what he dwells on is historical context, and he has his symbolic figures so behave as to signify the shape of the past. Their verse speeches are printed in unbroken sequence at the end, with a sentence of introduction and a stage direction.

The shows for 1609 and 1611, both by Munday, are represented by surviving texts, though that for 1609 is fragmentary. The 1611 *Chruso-thriambos*, however, evinces a movement toward verbal re-creation, in that Munday eschews background information, and, at least for the first half of his description, recognizes a relationship with his readers:

. . . supposition must needs give some graceful help to invention; and be as ready in apprehension, as the other in action. Imagine, then, that from the rich and golden Indian mines, sundry ships, frigates, and galleys, are returned home . . . Divers sea-fights and skirmishes are actively performed, both in the passage on to Westminster, and back again . . . No sooner landeth the Lord Mayor at Baynard's Castle, but there he is saluted by Leofstane a goldsmith . . .[16]

Our author moves gradually away from the present into realms of story; with the following sentence the shift to supposition's graceful help is complete:

After a supposed long and tedious journey, which all her daughters, Gold and Silver, may seem to have had, through their mother's large limits and rocky kingdoms, leaving in every vein, sinew, and artery, the rich and valuable virtue of their splendor: they are returned again, and seated by her to fulfill this solemn day of triumph, prepared for her eldest daughter, Gold.

(pp. 24–25)

As in 1605, Munday puts all the speeches at the end, so that they read much more like the script of a contemporary play than like an account of

15. *MSC* III, 68–69.
16. Pafford, ed., *Chruso-thriambos*, p. 22. Munday is even more apologetic about the inadequacy of the visible structures in later shows, especially *Himatia-Poleos* (London, 1614) and *The Triumphs of the Golden Fleece* (London, 1623).

public experience. In short, though print necessarily commemorates, Munday tends to withdraw from rather than to recapture the ephemeral.

But in the next year, 1612, Dekker's *Troia-nova triumphans* shows a decisive difference. Dekker's introduction is mostly about the "sumptuous thriftiness" of the sponsoring company (the merchant-taylors, again), stressing decorous cost and liberality (carefully distinguished from excess). This is obviously a puff for the patrons; the ensuing description, however, characteristically bids us "launch into the river":

> By this time the Lord Mayor hath taken his oath, is seated in his barge again; a loud thundering peal of chambers give him a farewell as he passes by. And see! how quickly we are in ken of land, as suddenly therefore let us leap on shore, and there observe what honorable entertainment the city affords to their new Praetor, and what joyful salutations to her noble visitants.[17]

"By this time": Dekker implies that even while we have been reading, the inaugural ceremonies have been running their course; we are to join them, here and now: "let us leap on shore, and there observe . . ." As in 1604, Dekker gives us a place to stand and guides the mind's eye toward its object. The pageant's dolphins and mermaids, Dekker further assures us,

> are not (after the old procreation), begotten of painted cloth, and brown paper, but are living beasts, so quaintly disguised like the natural fishes, of purpose to avoid the trouble and pestering of porters, who with much noise and little comeliness are every year most unnecessarily employed.
>
> (p. 233)

The glimpse of painted cloth and brown paper; the use, in other passages, of imperative verb and first-person plural; the present-oriented phrases (e.g., "as he passes by"; "And see!"); the reminders of the spectators' responses and of the spatiotemporal sequence of the procession—these features are the marks and the means of Dekker's rhetoric of presence.

This particular show is unusual for its morality-play ingredient, a dramatic encounter between Virtue and Envy. The latter character inhabits the third device, "a Forlorn Castle, built close to the Little Conduit

---

17 *The Dramatic Works of Thomas Dekker,* ed. Fredson Bowers (London, 1961), III, 231. See *MSC* III, 84, for evidence of Dekker's collaboration with "Mr. Heminges."

in Cheapside" (a typical collocation of the emblematic and the material).
Envy's henchmen attack the chariot of Virtue; but "their arrows, which
they shoot up into the air, break there out in fire-works, as having no
power to do wrong to so sacred a deity as Virtue." Speeches from Envy
and Virtue follow; Envy's faction "all retire in, and are not seen till the
throne comes back again. And this concludes this triumphant assault of
Envy: her conquest is to come." Read on, our author implies; there's more
excitement in store. The "conquest yet to come" suitably involves more
gunpowder. Virtue's honor guard, representing the twelve companies,
"discharge their Pistols, at which Envy, and the rest, vanish, and are seen
no more." A valediction, spoken by Justice, "mounted on some convenient
scaffold" near the gate of the Lord Mayor's house, concludes the description, except for a postscript:

> The title page of this book makes promise of all the shows by water, as of
> these on the land; but Apollo having no hand in them, I suffer them to die
> by that which fed them; that is to say, powder and smoke. Their thunder
> (according to the old galley-foist-fashion) was too loud for any of the nine
> muses to be bidden to it. I had devised one, altogether musical, but Time's
> glass could spare no sand, nor lend convenient hours for the performance of
> it. Night cuts off the glory of this day, and so consequently of these triumphs,
> whose brightness being eclipsed, my labors can yield no longer shadow.
>
> (p. 247)

The next year after *Troia-nova triumphans,* in 1613, another writer
joined the roster of pageant poets. This was Thomas Middleton, whose
Triumphs of Truth is written, and invented, in Dekker's vein. Middleton,
however, was by this date a mature and successful dramatist, and his
imitation is far from slavish. This is also Middleton's first show, as the
1612 one was Dekker's; and in this limited genre first efforts are often
a writer's best.

Middleton shares Dekker's preference for moral over historical allegory, and adopts the idea of enacting the conflict, here and now, of
virtue and vice. Munday's manner, he firmly rejects:

> [The planner of a civic festival should have] knowledge that may take the
> true height of such an honorable solemnity,—the miserable want of both
> which, in the impudent common writer, hath often forced from me much
> pity and sorrow; and it would heartily grieve any understanding spirit to
> behold, many times, so glorious a fire in bounty and goodness offering to

match itself with freezing Art, sitting in darkness, with the candle out, looking like the picture of Black Monday.[18]

This invidious brag shows us another aspect of the rhetoric of presence, one less apparent in, though not absent from, Dekker's 1612 booklet. The writer makes us explicitly aware of himself as writer; concomitantly, he addresses us readers directly as readers (not yet as spectators of the imagined event): "If any shall imagine that I set fairer colors upon their [the grocers' company's] deserts than they upon themselves, let them but read and conceive, and their own understandings will light them to the acknowledgement of their errors." From this, Middleton proceeds into the anamnesis of the day: "First, they may here behold . . ." The ambiguous phrase mediates between the *here* of the text and the *here* of the scene to be visualized. In a similar way, the readers addressed are to enact within themselves that deliverance from error that the pageants are about to enact visibly. In the description of that process Middleton, like Dekker, pursues an experiential sequence, putting each poetical address in its temporally proper place—not, like Munday or Jonson, saving up all the speeches till last. The account is less aggressively engaging than Dekker's but the visual description is more vivid. Here and there is a reminder of our presence at the festival:

. . . the Waits of the city there in service, his lordship, and the worthy company, are led forward toward the waterside, where you shall find the river decked in the richest glory to receive him . . .

(p. 239)

No sooner can your eyes take leave of these, but they may suddenly espy a strange ship making toward, and that which may raise greater astonishment, it having neither sailor nor pilot . . .

(p. 247)

Once Middleton has brought us onto the scene, he keeps us there not so much with elbow-nudging chattiness as by intense and minutely detailed visualization:

18. Middleton, VII, 233. For evidence of collaboration with Munday, see Middleton's concluding statement, and *MSC* III, 87. The two playwrights worked together also in 1623; see Withington, "The Lord Mayor's Show for 1623," *PMLA,* xxx (1950) 110–115. Munday's defensive introduction to *Sidero-Thriambos* (London, 1618), which refers to "the despite of envy and calumnious imputations," may be a belated reply to Middleton.

Zeal, stirred up with divine indignation at the impudence of these hell-hounds [Error and Envy], both forces their retirement, and makes way for the chariot wherein Truth his mistress sits, in a close garment of white satin, which makes her appear thin and naked, figuring thereby her simplicity and nearness of heart to those that embrace her; a robe of white silk cast over it, filled with the eyes of eagles, showing her deep insight and height of wisdom; over her thrice-sanctified head a milk-white dove, and on each shoulder one, the sacred emblems of purity, meekness, and innocency; under her feet serpents, in that she treads down all subtlety and fraud; her forehead empaled with a diadem of stars, the witness of her eternal descent; on her breast a pure round crystal, showing the brightness of her thoughts and actions; a sun in her right hand, than which nothing is truer; a fan, filled all with stars, in her left, with which she parts darkness, and strikes away the vapors of ignorance. If you hearken to Zeal, her champion, after his holy anger is past against Error and his crew, he will give it you in better terms, or at least more smoothly and pleasingly.

(p. 244)

The effect is a suspended visionary moment, as meanings unite with details of costume to create "nearness of heart." The second-person pronouns in the final sentence quoted, rather like Dekker's juxtaposition of the Forlorn Castle and the Little Conduit but on a larger scale, remind the reader that he is reading, now, and turn him toward the verse speech that follows.

The advancing procession collects, in Cheapside, London's Triumphant Mount, an elaborately peopled pageant, "but the beauty and glory thereof spread with a thick, sulphurous darkness, it being a fog or mist, raised from Error." At Truth's command, the "cloud suddenly rises and changes into a bright-spreading canopy, stuck thick with stars, and beams of gold shooting forth round about it . . ." Error succeeds in calling down the mist again several times more; each time, Truth disperses it. Finally,

a flame shoots from the head of Zeal, which, fastening upon that chariot of Error, sets it on fire, and all the beasts that are joined to it. The firework being made by master Humphrey Nichols, a man excellent in his art . . . this proud seat of Error lying now only glowing in embers—being a figure or type of his lordship's justice on all wicked offenders in the time of his government—I now conclude . . .

(p. 262)

The abrupt shift from the figural chariot of Error to master Humphrey Nichols's firework is a nice example of how the rhetoric of presence keeps the reader in touch with ephemeral actuality. Middleton's variant of this rhetoric oscillates between the represented fiction and its means of representation; but it never treats those means as a mere, dispensable "body."

Anthony Munday had been displaced—if not quite wholly—from the job later referred to as that of "city poet" for two years while Dekker and Middleton invented and innovated the annual shows. Whether Munday was impressed with the multiplication of pageants or the literary quality of the 1612 and 1613 booklets, or whether he was simply trying to meet the competition on its own ground—or all of these—we don't know; but in 1614 he has changed his technique. The account of *Himatia-Poleos,* the show for that year, and of *Metropolis Coronata* in 1615, follow the order of experience, inserting the verse speeches where they belong in the prose narrative sequence. The latter text ends with a lively song by Robin Hood and his merry men, which is among Munday's more pleasing poetical efforts.[19]

The precedent for the order and style of description, once set, was gradually reduced to formula. Munday in 1616 reverted to his former practice of lumping all the speeches together at the end; but Middleton, the most frequent pageant writer from 1617 through 1626, standardized and abbreviated the exemplary compositions of 1612 and 1613. Though the 1617 *Triumphs of Honor and Industry* is remarkable for the vividness of Middleton's I-thou relation to the reader (a point noted also in connection with *The Triumphs of Truth*), on the whole his commemorations, though always retaining the focus on the present, become more and more perfunctory with the passing years. Middleton's sequence of shows, however, was twice interrupted by one-time writers.

John Squire, the author of *Tes Irenes Trophaea, or, The Triumphs of Peace,* 1620, is otherwise and deservedly unknown to literary history. His description reduces Middleton's formula to its most pedestrian; but it nonetheless merits a word or two. Squire dispenses with introductory discourse and launches immediately "the first show or presentment on the water." He then proceeds in temporal order and formulaic fashion to describe the pageants in turn, ending each description with the verse speech (if there was one) of the main character. The events are located

19. Nichols, III, 107–118.

with geographical precision at Three Cranes Wharf, Paul's Churchyard, The Upper Conduit in Cheapside, Saint Lawrence-Land-End, the Lord Mayor's gate. But Squire is, if anything, a Jonsonian, taken up rather with the visualized emblem than with the visible moment. Like Jonson on such occasions, Squire is careful to note colors:

[Oceanus is on a chariot,] his azure locks and beard o'ergrown, hung like the careless emblem of a reverend age, disheveled o'er his naked limbs, which were shadowed off with a mantle of seagreen taffaty, limned with waves and fishes . . . Asia was attired in an antique habit of peach-colored satin, and buskins of the same, a coronet on her head, and a censer in her hand, reeking with Panchaian spices; . . . Europa in a robe of Crimson taffaty, on her head an imperial crown . . . and holding in her hand a cluster of grapes, to signify her full-swollen plenty.[20]

Whatever the actual occasion may have been like, Squire's booklet is tidy but uninspiring. It is no surprise to find better things in the unique show by John Webster, who produced the 1624 *Monuments of Honor* for the inauguration of his fellow merchant-taylor, John Gore. Webster is understandably conscious of literary precedent:

I could in this my Preface (by as great light of learning as any formerly employed in this service can attain to) deliver to you the original and cause of all triumphs, their excessive cost in the time of the Romans: I could likewise with no noble amplification make a survey of the worth, and glory of the triumphs of the precedent times in this honorable city of London: That, were my work of a bigger bulk, they should remain to all posterity . . .[21]

The literary awareness materializes in the first of the pageants on land, "a beautiful spectacle, called the Temple of Honor," wherein, below "five eminent cities,"

sit five famous scholars and poets of this our kingdom, as Sir Geoffrey Chaucer, the learned Gower, the excellent John Lidgate, the sharp-witted Sir Thomas More, and last as worthy both soldier and scholar, Sir Philip Sidney, these being celebrators of honor, and the preservers both of the names of men, and memories of cities above . . .

(p. 319)

20. *Ibid.,* III, ii, 620; see Bergeron, pp. 201–207, for a more favorable evaluation of Squire, based on thematic coherence and dramatic sequence.
21. *The Complete Works of John Webster,* ed. F. L. Lucas (London, 1927), III, 317. See also n. 7.

A distinguished company, and a distinguished context for a pageant writer to invoke. But throughout Webster is intent upon asserting his authorial presence:

I present riding afore this Temple, Henry de Royal . . .

(p. 319)

In the chariot I place for the honor of the company . . . eight famous kings of this land . . .

(p. 321)

The fourth eminent pageant, I call the Monument of Charity and Learning . . .

(p. 323)

. . . these twelve thus seated, I figure Loyalty . . .

(p. 326)

And so forth. These dignified claims of inventive omnipotence are a far cry from Dekker's racy intimacy.

In discussing his "fourth eminent pageant," Webster digresses into an apocryphal story about Sir Thomas White's founding of the college of Saint John Baptist at Cambridge, then explains that "this relation is somewhat with the largest, only to give you better light of the figure"— it's important that meanings, whether timeless or time-out-of-mind, be well apprehended. Webster constantly adds to this carefulness an attention to cost and spectacle—iconological exegesis supplemented by the lordly puff, as, videlicet,

Upon an artificial rock, set with mother-of-pearl, and such other precious stones, as are found in quarries, are placed four curious pyramids charged with the prince's arms, the three feathers, which by day yield a glorious show, and by night a more goodly, for they have lights in them, that at such time as my lord mayor returns from Paul's shall make certain ovals and squares resemble precious stones; the rock expresses the riches of the kingdom Prince Henry was born heir to, the pyramids, which are monuments for the dead, that he is deceased . . .

(p. 325)

Webster concludes, not with the compliment to the chief artificer which by this time was standard practice, but with a Jonsonian sneer at the less learned:

I could a more curious and elaborate way have expressed myself in these my endeavors, but to have been rather too tedious in my speeches, or too weighty, might have troubled my noble lord, and puzzled the understanding of the common people . . .

(p. 327)

If I frankly enjoy the talkative booklets better, that is no prejudice against *Monuments of Honor,* the last considerable attempt to ennoble the ephemeral show by linking its visible features to its atemporal significance. Dekker took over the pageant writing for two years after Middleton's death; his shows for 1628 and 1629 are so fully in the style of *Troianova triumphans* as to need no further comment here. Dekker, in his turn, was succeeded in 1631 by the most frequent Caroline author of the Lord Mayors' Shows, and the last of their inventors before the Civil War, Thomas Heywood. Heywood's method is consistent throughout his pageant-writing career; in his first show, *London's Ius Honorarium,* he is perhaps most explicit. A few brief extracts will suffice:

UPON THE WATER.

Are two craggy rocks, placed directly opposite, of that distance that the barges may pass betwixt them: these are full of monsters, as serpents, snakes, dragons, &c. some spitting fire, others vomiting water, in the bases thereof, nothing to be seen, but the sad remains of shipwreck in broken barks and split vessels, &c. The one is called Scylla, the other Charybdis, which is situate directly against Messana; [*sic*] Scylla against Regium: and whatsoever ship that passeth these seas, if it keep not the middle channel, it is either wracked upon the one, or devoured by the other; *Medio tutissimus ibit.*[22]

When the "rocks" join the procession on land, Heywood summarizes the above, adding, "I shall not need to spend much time in the description of them, the work being sufficiently able to commend itself." Despite this offhand attitude toward the "body" of the show, Heywood does not express contempt for the ignorant vulgar; rather, he commends the "master, wardens, and committees of this right worshipful company of haberdashers":

nothing here devised or expressed was any way foreign unto them, but of all these my conceptions, they were as able to judge, as ready to hear, and to

22. *Dramatic Works,* ed. J. Pearson (New York, 1874), IV, 270.

direct as well as to censure; neither was there any difficulty which needed a comment, but as soon known as shown, and apprehended as read . . .[23]

(p. 279)

The closing remarks recall Jonson's of 1604, quoted earlier, but with a difference:

I have forborne to spend much paper in needless and inpertinent deciphering the work, or explaining the habits of the persons, as being freely exposed to the public view of all the spectators. The main show, being performed by the most excellent in that kind, Master Gerard Chrismas hath expressed his models to be exquisite (as having spared neither cost nor care, either in the figures or ornaments). I shall not need to point unto them to say, this is a lion, and that an unicorn, &c. . . .

(pp. 280–281)

Jonson, it will be remembered, said that labels were unnecessary because the discerning spectator would read the iconographic truth without them; Heywood finds explanation unnecessary because of the representational exactness of the artificer. Though he follows his immediate predecessors in describing his show in temporal order, Heywood is much inclined to dismiss the visible with an "&c." and to dwell upon history and ancient authority. The loving care with which Jonson, Webster, and even Squire detailed costumes and properties and their meanings is gone. Gone, too, is the kinesthetic immediacy of Dekker and Middleton.

Except for their concluding paragraphs, which year after year compliment the skill and reliability of the pageant builders, Heywood's booklets read like what I suspect they were: proposals offered to the wardens of the relevant company, not after-the-fact commemorations. The confidence that the earlier writers show in the power of language to immortalize, through allegory and re-presentation, lapses in Heywood. And though the Lord Mayors' Shows resumed, even before the Restoration, the conviction of their lasting significance had proven little less ephemeral than their lath and plaster.

23. Cf. Munday, 1618: "For better understanding the true morality of this device, thhe personages have all emblems and properties in their hands, and so near them, that the weakest capacity may take knowledge of them . . ."

Ben Jonson and Captain Cox: Elizabethan Gothic Reconsidered

ALICE S. MISKIMIN

> Elizabeth and her train were attended by 400 servants of Leicester, all were in new liveries. His gentlemen who waited at table were cloathed in velvet. Sixteen hogsheads of wine, forty of beer, and ten oxen were consumed every day, besides a vast quantity of fruit and confitures. Their pastimes consisted of hunting, rustic revelry, comedies, concerts, and masquerades.
>
> Strype, *Annals* (1709)

THE ENTERTAINMENT of the queen by the earl of Leicester in the summer of 1575 at Kenilworth Castle was a triumph of Elizabethan hospitality. The magnificence and variety of the fete—nineteen days of diversion, from Saturday 9 July to Wednesday 27 July—provided a model for succeeding fetes to the end of her reign, none of which surpassed it in either artistic importance or expense.[1] The first full account of the Kenil-

1. Leicester's fete is said to have cost ca. £20,000, about £1,000 per diem. Recent discussions of Kenilworth include Howard Cole, *A Quest of Inquirie* (Indianapolis, 1973), Chap. 5 passim; John C. Meagher, *Method and Meaning in Jonson's Masques* (Notre Dame, Ind., 1966), p. 98; Stephen Orgel, *The Jonsonian Masque* (Cambridge, Mass., 1965), pp. 38–42.

worth revels, Robert Laneham's *Letter* to Humphrey Martin, a mercer of London, . . . *Whearin part of the Entertainment vnto the Queen Majesty at Killingworrth Castl in Warwik Sh'eer in this Somerz Progress 1575 iz signified,* was published in London that autumn. The brilliant events he described cast a very long shadow. Laneham's *Letter* speaks for itself as a document in social history; its after-images in literary history, however, invite closer scrutiny. I shall examine Laneham's *Letter* as it was read fifty years after Kenilworth by Ben Jonson, one of its most critical early readers. As Jonson did, I shall focus first on Laneham's Captain Cox, "a mason, an alecunner, & a fencer az hardy az Gawyn," who played a leading role in the Coventry guildsmen's history play performed for the queen at Kenilworth.

Laneham's *Letter* gradually acquired the status of primary historical source by the end of the eighteenth century. Warton quoted it in his *History* (1778); it was reprinted in full and annotated in John Nichols's massive *Progresses and Public Processions of Queen Elizabeth,*[2] and excerpted in Thomas Sharp's notes on "Hox Tuesday" in his *Dissertation on the Pageants or Dramatic Mysteries anciently performed at Coventry* (1825).[3] In 1821, two years before Nichols's *Progresses* came out in its enlarged and even more richly anecdotal edition, Sir Walter Scott took Laneham's *Letter* as the base for *Kenilworth,* the Waverly novel which synthesizes two kinds of romantic historicism—fiction and nonfiction—mutually corroborating the imagined events of Elizabeth's stay at Leicester's castle.

Scott uses Laneham's Kenilworth account as documentary backcloth, and in authenticating footnotes; his romantic medievalism advances a

2. Laneham's *Letter* was printed separately in 8vo in 1784 by J. Freen, twice in 1821 by T. Sharp and J. H. Burne, and in 1871 and 1880 with copious notes by F. J. Furnivall in *Shakespeare's England,* nos. 7 and 14, New Shakespeare Society Publications, ser. VI (London, 1871, 1880). John Nichols's *The Progresses & Public Processions of Queen Elizabeth . . . ,* 3 vols. (London, 1807, 1823), I, 408–452, prints Laneham, Gascoigne's *Princely Pleasures,* and *Hemetes the Hermit* from BM Royal 18A, xlviii. All quotations from Laneham are from Nichols's reprint.

3. "Hox Tuesday" is the Tuesday after the 2d Sunday after Easter. The play is described in Sharp's *Dissertation . . . ,* repr. with a new foreword by A. C. Cawley (New York, 1973), pp. 125–132. See also Mary D. Harris, *The Story of Coventry* (London, 1911), pp. 208 ff. and *idem, Ancient Records of Coventry* (London, 1924).

stage beyond Percy's, the Wartons', Ritson's, and Nichols's toward mythic realism, visionary "history" deeply indebted to their collections of literary evidence for the vaguely postmedieval Elizabethan world. Nichols and Laneham's *Letter* gave him a wealth of novelistic detail for settings, costumes, and minor characters against which to play out political and sexual intrigues among Leicester, Amy Robsart, the queen, and her entourage of courtiers (Lyly, Gascoigne, Raleigh). Among them appears Laneham himself, and to complete his picture of all the social elements involved in the Kenilworth affair, Scott introduces Captain Cox of Coventry, who twice at the queen's command produced the Hock-Tuesday play of the Saxon's defeat of the Danes in 1042 and the death of Hardicanute.[4] Scott's Elizabethan-Gothic prose *mise en scène* is the last step in the historical process that recreated romantic medievalism out of the surviving documents brought to light by eighteenth-century antiquaries.

The modern popular image of Renaissance royal spectacle has changed little since the turn of the nineteenth century. But well before the end of the reign of James I the neomedieval nostalgia of the Elizabethan court seemed withered, and to have lost its strength. While political and economic change may accelerate or retard such shifts in taste and style, the Jacobean turning away from the past seemed to contemporaries more deeply rooted in self-knowledge, and its expression became increasingly explicit in both moral and aesthetic terms. The polarizing sense of "the modern" in the seventeenth century is, of course, an intensification of Renaissance classicism: now, in retrospect, the medieval legacy—neither truly ancient, nor modern—was a historical embarrassment. The Kenilworth revels provide a case in point.

According to Laneham's *Letter,* Elizabeth's Captain Cox was a splendid actor, and also a notably literate man, whose library was worth recording in some detail. These two aspects of Captain Cox—his role in the Coventry history play, and his repertoire of postmedieval literature— provide an anamorphic perspective through which we may observe something of the mysterious process of cultural transformation that occurred

4. The play was presented on St. Kenelm's Day, Sunday, 13 July, and Tuesday, 15 July, 1575. Scott refers to Captain Cox in *Kenilworth,* Chap. xxxix passim; he is "a Paragon of Black-Letter Antiquities" and "an English Don Quixote" in Scott's notes. Cf. Arthur Johnston, *Enchanted Ground* (London, 1964), Chap. 7, for Scott's medievalism.

in the last quarter of the sixteenth century.[5] Set against Laneham's Kenilworth, the Jacobean devaluation of Elizabethan Gothic becomes perceptible. In Jonson's later masques, the "medievals" acquire an increasingly dubious aura, in the receding "doubtful darkness" which yields "the scene of light, discovered."[6] Given the difficulty of seeing the reciprocal relation of both aspects of Captain Cox, at once player and reader, it is best to separate his roles, to consider what each tells us about the meanings of "Renaissance Gothic." The later evolution of this concept belongs to the history of eighteenth-century antiquarianism and nineteenth-century medievalism, from Percy's *Reliques* to Blake's Chaucer and Spenser, a theme too large and complex to be pursued further here. We can, however, observe its beginnings, in the shifts of stress Jonson imposed on the Elizabethan Gothic image in his subtler readings of Laneham's *Letter*.

Before we consider Jonson's response to Laneham's *Letter*, we shall examine what most intrigued him: first, Captain Cox's medieval play, in the context of the 1575 fete, and then the catalogue of early modern printed books associated with him. Their history and influence are evidence of an elusive kind of postmedieval literacy important in itself. Together, Captain Cox's play and his books comprise the commoner level of a widely apparent phenomenon: the survival of the medieval in the Elizabethan Renaissance. Jonson's strong reaction to Captain Cox is far less famous than his comment on the Gothic in Spenser ("Spenser writ no language") but no less telling. His response to Laneham's *Letter* appears clearly in two late court masques, the *Masque of Owls* (performed at Kenilworth in August 1624) and *The Fortunate Isles* (January 1625),

5. "Anamorphosis" (a Renaissance trick perspective) is the distortion which renders objects unrecognizable unless viewed through a "prospective glass" or anamorphoscope. Wesley Trimpi, in "The Quality of Fiction: Rhetorical Transmission of Literary Theory," *Traditio,* XXX (1974), 67, n. 77, cites Galileo's critique of Tasso and oblique "anamorphic" perspective in illusionistic painting. Cf. John White, "Developments in Renaissance Perspective," *JWCI,* XII (1949), 58–79.

6. *The Golden Age Restored,* ll. 135–136; all quotations from Jonson's masques are from Stephen Orgel, ed., *Ben Jonson: The Complete Masques* (New Haven, 1969). Irena Janicka, *The Popular Theatrical Tradition and Ben Jonson* (Lodz, 1972) discusses his English literary sources and the arts, stressing continuities from medieval to Renaissance, the converse of the present essay's approach.

among the last he wrote for the Stuart court. Jonson's burlesque of Captain Cox and his ridicule of Cox's books reveal contempt for the Gothic nostalgia that Elizabeth's court at once self-consciously inspired and enjoyed.[7]

The Malorian medievalism apparent in the Kenilworth entertainments, considerably enlarged by the catalogue of the captain's books, gave Jonson a means to measure his own progress. Between antimasque and masque—a moral and aesthetic distance—the Gothic becomes grotesque: the contrast visibly heightens Jonson's celebration of the ideal, and the grandeur of the modern. In the first quarter of the seventeenth century, the "olde bokes" had become obsolete. However, between Jonson's satire on passé Tudor medievalism and the fragile, complex synthesis of Arthurian legend, Latinate humanist learning, and popular vernacular comedy of Leicester's Kenilworth fete, lies the world of the *Faerie Queene*. Jonson looks back ambivalently to Kenilworth and beyond it to medieval poetry, fully aware of the legacy he and his peers possess, both recent and remote. For all his critical clarity and detachment, Jonson's reverence for the ancients is not simply Augustan, but Christian conservatism, as the *Discoveries* testify.[8]

English literary history may be said to begin in the 1580s, in Sidney's and Puttenham's backward glances toward early Tudor poetry and the Middle Ages, Chaucer and Gower. Gascoigne published his *Certain Notes of Instruction* (an immediate precursor of the treatises of the following decade) in the *Posies* of 1575, with the *Princely Pleasures* that document the Kenilworth revels as aristocratic literature, worth preserving. In the atmosphere of *Arcadia,* Kenilworth, and Faerie Land, it was still possible to mix Gothic nostalgia with the new Italianate forms (as in Gascoigne's *Zabeta*) in poetry addressed to a still provincial English elite. But thirty years later, in the *Masque of Owls* and *The Fortunate*

7. The "Gothic Revival" in Elizabethan art is discussed by Roy Strong, *The English Icon: Elizabethan and Jacobean Portraiture* (London, 1969). See also H. W. Hintz, "The Elizabethan Entertainment and the *Faerie Queene,*" PQ, XIV (1935), 83–90; F. A. Yates, "Elizabethan Chivalry: The Romance of the Accession Day Tilts," *JWCI*, XX (1957), 4–25; Charles Mish, "Black Letter as a Social Discriminant in the 17th Century," *PMLA*, LXVIII (1953), 627–630.

8. See below, p. 200. For another statement of this view, see Alastair Fowler, "The 'Better Marks' of Jonson's *To Penshurst,*" *RES, N.S.* XXIV (1973), 266–282.

Isles, we see change, manifest in Jonson's appropriation of the play and books of Captain Cox as symbols of a decadent past no longer usable. Unlike Spenser's historicism, and equally unlike Scott's sentimental piety (which in *Kenilworth* trivializes the "vulgar barbarians" of early modern literary history), Jonson uses Captain Cox's play and his old books to confirm his own sense of advance: a new, higher form of English art, a purer language. In these masques, he deliberately contrasts his and Jones's Jacobean high court entertainment with the mélange of medieval and pseudoclassical fantasies that Gascoigne, Captain Cox, and their collaborators presented for Elizabeth.

One final witness to those pseudo-Gothic phenomena, who anticipates their revival, is worth noting in this context, to remind us of the continuous dialectic in historical criticism. Richard Hurd's essay on Elizabeth in his *Moral and Political Dialogues* of 1759 is a revisionary defense of the Elizabethan Gothic scene at Kenilworth, written three years before his more famous *Letters on Chivalry and Romance* in praise of Spenser (1762). Hurd says nothing about Jonson in discussing the moral and artistic propriety of the flattery of kings. Describing the fete at Kenilworth, however, he goes straight to the question—the synthetic mixture of heterogeneous secular symbols in the Renaissance high court festival:

What more decent . . . or so elegant way of complimenting [and] entertaining a great and learned Prince [than by] working through the veil of fiction (and taking) that fiction out of old poetical story? and if something of the Gothic romance adhered to these classical fictions, it was not for any barbarous pleasure that was taken in this patch-work . . . The deities introduced in the compliments at Kenilworth were those of the waters, the most artful panegyric on the Naval glory of this Reign, and the most grateful representation of the Queen of the Ocean, as Elizabeth was then called. . . .[9]

Later in this essay, we shall see how in the seascapes of *The Fortunate Isles* Jonson brilliantly develops the water imagery which (as Hurd saw) formed the natural center of the pageantry at Kenilworth. Laneham's *Letter* repeatedly notes that in addition to the aquatic spectacles and fireworks displays exhibited on and over the water, the queen's daily hunt finally ends when the deer are driven into the lake. In the evening, "it

9. Nichols, I, xxv–xxvi.

pleased her to stand, while vpon the Pool, oout of a Barge fyne appoynted for the purpoze, too hear sundy kinds of very delectable Muzik." The water is both symbol and scene for elaborate tableaux beginning on the day of the queen's arrival. From the *Masque of Blackness* (1605) to *Neptune's Triumph* (written for 1624, but never performed) and *The Fortunate Isles,* Jonson and Inigo Jones recreate such symbolic oceanic settings in the Banqueting House, by feats of artistic and poetic illusion far more complex and difficult to achieve than the "patch-work" of nature and art Hurd saw in the fete at Kenilworth castle.

I

As in the earlier municipal pageants officially welcoming the queen from 1559 on—at Greenwich, Oxford, Cambridge, Warwick—and later royal visits to great houses—Eltham, Nonesuch, Woodstock, Mitcham— there is a strong sense of place evoked in many of the records of these entertainments.[10] It is *this* city, *this* castle, *these* woods, *this* river, that awakens in joyous response to the approach of the sovereign. The *genii loci* rise up along the road to greet her, or (as in Sidney's *Lady of May* at Wanstead in 1578) suddenly appear in the forest. This traditional sense of locale is important in the Kenilworth fete, in its several kinds of exploitation of the setting, but nowhere more so than in Captain Cox's play. Since little is known about the Coventry Hock-Tuesday play be-yond what Laneham describes, the evidence can be briefly summarized.

One common emphasis that all surviving records share is the historicity

---

10. A full account can be found in Nichols's *Progresses* (see n. 2); cf. *The Queen's Majestie's Entertainment at Woodstock 1575 from the unique fragment of the edition of 1585 . . . The Tale of Hametes the Hermit,* ed. A. W. Pollard (Oxford, 1903 & 1910); J. W. Cunliffe, "The Queenes Majesties Entertainment at Woodstock," *PMLA,* XXVI (1911), 92–141; David M. Bergeron, *English Civic Pageantry, 1558–1642* (Columbia, S.C., 1971), pp. 30–35; Orgel, *The Jonsonian Masque,* pp. 44–56. See also George Adelard, *Amye Robsart, the Earl of Leycester, & Kenilworth* (London, 1870); John P. Cutts, "An Entertainment for Queen Elizabeth, 1591," *SMC,* IV (1974); Leslie Hotson, *Queen Elizabeth's Entertainment at Mitcham* (New Haven, 1953). For Gascoigne's role, see Charles Prouty, *George Gascoigne* (New York, 1942).

of the play, and its deeply local roots; the folklore traditions of the city
and Kenilworth Castle seem to intertwine. The castle is at the center of
all the Kenilworth spectacles, and provides their visual format, in the
lake, the tiltyard, and the Gothic hall as well as the surrounding park.
But the Hock-Tuesday play records events even older than the castle,
which goes back to the Barons' Wars and Simon de Montfort. It was
enlarged by John of Gaunt and remodeled again by Leicester for Elizabeth's visit. In the thirteenth century, Kenilworth was the site of one of
the great Round Table tournaments staged by Roger Mortimer in 1279;
one hundred knights and one hundred ladies were invited to the tourney,
the prize was a golden lion, and the impact of the Arthurian imagery on
Edward I was evident for the rest of his reign. Edward III's Round Table
in 1344, and his institution of the Garter in 1348, link his restoration of
the mystique, its political and aesthetic power, with the chivalric scenes
Loomis and Cline document from 1252 on, and which Sydney Anglo
analyzes at the turn of the sixteenth century at the court of Henry VIII.[11]
But Captain Cox and his Coventry guildsmen brought to Kenilworth
Castle their own civic "historial sheaws," not Arthurian, and datable to
the earlier eleventh century. In their play the mounted commoners, clerks,
and merchants fight the Danes on the same ground on which Elizabeth's
knights display their prowess in romantic costume at the barriers.

On her first official visit to Coventry (17 August 1565), ten years before
the Kenilworth fete, Elizabeth was greeted by the recorder with a speech
in which he described the city's medieval history, making special note of
the Hock-Tuesday play as an ancient and honored tradition:

And after the arrivall of the Daynes who miserably afflicted the people of
this realme, the inhabitants of this Citie . . . vtterly ouerthrew them in the

---

11. R. S. Loomis, "Chivalric and Dramatic Imitations of Arthurian Romance,"
in W.R.W. Koehler, ed., *Medieval Studies in Memory of A. Kingsley Porter*, 2
vols. (Cambridge, Mass., 1939), I, 79–97; *idem*, "Edward I, Arthurian Enthusiast,"
Speculum, XXVIII (1953), 114–127; R. H. Cline, "The Influence of Romances on
Tournaments of the Middle Ages," *Speculum*, XX (1945), 204–211; Sydney Anglo,
"The Evolution of the Early Tudor . . . Mask," *RenD*, N.S. I (1968), 3–44; Bruce
R. Smith, "Sir Amorous Knight and the Indecorous Romans . . ." *RenD*, N.S. III
(1973), 3–28.

last conflict with the Saxons. A memoriall wherof is kepte to this daye by certain open shewes in this Citie yearely.[12]

The earliest record Sharp found of actual performance of the play is a note in the MS *Annals* of the city for the year 1416, when Henry V was present: "The Pageants and Hox Tuesday inuented wherein the King and Nobles took great delight." In the Companies' books of accounts he discovered nothing more than entries for 1568, 1569, and 1576 (payments for "harness and poynts" by the Smiths', Cappers', and Drapers' Companies), which relate to the play Elizabeth heard about in 1565 and saw performed a decade later on St. Kenelm's Day.[13] Unlike the *Princely Pleasures at the Courte at Kenelwoorth . . . the Copies of all such Verses, Proses, or poetical inuentions and other Deuices of Pleasure, as were there deuised and presented by sundry Gentlemen . . .* (London, 1576), in which were published Gascoigne's masque, *Zabeta,* the Latin verse of Richard Mulcaster, and the elaborate dialogues and tableaux provided by the London poets and musicians at Kenilworth, there is no surviving text of the Hock-Tuesday play. That it contained speeches as well as vigorous action is indicated by Laneham's description, which also suggests reasons why the Coventry guildsmen chose the play for this occasion, as the means of "pleazaunt recreation [by which] her Highness myght best find herself wellcome." They hoped its success would move the queen to intercede with the Puritan authorities, whose interdict had stopped the Coventry plays ca. 1570. Thus, Laneham remarks, the display of valor of the Coventry women especially might "move some mirth to her Majestie the rather." The "old historiall sheaw" is not only good sport, but true and politically relevant:

12. Sharp, *Dissertation,* p. 125; Nichols, I, 193–197. Nichols (p. 190) records the "gift of the manor of Kenilworth to Robt. Dudley on 29 September, 1564, on the occasion of (Elizabeth's) conferring on him the dignity of Earl of Leicester and Baron of Denbigh."

13. Sharp, *Dissertation,* pp. 11–12: "1575 [*sic*]: Thomas Nicklyn, Mayor. This yeare the said maior caused hoc twesday wherby is mencioned a ouerthrowe of the Danes by the inhabitants of this Citie to be againe set vp and shewed forthe, to his great commendacion and the Cities great commodity which said hoc twesday was the yeare before plaide before the Quene at Kenelworth in the tyme of her progresse by the commaundment of the Quenes Counsell." *MS Annals.*

Of argument how the Danez whylom heere in a troublous seazon wear for quietness born withall and suffered in peas; that anon, by outrage and importabl insolency, abuzing both Ethelred the King . . . and all Estates every whear bysyde; at the grevous complaint . . . wearall dispacht and the realm rid. And for becauz the matter mencioneth how valiantly our English women for loove of their countree behaued themselues, expressed in actionz and rymez after their manner. . . . they thought it moought moove sum myrth . . . the rather. The thing iz grounded on story [history] and for pastime woont to be plaid in oour citee yeearly; without ill example of mannerz, papistry, or ony superstition . . . till noow of late laid dooun, they knu no cauz why . . .[14]

On the last point, Laneham notes, "they woold make theyr humbl peticion vnto her Highnes, that they might haue theyr Playz vp again."[15] As we shall see, Ben Jonson picks up the thread of Reformation censorship and its effects in the *Masque of Owls,* but in 1624 the topic was still too touchy to be mocked in the environs of Coventry: the allusion to Puritans was cut from the performed script, and another (on inflation and the interest rate, hence "safe") substituted.

The first performance, as Laneham describes it, began early in the afternoon in the great courtyard under the queen's windows. Three episodes can be deduced from Laneham's account, which is worth extended quotation. He describes first the entrance of Captain Cox, "cleen trust and gartered aboue the knee, in a veluet cap," flourishing a two-handled sword to marshal the procession. The action he directs consists of a horse parade, followed by mounted skirmishes between the opposing Saxon and Danish knights; then, a series of apparently choreographed close-order marching drills, and finally a free-for-all of hand-to-hand fighting, which ends with the defeated Danes led captive by the victorious Coventry women (presumably played by boys):

Captain Cox cam marching on valiantly befor. . . . and another fens master with him; thus in the forward making room for the rest. And after them, proudly prikt on formost the Danish launce knights on horsbak, and then

14. Nichols, I, 446–448.

15. Sharp notes the last recorded performance of the Hock-Tuesday play, dated 1591, in the Common Council Book: "The Conquest of the Danes, or The History of King Edward the Confessor." The documents Sharp copied were destroyed in a fire in the Birmingham Library in 1879.

the English; each with their alder poles martially in their hand. Even at the first entree, the meeting waxt sumwhat warm; that bye and bye kindled with corage a both sides, gru from a hot skirmish unto a blazing battail; first by spear and shield, outragious in their racez as ramz at their rut; with furious encounterz, that togyther they tumbl too it with sworde and target, good bangz a both sidez. The fight so ceasing, but the battail not so ended; folloed the footmen; both the hostes ton after tother; first marching in rankz; then warlike turning; then from rankz into squadrons; then into trianglez; from that into ringz, and so winding oout again. A valiant Captain of great prowez waz so hardy to give the first stroke; then get they grisly togyther . . . ton very eager for purchaz of pray, toother utterly stoout for redemption of libertie; thus, quarrell enflamed fury a both sidez. Twise the Danes had the better, but at the last conflict, beaten doun, overcom, and many led captive for triumph by our English weemen. . . .

Distracted by the dancing also going on in her chamber, Elizabeth did not see the full show, and commanded that it be repeated the following Tuesday. On that day, "her Majestie laught well." The players

wear the jocounder . . . becauz her Highnes had given them too buckes and five marke in mony, to make mery togyther. They prayed for her Majesty long, happily to reign, and oft to cum thither, that oft they moought see her; and what rejoycing vpon their ampl reward and what triumphing vpon the good acceptaunce, they vaunted their play was neuer so dignified, nor euer any players before so beatified.[16]

The Hock-Tuesday hippodrama stands at about mid-point on the scale of styles and kinds of pageantry produced during the queen's visit. The unparalleled range and variety of the Kenilworth revels are in part the result of the ample length of time available, which gave opportunity to a large number of writers, actors, and musicians to invent many kinds of theatrical spectacle. The participation of such men as Richard Mulcaster (then master of the Merchant Taylors' School), Gascoigne, George Ferrars (Elizabeth's Lord of Misrule), the court musician Henry Goldingham, and William Hunnis (master of the Queen's Chapel) establishes one frame of reference for the shaping of Leicester's fete. The London intellectual world was brought to Kenilworth, an aristocracy of talent in both poetry and music. Captain Cox and the Coventry guildsmen pro-

16. Nichols, I, 455–456.

vide a second frame, too quickly perceived as merely offsetting counterparts—provincial, amateur, and crudely vernacular. Laneham's account, however, picks out Captain Cox for distinction in the social and intellectual complex at Kenilworth. As Jonson saw too, the captain's sixty-odd books separate him from the ruder provincial comedians whose performances also pleased the queen.

The Kenilworth entertainment has been so often described that it may suffice to summarize the extraordinary neomedieval mélange of courtly and plebeian theater it brought together. At one extreme were the old comedies provided by medieval proletarian parody of high aristocratic forms: the Bride-Ale, a mock-wedding of a pair of ugly rustics, a burlesque tilt at the quintain and a comic morris dance; an old Middlesex minstrel, singing praise of the local cheese and an Arthurian ballad.[17] In the tiltyard, the joust and tourneys, an Italian tumbler ("I may gess hiz bak be metalld like a lamprey, that haz no bone but a lyne lik a lute string") and thirteen bears, baited by packs of dogs.

At the other extreme, Gothic themes and styles are taken seriously, elegantly performed, and mingled with Latinate learning and classical mythology. From the start, Arthurian imagery surrounded Elizabeth. Six giant trumpeters eight feet high stood at the portcullis, to symbolize the Briton ancestors whose realm she now rules. In the lake, floating islands appear for Merlin's prison and the Lady of the Lake,[18] dolphins for Proteus and Tryton, and fireworks displays of dragons. In the park, she met a Green Man (*hombre salvaggio,* the "Salvage Man") dressed in ivy and moss, "with an oken plant plvkt vp in his hond"—the poet Gascoigne, who (with Echo) reappeared later as "Silvanus." These heterogeneous native pastoral and Arthurian motifs blend with more elaborate humanist themes. On the bridge stood seven huge pairs of pillars, bearing live birds, fruit, fish, game, wine, musical instruments, and weapons: emblems signifying the gifts of "Silvanus," Ceres, Pomona,

17. "Warraunted for story oout of King Arthurz Acts, the first booke and 26 chapter"; i.e., "How the tydyngs came to Arthur that Kyng Ryons had ouercome the XI Kynges, and how he desyred Arthurs berde to purfyl his mantel," in Caxton's ed. (1485); printed in Percy's *Reliques,* vol. II, Bk. 1, no. 3.

18. Her speech, Gascoigne's dialogues, and *Zabeta* are printed in Nichols, I, 485–523.

Bacchus, Neptune, Mars, and Apollo, explained in Mulcaster's allegorical Latin poem delivered to the music of flutes, and inscribed in gold on the tower.[19]

Upon arrival, Elizabeth met "Hercules," the porter, and ten classical sibyls, one of whom prophesied the performance of Gascoigne's *Zabeta,* but bad weather spoiled the play.[20] It was never performed, but in the printed text Diana and her nymphs dispute the question of marriage, as do the Lady of the Lake, Proteus singing on his dolphin, "Silvanus" in dialogue with Echo, and the debate of "Deepedesire" and "Dewdesert" (the holly and the laurel) in the forest.

Even reduced to brief synopsis, Laneham's *Letter* describes a very wide range of Elizabethan modes in several arts, most of them well enough known not to need further discussion. I would call to attention, however, the predominantly English and medieval literary traditions the Kenilworth revels exploit. The entertainment for Elizabeth projects a magnified medieval image, more reminiscent of her father's court than modern. Much of its mixed inspiration derives from the most important new book published in England since the death of Chaucer—another anachronism, a translation, and prose: Malory's English *Arthur,* published ninety years before, and the first of Captain Cox's sixty-odd books. But Malorian themes are not the only Gothic influences at work in the Kenilworth pageants. As we have seen, the Hock-Tuesday play of Captain Cox reenacts a ritual celebrated at Coventry since as early as 1416; at least three other traditions of medieval and early Tudor court entertainment are brought together at Kenilworth. These too are well known, and have been so fully described by Pearsall, Anglo, and others that they need only brief discussion. The evidence for late medieval courtly entertainment is mainly non- or semidramatic. One major exception is of course the reading aloud of poems, as we know Chaucer read the *Troilus* to the court of Richard II. In the *Canterbury Tales* and *House of Fame* he satirized

19. Mulcaster's poem is discussed in Richard de Molen, "Richard Mulcaster and Elizabethan Pageantries," *SEL,* XIV (1974), 209–221.

20. The Sibyl's verses (by Hunnis) are printed in Gascoigne's *Princely Pleasures;* see above, n. 18. The Italianate *Zabeta* and the Kenilworth revels follow shortly the completion of portraits Leicester commissioned from Zuccarro of both the queen and himself, made in London and dated May 1575, hers inscribed "La Regina Elizabeta de Ingilterra in Londra Magio 1575." Cf. Nichols, I, xiv, n. 2.

minstrelsy, French and English romance, both popular and "high style" fashions of fourteenth-century nobles.

Lydgate, Chaucer's successor, who was at Oxford with Henry V and supplied his taste for moral-historical poems, wrote a rondel and ballade for the coronation of Henry VI, "Soteltees for the Coronation Banquet" and for the Triumphal Entry (21 February 1432) as well as at least seven mummings, precursors of the Renaissance court masque. The latter are significant in the present context for their bearing on Captain Cox. He and the Coventry guildsmen can be seen as the lineal descendants of the patrons of four of Lydgate's protomasques, the *Mummings* for the Mercers', Goldsmiths', Merchants', and Sherriffs' Companies of London, which date from 1426–30.[21] Lydgate's mummings consist of speeches and dumbshows with musical interludes. Those performed for London civic audiences, for May Day and Christmas banquets, are almost indistinguishable in style from those written for the court (Eltham, 1426, Windsor, 1429, and Hertford, 1430). Except for the last, Lydgate's royal and commoners' mummings are allegorical pageants: elaborately descriptive, mingling popular mythology with didactic passages in processional, pictorial "tapestry" poems—"Bacchus, Juno, and Ceres present olives, wheat, and wine." However, the Hertford pageant for the king is not high, Latinate, and allegorical, but rather low, rambunctious, colloquial, and comic: "Þe rude vplondisshe peple compleynyng on hir wives, with þe boystous aunswere of hir wyues"—clearly based on the *Wife of Bath's Prologue.*

The third kind of medieval court entertainment has already been mentioned, apropos Kenilworth castle itself: the jousting and pseudo-Arthurian chivalric exercises revived in the later fifteenth century in the patriotic milieu through which Henry VII reestablished the image of dynastic succession, and in which Prince Arthur and Henry VIII took part. The early Tudor tournaments were based on romantically nostalgic rituals performed at the court of Edward III in the 1340s and 1350s, themselves revivals of Edward I's imitations of the legends of Arthur. Plan-

21. Texts in H. W. MacCracken, ed., *Lydgate's Minor Poems,* 2 vols., EETS 107, 192 (London, 1911, 1934), II, nos. 28–32, 40. The mummings are discussed in Derek Pearsall, *John Lydgate* (London, 1970), pp. 180–188, and by Enid Welsford, *The Court Masque* (London, 1926, repr. 1962).

tagenet literary and political symbolism provided models for the more elaborate spectacles of the sixteenth-century Tudor court. In brief, these variously surviving Gothic formulas—pseudo-Arthurian tourney, pseudo-Ovidian allegorical pageant, Chaucerian estates' satire—underlie the collage of heterogeneous neomedieval spectacles Laneham describes at Leicester's Kenilworth fete.

The medieval literary antecedents of Elizabethan pageantry are well known, if sometimes understated, in their Renaissance context. Let us return to Captain Cox, and examine the second dimension of his portrait in Laneham's *Letter,* the catalogue of books which precedes the description of the Coventry play. Jonson found Laneham's admiration for Captain Cox's library ludicrous—symptomatic of a kind of decadence broader than bad taste, and perhaps ultimately more dangerous than vulgarity. The intellectual ambition of Captain Cox's class in the 1570s had been replicated and reinforced by two generations of new men by the end of James I's reign, when Jonson looked back to Kenilworth.

II

Given the range and richness of Laneham's list of Captain Cox's books, a full study of the evidence is not feasible here, nor can any of the individual titles be described in detail.[22] Proper evaluation would entail the sociology of literature and the history of ideas, leading far beyond the limits of Elizabethan Gothic in the half-century 1575–1625. Nevertheless, Laneham's catalogue can be set in its Renaissance frame of reference, with a brief review of the century of English printing, 1475–1575, to which Captain Cox's books belong. The titles and genres Laneham lists enlarge the context in which Elizabethan medievalism is frequently understood; just as the Kenilworth revels include more than chivalric tournaments and court tableaux, neo-Gothic taste is not reducible to aristocratic Malorian romance. Both middle and low postmedieval styles and forms

22. See Appendix below. W. D. Macray, *Annals of the Bodleian Library 1598–1867* (Oxford, 1868), pp. 86–87, lists some rare black-letter romances like Cox's among the tracts in 4° C. 32. Art. Selt. in the Selden collection, acquired ca. 1620. H. L. D. Ward's *Catalogue of Romances in the Department of MSS of the British Museum,* 3 vols. (London, 1883, 1893, 1910, repr. 1962).

—the history play, folk dancing, and folk mythology (the "Savage Man") were as conspicuous to contemporaries and as important for their antiquity in 1575 as the more spectacular, deliberately archaized rituals of the joust.

There is a necessary caveat to be made, concerning over- and underinterpretation of the evidence we have. Laneham's *Letter* is far from fragmentary, but since it is unsupported by other witnesses, it should be read with caution.[23] His list of Captain Cox's library is somewhat suspect, in that it purports to record many of the books possessed by a Coventry mason of whom no other record exists. The catalogue may equally reflect the taste, memory, or even the bookshelves of Robert Laneham himself. Nevertheless, the value of the inventory remains unchanged, whether it be of Captain Cox's books or Laneham's own. It is significant early evidence of what Raymond Williams calls the Long Revolution—the shift from oral to textual literacy.[24]

While modern criticism should not overemphasize the symbolic Arthurian frame of Elizabethan Gothic nostalgia, it is clear that the dominant neomedieval context was Malorian in the Renaissance as it was to

23. A case in point is that of the Kenilworth library. Given Leicester's reputation as patron and dedicatee of English letters, and that the evidence of inventories is notoriously difficult to interpret, one may reserve judgment of the Dudley household records, now at Penshurst, which account for the contents of Kenilworth Castle in 1583. None of Leicester's books is mentioned, other than one Bible and seven psalters. The list includes paintings (Rafel's *Fornarina*, portraits, a *St. Jerome*, and twenty-three maps), metalwork, and tapestries, but no mention of his magnificently bound Continental folios of Plato, Aristotle, and Renaissance humanists in history and science, which are known to include (in English) Jewel's *Defence of the Church of England* (London, 1567) and Foxe's ed. of the *Anglo Saxon Gospels* (London, 1571). See William E. Moss, *Bindings from the Library of Robt. Dudley* (Sonning-on-Thames, 1934); Adelard, *Amye Robsart*, prints the Kenilworth inventory. See Eleanor Rosenberg, *Leicester, Patron of Letters* (New York, 1955).

24. *The Long Revolution* (London, 1961); cf. L. B. Wright, *Middle Class Culture in Elizabethan England* (Chapel Hill, N.C., 1935); M. C. Bradbrook, "The Status Seekers: Society and the Common Player in the Reign of Elizabeth I," *HLQ*, XXIV (1960-1961), 111-124; M. B. Parkes, "The Literacy of the Laity," in Daiches and Anthony Thorlby, eds., *The Medieval World* (London, 1973), pp. 555-577; J. W. Adamson, "The Extent of Literacy In England in the 15th and 16th Centuries," *The Library*, 4th ser. X (1929), 163-183.

be in subsequent renewals in the eighteenth and nineteenth centuries. In effect, the history of Captain Cox and his books forms a running parallel with the rise, decline, and revival of Malory's *Arthur*. In Caxton's edition, *Kyng Arthur* was reprinted six times between 1485 and 1585, once more in 1634, and then not again until 1816. Similarly, the postmedieval catalogue of Middle English heroes remained roughly the same, down through the eighteenth century. In 1709, Steele reported in the *Tatler* that Isaac Bickerstaff's eight-year-old godson scorned Aesop's *Fables,* because they are untrue; he preferred "Guy of Warwick, Bevis of Southhampton, and St. George, the Champion of England, whom nobody can prove did not exist!" The Renaissance Gothic tradition remained superficially intact, a litany of secular names that invoke the Middle Ages. They are (except for Arthur) unlike the artificial names of Spenser's heroes—Sir Guyon, Artegall, Calidore, which belong to Elizabethan poetic fiction. An aside in the first book of Puttenham's *Arte of English Poesie* (I, xix) suggests the difference. It images a scene of aristocratic entertainment, and at the same time echoes the more famous allusion to such a moment in Sidney's *Apologie* ("Certainly, I must confesse my owne barbarousness: I neuer heard the old song of Percy and Duglas that I found not my heart mooued more than with a Trumpet . . ."). On his own attempt at poetry, Puttenham confesses;

We ourselves haue written for pleasure a little brief *Romance* or historicall ditty in the English tong, of the isle of great *Britaine,* in short and long meetres, and by breaches or diuisions to be . . . song to the harpe in places of assembly, where the company shalbe desirous to heare of olde aduentures & valiaunces of noble knights of the round table, Sir Beuys of Southampton, Guy of Warwick and others like . . .[25]

The historic names, "King Arthur, Sir Bevis of Southampton, Guy of Warwick . . . ," are valued for their archaic authenticity, the impossibility of proof that they never existed, their *fantasie.* The "aduentures and valiaunces of noble Knights," sufficiently ancient and stale for Chaucerian

---

25. Texts in G. G. Smith, ed., *Elizabethan Critical Essays,* 2 vols. (Oxford, 1904), I, 178; II, 43–44; cf. the catalogue of heroes collected by L. H. Loomis for *Sir Thopas* in W. L. Bryan and Germaine Dempster, eds., *Sources and Analogues of Chaucer's Canterbury Tales* (New York, 1941), pp. 486–559. Ca. 1555, Copeland printed *The Squire of Low Degree* (?1450), one of the last romances to use "straight" the formulas Chaucer parodied in *Thopas.*

parody before 1400, remain defensible as aristocratic entertainment by Sidney, Spenser, and Puttenham in the 1590s, at the height of the neo-medieval revival, against protests already being made.

Certainly, oral performance ("song to the harp in places of assembly") was by the mid-sixteenth century no longer the dominant mode of trans-mission of vernacular poetry, either popular or elite. Puttenham's phrase reveals the self-consciousness implicit in such nostalgia—like the mag-nificent armor-costume of the joust. But the Renaissance Gothic revival rested on a broader base than the intellectual aristocracy and the court. What Sidney calls his own "barbarousness" is, in a loose sense, an allu-sion to popular culture, the larger Elizabethan audience, whose taste Laneham's *Letter* (to "Humphrey Martin, mercer of London") and Captain Cox reflect.

The early English printers quickly recognized the market implications of the shift from MSS to print. N. F. Blake, H. S. Bennett, L. B. Wright, and others have established the booksellers' awareness of the expansion of literacy their business depended upon, and the gradually increasing change in the nature of literary patronage. One immediate effect of wider audiences was the perpetuation, after 1500, of more popular vernacular literary forms. What were formerly ephemera—ballads, tales, folklore, and songs—were given the same semipermanence as high aristocratic, learned, and sacred literature. Since Captain Cox's books include a wide range of early titles which acquired a new life in print between 1475 and 1575, it will be useful to survey the period in which medieval secular literature was not in fact discarded, but published and redistributed, when the atrophy of memory began. In 1508, Erasmus complained of the rising demand for books, but it was for copies of more of the medieval, not the newly recovered truly ancient authors. The Gothic image after 1500 is black letter, a commodity one could possess, a pattern book of medieval clichés.

The bookshops sold some new "trade" books—secular, nonscholarly works in English (Elyot's *Governor, Lyttleton on Tenures, The Ship of Fools,* Barclay's pastorals)—but the great mass of fifteenth- and early sixteenth-century printing was both deeply and superficially late medie-val: Aesop, allegorized Ovid, anti-clerical and misogynist satire, courtly love, Boethian tragedy, the myths of Troy. More's *Utopia* remained in Latin until mid-century; his comic *Sergeaunt and Friar* and *Book of*

Fortune (on the chance of the dice) are on Captain Cox's list, but not *Utopia*. In the interlude *The Four Elements* (1519), Rastell complains

> What nombre of bok[s] in our tong maternall
> Of toyes and tryfellys be made and imprynted
> And few of them of matter substancyall
> For though many make bok[s] yet vnneth ye shall
> In our englyshe tong fynde any marks
> Of connyng that is regardyd by clerks . . .[26]

Rastell is criticizing not only the insubstantiality of "toys and tryfellys" in English, but the sense of déjà vu. The Tudor poets did not reject the examples of their poetic fathers, or express contempt for "primitive Gothic barbarism," until the second quarter of the century. Vives and Erasmus (in both Latin and English by 1540) condemn "Lancelot, Amadis, and other nonsensicall fictions" for not stylistic but moral decadence.[27]

The evolution of the language was a more immediate impediment to poetry. By the 1530s, both the high aureate style and post-Chaucerian realism had been taken to unprecedented extremes in imitation; the high Gothic aureation in Douglas, Dunbar, and Hawes parallels the grotesque Gothic realism at the lower end of the spectrum. Alice of Bath is the model for not only Skelton's Elinor Rumming, Dunbar's *Twa Marrit Wemen,* and "Jill of Brainford," but a swarm of subliterary misogynist satires which multiplied her image in crudely pornographic forms. The debasement of style by increasing imitation did not, however, entail loss of esteem for familiar medieval models. "Trite" is a neologism in Hall's *Chronicles* (1548), and it does not gain force until fifty years later, in Ben Jonson. Booksellers continued to respond to rising demand, for Chaucer's *Works, A Hundred Merry Tales,* Skelton, and *Guy of Warwick.* The last three titles, as expected, are found in Laneham's list of Captain Cox's library.

This long anecdotal preface, placed at the beginning of the account

26. Quoted in Lucy Sweeting, *Early Tudor Criticism, Linguistic and Literary* (Oxford, 1946, repr. New York, 1964), p. 134.

27. Vives's *de instrucione feminae Christianae* (1523), trans. Richard Hyrde, published ca. 1540, denounces the predictable list; see J. W. Atkins, *English Literary Criticism: The Renaissance* (London, 1955), p. 60, and D. Bayne, *Moreana* XLV (1975), 5–16.

of the Coventry play, is perhaps as revealing of Laneham himself and his background as it is of his ostensible subject. He is impressed by Captain Cox's learning and taste, and wants to impress his reader with the extent and quality of Cox's "great ouersight. . . . in matters of storie." The list accounts for sixty-two titles of the Captain's books, with allusions to "a hundred others . . . many mo than I reheerse here" in his possession.

As we would expect, the great weight of the list is the "old poetry": thirty-three romances and tales, from *Kyng Arthurz Book* to the *Nutbroun Maid,* most of it in print from the beginning of the century—Lydgate, Skelton, Barclay, More, "Howleglas," Rabelais. The catalogue provides a summary of the literature of diversion, postmedieval fantasy, *moralitas,* obscenity, and wonders. The more "philosophical" portion of the list (*The Shepherdz kalendar, Daniells dreamz,* and twelve others) is both eclectic and archaic, dating from ca. 1492 to the 1550s.[28] The level of these "moral and naturall sciences" compares in sophistication with any recent popular *Digest*—"Tell Me, Doctor," Billy Graham, and Ann Landers in Tudor form. Like the eighteenth-century middle-class miscellanies, these are topical tracts of information and advice on the education of children, the control of women, how to outwit rogues and fools, nature lore, astrology.[29] The range is relatively narrow, the emphasis on social behavior, the tone in general colloquial and conservative.

As in the lists of poems, interludes, and songs, Laneham expects immediate recognition, citing short titles alone. Everyone knows these "auncient playz"—*Impacient Pouerty, Nugize, Hikskorner, Yooth & Charity;* the ballads ("all auncient") are cited by refrain ("So wo is me bigone," "Broom broom on a hil") though "he hath a hundred mo fair

28. See A. W. Pollard and G. R. Redgrave, *Short Title Catalog . . .* (London, 1926); Arundel Esdaile, *A List of English Tales and Prose Romances Printed Before 1740, I (1475–1642)* (London, 1912, repr. 1976); W. Carew Hazlitt, *Handbook to the Popular Books and Dramatic Literature of Great Britain* (London, 1867); H. S. Bennett, *English Books and Readers, 1552–1603* (Cambridge, Eng., 1965); David C. Fowler, *A Literary History of the Popular Ballad* (Durham, N.C., 1968).

29. See *Short Title Catalog,* Esdaile, *List,* and A. Rodger, "Roger Ward's Shrewsbury Stock: An Inventory of 1585," *The Library,* 5th ser. XIII (1958), 247–268; F. R. Johnson, "Notes on English Retail Book Prices, 1550–1640," *The Library,* 5th ser. V (1950), 83–112; H. F. Bell, "The Price of Books in Medieval England," *The Library,* 4th ser. XII (1932), 312–332.

wrapt vp in a Parchment and bound with a whipcord." Such a detail links Captain Cox with past, present, and future: with Chaucer's pimping Friar, Shakespeare's Autolycus, and the contemporary Kenilworth minstrel, performing his ballad "to the harp." Four of the captain's books are general reference, practical prose "of Antiquitee": *Dr Boord on heelth,* and three almanacs, English, French, and Dutch.[30]

Captain Cox's library is worth considerably more than a brief summary; his romances and poems alone span three centuries of European literary tradition. L. B. Wright has described the wider context of such urban bourgeois literacy, for which the masons, mercers, and newly prosperous clerks of major towns strongly desired recognition. Like a modern Rotarian's button, their acquired medieval legacy is conspicuous, rich, and a matter of symbolic pride to the Coventry guildsmen. In Laneham's admiration for Captain Cox, such "auncient learning" and fashionable taste are not laughable or absurd. The awkward antics of illiterate peasants did make Laneham laugh; he ridicules the obvious, the clownish wedding, the burlesque tilt, the unserious minstrel's comic song. While Laneham may have exaggerated Captain Cox's library, perhaps supplementing it with his own, his tone is not ironic. He describes a broad range of traditional postmedieval secular literature he assumed to be worthy of respect, and significant of mobility.

III

Before we turn to the revival of the Ghost of Captain Cox in 1624, two of Jonson's earlier court masques that employ Renaissance Gothic themes and symbols should be considered first: the *Speeches at Prince Henry's Barriers* (6 January 1610) and the spectacular *Golden Age Restored* (performed twice, 6 and 8 January 1615), which concludes the first *Folio* of 1616. Then we shall examine the *Masque of Owls* and *The Fortunate Isles* of 1624–25, which more directly respond to the Elizabethan medievalism of Kenilworth and its milieu. While his masques represent only a single facet of Jonson's *oeuvres,* and his critical attitudes toward the past reflect only one aspect of Jacobean intellectual history, these works

30. See Carroll Camden, Jr., "Elizabethan Alamanacs and Prognostications," *The Library,* 4th ser. XII (1932), 83–108, 194–207.

reveal significant change, and are evidence of complex redefinitions being made in English thought at the beginning of the seventeenth century.

In other masques which will not be taken up here (*The Gipsies Metamorphosed,* the *Masque of Augurs*) and in his greater comedies, Jonson exhibits the climactic change in the new London of King James and a more sharply divided world: the coterie court, and the mass of fools outside in the teeming streets. Neomedieval nostalgia was becoming irrelevant; it had begun to fade with James's accession, and was almost gone by the second decade of his reign. A saturation point had been passed, perhaps signified in the king's own ambivalence about magic and witchcraft. Although Prince Henry's *Barriers* invokes the Arthurian scene of Hunnis's *Lady of the Lake* at Kenilworth, the mock solemnity of these tedious pageants had become apparent. Later, Jonson's archaism becomes increasingly satirical, and the medieval is reduced to burlesque.

The speeches Jonson wrote for Henry's investiture as prince of Wales in 1610 provide an ornate historical frame for the dancing of the "Barriers," a symbolic joust performed by the prince as "Meliadus" (the chivalric lover of the Lady of the Lake) with six dancing knights.[31] In effect, this masque is virtually parodied fifteen years later in the *Masque of Owls,* where Captain Cox and his six dancing owls perform before Prince Charles on his first visit to Kenilworth as new owner of the castle. But *Prince Henry's Barriers* is unrelieved by comedy; it rather stiffly maintains the pseudo-Gothic façade of Malorian myth. There are no songs, the verse form is pompous, end-stopped pentameter couplets, without metrical variation; the ceremory of Meliadus's symbolic shield and drum, the discovery of Arthur ("Arcturus") above, as a star illuminated, and Merlin's and Chivalry's emergence from "caves of sleep" supply the spectacle.

The main speech is Merlin's history of the realm and prophecy to the prince, which occupies 200 of the 426 lines of the masque. Its main theme is,

> . . . it is not since as then.
> No giants, dwarfs, or monsters here, but men.
> His arts must be to govern and give laws
> To peace. . . .
>
> (ll. 165–168)

31. Text in Orgel, *Complete Masques,* pp. 142–158.

The distance between the present and the past is constantly stressed, in both Merlin's and the Lady of the Lake's speeches; allusions to the Crusades give way to Edward III's founding of the wool trade, Elizabethan shipping, and the maintenance of peace ("If industry at home do not decline," l. 190).

> How brighter far than when our Arthur lived
> Are all the glories of this place revived! . . .
> All that is high or great or can comport
> Unto the style of majesty . . . this place here shows.
> Only the house of chivalry . . . decayed
> Or rather ruined seems, her buildings laid
> Flat with the earth that were the pride of time. . . .
>
> (ll. 24–36)

Jonson's similes link decayed medieval architecture with the Egyptian pyramids ("barbarous Memphian heaps . . . obelisks and columns broke and down . . . ," ll. 37–38). The House of Chivalry is a ruin,

> . . . (O that it yet not stands!),
> More truth of architecture there was blazed
> Than in all the ignorant Goths have razed . . .
>
> (ll. 53–55)

As expected, Arthur appears, calling upon Meliadus to restore glory to "these ruined seats of virtue, and build more," to take up the "cobwebbed and rusty . . . shields and swords" which afford "not a spark of luster." For all its severe decorum, the *Barriers* does not revive the "dusty shield and rusty lances" of chivalric romance. The medievalism is stale, and the obeisance to Gothic ancestors perfunctory, as if Jonson found little inspiration or imaginative power in Merlin and the Lady of the Lake, or Chivalry, "dead as a lethargy." When Arthur commands, "Let him be famous, as was Tristram, Tor / Lanc'lot and all our list of knighthood . . ." (ll. 84–87), the more recent "list" of Meres' *Palladis Tamia* (1598) strikes a discordant echo to Arthur's pun. Meres' censure of "books . . . stale when they be printed, in that they be common" is a moral denunciation of fiction as "no lesse hurtfull to youth than the works of Machiavell to age . . . ," viz.,

Bevis of Hamptoun, Guy of Warwick, Arthur of the Round Table, Huon of Burdeaux, Oliver of the Castle, The Four Sons of Aymon, Gargantua . . .

The Seven Champions, Howleglas, The Black Knight, The Castle of Fame. . . .[32]

Here, of course, are categorized many familiar titles of Captain Cox's books, not only "low," but evil and obscene. Arthur's Gothic heroes, already condemned in Ascham's *Schoolmaster* (1568), are faded, barbaric, and better destroyed than revived, in the opinion of many men of the world outside the courtly game played out in Henry's *Barriers*.

In *The Golden Age Restored* of 1615[33] Jonson confronts the grandeur and the decadence of past and present more directly, and makes a revisionary shift in their relations. The Iron Age of the Vices in the antimasque is banished by the Renaissance Astraea, who brings in the new Age of Gold. To celebrate the present, Pallas reawakens the "far-famed spirits of this happy isle," the ancient poets—Gower, Chaucer, Lydgate, Spenser. Their "buried arts . . . shall flourish" in the new light cast by Pallas' shield, the new age of plenty, liberty, and love. In the masque, the Gothic darkness is gone, "metamorphos'd" by the vision the goddesses produce. The four poets who have been revived descend to speak the new language of Jonson's verse, untinged by nostalgic archaism: "[their] sacred songs have gained the style / Of Phoebus' sons . . . or the Thracian lyre" (ll. 113–115). The old poets are called upon to restore the purer image of love, to teach the masquers, but in Jonson's perfected language of highly idealized memory, which transmutes medieval romance:

> It was a time of no distrust,
> So much of love had nought of lust,
>   None feared a jealous eye.
> The language melted in the ear . . .
>
>   (ll. 176–179)

Jonson's four spirits of ancient English poetry symbolize not history, but the art that transcends time; they represent not neomedieval nostalgia, but the self-awareness of the poet who gives them new language, his own —neither "barbarous" ancient verse, nor its drab imitation, for which Jonson condemned Spenser in 1619.

32. Smith, *Elizabethan Critical Essays,* II, pp. 308–309; cf. I, 4 (Ascham) and I, 323 (Nash).
33. Text in Orgel, pp. 224–232.

Both the high Gothic revival and the low postmedieval realism of the Elizabethan fete at Kenilworth that Jonson found in Laneham's *Letter* emerge in new terms in his masques of 1624. The *Masque of Owls* (19 August 1624)[34] is a monologue of 164 lines spoken by Captain Cox's Ghost, mock-heroically mounted on a paper and buckram horse, with six silent dancers dressed as owls. It satirizes mediocrity—the rough and the barren—both in the bourgeoisie as a socioeconomic class and in the "old" poetry. What is now archaic—"Gothic"—is therein ugly, comic, and stupid. Jonson uses Laneham's *Letter* to burlesque the passé medievalism that had entertained the court in the same setting fifty years before. The Ghost of Captain Cox appears riding on a hobby horse, a prop Jonson exploits in double ironies, on both the crude Coventry hippodrama, and Cox's "ancient" literature:

> Room, room, for my horse will wince
> If he come within so many yards of a prince,
> And though he have not on his wings,
> He will do strange things.
> He is the Pegasus that uses
> To wait on the Warwick muses,
> And on gaudy days he paces
> Before the Coventry graces . . .
> For to tell you true, and in rhyme,
> He was foaled in Queen Elizabeth's time. . . .
>
> (ll. 1–10)

This famous Captain Cox was "at Bullen with King Harry . . . [and] has a goodly library / By which he was discerned / To be one of the learned . . ." (ll. 24–28). Jonson's contempt for Cox's books hits the middle class for its vulgar pretension to significant culture and economic status. The six silent owls are modern bourgeois failures, laughable because they are aspiring, incompetent, and bankrupt: merchants of blue thread, cheese, and tobacco, an unemployed Spanish teacher, a penniless huntsman out on bail for swearing. Originally, the third owl was a Coventry Puritan and thread spinner whose trade is undone by the losses that follow on his own morality. Since the "wise town" has again put down the "May-games and morris," the threads once bought by the dancers and tourists who came to Coventry for the plays "now lies on

34. *Ibid.*, pp. 425–432.

his hands, . . . ready to choke him / In a skein of that broke him" (ll. 131–135). As noted earlier, this speech was cut in performance, as offensive to Coventry Puritans, and a usurious scrivener substituted.

Jonson's "Owls" are, of course, ultimately Horatian satiric clichés; they are also postmedieval estates' satire, like Chaucer's *General Prologue* portraits, flattering an elite urban audience's superiority to inarticulate provincials. Captain Cox and his historic play have become self-satirized symbols of a dead past:

> I come to play your host
> And feast your eyes and ears
> Neither with dogs nor bears
> Though that have been a fit
> Of our main shire wit. . . .
>
> (ll. 58–62)

The legacy of Cox's library has become a joke.

Jonson's separation of styles and strong sense of advance beyond "auncient" English poetry are even more clearly stated in *The Fortunate Isles* (9 January 1625),[35] the last masque he produced before King James's death, and I think also inspired by Laneham's *Letter*. The antimasque ridicules Captain Cox's favorites: *Howleglas,* Scogan, and Skelton enter (in "historic costume") and parody Skeltonic meters, at the bidding of the genius figure Johphiel. The Rosicrucian student, Merefool, is struggling to attain a dream vision, but when he asks for "Ellen of Troy," he gets Elinor Rumming. Jonson quotes Skelton at length, with relish:

> That comely Jill
> That dwelt on a hill . . .
> Her face all bowsy
> Droopy and drowsy
> Scurvy and lousy . . .
> Wonderly wrinkled
> Like a roast pig's ear
> Bristled with hair. . . .
>
> (ll. 235–244)

"Lean-witted Scogan" and Skelton's medieval Latin are burlesqued ("O, vir amplissimus . . . et gentilissimus!" ll. 208–210); the scorn of the

---

35. *Ibid.,* pp. 433–453.

modern poet for retrospective folly comes alive when the two "ancient poets" materialize before Merefool, "this Master of all knowledge in reversion" (l. 192). Then the ugly, noisy confusion of the Gothic comedy (Howleglas, Westminster Meg, Tom Thumb, Doctor Rat, among twelve zany antic dancers) vanishes by one of Jones's machines, to bring forth the realm of Neptune: the sea kingdom of Apollo, Proteus, Amphion, and the incredibly lovely nymphs who sing in such neoclassical palaces, celebrating the great lord of waters and of isles.

The decor of this luminous world is Ocean's riches and sea-born Venus, silk and pearls, the splendor and gold of Neptune's kingdom in triumph over the harsh Gothic darkness it has overcome. The "medieval" now fully symbolizes the grotesque, in the last brilliant masques of the Stuart court, which quite consciously measure the new art against the obsolete medievalism of early Elizabethan taste:

PROTEUS

Aye, now the heights of Neptune's honors shine
And all the glories of his greater style
Are read, reflected in this happiest isle . . .

SARON

These are the true groves
Where joys are born—

PROTEUS

Where longings—

PORTUNUS

And where loves!

SARON

That live!

PROTEUS

That last!

(ll. 484–500)

The Fortunate Isles ends with three shifts of scene: the advance and recession of Proteus's island, the discovery of Oceanus's maritime palace (with loud music), and finally, the prospective of the sea upon which the fleet appears, "while three cornets play," for the final celebration of

Neptune's power, and the king's. As in all of Jonson's masques, the
staging depends upon single-point perspective, fixed at the center where
the royal audience is seated. Within the coherent framework thus in-
visibly established, the dancing floor becomes the world of dramatic
illusion which Jonson's and Jones's arts transform. So focused, enclosed,
and confined, it becomes neutral space where the imagination can do its
work, paradoxically freed from the limitations of temporal and spatial
boundaries.

It is quite otherwise in Laneham's account of Elizabeth's Progress at
Kenilworth; we are made frequently aware of the heterogeneity of the
entertainments, and their cumulative incoherence. They are unified only
by the fixed backdrop of the castle and its environs, and the central figure
of the queen, as she moves from place to place—always the point of focus
and the pivot—but a moving center, whose attention is renewed by a
series of extremely varied, episodic spectacles. Read in retrospect through
Laneham's eyes, Leicester's fete resembles a gorgeously magnificent
country fair, offering some wonderful new diversion every day, inclusive
of many traditions and styles of ritual celebration of the queen's ancestors
and of Warwickshire itself.

When Jonson looked back to that already departed pageantry, he was
aware of the degeneration of the modern present and at the same time
of the barbarous and primitive past the Jacobean world superseded. He
includes both—and the visionary ideal world of art—in the clearly separated levels of illusion of his court masques. As others have well argued,
Jonson raised the ephemeral entertainment of the spectators to the level
of literature that lasts.

In Scott's *Kenilworth,* the Elizabethan revels will be trivialized, senti-
mentalized, and made quaint—"toyes and tryfellys" no more real than
child's play with miniature antique tin soldiers. In the detachment of
Discoveries, Jonson meditated on such folly, the desire to save such toys.
In a passage marked *de Stultitia,* he recognized and defended the necessary illusion of all art, ancient, medieval, and modern:

What petty things they are, we wonder at? Like children that esteem every
trifle; and preferre a Fairing before their Fathers; what difference is, between
us, and them? but that we are dearer Fooles, Cockscombs at a higher rate?
They are pleased with Cockleshels, Whistles, hobbyhorses, and such like; we
with Statues, marble pillars, pictures, guilded Roofes, where underneath is

Lath, and Lyme, and perhaps Lome. Yet we take pleasure in the lye, and are glad, we can cozzen ourselves.[36]

With the death of James in 1625 and the coronation of a second Stuart, the distances separating the modern world of the kingdom of Charles I from the postmedieval Elizabethan court dramatically increase. In the literary history of the age to come—that of Milton, parliament, and the triumphant Restoration—the epic themes of Arthurian romance will be found increasingly inadequate, while the implications of Captain Cox's literacy steadily advance.

36. *Ben Jonson*, ed. C. H. Herford and Percy and Evelyn Simpson (Oxford, 1925–1952), VIII, 607, ll. 1437–1445.

APPENDIX

The Repertoire of Captain Cox

"Great ouersight hath he in matters of storie: as for King Arthurz book, Huon of Burdeaus, The foour sons of Aymon, Beuys of Hampton, The sqyre of lo degree, The knight of courtesy and the Lady Faguell, Frederik of Gene, Syr Eglamour, Sir Tryamour, Sir Lamwell, Syr Isenbras, Syr Gawyn, Clyuer of the Castl, Lucres and Eurialus, Virgils life, The castle of Ladiez, The wido Edyth, The King & the Tanner, Frier Rous, Howleglas, Gargantua, Robinhood, Adambel, Clim of the clough & William of cloudesley, The Churl & the Burd, The seauen wise Masters, The wife lapt in a Morels skin, The sak full of nuez, The seargeaunt that became a Fryar, Skogan, Collyn clout, The Fryar & the boy, Elynor Rumming, The Nutbroun maid. With many moe then I rehearz heere: I beleeue hee haue them all at his fingerz endz. Then in Philosophy, both morall and naturall, . . . besides poetrie and Astronomie, and oother hid sciences . . . whearof part as I remember, The Shepherdz kalender, The Ship of Foolz, Daniels dreamz, The book of Fortune, Stans puer ad mensam, The hy wey to the Spitlhous, Iulian of Brainfords testament, The castle of Loue, The booget of Demaunds, The hundred Mery talez, The book of Riddels, The Seauen sorowz of wemen, The proud wiues Pater noster, The Chapman of a peniwoorth of Wit. Beside his auncient playz, Yooth & Charitee, Hikskorner, Nugize, Impacient pouerty. And herewith Doctor Boords breuiary of health. What shoold I reherz heer, what a bunch of ballets & songs, all auncient: As Broom broom on a hil, So wo iz me begon, troly lo, Ouer a whinny Meg, Hey ding a ding, Bony lass vpon a green, My bony gaue me a bek, By a bank az I lay, and a hundred more he hath, fair wrapt vp in Parchment and bound with a whipcord. And az for Allmanaks of antiquitee . . . I weene he can sheaw from Iasper Laet of Antwerp vnto Nostradam of Frauns, and the vnto oour John Securiz of Salzbury. To stay ye no longer therin, I dare say hee hath az fair a library for theez sciencez & az many goodly monuments both in prose & poetry, & at afternoons can talk az much without book, az ony Inholder betwixt Brainford and Bagshot. . . ."

Festival in Jonsonian Comedy

MICHAEL McCANLES

I N Epigram 101, "Inviting a Friend to Supper," Jonson declares that his festivity will celebrate a dedication to controlled liberty. The courses will be plain but well chosen, and of "rich Canary-wine, / Which is the Mermaids, now, but shall be mine," he says, "we will sup free, but moderately" (ll. 29–30, 35). The supper will hold in balance reason and appetite: "my man / Shall reade a piece of Virgil, Tacitus, / Livie, or of some better booke to us" (ll. 20–22), thereby feeding the revelers' minds while they feed their bodies. The talk will be sophisticated and humane, and "No simple word, . . . [shall] afright / The libertie, that wee'll enjoy to night" (ll. 39–42).[1] The notion of festivity described here, and

1. *Poems of Ben Jonson*, ed. G. B. Johnston (Cambridge, Mass., 1962), pp. 50–51. All citations from the plays are from *Ben Jonson*, ed. C. H. Herford and Percy and Evelyn Simpson (Oxford, 1925–1952). A similar balance is announced in the versified rules which Jonson wrote for the meetings of his Tribe in the Apollo room at the Devil Tavern:

> And let our only emulation be
> Not drinking much, but talking wittily.
> Let it be voted lawful to stir up
> Each other with a moderate chirping cup;

more completely in his comedies, forms part of Jonson's complex ethical ideal of man as literate humanist, whose mastery of the decorums of language enables him to discriminate the forms of verbal address appropriate to his own status, his audience, and his subject matter. Jonson's guest will be expected to manifest in his gestures and speech the inner qualities of self-control, self-knowledge, and considered judgment of his relations with others.

These ideals are defined in Jonson's comedies through their perversions. And a major definitive action is the perversion of festival, where the allowed freedom of festival is either rejected through hypocritical moral rigorism, or debased into license and debauchery. More positively, Jonson celebrates human and social bonds by exploiting characters who in the one way or the other exhibit an incapacity for such celebration. Several of Jonson's comedies not only include various true and perverted festivals, but taken together exhibit a single archetypal "festive action," a pattern of celebration that controls the actions of specific plays, and illuminates Jonson's understanding of dramatic comedy as well.[2]

> Let not our company be, or talk, too much;
> On serious things, or sacred, let's not touch
> With sated heads and bellies. Neither may
> Fiddlers unask'd obtrude themselves to play.
> With laughing, leaping, dancing, jests, and songs,
> And whate'er else to grateful mirth belongs,
> Let's celebrate our feastes: and let us see
> That all our jests without reflection be.

This is from Alexander Brome's translation of Jonson's Latin (ll. 13 ff.), quoted in Katherine A. Esdaile, "Ben Jonson and the Devil Tavern," *Essays and Studies,* XIX (1943), 93–100.

2. The festive element in Jonsonian comedy has not gone unnoticed. Devra R. Kiger, *"The Staple of News:* Jonson's Festive Comedy," *SEL,* XII (1972), 329–344, finds in that play an opposition between true and perverted festival similar to the one I deal with here. Two recent dissertations are concerned with patterns of action derived from contemporary seasonal festivals: Frances Dodson Rhome, "Variations of Festive Revel in Four English Comedies, 1595–1605" (Indiana University, 1969), regarding *A Tale of a Tub;* and Shirley Farley Ransom, "Myth and Ritual in Ben Jonson's Earlier Dramatic Satires" (Purdue University, 1972). Other studies that deal with festive elements in Jonson's plays include the following: Ian Donaldson, " 'A Martyr's Resolution': Jonson's Epicoene," *RES,* N.S., XVIII

Festivity and its perversion occur in Jonson's comedies in four distinct though related versions. The first of these versions opposes the rational liberty of true festival, and two parodic extremes where freedom and control are sundered and one is grotesquely exaggerated at the expense of the other. At one extreme are characters who, in their moralistic rigor, humorlessness, or lack of self-knowledge, cannot bend far enough to be capable of rational pleasure. At the other extreme we find festivity that perverts liberty into license. In the second version characters cut themselves off from the quotidian world of labor and social intercourse, and blindly pursue dreams of transcendence into another world of illusory freedom, power, and infinite wealth. Festivity becomes a delusive realm of unending self-gratification, an ever-beckoning chimera promising infinite pleasure and appetite, wherein the pressures of bodily limitations, common sense, reason, self-knowledge, and social duties are drowned in never-ending holiday.[3] The third version is the festival as confidence game. Here, intriguers play on the self-delusions of the would-be escapers from the everyday, debunking their fantasies while enticing them with offers of fulfillment. In this version, the intriguers' wit and intelligence mark them as the only ones who can laugh, while the gulls' susceptibility to gulling shows them likewise incapable of true festivity.

A fourth and final version of festival includes Jonson's audience as well. For not only do these plays exhibit various examples of festive celebration both upright and debased, but they also enact for the audience a festive occasion: the performance of a Ben Jonson comedy.[4] The audi-

---

(1967), 1–15; and Jonas A. Barish, "Feasting and Judging in Jonsonian Comedy," *RenD*, N.S. V (1972), 3–35. On the larger question of the place and function of festival and carnival in Renaissance culture, two studies which have been generally neglected by students of Renaissance drama are Mikhail Bakhtin, *Rabelais and His World,* trans. Helene Iswolsky (Cambridge, Mass., 1968), and his earlier study *Problems of Dostoevsky's Poetics,* trans. R. W. Rotsel (Ann Arbor, Mich., 1973).

3. Alvin Kernan takes this point in another direction: "Jonson's characters are all satiric portraits of Renaissance aspiration, of the belief that man can make anything he will of himself and of his world, that he can storm heaven and become one with the gods, or make of earth a new paradise." *The Cankered Muse: Satire of the English Renaissance* (New Haven, Conn., 1959), p. 181.

4. In the Prologue to *Epicoene* Jonson invites his audience to his play as to a feast:

ence is invited to join with the playwright and his surrogates on stage in
exorcising through laughter a wide range of pervertedly festive and
antifestive characters. Like the normative and redeemable characters in
the play's fictive world, the audience can participate in a Jonsonian festival only by banishing antifestive attitudes through mocking laughter.
This means not only that reason, common sense, and ethical restraint are
the operative norms in Jonson's comic vision—a notion universally agreed
upon—but that the capacity for pleasure and festivity are norms likewise.

One or more versions of festive action just outlined occur in most of
Jonson's comedies. In the earlier plays we find the antics of the would-be
courtiers in *Cynthia's Revels* and Ovid's blasphemous feast in *The
Poetaster*. Another example is Volpone's and Mosca's seamy vision of a
never-ending game of gulling and seduction, and I will refer to *Volpone*
in this connection later on. Among the later plays, *The Staple of News*
offers Penniboy Junior's feast of prodigality, while *The New Inn* explores
the games of love and wit sponsored by Goodstock at the sign of the
Light-Heart. However, the plays where festive actions most completely
carry thematic concern are *Every Man In His Humor, Epicoene, The*

> Our wishes, like to those make public feasts,
> Are not to please the cook's taste but the guests'.

At the end of *The Alchemist* Jonson speaking through Face addresses the audience
and says, referring to the commodities tricked out of the gulls:

> And this pelf
> Which I have got, if you quite me, rests
> To feast you often, and invite new guests.

The Staple of News, as Devra R. Kifer has noted (*SEL,* XII, 329–344), is connected with a pre-Lenten, Shrovetide feast. Finally, we find in Jonson's uncom-
pleted *The Sad Shepherd* a play directly concerned with festival, wherein Robin
Hood (described in the dramatis personae as "Master of the Feast") confronts the
mirth-destroying malevolence of the witch Maudlin, who in her opening speech
presents the exact perversion of the ideal festival described in Epigram 101 and
Jonson's Rules:

> Have I not left 'em in a brave confusion?
> Amaz'd their expectation? got their Venison?
> Troubled their mirth, and meeting? made them doubtfull,
> And jealous of each other? all distracted?
> And, in the close, uncertaine of themselves?
>
> (II.i.1–5)

Alchemist, and *Bartholomew Fair;* and it is on these plays that I intend
to concentrate here.

Every Man In His Humor opposes characters who have achieved a
balance between reason and mirth and characters who sacrifice one for
the other. From this viewpoint the pranks of Wellbred, Edward Knowell,
and Justice Clement contrast sharply with the mummery of Matthew,
Bobadil, and Stephen, who are incapable of either the intelligence or the
mirth of Jonson's ideal revelry. The play's central plot comes down to
this: Old Knowell is determined to save his son from what he interprets
as an idle life of debauchery. In turn, Edward Knowell and Wellbred
blithely pursue their *divertissements* up to the point late in the play when
Wellbred evolves the plan to marry Edward to Mistress Bridget. The
concluding marriage feast, presided over by the master of the revels
Justice Clement, is thus the final goal of the play, the achievement of the
play's norm of festivity. The rest of the characters—Kitely, his wife,
Downright, Cob, and Old Knowell—are all admitted to the feast only
after each has recognized his previous enslavement to obsessive illusion
and incapacity for laughter. Matthew and Bobadil, however, are found
totally incapable of sharing in the concluding celebration and therefore
are cast out from it: Justice Clement condemns them to "penitently fast
it out in my court, without; and, if you will, you may pray there that we
may be so merrie within, as to forgive or forget you, when we come
out" (V.v.52–54).

Here humorous obsession is registered mainly in opposition to intelligent play, which has to contend with two kinds of enemies. One of
these, figured forth in various degrees by Old Knowell, Kitely, and
Downright, is the stance of antifestivity. Though these characters exhibit
a certain amount of common sense and to that extent fulfill the Jonsonian
norm, it is at once apparent how far they fall short of it. Kitely's continual fantasizing about his wife's being taken in adultery, Downright's
belligerent railing at the festive characters, even Old Knowell's huffy
exclamations against youth's permissiveness and lack of reverence for
old age: all of these attitudes are subject to correction precisely because
they deny or ignore man's natural inclination to manifest his human
rationality in laughter.

On the other hand, if these characters represent only part of the required balance and so represent it falsely, the same is true in reverse of

Matthew, Bobadil, and Stephen. These three hangers-on strive mightily to mimic the graces of true poet, soldier, and man-about-town respectively, and represent the false mirth that Jonson will pillory more corrosively in the following comical satires. Mindlessly they parody festivity just as the humorlessness and suspicions of Downright, Kitely, and Old Knowell parody reason. They cannot achieve the ideal union of mirth and reason simply because they lack the latter, and consequently their mirth is deficient also. Unable to laugh as Wellbred and Edward Knowell do at them, they can only jeer at Downright's unfashionable sententiousness. And it is of course appropriate that Downright, the most extreme representative of reason without mirth, should be the mortal enemy of Matthew and Bobadil, the most extreme representatives of mirth without reason.

The play is about festivity struggling to be born and achieving its full maturity only after various incomplete parodies of it have first been unmasked and exorcised. What distinguishes the festive gambols of Wellbred, Edward Knowell, and Justice Clement is precisely what characterizes Jonson's comedies vis-à-vis their audience: both festive characters and audience are enabled to enjoy festivity to the exact degree that they laugh at the fatuities of those who can laugh neither at themselves nor at others. If festivity equals a release from care, the recognition that beyond all delusions and fears all is well, then here festivity itself is laughter at those who cannot achieve such freedom. The truly festive characters in Jonson's comedies can confront the fatuous obsessions of others without obsessive responses of their own (as Downright responds to the absurd Bobadil and Matthew), but rather with the recognition that all absolutes are relatives, and all obsessions are finally tempests in a teapot. The antifestive attitude can make no distinctions except one— between the absolutizing categories of the self, and a world of fools and knaves that these categories are posed against. Downright, Old Knowell, and Kitely see nothing but prodigality around them; Stephen dreams only of the beau monde to which mastery of the appropriate manners and fashions will introduce him; while Bobadil can conceive only of a world inhabited by no other persons save himself and a host of enemy swordsmen whom he perennially routs.

All of Jonson's normative festive characters in the plays I discuss here possess some or all of the following capabilities: (1) a large view of the field of play which enables them to perceive the possible trajectories of motivations and actions hidden to the gulls and fools, whose destiny it is to be carried blindly from intention to unforeseen consequence; (2) a refusal to believe that there is only one good (usually the security or aggrandizement of the self), and only one evil, namely, all those who would obstruct or threaten the self; (3) a recognition of the need to unmask the high pretensions that cloak low motives, of bringing out into the open the hidden springs of human action; (4) freedom from the entropy of human behavior toward rigidification and enslavement to mechanical actions and reactions; (5) finally, an understanding that festive laughter is the ultimate sign of the assertion of reason rather than a holiday from it. Unlike the description of Renaissance festival given by Mikhail Bakhtin,[5] for Jonson, to equate festival with the reduction of all human motivations to bodily appetite is to pervert it. Such reduction usually accompanies a corresponding transformation of these appetites into high idealism, a point made in *Volpone* as well as in the play that most strikingly unmasks meretricious antifestivity, *The Alchemist*. To set holiday over against the quotidian world without recognizing the ways in which holiday can itself degenerate into stultifying rigidity, is to fall into still another rigidification, another narrowing of vision. Consequently, Jonson's true revelers always seem able to encompass at once the everyday world of common sense and the festive world of laughter and ridicule, without either confounding the two or setting them in malign opposition.

5. In *Rabelais and His World* (pp. 285 ff., 316 ff., and *passim*) Bakhtin describes carnival as the obliteration of the boundaries, closures, and idealizations of official society, and the celebration of bodily processes, particularly eating, defecation, and sex. His description of the symposium (p. 285) as it descends from the ancient world and enters Rabelais sets up intricate cross-currents between itself and the Jonsonian symposium referred to in his Rules and Epigram 101. Bakhtin says: "The themes of table talk are always 'sublime', filled with 'profound wisdom', but these themes are uncrowned and renewed on the material bodily level. The grotesque symposium does not have to respect hierarchical distinctions; it freely blends the profane and the sacred, the lower and the higher, the spiritual and the material. There are no *mésalliances,* in this case," pp. 285–286. It is interesting to note that *The Alchemist* is particularly critical of Sir Epicure Mammon whose goal is precisely to blend "the profane and the sacred, the lower and the higher."

In *Epicoene* the perversion of festival takes several forms. Precisely because he possesses no balanced vision of quotidian order and decorum, Morose is the main embodiment of antifestivity. On the other hand, the two humorous knights, Sir Amorous La-Foole and Sir Jack Daw, would make every day a holiday with the Collegiate ladies. In these characters the incapacities for either festivity or seasoned observance of ordinary behavior mutually confirm each other. The festive norms in the play are Dauphine, Clerimont, and Truewit. Truewit in particular holds in balance festive and quotidian values, and the wit that sponsors this balance enables him to manipulate those less witty than himself. As Barish notes, Truewit is very hard to pin down to a particular attitude.[6] His flexibility fulfills one of Jonson's ethical ideals, of which moral relativism is only a perversion. More broadly, the art with which these three characters manipulate the plot of the play measures their freedom from the inflexible compulsions that drive their victims.

The Collegiates, the Otters, and the two knights are noisily gregarious out of pure egoism; Morose would reduce all society to rigid silence. However, the insight of Clerimont, Truewit, and Dauphine into the hidden springs of fear and desire that motivate the other characters manifests their own true sociability. And just as in the play art corrupts nature by rejecting it and egoism perverts social intercourse to the ends of self-aggrandizement, so all the would-be revelers pervert festivity because they cannot relate it to ordinary human behavior. Sir Amorous La-Foole invites people to dinner out of an upper-story window as they drive by in their carriages; Captain Otter's highest joy is a drinking contest with his huge cups; the Collegiate ladies make spectacles of themselves as pseudo-intellectuals while secretly cultivating adultery. All these characters aspire to a perpetual holiday in which festivity is all the order there is. The appropriate enemy of their perverted festivity is thus not sobriety, but Morose's compulsive misanthropy. Morose's desire to muffle the entire auditory world, leaving his own voice the sole sound to be heard, a cosmos turned anechoic chamber, asks for and indeed demands the raucous explosions of the revelers' festive noise. The glee with which the audience watches the revelers drive Morose up into the

6. Jonas A. Barish, *Ben Jonson and the Language of Prose Comedy* (Cambridge, Mass., 1967), pp. 156–157.

attic, his head swathed in nightcaps, ought not to obscure the fact that, while Morose's antifestive rigidity offers no reasonable norm, the debauches of folly and knavery among his tormentors do not offer one either. Rather, Morose and the revelers all pervert the rational festivity Jonson would offer us, and this perversity is signaled to us by the way that both extremes at once generate and attack each other.

The play's festive action might be summarized as follows: Each character believes he controls one intrigue while becoming unwittingly the tool in another. Dauphine is the only one, besides Cutbeard, who knows the truth of the Epicoene intrigue. In turn Clerimont and Truewit control the rest of the intrigues while ignorant of Dauphine's plot. Sir Jack Daw and Sir Amorous La-Foole participate in the plot against Morose, only to find themselves gulled by Clerimont and Truewit into challenging each other to a duel. In the second half of the play, Dauphine inveigles Morose into a plot to annul his marriage to Epicoene, but he in turn is victimized by the noise of the wrangling divine and canon lawyer, played by Otter and Cutbeard. These latter two likewise cooperate ignorantly in their own gulling, in that the pedantic roles they play ironically extend to absurdity their own pretensions to Latinate learning.

As in *Volpone,* the line between fools and knaves continually shifts. Each becomes vulnerable to comic manipulation to the exact degree that he believes his own view of the field of play to be the only one possible (like the blind men and the elephant), and each presumes on his power to manipulate someone else.[7] Truewit's attempt to help Dauphine by disrupting the marriage between Morose and Epicoene runs afoul of Dauphine's larger intrigue which depends on Morose's believing that he

7. See my section on *Volpone* in "Mythos and Dianoia: A Dialectical Methodology of Literary Form," in *Literary Monographs 4,* ed. Eric Rothstein (Madison, Wis., 1971), pp. 56–65: The fools and gulls in Jonson's plays "are motivated by rigid, univocal purposes which project and imply a society of mechanical monomania as the ideal context in which to realize their desires. Whether they are thwarted by the more flexible Lovewits and Truewits, or by characters of their own ilk like Volpone and Mosca, they come to suffer themselves the reflex of their intentions and actions, because they are constitutionally unable to take into account the demands of flexibility and common sense which Jonson's [themes] press in upon them. They move encumbered by the blinders of their own obsessions and cannot see beyond the unidimensional thrusts of their understanding of themselves and of the world around them," p. 57.

is married to Epicoene. Jonson's ironies thus play across the blindered visions of all the characters, although some have more peripheral vision than others. In fact, blindered vision proves to be the lever that sets in motion the play's festive action. Almost every character equivocates in wishing to remain outside the arena of festive play, while at the same time indulging his own imagined festive freedom of control. Festivity in this play equals the attempt to impose one's own will on others, to create a world in which one's self alone is master of the field of play. And as always in Jonson's dynamic ethic the difference between folly and wisdom is a matter of degree rather than of kind.

The Alchemist's festive action links the confidence games of Face, Subtle, and Dol with the dreams of unrestrained self-gratification with which they entice Mammon, Dapper, Drugger, Ananias, and Tribulation Wholesome. The "itch of mind" (IV.vi.93) that lures all the gulls here is most clearly and pervertedly festive in Mammon's fantasies of unending lust:

> Wee'll therefore goe with all, my girle, and live
> In a free state; where we will eate our mullets,
> Sous'd in high-country wines, sup phesants egges,
> And have our cockles, boild in silver shells,
> Our shrimps to swim againe, as when they liv'd,
> In a rare butter, made of dolphins milke,
> Whose creame do's looke like opalls: and, with these
> Delicate meats, set our selves high for pleasure,
> And take us downe again, and then renew
> Our youth, and strength, with drinking the *elixir,*
> And so enjoy a perpetuitie
> Of life, and lust. And, thou shalt ha'thy wardrobe,
> Richer than *Natures,* still, to change thy selfe,
> And vary oftner, for thy pride, then shee:
> Or Art, her wise, and almost-equall servant.
>
> (IV.i.155–169)

For the gulls the philosopher's stone becomes a fetish, a mythical key to some fabulous domain where the limits and debilities of everyday existence, the entropy of mere flesh and blood, will have been finally escaped, and festival reigns unendingly. As Bakhtin points out, a central piece of carnival business is the hawking of spurious wares, prodigies, food, drink, and medicines[8] (*Volpone* gives us an extended version of this sort of thing), all promising an ever-increasing appetite fed by an inexhaustible cornucopia of commodities. In this respect, the confidence game of Subtle and Face is overtly carnivalesque. Still another aspect of medieval and Renaissance carnivals was the costumed characters in whom the people could behold distorted versions of themselves.[9] Subtle, Face, and Dol all play different roles for each of the gulls, ironically reflecting the truth of their own concealed expectations. If Mammon confounds the purity of spiritual discipline with the basest of carnal appetites, then this confusion is mirrored back to him by Subtle, who dresses in the role of an ascetic priest of alchemy and enjoins on Sir Epicure nothing but abstinence and high sentiments. In another direction, the philosopher's stone becomes for the Separated Brethren the key to gaining all those earthly powers that their persecuted state deprives them of. The covertly materialistic goals of Ananias and Tribulation Wholesome are thus unmasked when with much evangelistic rhetoric they pursue transformation of widows' and orphans' goods into gold.

It is interesting to note that Mammon's fantasies are not limited to pursuing "a perpetuitie Of life, and lust." He also imagines that he will "undertake, withall, to fright the plague / Out o'the kingdome, in three months" (II.i.69–70). And after the alchemical furnace and retorts have all exploded, Face bathetically recalls one of Mammon's pet projects:

> he would ha'built
> The citie new; and made a ditch about it
> Of silver, should have runne with creame from *Hogsden:*
> That, every sunday in *More*-fields, the younkers,
> And tits, and tom-boyes should have fed on, *gratis.*
>
> (V.v.76–80)

For Mammon holiday freedom vanquishes the constraints of the quotidian world, and his corrupted vision conjures up something of the millennial yearning which, as Bakhtin points out, seems to have hovered around medieval carnivals.[10] This attempt to domesticate festival, to

8. Bakhtin, *Rabelais and His World,* pp. 159–162.
9. *Ibid.,* pp. 265 ff.
10. *Ibid.,* p. 256.

methodize dreams and bring them into the everyday service of peasants and citizens is for Jonson one of Mammon's most meretricious goals, for it eradicates the boundary line between reason and festivity on which the true man of wit must balance.

As I have suggested, the true man of wit is enabled to live at once in the festive and quotidian worlds. Like Wellbred, Edward Knowell, Truewit, Clerimont, and Dauphine, Lovewit in this play has succeeded in domesticating festivity—not through an escape from reason, but rather by recognizing that reason is also play, and that the highest goal of reason is to exercise itself in witty entertainment. This is why Jonson has Lovewit refuse to chastise his servant Jeremy, but say to him:

> Come sir,
> You know that I am an indulgent master:
> And therefore, conceale nothing. What's your med'cine,
> To draw so many severall sorts of wild-fowle?
> *Face:* Sir, you were wont to affect mirth, and wit: . . .
>
> (V.iii.76–80)

And Lovewit joins the masquerade himself by putting on Surly's Spanish costume to marry Dame Pliant; as Kastril says to him, "thou are a Jovy'Boy!" (V.v.144). The final marriage between wit and festivity is celebrated when Lovewit agrees to seize all the goods Face and Subtle have accumulated:

> That master
> That had receiv'd such happinesse by a servant,
> In such a widdow, and with so much wealth,
> Were very ungrateful, if he would not be
> A little indulgent to that servants wit,
> And helpe his fortune, though with some small straine
> Of his own candor. Therefore, gentlemen,
> And kind Spectators, if I have out-stript
> An old mans gravitie, or strict canon, thinke
> What a yong wife, and good braine may doe:
> Stretch ages truth sometimes, and crack it too.
>
> (V.v.146–156)

In an archetypal action of carnival, where age is transformed into youth,[11] reason and pleasure join in Lovewit, and an "old man" is rejuvenated.

11. *Ibid.,* pp. 352, and *passim.*

Such real alchemy as this play affords lies, of course, not in the philosopher's stone, but in the "magic" by which Subtle, Face, and Dol transform the ridiculous delusions of the gulls into somewhat more homely profits. For them, there are no delusions of escape into a world of unending power and pleasure; on the contrary, life is something one lives by one's wits. And it is here that Jonson makes one of his most important points. Like Volpone and Mosca, Subtle, Face, and Dol are intriguers, manipulators of fools and gulls, perverted commentators on the moral and psychological perversions of their victims. They are, in other words, corrupted satirists, corrupted versions of the true master of the revels, in short, corruptions of Jonson himself. What these set up in Lovewit's house is a version of Jonson's own play, complete with costumes, phony dialects and cant, and the stage properties of alchemical equipment. The confidence men and woman are consummate actors, and they offer their victims, in effect, a perverted festival play, a performance dedicated to battening on the delusions of their audience. Jonson exhorts his own audience to self-recognition specifically by inviting it to see in his festival play another kind of festival play, one wherein people like themselves are inveigled to act out their potentialities for false festival. As in *Every Man In His Humor, Epicoene,* and *Bartholomew Fair,* the audience learns that it may securely laugh with and participate in a Jonsonian festival only by joining with the playwright in banishing perverted festival, a banishment which constitutes Jonson's play itself.

The Smithfield fair portrayed in *Bartholomew Fair* exhibits the most extensive similarities and differences in comparison with the medieval and Renaissance carnivalesque described by Bakhtin. The similarities are these: (1) it offers an escape from the workaday restrictions on the appetites; (2) it subverts the pretensions of established morality, the law, and respectability; (3) it transforms downward into bodily appetite the characters' aspirations to transcendent norms of behavior and belief; (4) it opens up unrestricted preying of one person on another: filchings (Edgeworth), games of abuse (the Vapors), and soliciting (Captain Whit's and Knockem's soliciting of Win and Mrs. Overdo to become prostitutes).[12] However, these items constitute only part of the action within the fiction of Jonson's play, and by no means do they exhaust

12. *Ibid.:* for (1) and (2) see pp. 88 ff.; (3) pp. 94 ff.; (4) pp. 147 ff.

Jonson's own presentation. Unlike contemporary Renaissance notions of the carnivalesque such as Bakhtin defines, for Jonson the shifting and dynamic reciprocity between the quotidian and the festive dictates a dual potentiality for both a harmony between them, and mutual corruption of one by the other. This dual potentiality will not allow Jonson simply to pose ideal festival off against the narrow workaday world, or regenerative bodily appetite against the stultifying claims of reason. Rather, he distinguishes more complexly between a balanced accommodation of both values, and the possible corruption of the values of one stance by those of the other. Not only may rigid antifestivity yield to a festive freedom perverted into license, but festivity itself may generate a waspish and quarrelsome rejection of festivity. Some characters in the play act as if festivity can stand unbalanced by quotidian values, while others believe that it must be quashed by moral rigorism. And since true festivity must harmoniously accommodate its opposite, while false festivity and rigid moralism at once dialectically generate and fight each other, the perversions of either stance can be annulled only if they are annulled together.

In *Bartholomew Fair* the perverse relation between festivity and the everyday appears in two forms that are really versions of each other. On the one side, the fair is viewed with varying degrees of indignation as a place of "enormities" and depravity (Justice Overdo), of idolatry and sin (Zeal-of-the-Land Busy), or of mere folly (Quarlous and Waspe). On the other side are those who see the fair as an escape from the restrictions of orthodox morality: John Littlewit and Win his wife, Zeal-of-the-Land Busy (again!), Mrs. Overdo, and Dame Purecraft are all secretly titillated by the gaminess of the fair and its sleazy reputation. Fittingly, all of these characters are transformed into opposites of themselves, secret identities that they covertly seek in the fair and yet would deny. Win and Mrs. Overdo finally come to wear the green gown of the prostitute; Zeal-of-the-Land Busy along with Justice Overdo end up in the stocks, victims of their own moralism; Waspe enacts an extreme version of himself in the game of Vapors; while Dame Purecraft pursues her silly belief in fortunetellers by wooing the insane Trouble-All under the delusion that she is destined to marry a madman. The fair is at once the negation of the everyday world and its negative image. All confront their own secret selves here, blown up and distorted as in a fun-house mirror, images which yet, like the distortional art of Jonson's comic practice, tell an essential truth.

For other characters in the play the festive world *is* the ordinary world. For Ursula, Edgeworth, Jordan Knockem, Captain Whit, Lanthern Leatherhead, Joan Trash, their very livelihood depends on catering to and battening on the festive appetites of others. In this respect, the Smithfield fair is only relatively removed from the busy bustle of London. For the fair's denizens pleasure is truly their business, and Jonson is the first playright to exploit the equivocal status of the public entertainer, moving his audience back and forth between platform and tiring-house to confront the sweat and humorless effort that lie behind the projected fantasies. Like *Epicoene* and *The Alchemist, Bartholomew Fair* is a play about playing in several senses of the term, not the least of which deals with the art of the playactor, the putter-on of shows. We are left, of course, with the realization that whatever enticements the fair offers are very much a function of the projections of those who come to it. These, like the would-be intriguers in *Epicoene* and the customers in *The Alchemist*, believe that the offered enticements are in fact real and palpable, and not simply the projections of their own desires—and this belief makes them eminently vulnerable to gulling. By portraying the earnest labors of Lanthern Leatherhead, Joan Trash, and Ursula, along with the equally earnest desperation of Subtle, Face, and Dol, Jonson opens out for his audience how susceptible to attack is a festive desire which maintains no anchorage in the world of everyday common sense. Ultimately, the fair is nothing but a heap of trash and greasy booths, all transformed like a sort of *materia prima* by the uncontrolled invention of the fairgoers themselves.

If Jonson's comedies are themselves festive occasions, the dramatic mimesis of men and women just like the audience, acting out for the latter its own potential for perverted festival, then Jonson's comic practice can likewise be seen as a continual exploration of the ethical strengths and social values of the comic-festive genre itself. As Paul Goodman has pointed out, the typical Jonsonian comic plot is like a balloon that blows up larger and larger until it finally explodes.[13] In the comedies I have

13. Paul Goodman, *The Structure of Literature* (Chicago, 1954), p. 86.

discussed here we find Jonson eliciting in the audience a growing expectation and suspense, as it awaits the final explosion to shatter the frail fantasies of intriguers, confidence men, and victims alike. The audience's expectations are guided by its awareness of the comic hubris that attends a feverish and unqualified belief in the power of cunning, disguise, and foresight to control the rest of the world according to a lust after infinite holiday. It expects the final catastrophe knowing full well that such intricate planning cannot indefinitely ward off the pressures of the accidental and the unforeseen, all those chances and changes of the workaday world that Jonson's characters dream of escaping.

If this adequately sums up the dynamics of comic emotion that Jonson's comedies create in their audience, then we may ask further whether the playwright is not benignly manipulating his audience, just as the Wellbreds, Truewits, and Lovewits, and their debased counterparts, the Volpones, Subtles, and Edgeworths, manipulate their chosen gulls within the plays themselves. In this respect, Jonson's plays invite the audience to participate in a dramatic festival-gone-haywire, but with this important addition: the plays dictate the norms of true festival which the audience must agree to as the condition of this participation. Part of the essential action of festivals, as C. L. Barber points out, is the exorcising of characters incapable of revelry.[14] These characters become scapegoats for the revelers, who load on them their own potential for festival-destroying care, obsession, and antisocial sterility. To the extent that Jonson's plays themselves portray the banishment of perverse festival, the audience participates simultaneously in this banishment and consequently in the true festival which is a Jonson play, the moment it begins to anticipate with growing laughter the final hooting from the stage of the perverters of festival. In short, Jonson's plays are festival actions in which the liberty of

---

14. C. L. Barber, *Shakespeare's Festive Comedy,* pp. 8-9:

The butts in the festive plays consistently exhibit their unnaturalness by being kill-joys. On an occasion "full of warm blood, of mirth," they are too preoccupied with perverse satisfactions like pride or greed to "let the world slip" and join the dance. . . . Craven or inadequate people appear, by virtue of the festive orientation, as would-be revellers, comically inadequate to hear the chimes at midnight. Pleasure thus becomes the touchstone for judgment of what bars it or is incapable of it. . . . While perverse hostility to pleasure is a subject for agressive festive abuse, highflown idealism is mocked too, by a benevolent ridicule which sees it as a not unnatural attempt to be more than natural.

true festival is released at the same moment that the license of false festival is exorcised by laughter. Only an audience made up of persons open to recognizing themselves identified in Jonson's fools and knaves can earn the right to deny that identification as the play progresses to its comic peripeteia. The release by laughter, the comic analogue to tragic catharsis, is ultimately twofold: a release from enslavement to self-delusive fantasies of perverted festival, and a release for participation in true festival. And it was the triumph of Jonson's genius as both playwright and public moralist that his plays should enact at once with wondrous economy the exorcism of mirth-destroying obsessions and the celebration of that exorcism.

Merlin and the Prince:
The Speeches at Prince Henry's Barriers

MARY C. WILLIAMS

PRINCE HENRY'S BARRIERS was a festive tourney held at the banquet house at Whitehall on 6 January 1610. The setting was designed and constructed by Inigo Jones, and the speeches which framed the combats were composed by Ben Jonson.[1] Already King James had set the following 4 June 1610 for the ceremony of investing his fifteen-year-old elder son with the title of Prince of Wales. The young prince, who was skilled in arms and chivalric exercises, was eager to demonstrate his worth and his promise as future ruler. In December 1609, using the name Meliades, Lord of the Isles, he had issued a challenge to combat to the knights of Great Britain. The opportunity to accept the challenge, or still better, to be one of the prince's assistants at the Barriers, was of course, much desired by gentlemen of the court. Elaborate preparations were undertaken to make the occasion a splendid one. In fact, the whole bill for "perles, Silkes & other necessaries," the weapons, "the works" provided by Inigo

1. Ben Jonson, *The Speeches at Prince Henry's Barriers*, in *Ben Jonson, The Complete Masques*, ed. Stephen Orgel (New Haven, Conn., 1969). Citations to the *Speeches* in the text are to this edition.

221

Jones, and the fees paid to actors and to Inigo Jones and Ben Jonson finally reached £2,466. Expenses for settings alone came to £550. In the tourney itself, the prince and his six assistants each fought with eight opponents in two separate combats, push of pike and swords, across a barrier positioned in the middle of the banqueting house. The king, the queen, two ambassadors, and a multitude of courtiers viewed the combats, which began before 10:00 P.M. and lasted through the night. Naturally, the spectators were overjoyed to witness the young prince's bravery, strength, and agility.[2] They must have been deeply stirred by the vision of England's future under such an able and valiant prince.

It is to the patriotic and political aspects of the affair that Ben Jonson and Inigo Jones address themselves in the spectacle and speeches that surrounded the combats. These speeches represent Jonson's only work based on Arthurian legends. What use Jones and Jonson make of Arthurian material for thematic effects, informing it with other values and materials, historical, political, ethical, and personal, is the subject I wish to discuss. Arthurian characters and events appear to have been selected to emphasize that for proper interpretation of his role in reviving British chivalry, the young prince has need of the guidance of the poet.

An Arthurian setting for the *Speeches* was not required, despite Herford and Simpson's statement that because the prince had styled himself "Meliadus, Lord of the Isles," Jonson's "cue was already in a great degree defined."[3] Other authors do not connect Meliades, the prince's title, with an Arthurian Meliadus. Daniel, in his masque, *Tethys Festival,* presented in June of 1610 as part of the celebration accompanying the prince's investi-

2. Contemporary accounts of the Barriers and reports of expenditures are to be found in *Ben Jonson,* ed. C. H. Herford and Percy and Evelyn Simpson, 11 vols (Oxford, 1925-1952), X, 508-514 (hereafter cited as "Herford and Simpson"). Both Herford and Simpson (II, 283; X, 512 n) and Stephen Orgel (*The Complete Masques,* p. 480) appear to be confused about the relationship of the Barriers (January 1610) to the investiture ceremony (June 1610). Herford and Simpson first reverse the order of the two occasions (II, 283) and then, in attempting a correction, transfer the investiture from 4 June to 6 January, the date of the Barriers (X, 512 n); Orgel says that "the Barriers celebrated the investiture of James's eldest son as Prince of Wales" (p. 480), without noting that the investiture ceremony would not be held for five months.

3. Herford and Simpson, II, 283.

ture as Prince of Wales, speaks of Meliades as Neptune's son and creates a masque of classical gods and of nymphs who represent rivers.[4] And William Drummond gives a non-Arthurian source for Meliades: in a note to his elegy on Prince Henry, "Tears on the Death of Moeliades," he comments that the name "which in these verses is given to Prince Henry, is that which he himself, in the challenges of his martial sports and masquerades, was wont to use, MOELIADES, PRINCE OF THE ISLES, which, in anagram, maketh MILES A DEO." [5]

It seems, then, that Jonson was not restricted to Arthurian legends. Nor was he by temperament attracted to Arthurian romance; his references to it are mainly disparaging, and he once nominated as fit for burning "the whole summe / Of errant Knight-hood" along with Merlin's marvels.[6] On the other hand, William Drummond notes about Jonson: "for a Heroik poeme he said ther was no such Ground as King Arthurs fiction." [7] The speeches for the Barriers gave Jonson an opportunity to treat Arthurian material in a heroic manner; and because King James was viewed as King Arthur come again, the use of Arthurian legend was highly appropriate. But even when he had settled on identifying Meliades as an Arthurian Meliadus, he had a variety of characters and incidents available to him, since there are two Arthurian characters named Meliadus. King Meliadus, the father of Tristan, who appears briefly in Malory's *Morte Darthur,* is featured in *Meliadus de Leonnoys,* the first part of a thirteenth-century romance, *Palamedes.* Among other adventures, Meliadus participates in a great tournament in which he injures Le Bon Chevalier Sans Peur and carries off Le Bon Chevalier's paramour, the Queen of Scotland.[8] In this work Meliadus is a heroic figure.

But Jonson, ignoring this chivalric hero, uses instead the Meliadus of *Les Prophécies de Merlin,* a late-thirteenth-century work which contains

4. Samuel Daniel, *The Complete Works in Verse and Prose of Samuel Daniel,* ed. Alexander B. Grosart, 5 vols. (1885; repr. New York, 1963), III, 301–323.

5. *The Poetical Works of William Drummond of Hawthornden,* ed. William B. Turnbull (London, 1890), p. 72 n.

6. Herford and Simpson, VIII, 205.

7. *Conversations with Drummond,* in Herford and Simpson, I, 136.

8. Cedric E. Pickford, "Miscellaneous Prose Romances," in *Arthurian Literature in the Middle Ages,* ed. Roger Sherman Loomis (Oxford, 1959), pp. 348–349.

many cloudily expressed political prophecies of events of the twelfth and thirteenth centuries, intermixed with romantic tales. Throughout most of this work Merlin has already been immured in his tomb by the Lady of the Lake, to be released only by Christ. Meliadus, the son of Meliadus of Lyonnesse and his mistress, the Queen of Scotland, is a lover of the Lady of the Lake, who persuades her to take him to Merlin's tomb.[9] Through him a number of Merlin's prophecies are transmitted from the sage within the tomb to scribes in other places. Far from being Lord of the Isles, this Meliadus is only a go-between.

Jonson was drawn to *Les Prophécies,* I believe, because of its political nature and because of the centrality of Merlin. From it Jonson takes the Lady of the Lake, King Arthur, Merlin, and Meliadus. He adds one other character, the allegorical figure Chivalry. Jonson then devises a ceremony, adapted from *Les Prophécies:* the presentation by the Lady of the Lake of Meliadus, long-preserved for this occasion, at the court of King James.[10] Meliadus, who is not the Lady's lover but her foster child, has been transformed into a heroic champion by combining his story with another, also told in *Les Prophécies*—that of Sir Lancelot, the foster son of the Lady of the Lake who takes him to King Arthur's court to be made knight. Jonson gives the presentation historical significance: Meliadus has been brought here at this particular time because the court under James, the new Arthur, has regained its ancient fame. Yet the Lady's speech stresses that chivalry is still in decay, and the scene painted on the shutters beside which she stands is one of most impressive ruins.[11] Depicted there is the Fallen House of Chivalry—not a house but a scene of a road surrounded by broken arches and columns with trees growing from the ruins of buildings.

Presumably there is a cloudscape above the shutters, and as the Lady's voice pierces the clouds, the cloudscape parts, revealing King Arthur, who

9. *Les Prophécies de Merlin,* ed. Lucy Allen Paton, 2 vols. (New York, 1926), I, 184.

10. W. Todd Furniss declares that "the ritual ceremony forms a part of every masque" Jonson composed. "Ben Jonson's Masques," in Richard B. Young, W. Todd Furniss, and William G. Madsden, *Three Studies in the Renaissance* (New Haven, Conn., 1958), p. 106.

11. Stephen Orgel and Roy Strong, *Inigo Jones: The Theatre of the Stuart Court,* 2 vols. (Berkeley and Los Angeles, 1973), I, 158, Plate 36.

has been "translated to a star" (l. 67).[12] Arthur explains that "Merlin's mystic prophecies" are now fulfilled in the union of England and Scotland and the coming of the second Arthur to the throne (ll. 74–77). He then lowers to the Lady a shield for presentation to Meliadus; on it is "wrought / The truth that he must follow" (ll. 94–95). Arthur next instructs the Lady to release the prophet Merlin to interpret the shield for Meliadus. Merlin rises from his tomb and summons Meliadus, whereupon the shutters part to reveal a new scene, reminiscent of the first, though the buildings are in less disrepair. But at the center now is St. George's Portico, an ornately decorated little building.[13] In the central archway of the Portico, where the lines of perspective meet, stands the new champion Meliadus.

Through a discourse on British history, the longest and most important speech of the Barriers, Merlin sets forth the truth that Meliadus must follow. Then, after King Arthur's shield is presented to Meliadus, Chivalry herself appears from her cave at the right of the stage set. The combats of the Barriers follow, concluded by a short speech from Merlin. The immurement of Merlin, the presentation ceremony, the importance of Merlin, his transmission of prophecies to Meliadus, and the application of the prophecies to political affairs of the author's own time and country have been taken over and adapted by Jonson from his source. The dignified and heroic tone of the *Speeches* is quite different, however, from that of *Les Prophécies,* which ranges from romantically pedestrian to grandiosely apocalyptic.

Also, all the drama of the spectacle—the appearances of Arthur from the heavens, Merlin from his tomb, Meliadus in his Portico, Chivalry from her cave—has been added by Jones and Jonson. Still another aspect of the spectacle contributed by the author and designer is noteworthy: the mixture of classical with medieval elements in the architecture depicted. In Inigo Jones's design the Fallen House of Chivalry includes the pyramid of Cestus, the temple of Antoninus and Faustine, the arch of Titus, and other Roman ruins.[14] The perspective stage set includes a Norman castle,

12. Since the Middle Ages, the identification of Arcturus with Arthurus had been common, and both the star Arcturus and its constellation Bootes were known as Arthurus, according to Herford and Simpson, X, 514–515.

13. Orgel and Strong, *Inigo Jones,* I, 164–165, Plate 37.

14. *Ibid.,* I, 163.

Trajan's column, and a triumphal arch,[15] while the domed Portico, with Romanesque and Gothic arches, is decorated with statues in niches. That Jonson as well as Jones envisioned a scene symbolic of Britain's past as having classical elements is clear from the Lady's speech, which refers to "those obelisks and columns broke and down / That struck the stars and raised the British crown / To be a constellation" (ll. 38–40). As Gail Kern Paster points out, Jonson conceives of classical architecture as didactic; the "truth of architecture" (l. 54) here instructs in "human potentiality and . . . universal mutability," in national greatness, and in chivalric valor.[16] The Roman buildings in these sets suggest, furthermore, that chivalry is not simply a matter of romantic adventurousness or even comradeship of loyal knights; it represents formality, dignity, order, harmony—classical as well as medieval qualities. In restoring chivalry, the prince will restore classical splendor and classical ideals.

In the speeches that accompany the scenic effects, Jonson explores the meaning objectified by this setting and by the goddess Chivalry. He also affirms the present glory of the British court, instructs the prince in political wisdom, and presages a glorious future for Britain. In these speeches, Arthur, the ideal king, and Merlin, the prophet, are given associations and symbolic values with specific applications for the occasion.

The associations that Jonson summons up in connection with Arthur are, first of all, political. The legendary King Arthur united England and Wales and reigned over England in what was commonly thought of as England's Golden Age. Like Henry VII, King James traced his ancestry to this great king. Because James united England and Scotland, he was hailed as King Arthur come again to restore the Golden Age of Britain.[17] When he "claimes Arthurs seat" (l. 21), the words constitute an anagram for Charles Iames Stuart.[18] The audience is not only warmed with patriotic feelings about the greatness of Britain in chivalric times under an ideal king but reminded of the political benefits that King James has brought to Britain, as well as of his claim to the throne through his Arthurian descent. Both King Arthur and the Lady of the Lake, moreover, speak of

15. *Ibid.*, I, 39.

16. "Ben Jonson and Architecture," *RQ*, XXVII (1974), 318–319.

17. Roberta F. Brinkley, *Arthurian Legend in the Seventeenth Century*, Johns Hopkins Monographs in Literary History III (New York, 1967), pp. 6–13.

18. Herford and Simpson, X, 514.

James as a monarch even greater than Arthur. The past is used to compliment the present.

Also, the appearance of Arthur as a star suggests heavenly direction for the prince and gives visual embodiment to a continuing metaphor of chivalry and glory as brightness.[19] Brightness represents not only the blaze of glory and fiery daring as in the fiery victories of the Black Prince (l. 263), but the ideal qualities of James's kingdom ("the golden vein / Of Saturn's age is here broke out again," ll. 333–334) and the heavenly "light" of the king's virtues (justice, fortitude, prudence, peacefulness, ll. 398–400), as well as of the bright fortune to come (ll. 408–409). Through this metaphor, the honor and daring of knighthood are allied to the virtues of wise and peaceful government and to the ideal and heavenly sources of all virtue.

As the metaphor of light, objectified by King Arthur, draws together feudal and classical ideals, so also does the figure of Merlin, who issues from his tomb suggesting not so much prophet as poet. Orgel and Strong "make a very tentative suggestion" that Inigo Jones's drawing of a huge, bearded, laurel-crowned man, derived from the figure of Homer in Raphael's *Parnassus,* is the sketch for Merlin.[20] This identification seems to me exceedingly likely, for Jonson clearly wishes Merlin to be seen as *vates*— prophet and poet. He is not at all Merlin the shapeshifter, the devil's son touched by grace. Arthur says of him to the Lady of the Lake:

> And for the other mysteries here, awake
> The learned Merlin; when thou shut'st him there,
> Thou buried'st valor too, for letters rear
> The deeds of honor high and make them live.
> If then thou seek to restore prowess, give
> His spirit freedom; then present thy knight:
> For arms and arts sustain each other's right.
>
> (ll. 101–107)

This Merlin is first of all the poet. And the poet does not simply preserve deeds of honor; through his art he makes them live again and keeps them alive. For this purpose, his spirit must be free.

19. See John C. Meagher, *Method and Meaning in Jonson's Masques* (Notre Dame, Ind., 1966), pp. 107–124, for a discussion of the symbolism of light in Jonson's masques, including *Prince Henry's Barriers.*

20. Orgel and Strong, *Inigo Jones,* I, 167.

In interpreting the shield for Meliadus, Merlin is illustrating the role of the poet with respect to the prince. The pictures on the shield are "not the deeds / Of antique knights, to catch their fellows' steeds" (ll. 159–160); there are "no giants, dwarfs, or monsters here, but men" (l. 166), great kings of Britain. As Furniss has shown Merlin's emphasis is not on war but on peace—peace, order, and prosperity.[21] First he speaks of the justice Edward I strengthened in England; the beginning of the wool trade under Edward III; the riches amassed by Henry VII; and the defensive might created by Henry VIII and Elizabeth. Such "civil arts" the prince must learn. Then great martial kings are praised and their victories recounted. But Merlin makes clear that the battles were undertaken in worthy causes; these leaders fought for their faith (the highest cause) or their rights by law of nations (ll. 245–247). Words of praise for victories are counteracted by terrifying metaphors of destructiveness: rivers of infidel blood, the plowing up of whole armies, a wasting fire. Henry V, whom Prince Henry is considered to resemble in face as well as name (ll. 278–279), is set up as an example of virtue. So British kings are praised for valor and conquest, but the prince is counseled to learn the arts of peace. Finally King James, the supreme model, is praised for bringing union to the British Isles and for being a master of political wisdom. This godlike king is also a being impervious to mutability. The wheel of Fortune has been fixed, the country's strength has been set "conterminate with heaven" (l. 333), and the Golden Age has returned. Here is the merging of ideals of medieval chivalry with the classical ideal of peace and the tradition of the Golden Age, a merging which we have already observed in tne Inigo Jones designs. As Furniss says, "The symbolic nature of the barriers has been subordinated to the symbol of the wise and peaceful king who sits *unarmed* in the center of the hall." [22]

He who praises the king, interprets history, advises the prince on the arts of government, and gives true significance to the occasion is Merlin —the poet and the prophet. The relation of poet to this prince and to his society is made visible, as it is also in *Poetaster*. Merlin, garbed, coiffed, and bearded like Homer, reads the shield to Meliadus and so illustrates the function of the masque: the poet offers sound principles of rule to the

21. Furniss, "Ben Jonson's Masques," p. 126.
22. *Ibid.*

monarch.[23] Merlin's long speech has little to do with Meliadus but every-thing to do with the real Prince Henry, and with Jonson himself.

In the previous year, 1609, in the letter to Prince Henry that had accom-panied the manuscript of *The Masque of Queens,* beautifully copied out and elaborately glossed for the prince at Henry's request, Jonson spoke of his pleasure at the happy combination of virtue and heroic form he ob-served in the prince. He added that the poet, who has power to immortal-ize, should be "the care of princes." [24] In *Prince Henry's Barriers,* Jonson through Merlin is showing the prince that the poet can be adviser, educa-tor, interpreter, celebrator. Merlin's speech, over two hundred lines long, is by far the most important of the masque. Also, it is Merlin who puts an end to the combats at the barriers, advising the prince not to tempt fortune but to use it "reverently," and to forgo deeds of arms for the task of bear-ing up heaven (ll. 393–402).

Merlin's advice is both idealistic and practical. It is in fact the advice of a seasoned Renaissance humanist, Ben Jonson. Perhaps in setting up standards of rule for this young prince and showing him the importance of the poet for the king, Jonson is also being quite personal. When Me-liadus is turned over from the legendary foster mother, the Lady of the Lake, to the legendary prophet who is also well known as a father figure to the young King Arthur, Prince Henry may be meant to see himself in a similar relationship with the author who has so much wisdom and also so much admiration for him. As Herford and Simpson point out, there is "an almost fatherly tenderness and pride" in the dedication to the *Masque of Queens,* which may reflect some of Jonson's feeling for his own son who, had he lived, would be two years younger than Prince Henry.[25] And perhaps, imagining himself blessed by the care, appreciation, and favor of a noble young ruler, Jonson feels his spirit freed, like Merlin's, from a tomb.

After the Barriers, Merlin offers a prophecy: of the bright fortunes of James's family. Ironically, the prophet's vision failed. King James could not fix fortune's wheel, and in 1612 the young prince died.

23. Ernest W. Talbert, "The Interpretation of Jonson's Courtly Spectacles," *PMLA,* LXI (1946), 473.

24. Orgel, *The Complete Masques,* p. 478.

25. Herford and Simpson, II, 282.

The scenes and speeches of *Prince Henry's Barriers*, nevertheless, must have made a grandly patriotic and thrilling occasion of the tourney. Arthurian characters and incidents from *Les Prophécies de Merlin* have been greatly transformed and given new ethical and political values. Gothic arch and Norman castle are combined with Roman temple, heroic ideals of honor and prowess with classical traditions of Saturn's Golden Age and the ideal of peace. Arthur is both ideal king and a symbolic star. Merlin is adviser and prophet, also perhaps Jonson himself. Prince Henry is at once himself and Meliadus, an ideal, heroic champion; King James, watching, is himself and King Arthur come again.

The spectators, representing the highest nobility and political power, are part of the scene, too. As the Lady of the Lake says,

> What riches do I see, what beauties here!
> What awe, what love, what reverence, joy, and fear!
> What ornaments of council as of court!

(ll. 26–28)

They are the "gentry" who have neglected the House of Chivalry, and now they must help the prince restore and then "sustain" it (ll. 32–34). They are those who admire and respond to the poet's and artist's celebration of king and prince and country. They are citizens who prosper under a good king. Some of them will participate in the long night of combats which will test the prince. All are caught up in a celebration, created by Ben Jonson and Inigo Jones, of the splendor of power, the ideal of civilized rule, the heroism of Arthurian legend, the significance of a poet, the nobility of a prince, the greatness of a unified Britain, and the vision of a future where the country's shore will stretch to the sky (l. 426).

Love Restored: *A Defense of Masquing*

JEFFREY FISCHER

I N JONSON's *Love Restored,* the daringly provocative antimasque centers
on a defense of masquing as an expression of the court's beleaguered
values. Jonson transforms the generally symbolic figure of vice, excess, or
misrule into a spokesman for topical political criticism of court profligacy,
and then overturns his biting attack by means of a carefully structured
metaphor that distinguishes the values of the court as superior to those
upon which the criticism is founded.

The antimasque represents an attempt by Plutus, the god of money, to
prevent the revels from taking place. Behind this is the complex historical
tension between a nearly bankrupt royalty and the religious movement
and economic class on its way to supplanting its role. Jonson defends
masquing by turning the tables on the critics, transforming the world's
attack on court extravagance into the court's unmasking of a hypocritical,
misguided world.

The basic structure of the antimasque is a confrontation between Plutus, disguised as Cupid, and the English country spirit Robin Goodfellow, who has come to court to see the performance. It opens with a
masquerado (a "strayed reveller") announcing to the audience that no

masque will be performed. The disguised Plutus interrupts this apology to condemn the practice of masquing. Robin then enters, disappointed at the news, and recounts his difficulties in obtaining admission, in a comic monologue which also serves to satirize the kind of people who will become associated with the god of money. Plutus assaults masquing a second time; but Robin now unmasks him (fully identified as Mammon), and carries the action into the masque proper, the court, or domain of the genuine Cupid, where Plutus does not hold sway. The songs of the masque complete the dissociation of the court world from the world of Mammon and lead first into the presentation of ten courtiers disguised as virtues, then into general dancing.

From the beginning, with the announcement that the performance has been cancelled, our expectations of theatrical illusion are turned upside-down. When the masquerado insists further that "Though I dare not show my face, I can speak truth under a vizard,"[1] we are encouraged to question the nature of the relationship between disguise and truth, to admit the possibility that it might be paradoxical or many-sided. This initial disruption of illusion will emerge as the controlling metaphor of the masque, ultimately to distinguish between those who hide behind disguise and those for whom disguise is a way of revealing truth.

The masquerado's apologetic induction tells us that the masque in its narrow definition, as the entrance of courtiers in allegorical disguise and as choreographed dancing, cannot be performed; instead there is "wild music" more characteristic of the antimasque. When Plutus enters, dressed as Cupid, we have, ostensibly, a premature attack on the disorder of the antimasque. By nature Cupid belongs to the masquing proper, and his first lines, "Away, impertinent folly! Infect not this assembly" (ll. 20–21), would normally be a cue for the antimasque stage-flats to be whisked away and the sumptuous masquing scene revealed, a transforming moment like the sudden blare of trumpets in *The Masque of Queens* or the awakening of Hercules in *Pleasure Reconciled to Virtue*.

But something is wrong. This Cupid is not really Cupid, but Plutus, the god of money. Instead of introducing a triumphant masque he suppresses it. Moreover, his claim that "I am neither player nor masquer, but

---

1. All references to *Love Restored* are to Ben Jonson, *Selected Masques,* ed. Stephen Orgel (New Haven, Conn., 1970).

the god himself" (ll. 26–27) adds to the confusion of truth and disguise. Uncertain of how and where the production separates theatrical illusion and reality, the audience is apt to maintain a skepticism and make critical judgments of "Cupid" 's speeches.

Of central importance here is the problem of Jonson's stage direction *"Enter Plutus disguised as Cupid"* (l. 16). No explicit statement is made about whether or not the audience is meant to see through this disguise, and it makes an important difference. If the audience thinks Plutus is really Cupid, it is fooled by the appearance, and, like the masquerado, will be genuinely surprised by the unmasking scene. If the audience knows Plutus isn't really Cupid, it views the proceedings with irony. Both in terms of the generic demands of the masque and the particular metaphorical structure of *Love Restored,* the second possibility seems more likely.

We must notice here the special relationship of audience to production found in the masque. Unlike most dramatic forms, the masque does not demand a "willing suspension of disbelief" as a way of keeping the audience in contact with the play's illusion. It is written for a particular audience on a particular occasion—and to praise (and thereby instruct) its audience by creating its audience in the work itself. It alters the dramatic structure for ulterior, and one might say political, reasons. Or to distinguish another way, the impetus of the drama normally comes from within the work; the impetus of the masque comes ultimately from the audience, and especially the king, who is at once the center of the audience and of the performance.[2] If the king himself were deceived by Plutus, this would be a serious violation of the masque's formalities, a usurpation of the king's ultimate control over the performance.

The structural development of *Love Restored* is toward a distinction between the kind of people who are fooled into believing that Plutus is Cupid and those who can see through his disguise. Jonson uses the

2. The most suggestive discussions of the thematic and structural patterns at work in the masque form are found throughout Stephen Orgel, *The Jonsonian Masque* (Cambridge, Mass., 1965). Other valuable theoretical discussions are in John C. Meagher, *Method and Meaning in Jonson's Masques* (Notre Dame, Ind., 1966); Enid Welsford, *The Court Masque* (1927; rpt. New York, 1962); and Dolora Cunningham, "The Jonsonian Masque as a Literary Form," *Ben Jonson: A Collection of Critical Essays,* ed. Jonas Barish (Englewood Cliffs, N.J., 1963).

resources of his scholarship to help achieve this. In reading Cephisodotus, Parsanias, and Philostratus, he found Plutus described as "a little boy, bare headed, his locks curled, and spangled with gold, of a fresh aspect, his body almost naked, saving some rich robe cast over him." This is the description of a figure remarkably like, and easily mistaken for, Cupid. On the other hand, he found in Aristophanes, Theognis, and Lucian a Plutus "blind and deformed."[3] Jonson exploits these differences by making them functions of the beholder's insight—some people, like the masquerado, see Plutus as a Cupid-like youth, but to the more perceptive, he is a lame old man. Robin Goodfellow can recognize the villain's true identity, because he possesses that superior perception: "We spirits I see are subtler yet, and somewhat better discoverers" (ll. 159–160). Later on, the real Cupid states that Plutus is also incapable of deceiving the court:

> When thus the world thou wilt deceive
> Thou canst in youth and beauty shine,
> Belie a godhead's form divine,
> Scatter thy gifts, and fly to those
> Where thine own humor may dispose;
> But when to good men thou art sent
> By Jove's direct commandement,
> Thou then art aged, lame, and blind,
> And canst nor path nor persons find.
>
> (ll. 217–225)

For the audience to have been fooled by the disguise would have indecorously connected them with the foolish world rather than with the elevated, discriminating ideal world which is their proper sphere.

Even though Plutus is probably recognized as a fraud from the first, he nevertheless attacks the masque in a manner that cannot be summarily dismissed. He argues that the pleasures of the masque are "false and fleeting" and will cost the audience "the repentance of an age."

'Tis thou that art not only the sower of vanities in these high places but the call of all other light follies to fall and feed on them. I will endure thy

3. Allan H. Gilbert, *The Symbolic Persons in the Masques of Ben Jonson* (Durham, N.C., 1948), p. 199. The sources are all Jonson's own, cited in "The King's Entertainment in Passing to His Coronation," *Ben Jonson*, ed. C. H. Herford and Percy and Evelyn Simpson (Oxford, 1925–1952), VII, 97, ll. 436 ff. There Jonson describes Plutus in Cupid fashion and includes the alternate description in his footnote only.

prodigality nor riots no more; they are the ruin of states. Nor shall the tyranny of these nights hereafter impose a necessity upon me of entertaining thee. Let 'em embrance more frugal pastimes!

(ll. 135–141)

This is the familiar voice of the Puritan critic of the stage, and signifies a serious attack that would eventually see the closing of the theaters in 1642. In general, the Puritans attacked the theater for its effects on popular morality, its competition with churchgoing, the evils of the acting profession and its connection in their minds with London's underworld. But, in addition, there was a sharp criticism of the court's indulgences in theater and spectacle, centering not on issues of popular morality but on the court's neglect of the more serious duties of state, its failure to project a suitably dignified image of itself, and especially on the inexcusable extravagancies of court entertainment intended to uphold an image of magnificence. Herford and Simpson identify two main groups of critics:

To the Puritan the Masque was a branch of the abhorred drama, and the fact that it was designed to amuse, at an extravagant cost, an aristocratic audience and a royal champion of divine right did very little to qualify his disesteem. And many grave citizens who were not Puritans took exception to the enormous sums spent upon the soon forgotten pastime of an hour.[4]

Plutus carries on his argument with a sense of outrage. A more restrained, but similar note was sounded by the Puritan historian Arthur Wilson, in his 1653 history of King James's reign:

The King himself being not a little delighted with such fluent Elegancies, as made the nights more glorious than the dayes. But the latitude that these high-flying fancies, and more speaking Actions, gave to the lower World to judge and censure even the Greatest with reproaches, shall not provoke me so much as to stain the innocent Paper. I shall onely say in generall, That Princes, by how much they are greater than others, are looked upon with a more severe eye; if their Virtues be not suitable to their Greatness, they lose much of their value: For it is too great an allay to such refinedness to fall under the common cognizance.[5]

Admittedly, Plutus's arguments against the extravagance of masquing border on being petty. He suggests that the courtiers busy themselves

---

4. Herford and Simpson, II, 289.
5. Arthur Wilson, *The History of Great Britain, Being the Life and Reign of King James I* (London, 1653), p. 54.

with card games instead, encourages the ladies to occupy themselves with domestic chores "a dozen of 'em to a light, or twenty—the more the merrier—to save charges" (ll. 146–147) (presumably alluding to the incredible candlelit stagings of Inigo Jones), suggests that they stay at home in "old nightgowns" instead of throwing away their money on the lavish costumes that are, in any case, bought on credit. Most critics of *Love Restored* agree with Herford and Simpson in characterizing Plutus as a "despot of frugal pastimes, gloomy countenance, and utilitarian economics." [6]

Despite its petty nature, Plutus's criticism does touch on some of the key political issues of James's rule and suggests the deeper divisions that ultimately led to the English Revolution. James himself could not have dismissed the arguments lightly, for around the time of *Love Restored* he appears to have taken some heed of his critics. *Love Freed from Ignorance*, which immediately preceded *Love Restored*, cost only a little over £700, a considerable bargain compared to figures of over £1,000 both before and after this period. *Love Restored* itself appears to have required much less elaborate staging on the whole than most other masques, since so much of it is taken up by a scene of prose comedy. Herford and Simpson cite its budget at £280. 8s. 9d., although there is some dispute as to whether this figure includes all expenses. W. Todd Furniss notes that this comparatively cheap production was mounted just after James had disrupted negotiations with Parliament over his income. [7] Parliament had refused the

6. Herford and Simpson, II, 290. Jonas Barish, *Ben Jonson and the Language of Prose Comedy* (Cambridge, Mass., 1960), p. 253, says that "Once again, Jonson is crusading against visible, social forms of folly, this time the officious purse-pinching of those who would hoard but not spend, who would restrict the court in its necessary function of 'magificence,'" while Orgel, p. 74, calls Plutus a miser: "It is he alone who makes a virtue of parsimony and conceives of morality in terms of buying and selling."

7. Herford and Simpson, X, 533. Marchette Chute, *Ben Jonson of Westminster* (New York, 1953), p. 175, records the cost of *Love Freed*, while the notes to the masques in Herford and Simpson, vol. X, give thorough accounts of expenditures for some of the masques. They record the cost of *Oberon* in 1611 at £1,087. 8s. 10d., p. 522, and of *The Masque of Queens* in 1609 at £2,751, p. 493. G. P. V. Akrigg, *The Jacobean Pageant* (Cambridge, Mass., 1962), p. 151, records a figure of £4,000 for the Christmas masque of 1618, and estimates that its equivalent in modern British currency would be £32,000. W. Todd Furniss, "Ben Jonson's Masques," in Richard B. Young, W. Todd Furniss, and William G. Madsen, *Three Studies in the Renaissance*, Yale Studies in English (New Haven, Conn.,

crown's request for a £200,000 annual subsidy; the issue was not merely the royal family's extravagance but a question of whether the king or Parliament should have final control of taxation and spending. Surely Plutus's outrage at the extravagance of court entertainment must have seemed an uncomfortable intrusion of reality into the masque world, albeit an intrusion which the design of the masque works to counteract.

The court had, however, a powerful ideological defense of its extravagance. It insisted that magnificence was necessary for the dignity of the king. In 1609 James addressed himself to this question before Parliament: "It is trew I haue spent much: but yet if I had spared any of those things, which caused a great part of my expense, I should haue dishonored the kingdome, my selfe, and the late Queene." [8] Behind the king was a firm Renaissance tradition associating expense with virtue and dignity, especially with respect to royal entertainments, which were, incidentally, important political events, as witnessed by the complex protocol of invitations and seating arrangements for foreign nobility and diplomats. [9]

The significance of Plutus's assault extends far beyond simple annoyance at the cost of costumes or lighting of court entertainments. Its ultimate reach is toward the ideological and class divisions which associate Puritanism with the emergence of modern capitalism, and toward the struggle between monarch and Parliament—the ideological conflict between a social theory based on ideas of community, social harmony, and hierarchical order and one based on the supremacy of individual interest. [10]

1958), p. 168, links the cost of *Love Restored* with the king's general financial troubles. Furniss's brief commentary on the masque as a "Combat of Concepts" is especially incisive.

8. *The Political Works of James I*, ed. Charles Howard McIlwain (Cambridge, Mass., 1918), p. 319.

9. Meagher, p. 34, discusses this tradition of "magnificence," and ultimately traces it to Aristotle's remarks in the *Nicomachean Ethics*, in his insistence on "taste, decorum, and the appropriateness in the expenditures of the magnificent man."

10. L. C. Knights, *Drama and Society in the Age of Jonson* (London, 1937), *passim*, provides an abundance of information concerning the sociopolitical background to Jonson's time. He characterizes the age as the "heaviest period in the transformation to a money economy" (p. 7), and uses the clash between emerging capitalism and the old order as a framework for his discussion of major playwrights of the period.

If this interpretation seems to derive from modern notions of historical materialism, it nonetheless bears a remarkable affinity with the distinction Jonson himself draws in *Love Restored* between the Mammon- or Plutus-deceived world and the Cupid-inspired court.

Jonson defuses the potential explosiveness of Plutus's argument by setting against it the characteristically unifying and idealizing elements of the masque form. Plutus will ultimately be contrasted to the real Cupid who belongs at court, but for the purposes of the crucial transformation to masque proper, and in terms of the thematic design of *Love Restored,* the real restoring figure is Robin Goodfellow.

He enters after Plutus has declared his intention to block the masque. "How! No masque, no masque? I pray you say, are you sure on't? No masque indeed? What do I here then? Can you tell?" (ll. 35–37) The first thing we notice about Robin, in a play in which the roles of spectators and actors are already in confusion, is that he is himself a spectator, and a frustrated one at that. Indeed, his disappointment reflects the disappointment the royal audience might have felt had there really been no masque. In this way Robin stands for the audience; Jonson has chosen to handle the perpetual problem of how to bring the audience into the center of the play by a daring trick of role-reversal. He provides a character to "play" the audience. While it may be argued that Robin, as a figure from English folklore, is not sufficiently dignified for such a part, we should at least consider him a country cousin, whose "rude good fellowship," so severely criticized by Plutus, more genuinely befits the small, confident society at court, and the character of King James, than the severity of the god of money. We shall see that in crucial ways Robin provides the responses that make his identification with the values of the audience central to the structure of the masque.

His brilliant comic monologue about trying to get in to see the masque helps to draw him closer to the audience. He is, after all, one who does get in, part of a select audience in a hall small enough to have required a rigid limitation of spectators. In contrast are Plutus, who only gets in by guile, and those satirized in the monologue who do not get in at all. Robin's original plan is to watch "what kind of persons the door most opened to, and one of their shapes I would belie to get in with" (ll. 81–82). In each case he is frustrated and only finally gains entrance when he comes as himself. Enid Welsford, in *The Court Masque,* glances at one of the main points of this monologue, but without thoroughly exploring its thematic implications. She calls *Love Restored* "a comedy of manners . . . where [Jonson] gives a vivid picture of the difficulty that the bourgeoisie experienced in gaining admission to the great Court functions." [11] Among those whom Robin imitates are a group of "country ladies" who have been waiting at the door of the masquing hall since seven o'clock that morning. The coarse satire Robin allows himself marks these women as radically different from the kind of people who do attend the masques:

Marry, before I could procure my properties, alarum came that some o' the whimlens had too much; and one showed how fruitfully they had watered his head as he stood under the grices; and another came out complaining of a cataract shot into his eyes by a planet as he was stargazing.

(ll. 102–107)

When he attempts to gain entry in the guise of a "fine citizen's wife," he meets with a shocking scene of sexual indecorum which also must be taken as radically unlike the sexual manners (at least the public ones) of the court. Jonson is thus able to include the kind of ribaldry that apparently most pleased his royal audience without a breach of decorum, since he makes it a functional part of the antimasque, as the epitome of what the court is not like:

that figure [the fine citizen's wife] provoked me exceedingly to take it, which I had no sooner done but one o' the blackguard had his hand in my vestry and was groping of me as nimbly as the Christmas cutpurse. He thought he might be bold with me because I had not a husband in sight to squeak to. I was glad to forgo my form, to be rid of his hot steaming affection; it so smelt o' the boiling house.

(ll. 108–114)

At work behind this comedy is a deliberate drawing of a distinction between audience and uninvited. Robin falls in with the former, and it is significant, as Herford and Simpson note,[12] that he gets in on his own cognizance, as one who doesn't have to disguise himself.

The full meaning of the comedy becomes clear when Robin unmasks Plutus; he associates the satirized bourgeoisie with the deceitful, corrupt god of money. The masquerado, while recognizing that something is

11. Welsford, p. 188.
12. Herford and Simpson, II, 290.

peculiarly uncharacteristic of this "Cupid," is unable to see beyond the mask; he only gets as far as calling him a "reformed Cupid," unwittingly spelling out the irony of Plutus, the self-proclaimed reformer of court morals, as a Cupid altered or corrupted (presumably by the Reformation) from his true nature. But Robin sees right through:

Nay then, we spirits I see are subtler yet, and somewhat better discoverers. No; it is not he, nor his brother Anti-Cupid, the Love of Virtue, though he pretend to do it with his phrase and face. 'Tis that imposter Plutus, the god of money who has stol'n Love's ensigns, and in his belied figure reigns i' the world, making friendships, contracts, marriages, and almost religion; begetting, breeding, and holding the nearest respects of mankind and usurping all those offices in this age of Gold which Love himself performed in the Golden Age.

(ll. 159–168)

Plutus is discovered here as a pretender, different from the other kind of masquers who will appear—those whose disguises highlight rather than conceal their true characters. His masquing works toward deception; that of the others works toward truth.

Robin begins the counterattack by charging Plutus with hypocrisy, thus linking him to another hypocrite, mentioned in the comic monologue, a Puritan in whose shape Robin attempted to enter. In that instance he took the guise of a "feather-maker of Blackfriars," a recognizably Puritan stock figure.

In that shape I told 'em, "Surely I must come in, let it be opened unto me"; but they all made as light of me as of my feathers, and wondered how I could be a Puritan, being of so vain a vocation. I answered, "We are all masquers sometimes."

(ll. 92–96)

This mode of satirizing Puritans was common to many playwrights, as a defense against their attack on theater. Perhaps Jonson himself provided the most familiar example in his portrayal of the Puritan hypocrite Zeal-of-the-Land Busy in *Bartholomew Fair*. Not only is Plutus a hypocrite; he is also a usurper, one who "pretends to tie kingdoms" and performs all the duties and functions of an actual head of state. He rules in Love's place, and has banished Cupid to cold and darkness. This is the second indictment of the god of money, especially as it relates to the dominant political struggle of the day over control of financial appropriation; it ushers in the identification of Plutus with the "insolent and barbarous Mammon" and reflects a dismay at the money-mindedness of the growing middle-class.

As the pivotal figure in the masque, Robin brings about the transformation from antimasque to masque proper. He does not deprive Plutus of his powers of misrule, but rather moves the masque on, by a change of scene, to a place where Mammon's evil cannot penetrate. This is the penultimate step in the separation of the court from the bourgeois or Mammon-controlled world. "Come," says Robin: "Follow me. I'll bring you where you shall find Love, and by the virtue of this majesty, who projecteth so powerful beams of light and heat through this hemisphere, thaw his icy fetters and scatter the darkness that obscures him" (ll. 180–184). At no point is Plutus made to relinquish his control over the world; it seems, rather, allocated to him as his domain. In the world outside the court, Plutus's disguise is and remains effective, and he does reign over the social institutions which would otherwise be governed by Cupid "making friendships, contracts, marriages, and almost religion; begetting, breeding, and holding the nearest respects of mankind." The effect of Plutus's false rule has been to transform the Golden Age into an age of gold, and the real indictment here is not of Plutus/Mammon but of his worshipers: " 'Tis you, mortals, that are fools, and worthy to be such, that worship him; for if you had wisdom, he had no godhead" (ll. 177–178).

In contrast Robin shows us the world of the court, a world without foolish Mammon-serving mortals, where the real Cupid reigns, nourished by the heat and light emanating from the throne. Here the masque can at last be held "in despite of this insolent and barbarous Mammon." The first song of the masque proper continues this theme, proclaiming the triumph of majesty and magnificence over money-mindedness:

> To be so cold!
> Yes, tyran money quencheth all desire,
> Or makes it old.
> But here are beauties will revive
> O how came Love, that is himself a fire,

> Love's youth and keep his heat alive:
>> As often as his torch here dies,
>> He needs but light it at fresh eyes.
> Joy, joy the more; for in all courts
> If Love be cold, so are his sports.

(ll. 196–205)

Cupid's speech immediately after the song underscores the distinctions drawn in the antimasque between a world dominated by disguise and deception and a court governed by love and truth, by a "heat that inward warms" and allows him to be not covered up but "naked in these places / As at his birth, or 'mongst the Graces" (ll. 209–211).

Stephen Orgel regards this transformation point as the critical flaw of *Love Restored*. In *The Jonsonian Masque,* he argues that the early development of the antimasque into a scene of prose comedy created a disproportion between antimasque and masque proper that ran counter to the demand that the masque be used to glorify the court. He claims that the inherently dramatic quality of the antimasque makes the main masque, "the world of essence, ideal and unchanging," pale and uninteresting, and draws a contrast between the "vital and rich" invective of Plutus and the "singsong couplets" of Cupid. Moreover, he sees a failure in *Love Restored* to bring about what he calls "the ultimate goal in the masque form": "to create a symbolic figure that would be an adequate representation of the courtier beneath the masque. The aim is wholly achieved only in certain of the late masques."[13] Orgel does not see in Robin Goodfellow the same kind of transition figure as that represented by Hercules in *Pleasure Reconciled to Virtue* or by Silenus in *Oberon,* one who can "enter the world of misrule, assess it, and lead us from it into the masque."[14] The transformation scene does succeed, because Robin acts as a substitute for the audience, as we have seen earlier, so that through him the audience can prove its true worth by a rejection of Plutus and of those people who have been hoodwinked into seeing him as the god of love. Through Robin, the king sits firmly in the center of the masque. The transformation can occur in an organic way because the antimasque itself contains the elements of its own destruction, and because the drama of the unmasking

13. Orgel, p. 68. Orgel argues that, as a result of the weak transformation scene in this masque, the masque proper takes on the appearance of "tasteless flattery."
14. *Ibid.,* p. 162.

of Plutus is carried thematically into the material of the main masque. The conflict within the antimasque between Plutus and Robin is transfigured into the larger conflict between the world of misrule and the world of masquers.

It is Robin Goodfellow, too, whom Cupid orders to chase the god of money from the court:

> Chase him hence
> T' his caves, and there let him dispense,
> For murders, treasons, rapes, his bribes
> Unto the discontented tribes,
> Where let his heaps grow daily less,
> And he and they still want success.
>
> (ll. 226–231)

One cannot help but suspect that Plutus is sent back to the world with a vengeance. He will continue to hold sway there, and Cupid's wish for his "heaps" to decrease and his plans to fail among the "discontented tribes" of avaricious Puritans sounds suspiciously like the king's curse against an uncooperative Parliament. Plutus's attack on the court has become the court's castigation of the Mammon-serving world. Through Robin, the court has successfully defended itself and its pleasures.

Nevertheless, no one involved at all with the making or watching of masques could deny the usefulness of money. Cupid may be the true symbol of the masquing spirit, but money is still necessary to translate that spirit into the actual entertainments. The final solution of the masque, then, is not a wholesale rejection of money, but a reconciliation of money to its higher uses, in keeping with that described by *Pleasure Reconciled to Virtue,* in which pleasure is firmly brought under the guidance of the virtues of harmony and order.

> The majesty that here doth move
> Shall triumph, more secured by love
> Than all his earth, and never crave
> His aids, but force him as a slave.
>
> (ll. 232–235)

The true wisdom of the court is its ability to master money—to use it as a means to majesty—rather than be made a slave to it by deception. This is the ultimate distinction between the court and the world outside.

Having restored money to its proper role, Cupid can now call upon the masquers to display themselves. These masquers—both as allegorical virtues and as actual persons—are the ultimate representation of the kind of people, Robin's fellows, who have seen through Plutus and have banished him from the court; they are the antitheses of the immoral, ridiculous figures described in Robin's monologue. Plutus had tried to prevent their appearance, which signals now the full victory of courtly majesty over parsimony. As in all masques, the audience sees itself as its own ideal. Unlike the impostor Plutus, these masquers wear disguises to show who they really are. Cupid introduces them and announces the approaching finale, the merging of spectator and performer in the dance.

> The spirits of court and flower of men,
> Led on by me, with flamed intents,
> To figure the ten ornaments
> That do each courtly presence grace.
> Nor will they rudely strive for place,
> One to precede the other, but
> As music them in form shall put,
> So will they keep their measures true,
> And make still their proportions new,
> Till all become one harmony.

(ll. 240–249)

The lyrics contrast the harmony and mutuality of dancing, and of the greater ideal dancing represents, with the antimasque world of Mammon-worshippers, who do "strive for place / One to precede the other." The magnificence and proportion demonstrate the superiority of court values; the form of masquing itself becomes its final defense.

Milton's Arcades: *Context, Form, and Function*

CEDRIC C. BROWN

M ILTON's *Arcades* consists of an action designed in "honour and devotion" for the aged Countess Dowager of Derby at her seat at
Harefield in Middlesex. The gesture is evidently the responsibility of
members of her family, who dress up as shepherds and shepherdesses, together, probably, with one or more musicians. Pretending that they have
come from Arcadia, they are told that they should dance no more there,
but rather come and live at Harefield, to serve the lady of that place. The
countess creates a new Arcadia about her, by her bright presence. She is
the center of a place of blessedness, of innocent virtue and piety. In these
verses for Harefield, as in the prologue added to Guarini's famous pastoral
drama, *Il Pastor Fido,* the device is the transference of Arcadianism to a
new locality. Milton, like Guarini, expresses such transference with the
analogy of the well-worn tale of Alpheus and Arethusa.

I. The Device

Pan is god-king of Arcadians. They may be courtly as well as rustic,
as for example in Jonson's *Pan's Anniversarie,* written for the birthday of

245

James I in 1620, where the scene is Arcadia and it is the shepherds' holiday. In Milton's verses even Syrinx, Pan's mistress, would have to yield to the lady of Harefield, for she outshines all Arcadian queens whatever:

> Though Syrinx your Pan's mistress were,
> Yet Syrinx well might wait on her.
> Such a rural queen
> All Arcadia hath not seen.
>
> (ll. 106–109)

She sits in a "state," either really or imaginarily illuminated, and the Arcadians are drawn to her by radiant light. This is the familiar divinity of courtly compliment, "too divine to be mistook." More precisely, in one verse of the opening song, she is celebrated as like Latona, mother of Diana and Apollo, types of aristocratic youth; as like Cybele, *magna mater* and *mater deorum,* "mother of an hundred gods"; and as like Juno, *matrona* and *regina,* heavenly queen. For Juno Milton had once written Ceres in the manuscript, and Ceres is another matron, *quasi $\bar{\gamma}\eta$ μήτηρ.*[1] The terms suit the mother and grandmother to many noble offspring, and, as we shall see, some of her grandchildren are almost certainly among her celebrators.

The Genius of the Wood, a musician who seems to be either part of the establishment or familiar with it, acts the part of guide through the park, and he adds to the celebration by describing his protective and healing activities. This is an aspect of Jove's general providence, another image of blessedness, but particularly to be marked within the estate at Harefield. His work done, he says, he spends nights listening to the music of the spheres, as only the purely spiritual or chastely virtuous can. This reference he turns into further compliment by bringing heavenly harmony to earth for her:

> And yet such music worthiest were to blaze
> The peerless height of her immortal praise.
>
> (ll. 74–75)

As the Arcadians move across to the state, so that the nobles among them may kiss the hem of the lady's garment, they complete a gesture which is

---

1. Milton first wrote Juno, then substituted Ceres, then finally restored Juno by underlining. References to the manuscript are made through the Scolar Press facsimile of the Trinity Manuscript (Menston, 1970); for the printed text I have used *The Poems of John Milton,* ed. J. Carey and A. Fowler (London, 1968).

intended only to celebrate her and her residence, and only, I think, to be heard by her.

At the same time the device brings courtly entertainment to her house. Arcadians are singers and dancers, and to this place they bring their happy skills to honor the new mistress of Pan. Thus an "entertainment" is brought to her and to her house. The rest of the entertainment we do not have, but it would be a reasonable guess that *Arcades* was the presentation that opened "this night's glad solemnity" as a kind of dedication.

This old lady had known entertainments before. She and her second husband, Lord Keeper Egerton, had put on an entertainment in the same house for the visit of Queen Elizabeth on her last summer progress in 1602. Then Sir John Davies provided the text.[2] The countess herself had been welcomed in a royal-style entertainment at Ashby de la Zouch by her daughter and son-in-law, the earl and countess of Huntingdon, in 1607. For that occasion, Marston wrote the verses.[3] It can hardly be fortuitous that three surviving entertainments concern her: she must have liked them. By the time of *Arcades* she was in her seventies and rarely moved far from Harefield. Now younger members of her family bring courtly festivity to her as she sits in her own house, as a tribute of respect and affection, and probably, as will become evident below, in a gesture of familial gratitude.

Exactly how this festivity came about we do not know, and neither Milton's manuscript nor the edition of 1645 tells us. Interpreters have made a few guesses. Masson, far better informed than most of his successors, suggested the occasion of the dowager's birthday (4 May) or the Calverley-Hastings wedding of April 1634.[4] *Arcades* is usually assigned to some time in the period 1630–1634, often to the summer season, before *Comus*, which was performed at Ludlow on 29 September 1634. In fact, there is no absolute reason to assign it to the summer season, and we have

2. Recently identified properly in *The Poems of Sir John Davies,* ed. R. Krueger (Oxford, 1975).

3. Discussed in *The Poems of John Marston,* ed. A. Davenport (Liverpool, 1961).

4. D. Masson, *The Life of John Milton* (London, 1859), I, 562. Masson's dating of *Arcades* in 1633/4 seems to me sensible, though these two particular occasions do not receive much support from the family documents.

no incontrovertible proof that it preceded *Comus*. It has often been assumed, again with no proof, that the Egerton children, who took the leading parts in *Comus,* must have had a major role in *Arcades* too, with the help of their friend the court musician and family musical tutor, Henry Lawes. All in all, precious little work has seen the light on the family and household at Harefield since Masson examined many of the relevant documents last century, and after his time they were dispersed. Treated as some sort of slight masque, which it is not, and sometimes reconstructed in the manner of a welcome in a country-house entertainment for royalty, which it is not, *Arcades* has been misunderstood in its dramatic form and has been underinvestigated as a piece of occasional writing. Sometimes it has even been assumed that its text, in manuscript and print, might in some sense be defective, which seems to me an unnecessary and confusing inference. It turns out that it is possible to discover a good deal about the situation at Harefield in the early 1630s, to see that even Masson made a few errors, to make a fair guess about the kind of gesture from the family that *Arcades* represents, and to observe that misinterpretation of various kinds has been passed down more or less unexamined through generations of critical commentators. In these things, the reconstruction of the occasion must remain conjectural, of course, but we can at least establish some general groundwork about context and correct some common ideas about structure and staging. *Arcades* may seem a small, conventional, low-keyed, and rather privately intended work. Nevertheless, in the edition of 1645, like *Comus* and *Lycidas,* it was set apart from the body of other English poems and offered as a major example of occasional writing in the early career of the poet. This placement of it might suggest that we would do well to try to understand it better on its own terms.

II. Contexts: House and Family, Court and Theatricals

Harefield had been bought by Sir Thomas Egerton after his marriage to the countess of Derby at the beginning of the century. As an elderly woman the dowager lived on there almost exclusively until her death on 26 January 1636/7. The estate comprised the manors of Harefield and Moor Hall. The smaller Moor Hall manor house, by her time little more than a farm, stood down in the valley by an old Knights Templar chapel probably used as a stone barn.[5] The manor house of Harefield itself, surrounded by its park, stood on rising ground above the church, and commanded a view over the river Colne and across to Windsor Forest.

By 1630 the countess had rather a diminished household. For her station, she was not prosperous. On 14 June she wrote to her daughter Frances, countess of Bridgewater, that

> If you here any more speech of my Lady Killigray coming to see me I pray send me word with all the speed it may be, that I may send to London for provision because I am not so well furnished in mine owne house as I could wish. Besides, I am sometimes from home at the house which I am building to set it forward; that if it should please God to call me, I might have a place to lay my stuffe in, out of my Lord Castlehaven's fingering.[6]

The earl of Castlehaven, to whom we shall return, had married her eldest daughter, Lady Anne, widow of Lord Chandos, in 1624.[7] He had a claim to much of her stuff through his wife.

In order to understand the position at Harefield at the time that *Arcades* was performed, we must first understand the position of the dowager's three daughters, her only children, and her grandchildren. Her three middle-aged daughters were in differing circumstances, though all had married earls. The second daughter, Frances, was the most happily placed. She had married her stepbrother Sir John Egerton, later earl of Bridgewater. The Bridgewater estates were considerable, the earl was a privy councilor, and in 1631 he was selected to become the next president of Wales. However, thus far he had married off nothing but daughters, which must have called heavily on his resources. By 1634, when the three youngest and only unmarried children, Alice (b. 1619), John (b. 1623), and Thomas (b. 1625), performed in *Comus,* he had given away seven daughters in marriage.[8] This household was well off, but not unembarrassed by financial considerations.

The countess of Derby's eldest daughter Anne had, to begin with, made a rich match with Grey Brydges, fifth Baron Chandos, the so-called king

5. The best description of the estate I have found is a survey of 1636 now in the possession of the Fitzroy-Newdigate family at Arbury Hall, Warks.
6. Huntington Library MS. EL 6481.
7. Parish Registers at Harefield; 22 July 1624.
8. Huntington Library MSS. EL 6841, 6846, 6848.

of the Cotswolds, who died in 1621. Her second marriage in 1624, at Harefield, to Mervyn Touchet, Lord Audley, earl of Castlehaven, proved a bane when the family discovered that they had disposed of estates to a man who was untrustworthy and an infamous sexual pervert. Diplomatically, this marriage to an earl is unmentioned on the funeral monument in Harefield church. There were no children born of the alliance of Lady Anne and Castlehaven, but both had children by their previous marriages. Anne's children were two boys, George, Lord Chandos (b. 1620), and William (b. 1621), and two girls, Elizabeth (b. 1616?) and another daughter, possibly named Anne or Frances.[9]

The countess of Derby's third daughter, Elizabeth, had married Henry Hastings in 1603, and he had become earl of Huntingdon in December 1604. The Hastings estates had once been very large, but Henry's great-uncle, the open-handed Puritan earl, had had to sell off or mortgage most of his lands, and his estates were left in ruins at his death in 1595.[10] Neither George, the fourth earl, nor Henry, the fifth, could recover from the burden of inherited debts.[11] One single schedule of debts for 1621 shows that Henry at that time raised loans to the amount of £11,662 and that he also owed £600 further to the crown.[12] By 1630 he was living in reduced circumstances at Donnington Park, Leicestershire, seldom coming to court and repeatedly failing to pay his subsidies. As we shall see, the dowager gave some assistance to this branch of the family, to whom she was close, and in which she had four grandchildren: Ferdinand, Lord Hastings (b. 1608), recently married to Lucy, daughter of Sir John Davies; Henry (b. 1609); Alice (b. 1606) and Elizabeth (b. 1612).[13]

In order to understand the pattern of life at Harefield in the 1630s we need also to rehearse the disasters of 1631. In that year, when the dowager

9. I have not been able to fix name or date of birth of the second daughter. Huntington Library MS. EL 6524 is a copy of an agreement about the portion of Frances, daughter of Anne, countess of Castlehaven, in a marriage with Mr. Edmund Fortescue, dated 14 May 1635. This might settle the name as Frances.

10. The 1607 entertainment at Ashby was quite lavish: see Masson, I, 559–560; Davenport, pp. 40–45; a more modest impression of the household is given in Claire Cross, *The Puritan Earl* (London & New York, 1966).

11. Cross, pp. 61–111.

12. Leicester Record Office, DE 500, bundle 25.

13. I have supplied previously uncertain dates of birth from the Parish Register of Ashby de la Zouch, now in Leicester R.O.

was seventy-two, the regimen of life at Harefield changed radically, when the behavior of Castlehaven was brought to public notice by his son and heir, James Touchet, Lord Audley, as soon as he came of age. The Castlehaven affair was a scandal through the land, and there are several contemporary accounts of it.[14] Recently it has been described again in connection with Milton's Ludlow masque. The concentration on the ideal of chastity in *Comus,* and what look like cuts in passages concerned with sexual mores in the Bridgewater manuscript version, have been associated with it, so that the masque has been seen as a kind of public purgation for the family.[15] It is not the purpose of this piece to argue about the relevance of the Castlehaven scandal to *Comus.* It seems to me unlikely that it determined the masque thematically. It is more likely that it brought about a situation at Harefield which led to *Arcades.* In fact it is possible that there would have been no *Arcades* had the Castlehaven business not occurred.

Briefly, the events were these. Soon after his marriage to Lady Anne, Castlehaven submitted her to all sorts of sexual insults and outrages. He had some of his favorite servants assault her sexually while he watched and made others display their sexual organs in front of her. He himself seems to have had homosexual relations with a number of his servants, and to have kept a common prostitute in the house. He contrived a marriage between his own elder son and Anne's elder daughter, Elizabeth, in 1628. The girl was then about twelve. Having married her to his son, Castlehaven had her forced by one of his servants, while he watched, and had his servants sleep often with her, reputedly hoping to beget a further heir and to disinherit his own son. To add to the sadness of his case, he was suspected of popery. He was tried by his peers, and his execution took place in May 1631. In July, two of his servants were hung at Tyburn, talking to the last. Castlehaven always protested his innocence, but few can have believed him, and certainly none of his wife's family.

Much of the aftermath was reaped by the countess of Derby, whose daughter and granddaughter were the injured or tainted parties. She took

14. Printed source: *The Arraignment and Conviction of Mervin Lord Audley, Earl of Castlehaven* . . . , (London, 1642). Fullest MS source: S. P. Dom. 207.

15. Barbara Breasted, "*Comus* and the Castlehaven Scandal," *Milton Studies,* III (1971), 201–224; Rosemary K. Mundhenk, "Dark Scandal and The Sun-Clad Power of Chastity . . . ," *SEL,* XV, no. 1 (1975), 141–152.

in Lady Castlehaven's children and undertook their proper education. She would not welcome Lady Castlehaven herself or the ruined granddaughter Elizabeth. She wrote to Secretary Dorchester:

And that my daughter and she [Elizabeth] may be so happie to receive their pardon from the King. and till such time I shall never willinglie yeeld to see either of them. for the sight of them would but Increase my griefs, whoese hart is almost wounded to death already wth thinking of so fowle a businesse.[16]

Furthermore, she was frightened lest "there should be some sparkes of my Grandchilde Awdlies misbehaviour remaining, wch might give ill example to ye young ones wch are wth me." For she had in her house "two of her young Brothers, & sister, whoe as yet, (I humbly thanke God) are both hopefull & vertuous." It seems that she was going to do her best to "govern" these young ones and to reestablish them in respectable circles, and, quite realistically, she was taking no further chances with the damaged name of the family. Economics also concerned her. During the summer of 1631 she entered into negotiations with the crown for help in the maintenance of her new dependents. Without help from the king, she said, her daughter and granddaughter "are lefte most miserable in deed: destitute of all other meanes to mayntaine either of them, but that myselfe out of my poore estate am faine to releeve them, and all the children of my daughters besides: . . ."[17]

In 1631, then, the dowager had gained five noble dependents in desperate straits: two of these she helped to support away from her own home, and three of the children she maintained within her own household at Harefield. I have no evidence to suggest that the two ever came to reside at Harefield, although the desired pardons were granted in November of the same year.[18] By 1634, a year for which household accounts survive,[19] Elizabeth does not seem to be in the house, and Lady Castlehaven certainly lived elsewhere, for money is dispatched to her by servant for her

16. S. P. Dom. 192.11; cf. her letter to the king 192.11.1.

17. S. P. Dom. 198.18; the decision given in S. P. Dom. 195.30.

18. S. P. Dom. 203, 35 & 100; for Elizabeth 14 November, for Lady Castlehaven 30 November.

19. Huntington Library Hastings MS, unnumbered: a book of steward's accounts for Harefield from w/e 22 May 1634 to w/e 23 April 1635. My source of information about the household is this, where no other is stated.

to give away in charity. Nor can I find any mention of the other Brydges girl in 1634. Although of course she continued to bear some financial responsibility for this whole branch of her family, it may be that by 1634 she had only to watch over the boys in her house. When they came in 1631, George Lord Chandos was eleven, and William his brother ten. Masson suggested that the Brydges children might have been among the "noble members of her family" who put on *Arcades* for the dowager. This seems to be very likely indeed, as all were dependent on her, and two or three were permanent residents of her house.

It should be noticed also that other members of her family stood as debtors to her, and at least one of these was also a resident. A fixed member of the household during this period was Lady Alice Hastings, the elder daughter of the impoverished earl of Huntingdon. By 1631 she was a mature spinster of twenty-five. Whether she lived in the house before her Brydges cousins came, I do not know, but it looks likely that she performed the function of companion and helper in governing youth for the rest of her grandmother's lifetime. It is to Lady Alice Hastings alone that Ralph Codrington, writer of tedious and precious elegies, addresses his piece on the dowager's death. (Alice, or someone else with good sense, endorsed it with the word "troppo.")[20] She is referred to regularly in the accounts as Lady Alice, and some further measure of her permanence may be gained from the fact that she had become copyholder of some valley land in the manor, as a survey of 1636 shows.[21]

All the Hastings branch were frequent visitors at Harefield, and were endebted to the dowager in various ways. The countess of Huntingdon stayed quite often when she came toward London, as she did for a long period on family business during 1632. The other Hastings granddaughter, Elizabeth, was also a frequent visitor, perhaps for considerable periods at a time, and she seems to have been on good terms with her grandmother and sister there. Harefield was probably like a second home to her, as it had become a more or less permanent one for her older sister. In quiet ways the dowager probably helped Huntingdon's parlous finances. The housing of Alice must have been welcome to him. Moreover, in February 1633/4 the countess of Huntingdon died in Bridgewater's

20. H. M. C. Report, Hastings MSS, IV, pp. 341–342.
21. Arbury Hall MS.

house in London,[22] and the Leicestershire home was left without a mistress and with just one daughter, twenty-one-year-old Elizabeth. When Elizabeth married Hugh Calverley that spring, on 10 April 1634, she was married not at Donnington but at Harefield, and her grandmother seems to have borne the cost of the festivity.[23] There was a family gathering, to which Hastingses and Egertons came.

The large family group seems to have been quite closely knit and loyal. The grandmother supported all the Brydgeses to a considerable degree and gave aid also to the Hastings branch, to which she was close, and members of both these branches of her family were either residents at Harefield or frequent visitors. This group of people is most likely to have formed the basis of the band of nobles who presented "honour and devotion" in *Arcades*. The Egertons also visited periodically, and were on good terms as well, though, of course, they needed no support.[24] The general situation in the family from 1631 until the death of the countess suggests that the entertainment of which *Arcades* was a part might have been given partly out of a sense of obligation and grateful recognition for the way she had served as center to the family in a difficult and sensitive time. Milton's verses ensure that the whole festivity is dedicated to her honor, and that she is celebrated as the head of an ideal household, a "shrine" around which nature is blessed back into health each night, and where a spirit of rural innocence can demonstrate the presence of virtue by listening to the music of the spheres. If the gesture was the idea of those most closely associated with the house, it would seem likely that Alice Hastings took some role in its organizations. It may be symptomatic that it is she who has some of the musical instruments put into order for the Christmas holiday season of 1634, when the Lawes brothers are there.

If gratitude is one of the motives behind the invention of the entertainment, we are probably looking for a date some little time after 1631. The

22. Huntington Library MS. EL 6522.

23. The wedding took place several weeks before the beginning of the account book, but on w/e 11 September 1634 there is noted a sum to the confectioner "for banquetting sweetmeates served in at my La: Eliz: wedding & other times not entered before."

24. Despite Breasted's remark that the wealthier Bridgewater offered no help to his stepmother during the crisis, there is evidence to the contrary: for example, he paid her livery fees in October 1631 (Huntington Library MS. EL 6522).

boys would be older, the debts would be greater, and the times less harassed by scandal. The contact of the household and family with the court and its theatricals would also be greater, which may well be a contributing factor in the decision to put on some kind of courtly mannered festivity. From this point of view it may be worthwhile noticing the triumphs of about 1634 in this last great responsibility of the dowager's life, the proper bringing up of her Brydges grandchildren. By February of 1634 (and therefore presumably rather earlier) the young Lord Chandos, now thirteen and a half, had come into the eye of the court, joining his two younger Egerton cousins John and Thomas, as one of the pages in the King's Shrovetide masque, Carew's *Coelum Britannicum.*[25] Her grandsons danced with torches in their hands to precede the entry of the king with the other main masquers. In the summer of 1634, after his fourteenth birthday, Chandos went up to Oxford for his first term, returning in mid-December. Then after Christmas he spent some time in London, staying in Bridgewater House, attending a "cause" of some kind, and moving again in court circles, this time as spectator at the latest masque, Davenant's *Temple of Love.* A few years later his younger brother was also to be entered at Oxford. The period about 1634 seems to have been a gratifying one for the dowager and also a period of interest in theatrical entertainments in the minds of the family, for in 1634 also, of course, the first official residence of Bridgewater in Wales was marked by Milton's masque at Ludlow, and in the journey of Bridgewater's party to the north of the principality they had also been entertained theatrically at Chirk Castle in Denbighshire.[26]

Although it is not the purpose of this article to give detailed arguments concerning the possible dates of *Arcades,* which would occupy a great deal of space, an association with Carew's masque would of course imply that the Harefield entertainment took place some time reasonably soon after February 1634 or I suppose in the Christmas season immediately before. If we take Egerton children into account, we should consider *Coelum Britannicum* again, in which John and Thomas performed, and

25. The most convenient source for most court masques of this period is now S. Orgel and R. Strong, *Inigo Jones: The Theatre of the Stuart Court,* 2 vols. (London, Berkeley & Los Angeles, 1973).

26. B. M., Egerton MS. 2623.13; this is newly edited and identified by the present author in a forthcoming article in *Milton Quarterly.*

also Milton's own Ludlow masque of 29 September 1634. This might argue a date soon before *Comus* (for example, the very beginning of July when Bridgewater visited Harefield for farewells before leaving for Wales), or soon after, as at Christmas 1634, when the Laweses were in the house, having returned from Ludlow.[27] An earlier, and I think less likely, occasion would have been associated with Townshend's *Tempe Restored,* the queen's masque of 14 February 1632. Milton was not yet down from Cambridge. Playing in this masque were Lady Katherine Egerton as a main masquer and John (only nine and called Lord Ellesmere) and Alice Egerton among the children representing the influence of the stars. Whatever exactly was the context for *Arcades,* it would seem that some two or three years after the bad spring and summer of 1631, we have the sort of family situation, centered on Harefield and close in time to the participation of young members of the family in court and courtly theatricals, in which the gesture of *Arcades* might be thought to make sense.

III. The Fitness of the Invention

With the conjecture of some such context in mind, we may look more closely at the leading characteristics of Milton's invention in *Arcades.*

First, not only is a pastoral goddess honored, but the whole household and demesne of Harefield is also celebrated. The fiction ends in the gesture of honor to the countess, the kissing of her garment, and in the invitation to

> Bring your flocks, and live with us,
> Here ye shall have greater grace,
> To serve the Lady of this place.
>
> (ll. 103–105)

Not merely a ritual visitation but a residence seems to be proposed. Members of her family dress up as Arcadians, *pretending* to be aliens to the place with which they are familiar. Whichever branches of her family

27. W / e 11 December, stables account: "Bate by Mr Lawes horse"; w / 25 December, extraordinary expenses: "To Hussie for fetching Mr Lawes horse & his brothers from Lond."

participated in the gesture, at least two, if not three, of the Brydges children came among shepherds and shepherdesses, and at least Alice of the Hastings family, for these children were actually resident at the house. A fiction that suggests a "greater grace" in coming to live here would have been a fiction delicately apt, by which some of her family could express the happiness of their coming to a new home.

Second, the fiction of the quest also expresses the specific nature of the occasion. As we have said, Arcadians are singers and dancers, the dowager's relatives have put on dramatic disguise, and a particular function of the whole occasion would seem to be to delight the old lady by bringing theatrical and musical festivity to her house. At this time of her life she visited neighboring houses, like that of her friend the countess of Monmouth just up the hill toward Rickmansworth at Moor Park, but there is no indication that she ever went near the court any more. Yet evidently she delighted in courtly kinds of theatricals. So those who celebrate her as mother-goddess do so because they have determined to dedicate some kind of courtly entertainment to her, as she sits at home, bringing music and dance, poetry and disguisings, to the house. As the third song indicates, the Arcadians have been dancing somewhere else, and now they are to come and dance here instead.

On this last point it is tempting to speculate further. It may be merely part of the fiction to remind the chief beholder that shepherds and nymphs have been dancing somewhere else—that is, in Arcadia proper. The Arcadians travel overseas, as Alpheus to Arethusa. One could also see a topical reference. Have they been dancing at court perhaps? Or at least some of them? Or, being often at court, have they brought with them a taste of its arts? Could it be that the Arcadia they have come from is the place where a queen reigns who delights above all in pastoral celebrations?

I would put these things forward only as conjectures and would not want to suggest that the fiction is not elaborated in its own terms. The self-sufficiency of the poetic invention is both a mark of a poet's independent integrity and also a contribution to the tact and decorum of such a piece. The pretenses are satisfyingly complete, brief though they are. In their opening song the Arcadians feign surprise that "this clime" should hold "A deity so unparallelled," as if the Arcadia they have come from ought automatically, on first consideration, to be thought superior.

The transference of Arcadian excellence to this rural place is justified during the action, so that at the end Genius, being local, being partisan, being the informing spirit of the episode, can resort to a touch of triumphant mischief in the third song: was not Arcadia stony in comparison to these green lawns? Complete though the poetic pretenses are, if a reference to the court is a part of this comic celebration, it would give more point to the two lines inserted afterward into the Trinity manuscript, to the puzzlement of some commentators:

> Though Syrinx your Pan's mistress were,
> Yet Syrinx well might wait on her.
>
> (ll. 106–107)

Charles, like James before him, would be Pan, and the upstaged mistress would be the queen. "And the dame hath Syrinx grace!" wrote Jonson of James's queen at Althorp. Harefield centers on its own "rural queen," whose service must be recognized above all other, on this occasion, because the disguised ones are to acknowledge a particular obligation and kinship, and because their determination is to make a modest aristocratic household in the country display its own happiness, momentarily in a regal way.

If we look at *Arcades* in some such way, we may make an intelligent guess as to how Milton's verses were only a "part" of an evening's entertainment. It is called "Part of an Entertainment presented to the Countess Dowager of Darby at Harefield, by some Noble Persons of her Family," and we know nothing of the other parts. In the cancelled start in the manuscript, surely inaccurately and for a time only, Milton first called it "Part of a maske." Just in what sense the term masque might be applicable to *Arcades* will be discussed below, but that Milton flirted with the term at all might suggest that some kind of dancing took place during the evening, and this the invitation of the third song would also seem to imply. It is rather unusual and puzzling to have a part of an entertainment written by an author, with no indication given of an identity or occasion for the whole festivity, as, for example, the visit of some great personage, the most usual cause of entertainments at country houses. But if the intention was to present to the dowager, as a token of familial triumph in which she had a share, some sample of the kind of skills in dance and song (and if we think of *Comus,* in acting) that the children were acquiring in their courtly training, then it is easy to imagine that the "entertainment" was made up of some recapitulations or imitations or adaptations of masquing. The other parts of the festivity might have been derived from things seen and heard at court or at Ludlow. There were servants at Harefield who were musicians,[28] but if the family group had the assistance of the Lawes brothers, such a program would have been easier to sustain.[29] Because there was dancing and because the genesis of the entertainment was probably in some kind of masquing, Milton first fell into calling the whole event a masque, then realized that this could not really be right. He could give no clear indication of the identity of the whole entertainment, perhaps, since it probably had the structure of a miscellany or an adaptation. The occasion also was essentially private, even rather delicate, not to be published. Only his part, written to dedicate the whole affair to the countess, had a structural completeness of its own. Hence it was merely "part of an entertainment."

IV. Form and Staging

The formal characteristics and staging of Milton's contribution are usually misunderstood. The most obvious and prevalent misconception about it is that it is a masque. It is clear that critics have the masque and *Comus* in mind, not only when they call the Harefield verses a "little masque" but also, I suspect, when they dismiss it as a "slight affair."[30] Just as the masque is not quite the correct form by which to measure and assess this "part of an entertainment," neither is the common type of country-house entertainment for royalty, which usually began with an elaborate welcome in the park. By this pattern, however, it has been reconstructed more than once, partly because the general influence of Jon-

28. Messrs. Jones, Allen, and Cotton had the upkeep of their viols paid by the countess. In the house were also a harpsichord and a virginal.

29. However, music for *Arcades* is not included in Henry Lawes's manuscript in the British Museum, which seems to have been quite a full record of his compositions.

30. Phrases from A.S.P. Woodhouse and Douglas Bush, *A Variorum Commentary on the Poems of John Milton* (London, 1972), II, pt. 2, 526, and D. Daiches, *Milton* (London, 1957), p. 62.

son's earlier entertainments has been felt, especially that of *Althorp,* and partly because of the previous royal entertainment at this same house in 1602. *Arcades* does show certain likenesses in rhetorical procedure with these entertainments, but it does not share the same function or have the same staging arrangements.

The false identification with either masque or entertainment welcome (or sometimes both at the same time) leads to two most noticeable false assumptions about Milton's piece: first, that it embodied dance within the compass of the text, like a masque; and, second, that its "scene" was set out of doors, like the welcoming part of a country-house entertainment. The fact is that in itself *Arcades* is shaped like nothing else that survives from the period. One reason for its singularity may seem obvious enough —that it is only a part of some longer festivity. More importantly, the uniqueness arises out of the particularities of function and occasion. Form is dictated by function, and not vice versa, and it is the occasion itself, as far as we can understand it, that apparently has no exact analogue in any entertainment from the period. Of course, in making his contribution, the poet showed an awareness of the conventions of the nearest proximate forms, of masque and entertainment, and any poet of the time in his position would have done what the young Milton probably did, that is, browse through the 1616 Folio of Jonson, the most comprehensive pattern book in print.

Milton never called his "part" a masque, as far as we know. Nevertheless, one major characteristic of masque his piece does have, and this leads to other masquelike features in it. The performing nobility assume disguise symbolic of their own being, conceived in idealized fashion, and placed in a fiction appropriate to the occasion. Participants of lower standing also took part in masques, though usually in the burlesque or supporting roles—usually, in fact, in the acting roles or as musicians—but it was assumed that the chief symbolic presences in masque should be personated by the high nobility or royalty where that was possible. These chief figures were often "discovered" spectacularly, and stepped down to the dancing floor in front of the stage, to dance measures mimetic of order and virtue, and to begin the revels, the social dancing in which performers and beholders mixed. Culmination in such dance is crucial to masque proper at the court of this period, and the identity of the actual and the ideal, through the pretense of images, is a prerequisite for the function of exemplary celebration. In those masques that were printed, the list of chief masquers was often appended to the text.

The main pretense at Harefield was that the noble persons of the family were foreign Arcadians coming to find this new queen of which Fame had spoken. This is an aspect of Milton's "part" that makes it masquelike. By a curious reversal, it is in this respect more like a masque than *Comus,* in which the chief masquers of noble blood are limited to three children who assume virtually no disguise at all, act rather as in a play, and are not discovered in any spectacular fashion, though they do dance at the end of the action.

Added to masquelike disguisings in *Arcades* must be considered the masquelike quality of the central fiction of the quest. The quest is a natural extension of the idea of the action coming to serve a noble presence seated in a state. Among court masques, an analogy could be provided, for instance, in Jonson's early *Masque of Blacknesse.* Here questers also move toward the desired presence and are met or intercepted on the way. They are said to be daughters of Niger seeking the light of Britannia, and in a marginal note Jonson also resorts to the tale of Alpheus and Arethusa as support for the notion of freshwater Niger traveling across salt Ocean to Albion in the west. The fiction of the quest in *Arcades* is essentially a masquelike invention, though explored in more personal and less nationalistic terms than in *Blacknesse.*

For all this, Milton's piece lacks the one feature most essential to proper masque: it does not seem to me that the action leads into dance or revels within the compass of Milton's text, although critics have often tried to make out that dances feature somewhere in it. Dances belong to some later parts, not to this part of Milton's. It is among those who assume that *Arcades* is a slight masque that one finds assumptions being made that there are dances implied within the compass of the text. Woodhouse, for example, in the *Variorum Commentary,* claims that the usual narrative or directions of printed masques are missing from the text of *Arcades* at the point where dances would have been performed.[31] He takes it that we must infer that, as the Arcadians are invited to approach the state in the second song, the Genius invites them to dance. He conjectures that the beginning of the third song—"nymphs and shepherds dance no more

31. *Variorum Commentary,* p. 542.

/ By sandy Ladon's lilied banks"—halts the dance. Dances have been placed elsewhere in the action. Parker, in his biography, assumes a danced forward movement during the second song.[32]

This seems to me unjustified supposition. Nothing in the second song suggests dance. The most obvious reason for there being no prose direction in the text mentioning dance is that there were no dances within the compass of the text. I cannot see why both the carefully corrected Trinity manuscript and the printed texts should present an inconsistency, by including fairly explicit prose descriptions for *Comus* and not for *Arcades*. Or why we should have directions at the beginning of *Arcades* and not at the end. Milton's text was not constructed to contain dance, and therefore in no proper sense can it be treated as masque.

In its disguisings and invention Milton's Harefield piece is masquelike, then, without actually constituting a masque or even, probably, part of a masque. It was meant to evoke and introduce the masquing world. It seems to me that it has been the assumption that it ought to be a proper masque that has encouraged the idea that dances are implied in the text. This in turn has led to a conclusion that the text is defective. By prejudice, form has been imposed on *Arcades* from without. Confusions of similar order have arisen in assuming a likeness between *Arcades* and parts of country-house entertainments.

By the term "country-house entertainment" I refer to the kind of event put on at country houses for the visit of some great personage. Most commonly these feature on royal progresses or other royal journeys. In terms of structural convention the country-house entertainment is not so closely delineated as masque. Nevertheless, common conventions can be recognized. The type most often found, and closest in some of its aspects to *Arcades,* is that represented by Jonson's entertainments at Althorp (1603) and Highgate (1604). If one is thinking of what was available to Milton in print, and if one lays aside for the moment the great Kenilworth entertainment of 1575 as being distinct in scope, he would have had access to the early entertainments of Jonson in the 1616 Folio, Sidney's older *Entertainment at Wanstead* (*The Lady of May*), which was frequently reprinted with the *Arcadia* in the 1620s and 1630s, and Campion's *Caversham Entertainment* for Queen Anne and Prince Henry of 1613.

---

32. W. R. Parker, *Milton: A Biography* (Oxford, 1968), I, 83.

Caversham shares many of the characteristics of *Althorp* and *Highgate*. Sidney's piece for Queen Elizabeth, on the other hand, has a boldness and a playfulness about it, born of a familiarity on the part of the author, which no later poet for royalty in such a presentation could equal, although a spirit of comedy appears in others. It looks likely that Jonson's early entertainments were influential as models for the other entertainments of the seventeenth century.

Similar characteristics are also shown by entertainments which Milton could not have known or is unlikely to have known: Jonson's later *Entertainment at Welbeck* (1633) and *Love's Welcome at Bolsover* (1634), not printed until 1640; Marston's entertainment at Ashby in 1607 for the same countess of Derby, never printed; the mainly prose Harefield entertainment of Sir John Davies given in 1602 for Elizabeth by the same countess, mentioned above, never printed; the rather different but related indoor banquet-entertainment given to the earl of Bridgewater at Chirk Castle in 1634, also mentioned above and never printed. For some of these pleas could be made that Milton might have seen a manuscript copy. There also must have been other manuscript texts which have not survived.

Country-house entertainments for royalty often spread over several days. The exact arrangements were obviously related to such factors as the length of the visit. The easiest way to describe the features of these entertainments is to identify three parts. The first would be the elaborate welcome, given on the arrival of the great visitors. The third would be the speeches of farewell, given on the day of departure, sometimes with the presentation of gifts. These speeches were seldom long. The second, middle parts, much the most variable, would be whatever theatrical or spectacular diversions might have been organized on the middle day or days of the stay. In two cases, at Caversham and Ashby, proper masques were presented after supper in this middle period.

Insofar as *Arcades* has been compared to these entertainments, it has been an analogy with the first, welcoming parts that has taken the minds of Milton's commentators. The welcome was often the largest part of the whole festivities, from a theatrical point of view. Usually it began out of doors, frequently at the entrance to the park enclosure or at some convenient point within the park, where the visiting party could be intercepted. The speeches were generally spoken by actors playing local rustics or local deities. Sometimes apparent rudeness or ignorance was contrived to begin with, feigning absence of welcome or lack of decorum, so that this could be superceded by more courtly welcomes as the party was conducted toward the house. Thus, at Ashby, melancholy gives way to a spirit of generous festivity. In Jonson's Theobalds entertainment of 1607 the sad mood of Genius is corrected by the better wisdom of Mercury. At Chirk the ignorance of rustic Genius, who feigns not to know who the visitors are, is made good by knowing, courtly Orpheus. Such rhetorical devices were made to create a sense of progression and to define the proper spirit of celebration.

There seem to me to be several ways in which one might consider comparisons between *Arcades,* as the opening part of some kind of entertainment, and the welcomes of the type of country-house entertainment represented by *Althorp, Highgate, Caversham,* and the other extant texts. Some of the figures of compliment are similar, though commonplace elsewhere; the function of both extends to the encouragement of a state of mind in which the ensuing events might be enjoyed; both Milton's piece and these other entertainments focus on the spirit of a particular place, hence use a local deity as mouthpiece. But one analogy, thought of especially in connection with the previous Harefield entertainment of 1602, has been assumed which in my view is false, and it has caused considerable misunderstanding about the staging of *Arcades.* It has often been assumed that *Arcades* was played out of doors.

Early scholars sensed some kinship between *Arcades* and country-house entertainments. In his edition Todd gave a long description of the Ashby entertainment, which had not then been published, but he drew no conclusions from the analogy.[33] It seems to have been Masson who gave currency to the idea of outdoor performance. He described *Arcades* as "a little open-air pastoral of songs and speeches" and imagined it in the following manner:

The time is evening. Harefield House it lit up; and, not far from it, on a throne of state so arranged as to glitter in the light, the aged countess is seated. . . . Suddenly torches are seen flickering amid the trees of the park; and up the long avenue of elms, as we fancy,—the identical avenue which

33. *The Poetical Works of John Milton,* ed. H. J. Todd, 2d ed. (London, 1809), VI, 151–156.

had borne the name of "the Queen's Walk" ever since Elizabeth had passed through it two-and-thirty years before—there advance the torch-bearers, and with them a band of nymphs and shepherds, clad as Arcadians.[34]

In 1602 Elizabeth had been intercepted by a dairy farm out in the park, had been escorted down the avenue of elms, and had been directed to a chair placed on a stage especially built near the front steps of the house. It was, of course, summer. Masson has recreated *Arcades* in the same way, except that the countess is seated on her state all through, and the "visitors" move toward her. Modern critics have found such ideas congenial. ". . . arranged for an outdoor, evening performance, and his lines show some awareness of the actual setting," says Parker.[35] "A particular outdoor setting" is the verdict of Demaray, in his full-length account of Milton and the masque.[36] He reconstructs the event much as Masson did, with the 1602 entertainment, and other entertainments, in mind. The *Variorum Commentary* thinks it "reasonable to suppose that this preliminary part . . . may have been set out of doors."[37]

To ideas of *Arcades* as an outdoor performance there are serious objections. First, if the state was actually illuminated with torches or candles (of which we cannot be sure) to give a "sudden blaze," it is unlikely that it was placed out of doors. These chairs were sometimes put outside in the daytime, as at Harefield in 1602. Were illuminated states ever placed out in the elements? Orgel and Strong do not think so.[38]

Second, and most crucially, this is simply not the welcome of a country-house entertainment of the familiar type. Its function is different. It is true that Genius pays compliment to the noble "visitors," according to the pretense of the moment:

> Stay gentle swains, for though in this disguise,
> I see bright honour sparkle through your eyes,
> Of famous Arcady ye are, . . .

> (ll. 26–28)

34. Masson, I, 563–564.
35. Parker, I, 81.
36. J. G. Demaray, *Milton and the Masque Tradition* (Cambridge, Mass., 1968), p. 49.
37. *Variorum Commentary*, p. 531.
38. *Inigo Jones*, I, 128–129.

> And ye the breathing roses of the wood,
> Fair silver-buskined nymphs as great and good, . . .
>
> (ll. 32–33)

But the piece is not primarily in honor of the "visitors" at all, but in honor of the resident lady, whose presence is the goal of their quest. The preceding song of the Arcadians had already celebrated her, and the force of compliment in Genius's speech turns immediately on her:

> I know this quest of yours, and free intent
> Was all in honour and devotion meant
> To the great mistress of yon princely shrine,
> Whom with low reverence I adore as mine,
> And with all helpful service will comply
> To further this night's glad solemnity; . . .
>
> (ll. 34–39)

From this point of view the invention is more like that of a masque, like Jonson's *Masque of Blacknesse,* as we have seen, and the action moves to the state, as it does in the Ludlow masque.

Third, we may notice that this is performed in the evening, being "this night's glad solemnity." The "blaze" of the state suggests some degree of darkness, and the elms are said to be "star-proof." There are obvious, though I suppose not insuperable, difficulties in arranging something like a welcome, beginning outdoors, in too much darkness. Welcomes are characteristically daytime events, whereas of course other kinds of theatrical entertainment, including masques, were usually played after supper in the evening, most often during the winter festive season.

Fourth, it would have been difficult for the countess to hear what was said by the Arcadians and Genius at the opening of the action. All the speeches are in her honor, and must be heard by her. I cannot see how this could easily be possible outside, across the length of woods and lawns. Woodhouse's concession of making the state "visible from without" hardly helps the auditory problem. Parker has "the grand old lady peering into the darkness beyond from a shining and canopied throne," but no hearing. Demaray indicates a "suitable distance" between the position of the first song and the countess's chair, like Donne's "within convenient distance stood." In a proper welcome the problem does not arise, because it is always the moving party that is being addressed as it comes toward the house.

There seems to me no doubt that *Arcades* was played indoors, in whatever great chamber Harefield offered, in the evening, making artful though not extravagant use of artificial light. The use of the word "scene" might also be thought to be technical, to mean in this case a single standing set or playing place, however modest or perfunctory. It may have signified simply a part of the room in which the initial dramatic action took place.

It is reasonable to speculate about the arrangement in the room, since what immediately suggests itself is an organization derived on a modest scale from the normal staging of masques. The chief dramatic action, such as it is, is represented by the song of the appearing Arcadians and the intercepting speech of Genius. This takes place on or in front of a "scene" at one end of the room, facing the state, which is placed at, or toward, the other end. The Arcadians appear, sing, gesturing toward the state, and offer to come forward across the room. Genius stops them as they start to move forward, speaks his long speech, then conducts them across the intervening space of floor during the second song:

> O'er the smooth enamelled green
> Where no print of step hath been,
> Follow me as I sing, . . .
>
> (ll. 84–86)

The third song marks the arrival to her presence, to "kiss her sacred vesture's hem."

It is true that their journey across the room is made to sound as if it were through the park, over lawns and "under the shady roof / Of branching elm star-proof," but both lawns and overarching elms are equally suggestive of the *pretense* that they are outside in the park. The "smooth enamelled green" may perhaps be likened to the customary green carpeting used for the central dancing space in masques, set between stage and state, and referred to also in the interludes and dance features of plays. The general arrangement of "scene" at one end of the room, state at the other, and an intervening space of floor for dancing, is in conscious imitation of the usual arrangement for court masques, deliberately reminding all those present of court masques, but adapted to the limitations of little spectacle and smaller scale.

There may have been careful use of light. It seems unlikely that there was much scenery, and there may have been none. For the three "scenes" at Ludlow the salient features are mentioned in the text, and nothing is mentioned for Harefield. The intention was not for costly spectacle, but on the contrary to call up courtly show and then to establish the Arcadian superiority of this modest rural celebration, a truer Arcadianism resulting. Of course props and costumes could sometimes be borrowed, but an illuminated state would be fairly easily improvised or suggested, and so too the pastoral dress. Genius requires a more particular costume. It may or may not be significant that nothing is needed for *Arcades,* except the simple pastoral dress, which was not also required for *Comus,* assuming that Genius and the Attendant Spirit could make do with the same clothes.

Milton's piece, then, is in no simple sense either masque or country-house welcome. It has no dances within the compass of the text. It was played not out of doors, but probably in the great hall of the house, where the room had been arranged somewhat in the fashion of a masquing hall. As a text, it is a part of some larger festivity, but not in itself fragmentary or defective. What, then, may we call it, in terms that are properly descriptive? Milton had no word for it, except finally "part of an entertainment." Nor I think have we, if we are to be as careful as he in our choice of vocabulary. He had no scruples about the kind of *Comus:* he thought it was a species of masque, so he called it a masque: "A Masque presented at Ludlow Castle." His Harefield verses he could call neither masque nor entertainment, and, perhaps precisely because they could have no title accurately descriptive of kind except the untidy and rather unhelpful "part of an entertainment," he gave them instead a poetic identity, *Arcades.*

V. Comic Pretense and Sober Compliment

Daiches's remark that *Arcades* is a "slight affair" touches quite a common attitude among the commentators, even among some of those who find its "purely aesthetic attitude" and "aristocratic art" appealing.[39] This may provoke the question of just how we can call it limited or slight.

39. *Variorum Commentary,* pp. 524, 526.

Clearly, it is pointless to measure *Arcades* against the full expectations of masque. It does not get us very far to have in mind all the potential public aspects of the court masque, where all present were invited to see their court in the context of a mystique of virtuous power inherent in king and nation, and where the images were likely to be drawn up on a historical, heroic, or schematically moral and philosophical basis. Despite its use of the courtly Arcadian mythology and the evidence of its moral tone, *Arcades* has no public aspect of this kind at all, being a part of a small family celebration. It seems to me that it does not even have the references to England in it that some seek to find, making "this clime" a "new homeland for pastoral poetry."[40] If it is slight, it is largely because its occasional function was private and limited.

It seems to me that it is not slight if judged in the context of what it was apparently asked to do. In maintaining this, I would like to pick out several characteristics of the poetry and to relate them to the kind of function that I have conjectured Milton was to serve. I would like to describe what strike me as the particular sources of delight in the performance, in this epideictic mode in which delight and fitness ought to be hard to separate.

As the nobles enter at one end of the room, the first source of pleasure exploited is the delight in pretense and disguise itself. The countess sees those she knows dressed as shepherds and shepherdesses and hears that they are pretending to be strange to her. She is asked to pretend, with them, that they could think of mistaking this "she," or only guess at her identity, or be informed only by Fame. Genius adds to the pleasures of feigning by giving the disguised ones a poetic identity as Arcadians. In fact his opening words exploit pretense in more ways than one: it is plain that he is familiar with and privy to the play of the whole affair, yet he asserts that he can recognize them *despite* their disguise, "though in this disguise." The particular delight is always in the curious interplay of real and fictional identities.

His own fictional identity he gives out fully soon after. Again, I take it as a source of particular delight. There is a touch of comic portentous-

40. An idea of C. Brooks and J. E. Hardy in *Poems of John Milton: The 1645 Edition* (New York, 1951), pp. 163–168, adapted by S. D. Blau in "Milton's Salvational Aesthetic," *Journal of Religion*, XLVI (1966), 282–295.

ness in the announcement: "For know by lot from Jove I am the power . . ." At the same time he registers the self-sufficiency of a poetic dialect, in which it will be no embarrassment to figure God in Jove. Genius's identity also reinforces the whole scene as a wood, and it provides further elaboration on the delight of holding simultaneously in the mind the "real" identity of servant-musician and the "fictional" identity as guardian divinity of the wood. This sport with identity is given a new twist, when first, in the persona of deity (though with reference to his actual musicality), he states that he hears the music of the spheres

> which none can hear
> Of human mould with gross unpurged ear; . . .
>
> (ll. 72–73)

In part this is obsequious praise—the present company are to assume that they, too, are able to hear it—but it is also comic, in that the momentary suprahuman pride does not sort easily with a musician's subservient social station. A similar comic level operates with the Attendant Spirit in *Comus*.

The next lines, effecting a main turn in the speech, make the whole rhetorical strategy manifest:

> And yet such music worthiest were to blaze
> The peerless height of her immortal praise, . . .
>
> (ll. 74–75)

Then again the intimate delight of feigning: as Genius refers again to her, he becomes the opposite of divinely arrogant:

> If my inferior hand or voice could hit
> Inimitable sounds, yet as we go,
> Whate'er the skill of lesser gods can show,
> I will assay, her worth to celebrate, . . .
>
> (ll. 77–80)

The social reality of his subservience reasserts itself. The figure is saved from fulsomeness by the consistency of the rhetorical pretense and progression. Raised now to all-heavenly goddess by the logic of the application of the music of the spheres, it is no wonder that a lower, earth-bound god might hesitate to express her. Rhetorical assertion, delight in pretense, a kind of intimate comedy in acting—all these operate inextricably together.

There is nothing slight in the whole rhetorical conception of Genius's speech. It is sustained and confident in its procedures. The leisurely elaboration of his pastoral descriptions is remarkable. Fifteen whole lines go to the description of plant doctoring, after he has introduced the topic in lines 44–45. Similarly, ten lines elaborate "the celestial siren's harmony." The sustained rhetorical structure of the speech is itself offered as a source of delight, and there is also delight in the sheer detail of the poetry. Figures of pastoral healing can be met elsewhere, as in *Pan's Anniversarie* or Fletcher's *The Faithful Shepherdess,* revived for royal performance in 1634,[41] but noone does them with such resourcefulness as Milton, here and in *Comus*. At the same time, these figures of pastoral healing and of the music of the spheres convey a moral force: moral exemplification cannot easily be separated out, either, from the means of entertainment.

The second song, as we have seen, teases with the details of pretense, inviting the hearers to translate places in the room into the features of the park outside. The third song, as we have also noticed, ends the action with a note of not unmischievous triumph, for the whole action, like Genius's speech, needs a sense of rhetorical progression. So Lycaeus is remembered as "old," Cyllene as "hoar," and Maenalus as "stony," in the determination to celebrate now this new Arcadian place. Again, there is nothing obtrusive or forced in this device, for the epithets are in themselves unexceptional. The mischief is in context and rhetorical design. Then, with a snook cocked at Syrinx, the triumph is complete.

It may seem invidious or elementary to labor a description of the modes of pretense in *Arcades,* yet it seems to me that it has been the spirit of intimate play that has sometimes eluded those of Milton's commentators who have bothered with the piece. Too often the pretenses have been taken with inflexible literalness, or sometimes converted (for easier handling) into the more somber mode of schematic allegory.[42] The false identification with the royal welcome was all the easier when critics

41. G. E. Bentley, *The Jacobean and Caroline Stage* (Oxford, 1941–1968), VII, 91–92. The designs seem to have been by Jones, though the play is not fully considered in Orgel and Strong.

42. Apart from Brooks and Hardy, the most elaborate allegorization is by J. M. Wallace, "Milton's *Arcades,*" *JEGP,* LVIII (1959), 627–636.

thought in literal-minded terms of real visitors coming across the real park. So too with allegorizations of the piece, which cannot cope with the elusive and shifting effects of intimate disguise, or properly describe the structure of its rhetorical procedures. Some critics, perhaps, have been seeking the firmer symbolism of more public inventions like the court masque. It is interesting to see that similar problems have been acute in commentary on Milton's Ludlow masque, which does have the firmer symbolism and more programmatic idealizations and exhortations for a public occasion. But at the same time *Comus* also delights and teases with intimate pretenses, for the "family" context of *Arcades* is also present at Ludlow, and coexists with the masque's other modes.

If my suggestions are correct about the sort of context and occasion to which *Arcades* may belong, we could extract two main functions of Milton's dedicatory verses. They had to make a gesture of honor to the mother figure of the family, and in this regard the rhetorical devices of *Arcades* resemble those of other kinds of poetry of praise. They are not, in this sense, particularly original. They also had to delight her and to put her and all concerned into a fit mood for the presentation of the subsequent entertainments of song and dance or whatever. In this second function of defining a spirit for festivity, the purpose of *Arcades* shares some common ground with the welcome, which sought to settle the visitor and household into the best attitude for the occasion, a spirit both decorously respectful and gay. Or, to cast the net wider, it shares some common ground also with the technique of the opening acts of Shakespearian comedy, where a challenge is often issued to the audience to join in a mood of communal festivity, exorcising inappropriate sentiments. So also, incidentally, with Milton's twin poems *L'Allegro* and *Il Penseroso,* which are comic in spirit, and which begin with the banishment of melancholy in the opening of the first poem—the poems might belong to some festive occasion. In this function of creating a fit mood of comic celebration, commentators do not seem to me to follow Milton's text very closely. My suggestion that Syrinx makes a hit at court may only be conjectural, but there is further evidence of comic pretense and of an edge of playful extravagance in the speech and final song of Genius. And surely in many kinds of celebratory or complimentary composition some license of extravagant play is understood and expected, else the praise is apt to become a burden, and dull, and if dull, indecorous. That "comic" pretenses of *Arcades* cannot be disjoined from its function as dedicatory compliment is one mark of its success.

As to the moral integrity of *Arcades*, this quality critics have been quicker to see. Many have noticed the insistence on the figure of the music of the spheres, and with knowledge of Milton's other writings the critics can see better than the countess of Derby might have done the signs of a favorite Miltonic expression of high ethical import. Critical responses to implications of salvation or redemption do not seem altogether wide of the mark.[43] One knows the directions of Milton's very religious masque. What seems to me remarkable about this part of Genius's speech is that it is so much contained within the demands of decorum. It is not that Milton, impatient of the devices of aristocratic celebration, seeks to pervert the conventions into a new direction; or, at least, not simply that. The moral integrity of this passage of Genius's speech actually contributes to its art of compliment.

There is in fact a particular integrity about the whole of Genius's speech which amounts to a scrupulousness both aristocratic and religious. The praises offered to the countess in the first song are commonplace, and it is not unfitting that they are. The seeking of a divinity, the guessing at the goddess's name—these are acceptable gestures because they announce the pretenses, and recollect the kind of courtly aesthetic in which the masquing grandchildren had been practised. What Genius offers is both more elaborate and more serious, since it relates this aesthetic to considerations of moral purity and of God's providence. In terms of compliment, we know that it is part of a large rhetorical figure that special protective, healing powers, ordained by God, should be associated with the countess's estate. But a lesser poet than Milton would have made the connection explicit, would have *said* that it was because of her presence that such prosperousness and benediction reigned. Milton, for his part, insists with religious exactitude and artistic nicety that Genius is the servant of Jove, and feigns that the contact between Genius and the countess is rather remote. This is not simply the case of a poet stopping one short of idolatry in praise, acknowledging Grace, and setting his art in a new direction. It is in itself a compliment to the countess's

43. See S. D. Blau and J. S. Lawry, *The Shadow of Heaven* (Ithaca, N.Y., 1968), pp. 51–58.

apprehension, her perception both of religious nicety and of delicacy in an invention. It should have been a compliment and a delight to her, that the poet expected in her, the chief understander, that acuteness of judgment. The integrity of the poet in celebration is projected on to the chief recipient of the entertainment. Ben Jonson, of course, made demands on his beholders of masque, and was inevitably disappointed. However that may have been, with Milton, both at Harefield and at Ludlow, it is in some such sense of high-minded decorousness in invention that his art shows itself as incomparably aristocratic.

Richelieu's Theater: The Mirror of a Prince

TIMOTHY C. MURRAY

> A quoy peut-estre on m'objectera, que le Theatre est un lieu
> d'instruction publique, et que le Poëte Dramatique n'a pas
> moins intention d'instruire, que de plaire . . . car comme la
> Poësie Dramatique est l'Imitation des actions humaines, et c'est
> ce qu'elle doit faire directement.
>
> L'Abbé d'Aubignac

ARMAND JEAN DU PLESSIS, Cardinal de Richelieu, was highly praised by
the Abbé d'Aubignac for his instrumental patronage of the early
French theater. Theatrical instruction played a particularly important
role not only in this neoclassical dramatic poetry, but also in the private
theater built by Richelieu in his Palais Cardinal. The image reflected by
the ceremonial pageants of the Salle de la Comédie[1] always displayed a
specific moral theme: the power and order of its host, the Cardinal de

---

1. The large theater in the Palais Cardinal is identified as *la Salle de la
Comédie* by Henri Sauval in *Histoire et Recherches des Antiquités de la Ville
de Paris,* V.II (Paris, 1724), p. 161.

Richelieu. Whether as a hall for public ceremony, as a stage for the production of drama, or as a center for state balls and entertainment, the Salle de la Comédie was a signifier of the princely generosity and the political principles that were promoted by Richelieu. An analysis of the first production in the Salle de la Comédie will clarify exactly how this theater and its spectacle functioned as a mirror of Richelieu's political order.

The metaphor of theater as mirror was commonly used in the Renaissance to symbolize the instructive value of dramatic action. The French cherished the theatrical "miroirs publics"[2] because

> la Comedie apparoist un exemple
> Où chacun de son fait les actions contemple:
> Le monde est le theatre, et les hommes acteurs.[3]

By presenting the mirror of man's life, dramatic action imprints this moral image on the mind of the viewer. The viewer, in turn, translates the image into a message that he associates with it. For he brings to the theater a code of symbols that act as signifiers of dramatic action. The signs reflected by the theatrical mirror function as "summations and confirmations" of the symbolic meanings previously acquired. The Cardinal created an environment requiring a unified effort of author, player, and spectator to translate the actions of the stage into moral and political themes which could be reenacted in the world.

No better example of this process can be found than the opening night of the Salle de la Comédie. For the inauguration of his theater, Richelieu had commissioned *Mirame,* the play by Jean Desmarets de Saint Sorlin. But it was the opening of the theater itself that was of prime importance. The inauguration was given special grandeur by the "Comédie de pompe et de parade" that followed the play. Central to the entire occasion was Richelieu himself, in his role as author, audience, and player in the theater of France.

2. Molière, "La Critique de l'Ecole des Femmes," in *Oeuvres Complètes,* V.I, ed. Maurice Rat (Paris, 1956), p. 539.

3. Pierre de Ronsard, "Pour La Fin d'une Comédie," in *Oeuvres Complètes,* V.II, ed. Gustave Cohen (Paris, 1950), p. 472.

The Salle de la Comédie provided the French aristocrat in the early seventeenth century with a new theatrical experience.[4] It was the first private structure of major proportions to have a permanent stage.[5] Richelieu constructed the Salle de la Comédie for the purpose of presenting an ordered and hierarchical setting for the serious contemplation of drama. On the opening night of 14 January 1641, the hall itself was the

4. Before Richelieu inaugurated his *salle* in 1641, two permanent public theaters stood out as architectural examples of "ces édifices magnifiques" which frame "toute l'enceinte du lieu commun aux Acteurs, & aux Spectateurs." (A definition of *théâtre* cited by Antoine Furetière, *Dictionnaire Universel*, vol. IV [The Hague, 1727].) Their relation to the Palais Cardinal is of particular interest to our discussion. The Hôtel de Bourgogne boasted the oldest public theater in Paris. Its open and crowded *parterre* made for rowdy audiences which would have tried the patience of any serious viewer. The chaos exhibited in the hall was mirrored on stage by the Bourgogne's penchant for slapstick and farce and by its reliance on *decor simultané*. The scenery consisted of up to five compartments placed side by side which depicted different locations. In order to situate a scene, an actor would first place himself in or in front of a certain compartment. The compartment then served as the spatial referent for the entire scene—even if the actor moved down stage. (Refer to T. E. Lawrenson, *The French Stage in the XVIIth Century* [Manchester, 1957], pp. 81–85.) The combination of *decor simultané* with the audience of the *parterre,* who "ne cessent aussi de parler, de sifler, & de crier, & pour ce qu'ils . . . ne viennent-là qu'à faute d'autre occupation," must have resulted in a confusing, if not often nonsensical production. (François Parfaict, *Histoire du théâtre François* [Paris, 1745], VI, 128.) The Théâtre du Marais provided an alternative to the Hôtel de Bourgogne. If our accounts are at all accurate, the Marais, a converted *jeu de paume,* seemed to be a slight bit tamer than the Hôtel de Bourgogne. A partial reason for this difference might have been the Marais's tendency to present tragedy. In addition, machinery was accented at the Marais, as were the unities of place and *décor*. Richelieu's preference for the group of actors associated with the Marais probably originated from the seriousness of their drama, and from the order and unity of their machinery. However, the Cardinal did not frequent the public theater.

5. Preceding the Salle de la Comédie, there were probably a number of small private theaters in and around Paris. Richelieu himself had two. A small theater on his estate at Rueil was used for practices and impromptu performances. The Cardinal also maintained a larger theater seating 600 at the Palais Cardinal. However, the grandeur of this theater's spectacle was limited by its size. Moreover, neither theater was equipped like the *salle* to signify the political stature of its patron.

primary spectacle. The *Gazette de France* indicates that the audience was noticeably engrossed by "un si magnifique théâtre." [6]

Blondel's Plan du Palais Royal (Figure 1) depicts the auditorium, which was sixty feet wide and seventy feet long, excluding the stage area of similar dimensions. Although Blondel's drawing is a plan for the modification of the Salle de la Comédie undertaken in the 1670s,[7] the dimensions of both the *salle* and the stage area remained comparable after renovation. However, *Le Soir* by Michel van Lochon (Figure 2)[8] suggests that, in 1641, the auditorium was distinctly rectangular, as opposed to the rounded lines in Blondel's etching.[9] *Le Soir* also depicts the raised stage at one end that was flanked by "two rows of gilded boxes, one above the other, on either side." [10] Although van Lochon's engraving shows an open *parterre,* there was a striking *amphithéâtre* of twenty-seven tiers in the center of the hall. Henri Sauval wrote that the *amphithéâtre,* accounted for in Blondel's plan, was made of stone steps which were $5\frac{1}{2}$ inches high and 23 inches deep.[11] Their total depth, as calculated by T. E. Lawrenson was $51\frac{3}{4}$ feet.[12] Consequently, this structure occupied most of the hall. When movable benches for spectators were placed on these steps, the Salle de la Comédie boasted a rectangular auditorium that provided a strong contrast to the unruly *parterre* of the public theater. In reference to van Lochon's engraving, I am inclined to agree with Lawrenson that "the *Le Soir* engraver has suppressed the amphitheatre to show his royalty (and the stage) or that it refers to a performance before its installation." [13] Supporting the first premise, W. Deierkauf-Holsboer asserts that "dans un parterre vide, l'artiste a mieux dis-

6. Cited by Agne Beijer in "Une Maquette de décor récemment retrouvée pour le 'Ballet de la Prospérité des armes De France,'" in *Le Lieu théâtral à la Renaissance,* ed. Jean Jacquot (Paris, 1964), p. 378.

7. Lawrenson, pp. 172–173.

8. Beijer suggests that this engraving, which he attributes to van Lochon, is modeled after the sketch "Intérieur du Théâtre du Palais Cardinal" (Musée des Arts Décoratifs, Paris) (Fig. 5 in Beijer).

9. Lawrenson, pp. 172–173.

10. Henry C. Lancaster, *A History of French Dramatic Literature in the Seventeenth Century,* Part II, V.II (Baltimore, 1932), p. 20.

11. Sauval, p. 162.

12. Lawrenson, p. 171.

13. *Ibid.*

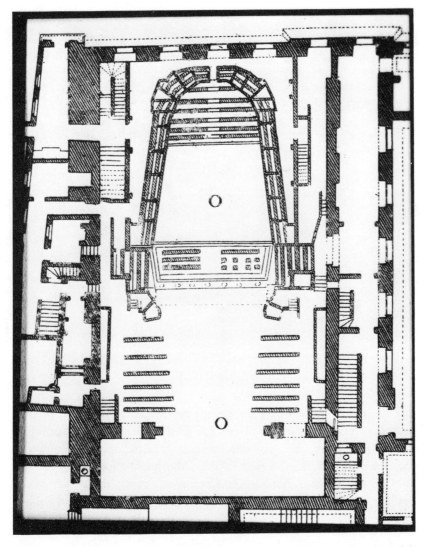

FIGURE 1. Plan of the *Salle de la Comédie* included in Blondel's Plan du Palais Royal (*Architecture française, 1754*). Courtesy of the Library of Congress.

FIGURE 2. *Le Soir* by Michel van Lochon. Courtesy of the Bibliothèque Nationale, Cabinet des Estampes, Paris.

posé de la place nécessaire pour son groupe de personnages."[14] Even if *Le Soir* emphasizes the central position of the prince at the expense of architectural verity, the *amphithéâtre* itself, whether installed before or after the opening night, served to stress the hierarchical setting of the Salle de la Comédie. Because, as Lawrenson insists, the *amphithéâtre* was not amphitheatrical in the general sense of the term—everything points to straight rows of steps rising backward—the hierarchy of seating and perspective was accented. Richelieu was also careful to adorn his meticulously planned auditorium with "majesteux ornamens." An arcade of three arches, painted in *trompe-l'oeil,* was directly behind the *amphithéâtre.* In addition, the roof beams were "poutres de chêne d'une longueur si extraordinaire & si prodigieuse," that they too were intrinsic features

14. Wilma Deierkauf-Holsboer, *L'Histoire de la mise en scène dans le théâtre français à Paris de 1600 à 1673* (Paris, 1960), p. 30.

of the opening-night spectacle.[15] The Salle de la Comédie, whose seating was ordered hierarchically, and whose decorations shared the elegance of baroque scenery, marked the beginning of an aristocratic trend away from the French public theater toward the grandeur of the court auditorium.

As an architectural addition to the Palais Cardinal, the Salle de la Comédie was presented to its first audience as a reflection of Richelieu in his domestic surroundings. On the opening night, Richelieu, the person responsible for the conception of this theater, whom we might as well call its author, showed off an interior of such grandeur and architectural harmony that it would have equaled the *grande salle* of any court. That such an association might have been made is assured by the seventeenth-century custom that transformed royal halls into temporary theaters. In fact, we can take this analogy one step further. Like any courtly domain, the Salle de la Comédie exhibited important people as well as "majesteux ornamens": for Richelieu, an essential element of serious drama was the careful construction of an audience. He not only planned the theater, but he also hand-picked the spectators. An account of this selection is provided by the *Memoires de Michel de Marolles:*

On n'y entroit que par billets, & ces billets n'étoient donnés qu'à ceux qui se trouverent marqués sur le Mémoire de son Eminence, chacun selon sa condition; car il y en avoit pour les Dames, pour les Seigneurs, pour les Ambassadeurs, pour les Etrangers, pour les Prélats, pour les Officiers de la Justice & pour les Gens de guerre.[16]

Such attention was given to the constitution of this premier audience that:

Les généraux Jean de Werth, Enkenfort et Dom Pedro de Léon, prisonniers de guerre, en eurent leur part, y ayant été conduits du bois de Vincennes.[17]

The theatrical presentation of both war captives and esteemed courtly personages is a sure referent to the mind behind the military and domestic strategies of France. The author of this spectacle, "son Eminence," combined orderly scenery with a well-mannered, highly significative

15. Sauval, p. 163.

16. Michel de Marolles, *Memoires* (Amsterdam, 1755), I, 236.

17. *Gazette,* 19 January 1641, cited by Léopold Lacour, *Richelieu dramaturge et ses collaborateurs* (Paris, 1925), p. 115.

audience. Of course, this synthesis was best appreciated by its author, now become spectator.

What Richelieu observed was an audience arranged in a similar order to the way they would be seated at court. The placement of his spectators was in fact indicative of their social position. The higher one's rank, the closer one sat to the monarch. Just as at court, Louis XIII, accompanied by Anne of Austria, shared the place of honor with Richelieu. The audience surrounding the court is here transformed into a "living and visible emblem of the aristocratic hierarchy."[18] The spectator is spectacle.

Yet, if we look again at the seating plan, it becomes apparent that the invited spectators are not the real spectacle, but only supporting players. The visual and verbal center of the hall belongs to the *"échafaud"* on which sat Richelieu, the king, and the queen. If there was an *amphithéâtre* on the opening night, the dais must have been placed at its center. If the *amphithéâtre* had not yet been built, the dais was positioned in the middle of the *parterre*. The dais must also have been equal in height with the raised stage so that the scenic perspective could achieve its full effect. In this position, the central party would have been the focus of visual attention from all sides. Consequently, the *échafaud* established the royal trio as players in the theater. A seventeenth-century definition of *théâtre* gives added force to this relationship: "un lieu élevé par degrez, un échafaut orné pour faire quelques ceremonies."[19] It might be said that the traditional platform used in the medieval and Renaissance ceremonies surrounding royal entries found a place in the Salle de la Comédie. Richelieu and his party were isolated on the royal scaffold. They were the primary company of players for this opening-night spectacle. Figure 3 also shows that this *échafaud* was centered in front of a proscenium arch, as it would have been in a royal entry. The medieval arch repeats its function as "a completely undifferentiated . . . form in which spectator and spectacle are integrated."[20] It should be stressed, however, that the centering activity no longer takes place *within* the proscenium arch. Whereas the arch once integrated spectacle and spectator by means of

18. Stephen Orgel, "The Poetics of Spectacle," *NLH*, II, no. 3 (1971), 378. Orgel uses this terminology to describe the same occurrence in the court theater of Inigo Jones.

19. Furetière, vol. IV; s.v. "théâtre."

20. Lawrenson, p. 138.

the monarch's position within it, this integration took place in the Renaissance theater by means of the monarch's position in relation to the stage's perspective as defined by the arch.

As in a royal entry, the princes were surrounded on all sides by their spectacular spectator-subjects. Being the actors in a theater-in-the-round, Richelieu and his royal guests had placed themselves at the center of attention. The over-all focus of vision and language associated with the opening of the theater moves from *spectacle* (architectonic equipment) to *spectator and spectacle* (the guests and their overpowering signification as subjects of the monarch) to the *royal players, spectators, and spectacle.* The first viewing of Richelieu's theater culminates in a mimetic vision of monarchical centralization. The theater of the Palais Cardinal is a mirror of the Cardinal's hierarchical society.

But what of the play, the tragicomedy *Mirame?* What happened when the theatrical production moved the viewer's attention from the royalty in the center of the *salle* to the drama at one end? Did Desmarets abruptly take from the Cardinal his rightful role as author? If this was so, the players of *Mirame* would have been the primary participants in the theatrical spectacle. The probability of an abrupt change of focus is further suggested by the presence of a proscenium-arch curtain: if, as Wiley asserts, this was indeed the first proscenium-arch curtain in Paris, it would have marked a significant boundary between stage and *salle,* and its opening would have commanded the attention of all spectators.[21]

Still, any contrast challenging the centrality of Richelieu's spectacle must be carefully viewed within the context of the entire event, the opening of the Salle de la Comédie. The inscription on the proscenium arch curtain, as recorded by Stefano della Bella (Figure 3), suggests that the "OUVERTURE du Theatre DE LA GRANDE SALLE" is the central event of the evening. We have already seen that the *ouverture,* as spectacle, provides an exciting example of theater as mirror. The lower position of "MIRAME Tragicomedie" (Figure 3) suggests that any dramatic activity ought to be understood as a subordinate part of the *ouverture.* Furthermore, della Bella's engraving shows that even the actors could not refrain from opening the drawn curtain in order to view the main event on the *par-*

21. W. L. Wiley, *The Early Public Theatre in France* (Cambridge, Mass., 1960), p. 198.

terre. If we are to discuss *Mirame* as something in contrast to, and yet a subordinate part of the *ouverture,* it can be understood as a play within a play. As a fictive extension of the activity in the *salle, Mirame* both challenges and enhances Richelieu's centrality of place, authorship, and action.

FIGURE 3. Proscenium arch curtain for *Mirame,* in the Salle de la Comédie, 14 January 1641. Engraving by Stefano della Bella in *Mirame* (Paris, 1641). Courtesy of the Prints Division, The New York Public Library—Astor, Lenox and Tilden Foundations.

It might still be suggested, however, that with the opening of the proscenium-arch curtain, the royal theater ceased to be a theater-in-the-round. But, on the contrary, the revealed stage area completed a missing fourth side of the *salle.* The length and grandeur of either the *amphi-théâtre,* or the *parterre,* were balanced by a carefully decorated stage area. Among other elements, an equal distribution of light in all parts of the theater, which "n'était éclairé que sobrement," [22] contributed to a uniform

22. Deierkauf-Holsboer, p. 76.

atmosphere of theatrical enchantment. What Agne Beijer calls "l'unité architectonique de la scène et de la salle" extended the saturation of theatrical intensity from the *salle* to the stage.[23]

Nor was it the case that Desmarets stole the authorial limelight from Richelieu. Just as he did with Lemercier, the architect of the Salle de la Comédie, Richelieu presented Desmarets with "une partie du sujet & des pensées de *Mirame*."[24] The playwright explicitly carried out his master's wishes. Richelieu's intentions in employing Desmarets are recorded by Paul Pellison-Fontanier:

Il [le Cardinal] pria encore Monsieur des Marests de luy en faire tous les ans une semblable [travaille pour le théâtre]. Et lors qu'il pensoit s'en excuser sur le travail de son Poëme heroïque de Clovis, dont il avoit déja fait deux livres, & qui regardoit la gloire de la France, & celle du Cardinal mesme; le Cardinal répondoit qu'il aymoit mieux jouîr des fruits de sa Poësie; autant qu'il seroit possible, & que ne croyant pas vivre assez long-temps pour voir la fin d'un si long ouvrage, il le conjuroit de s'occuper pour l'amour de luy, à des pieces de Theatre.[25]

Desmarets abandoned the authorship of his epic for the sake of becoming the Cardinal's dramatic scribe. Through Desmarets's transcription, Richelieu could see the fruits of his glory acted out on stage. A dramatization of the Cardinal's social stature was exactly what *Mirame* presented. As a play within a play, or, as a mirror of the "OUVERTURE du Theatre," *Mirame* was an "imitation des actions humaines" of the *grande salle*. The resulting instruction clarified Richelieu's role in the theater of France.

Mirame reiterated the central themes of any play sponsored by Richelieu: family honor, patriotism, and the monarchical principle.[26]

23. Beijer, p. 400.

24. Paul Pellison-Fontanier, *Relation contenant L'histoire de L'Academie Françoise* (Paris, 1653), p. 178.

25. *Ibid.*, p. 177.

26. Lancaster, Part II, V. II, p. 764, adds that "the prevailing political views expressed in the plays [of Corneille's time] are those of Richelieu." Mirame is aptly summarized by Lancaster, Part II, V. II, p. 377:

Arimant, favorite of the King of Colchose, makes war upon the King of Bithynia in order to win his daughter, Mirame, who had fallen in love with him when he had come to ask her hand for the Prince of Colchos, now dead. Mirame's *confidente* Almire, arranges a rendezvous for Arimant at night in the garden by the sea. There, reassured

However, as Lancaster and Lacour note, the strength of the plot is dissipated by numerous flaws. The hero Arimant, for instance, dominates but two scenes of the entire play, and fails to make an appearance in the final two acts. The plot is also weakened by the dialogue's *"préciosité"* and by many unconvincing *coups de théâtre,* such as three unsuccessful suicides, or Mirame's conflicting pledges to both Arimant and Azamor. Although she assures Arimant that his absence will not move her toward Azamor—"Il est mon ennemy; suiuray-je son conseil?"—she nullifies the pledge by her promise to Azamor: "Prince, ie n'auray point d'autre mary que vous." [27] Furthermore, Lancaster contends that "the scenes are not all linked and the unity of action is violated by the introduction of superfluous scenes and by a *deus ex machina* in the person of the ambassador from Colchos." [28] Doubtless, verisimilitude did not contribute to the success of *Mirame*. On the contrary, the play's very lack of verisimilitude, its disjointedness, and its shallow characters could be seen as a frame through which Richelieu's splendor was reflected. Whether in the playhouse or in Louis XIII's court, the Cardinal was quite accustomed to entertaining chaotic episodes for the purpose of making a final entry as the *deus ex machina* who could stabilize anything. [29] Furthermore, the play's emphasis on dramatic action and mechanical spectacle diminishes

---

of Mirame's love, he gets permission to carry on the war, provided he does not cause her father's death, but in the battle that follows he is defeated and, while trying to swim to safety, is captured by Azamor, King of Phrygia, also a lover of Mirame. After another meeting with Arimant, Mirame, hearing that he has had himself killed by a slave, decides to take poison. Her death and that of Almire are reported to the King of Bithynia. Azamor, in despair, is also contemplating suicide when Almire discovers that the draught she had shared with the princess is only a sleeping-potion. It is then learned that Arimant had been only slightly wounded. His fainting had been misinterpreted. An ambassador from the King of Colchos declares that Arimant is the brother of Azamor, who is so much moved by this information that he withdraws his request for Mirame, while the latter's father, perceiving that, since Arimant is Azamor's brother, he is of sufficiently high birth to marry her, makes no further objection to the match.

27. Jean Desmarets de Saint Sorlin, *Mirame* (Paris, 1639). See Act III, scene v, pp. 51–53; Act IV, scene ii, p. 65. As the publication date indicates, the play was commissioned and published prior to its inaugural year of 1641.

28. Lancaster, Part II, V.II, p. 378. A prime example of a superfluous scene is Act III, scene vi (*Mirame*, pp. 54–55) which consists of a mere nine lines, more fitting as the conclusion of scene v.

29. Refer to Carl Burckhardt's discussion of Richelieu's use of contrived chaos for his rise to power: *Richelieu: His Rise to Power* (New York, 1964).

the power of its poetic language. Michel de Marolles complained that "cette piece ne réussit pas si bien que quelques autres de celui qui l'avoit composée ausquelles on n'avoit pas apporté tant d'appareil." [30] However, this sort of mechanical heightening was typical of the schemes which Richelieu would employ to enhance his power, and his commission to the playwright must have reflected his self-conscious position.

The use of machinery in the Renaissance theater always signified the lavishness of the play's benefactor. As Sebastiano Serlio proclaimed:

The more such things cost, the more they are esteemed, for they are things which stately and great persons doe, which are enemies to niggardlinesse. This have I seene in some Scenes made by Ieronimo Genga, for the pleasure & delight of his lord and patron Francisco Maria, Duke of Urbin: wherein I saw so great liberalitie used by the Prince, & so good a conceit in the workeman, & so good Art & proportion in things therein represented, as ever I saw in all my life before. Oh good Lord, what magnificence was there to be seene. [31]

Mirame was above all a magnificent spectacle of theatrical machines. The audience, according to Marolles, marveled at "des machines qui faisoient lever le Soleil & la Lune, & paroître la Mer dans l'éloignement, chargée de Vaisseaux." [32] The *Gazette* gives a more elaborate description of the spectacle

dont la perspective apportât plus de ravissement aux yeux des spectateurs . . . de fort délicieux jardins, ornés de grottes, de statues, de fontaines et de grands parterres en terrasses sur la mer [see Figure 4], avec des agitations, qui semblaient naturelles, aux vagues de ce vaste élément, et deux grandes flottes, dont l'une paraissait éloignée de deux lieues, qui passèrent toutes

---

30. Marolles, p. 237. It is interesting to note that this tendency to subordinate poetry to spectacle was also common in seventeenth-century Italy. Louise Clubb provides a marvelous example of the dramatic text which "was often only a pretext for spectacle": "The depth to which the literary part of drama could fall is sounded by Coppola's pathetic explanation that he wrote *Le nozze degli Dei* (1637) in haste because the Duke of Florence suddenly ordered a spectacle of heaven, hell, and the seas, and that in performance the text had been abridged to suit the demand of music and machinery." *Italian Plays (1500–1700) in the Folger Library* (Florence, 1968), p. xxxvi.

31. Sebastiano Serlio, *The first [-fifth] Booke of Architecture* (London, 1611), chap. 3, fol. 26.

32. Marolles, pp. 235–236.

deux à la vue des spectateurs. La nuit sembla arriver ensuite par l'obscurcis-
sement imperceptible tant du jardin que de la mer et du ciel qui se trouva
éclairé de la lune.[33]

Pellison-Fontanier suggests that Richelieu "fit bastir cette grande sale
de son Palais" mainly to facilitate the production of such extravagant
spectacles.[34] Like the construction of the *salle*, *Mirame's* scenic displays,
"dont la representation luy cousta deux ou trois cents mille escus,"[35]
constituted what Stephen Orgel calls "a prime instance of royal liberality,
exemplifying the princely virtue of magnificence."[36]

The centrality of the prince is mirrored not only by elaborate machinery, but also by an exaggeration of perspective. Figures 4 and 5 show
the setting for *Mirame*. Lawrenson points out that only two wings were
used "so that the perspective must have been a sharply fleeing one to
give the necessary effect of distance."[37] The viewer could only enjoy
perfect perspective from a "single fixed eyepoint" in the hall.[38] The
proscenium arch bordered the vanishing point and the center point of
perfect vision in the Salle de la Comédie. As we have already ascertained,
the royal *échafaud*, positioned in the center of the *salle*, was centered by
the proscenium arch. Only the royal party had a perfect perspective of
Mirame. Because the spectators' position, in relation to the prince, established the clarity of their perspective, the play within the play enhanced
the audience as emblems of hierarchical order. For these viewers with
imperfect vision, the theatrical experience of *Mirame* was directed away
from the stage toward the one point in the *salle* from which the perspective achieved its greatest effect.[39] Richelieu and his party remained the
center of attention throughout *Mirame*.

---

33. Lancaster, Part II, V. II, p. 376. These scenic devices are illustrated in a
series of engravings by della Bella which depict a scene from each act of *Mirame*.
Originally appearing as illustrations in the 1641 edition of *Mirame,* the engravings
are reproduced in: Alexandre de Vesme and Phyllis Dearborn Massar, *Stefano
della Bella* (New York, 1971), Prints #937–941, pp. 200–202.

34. Pellison-Fontanier, p. 178.

35. *Ibid.*

36. Stephen Orgel, *The Illusion of Power* (Berkeley, Calif., 1975), p. 37.

37. Lawrenson, p. 128.

38. George Kernodle, *From Art to Theatre* (Berkeley, Calif., 1944), p. 178.

39. Orgel, "The Poetics of Spectacle," p. 378.

FIGURE 4. Pen and ink of elaborate scenery for *Mirame*, by Stefano della Bella. Louvre, Collection Edmund de Rothschild. Courtesy of Cliché Musées Nationaux, Paris.

FIGURE 5. Decor of *Mirame*, Act III. Engraving by Stefano della Bella in *Mirame* (Paris, 1641). Courtesy of the Prints Division, The New York Public Library—Astor, Lenox and Tilden Foundations.

The success of a play within a play always depends upon the under-standing of those performers viewing it. In a play with perspective set-tings, the spectator with the best vision is ultimately responsible for a clear interpretation of the work. Especially for a production that mixes histrionics with mechanical spectacle, the interpreter needs to exercise what Roland Barthes describes as *"ecumenical perception of sensuous artifice*—gesture, tone, distance, substance, light—which submerges the text beneath the profusion of its external language." [40] With the aid of ecumenical perception, the viewer could recognize *Mirame* in all of its diverse and disparate elements to be a model of the universe.[41] The suc-cess of *Mirame* depended on Richelieu's imaginative powers to see his own cultural setting in terms of the dramatic model of the universe.

Mirame, however, did not limit itself to the presentation of a realistic model. Disparity and a lack of verisimilitude were emphasized for the sake of exaggerating the dramatic role of a *deus ex machina.* No such figure was in fact to be found in early seventeenth-century France. Al-though Richelieu was the creator and controller of the opening night at the Palais Cardinal, he was far from maintaining absolute control over the many crises that beset his age. The role of drama, then, was to bolster the image of the fallible prince by imitating an ideal world. As an "illu-sion of power," *Mirame* is not necessarily a reflection of Richelieu's actual position in society, but a mirroring of the way he wished to see himself.

If *Mirame* is but a private illusion of power, how did its audience respond to a production so incoherent to a larger public? The reception of the play within the play was an important moment in the larger spectacle of the *ouverture.* A poor viewer's response to Richelieu's dra-matic creation for which "il témoigna des tendresses de père" [42] would have cast a pall over the entire event. In fact, accounts of the reactions to *Mirame* indicate that the play was not appreciated as a successful work of art. Campion, an agent of the Count of Soissons, wrote: "J'y trouve

40. Roland Barthes, "Baudelaire's Theater," *Critical Essays,* trans. Richard Howard (Evanston, Ill., 1972), p. 26.

41. Orgel, in *The Illusion of Power,* p. 47, maintains that all courtly masques presented a model of the universe which was brought under control by its viewer.

42. Pellision-Fontanier, p. 178.

quantité de defauts qu'il faudroit estre bien hardy pour publier icy."[43] The private diaries of two viewers also expressed dissatisfaction with the performance. The Abbé Arnauld shared "peu d'estime qu'on fit de cette pièce."[44] More specifically, Michel de Marolles took the machinery to task for cheapening the dialogue:

je n'en trouvai pas l'action beaucoup meilleure pour toutes ces belles ma-chines, & grandes perspectives. Les yeux se lassent bientôt de cela, & l'esprit de ceux qui s'y connoissent, n'en n'est guere plus satisfait.[45]

Marolles lamented a general lack of the verisimilitude which the Acad-emy proclaimed to be the primary ingredient of an effective play.

In contrast to these critiques, entered in the privacy of their authors' boudoirs, the *Gazette* of 19 January 1641, printed nothing but grandilo-quent praise for *Mirame:*

Le soir de 14° de ce mois fut représentée dans l'Hostel de Richelieu une pièce de théâtre composée par le Sr Desmarets, esprit poli & fertile tout en-semble: laquelle n'a point eu sa pareille de nostre aage, si vous la considerez dans toute son estendue. Le sujet en estoit excellent, qui fut traité avec une telle abondance de pensées délicates, fortes et sublimes, qu'il seroit mal-aisé de trouver dans tout l'amas des plus belles tragédies de l'antiquité, les rais-sonemens qui sont dans cette seule pièce.[46]

Alas, the *Gazette's* account of *Mirame* is most flattering. But how can anyone seriously entertain a suggestion that Desmarets's meager attempt at tragicomedy surpassed "tout l'amas des plus belles tragédies"? And how was it possible for an audience lacking perspective to appreciate the wholeness of a markedly fragmented performance?

Dramatic unity, or wholeness, was understood to depend on the *vraysemblance* of the production. The conceptual significance of *vray-semblance* is made clear in *La Pratique du Théâtre,* where d'Aubignac delineates the qualities of *vraysemblance* by comparing dramaturgy and

43. Tallemant des Reaux, *Les Historiettes,* V.II, eds. MM. de Monmerqué and Paulin Paris (Paris, 1854), p. 82.

44. Cited by Lacour, p. 116.

45. Marolles, p. 236.

46. Cited by Beijer, p. 378.

painting.[47] Both of these arts, says d'Aubignac, are intent on the production of an *image,* or a series of images which predicate a certain quality of vision. The image must be capable of maintaining a stability and consistency in all aspects of its animation. This prerequisite seems to negate the verisimilar validity of either the *coup de théâtre* or other disrupting, noncausal dramatic events. D'Aubignac suggested that *vraysemblance* is best achieved in theater through the presentation of a dramatic *coup d'oeil.* As in art, superfluous action and dialogue should be minimized "afin que d'un seul regard on pût avoir une suffisante connoissance de tout ce qu'il auroit voulu dépeindre." [48] A view of a single tableau or any part of a dramatic performance should call to mind and even foreshadow the whole. Marolles registered his frustration with *Mirame* because its machinery, "pour tromper la vue," discouraged any lasting *coup d'oeil.* The play's superfluous scenes and ineffective *coups de théâtre* contributed to a disjointed viewing. Indeed, Richelieu was probably the only spectator who could possibly have imagined a sustained *coup d'oeil* throughout *Mirame.* As author, he was familiar with the disjointed plot. He could perform a mental unification of the plot so that it might portray "the dramatic illusion of causal necessity on which conviction of unity depended." [49] In addition, Richelieu benefited from sitting at the point of perfect perspective. Only he could imaginatively unify both the visual and verbal inconsistencies of his play within a play.

The audience partook of an entirely different vision of verisimilitude. The lines of perspective directed the audience's attention to a tableau in which "le lieu où paroist un Acteur, soit l'image de celuy où lors agissoit le Personnage qu'il represente." [50] As *Le Soir* illustrates (Figure 2) the image and the character seen in this tableau was Richelieu himself watching *Mirame.* Although the clarity of the vision varied with one's

47. My discussion is informed by Michael Fried's article, "Toward a Supreme Fiction: Genre and Beholder in the Art Criticism of Diderot and His Contemporaries," *NLH,* V (Spring 1975), 543–585. In most cases, his discussion of Diderot's approach to painting and dramaturgy directly pertains to d'Aubignac's text.

48. L'Abbé d'Aubignac, *La Pratique du Théâtre* (Paris, 1927), pp. 83–84.

49. Fried, p. 569.

50. d'Aubignac, p. 100.

seating in the theater, all angles reflected a dramatic *vraysemblance*
which fulfilled d'Aubignac's formula. Being isolated on the platform,
Richelieu and his party exemplified the unities of place and time. Firsthand descriptions of Richelieu indicated that his actions during the play
contributed to this ideal dramatic tableau. By appearing satisfied with
the performance, Richelieu was careful "de ne rien montrer de tout ce
qu'on doit ignorer, et qui peut choquer." [51] The Cardinal played his part
well by seeming to have appreciated *Mirame* as a mirror of himself. His
performance was recorded by Campion:

je me suis trouvé assis près de Monsieur le Cardinal, qui avait tant d'attention
au récit de sa comédie qu'il ne pensait qu'à s'admirer soi-même en son propre
ouvrage.[52]

This indicates that Campion responded to the play within the play as a
true courtier should. He saw it as a device through the viewing of
which Richelieu might portray an image of himself, the prince.

Any princely tableau in Renaissance France would have been received
by its spectators in the context of this seventeenth-century definition of
mirror:

ce qui nous represente quelque chose, ou qui la met comme devant nos
yeux. C'est un *miroir* de vertu, un *miroir* de patience.[53]

Richelieu's carefully controlled visage imitated his courtly image as the
guardian of virtue and stability—an idealized image which *Mirame*
exaggerated by spectacle. The *Gazette's* praise of *Mirame* rests on a
statement of qualification, "si vous la considerez dans toute son estendue."
This excerpt instructs us to consider the play in terms of the circumstances of its performance. The courtly audience accepted the play for
its mirroring of Richelieu.

The nature of the audience's applause following *Mirame* indicates that
the play within the play was "instructif au public par la seule connoissance des choses representées." [54] Instead of giving recognition to Desmarets, who was the recipient of "un silence de glace, un ennui calculé," [55]

51. *Ibid.*, p. 38.
52. Cited by Lacour, p. 116.
53. Furetière, vol. III; *s.v.* "miroir."
54. d'Aubignac, p. 319.
55. Campion, as cited by Lacour, p. 116.

the audience responded warmly to Richelieu—the actor, author and audience. It appears that they recognized his tableau of virtue, harmony, and centralization of the monarchy. Fontanelle wrote that

les applaudissements qu'on donnait à cette pièce, ou plutôt à celui que l'on savait qui y prenait beaucoup d'intérét, transportaient le cardinal hors de lui.[56]

As if to take advantage of a captive audience, Richelieu then exaggerated his acting in the presentation of a dramatic epilogue:

il se levait et se tirait à moitié corps hors de sa loge pour se montrer à l'assemblée, tantôt il imposait silence pour faire entendre des endroits [passages] encore plus beaux.[57]

Richelieu may have terminated the play within the play by clarifying its meaning for the Campions and the Marolles who were not willing to appreciate the beauty and significance of his production. Even though the exact words of this speech are not known, the act of Richelieu's poetic delivery is significant in itself. By presenting this captivating monologue concerning the play—the poetic epilogue lacking in *Mirame* —the Cardinal was once again the sole focal point of the spectacle.

"Dans toute son estendue," from dramatic spectacle to princely tableau and epilogue, *Mirame* proved to be an impressive production of *vraysemblance;* the sustained *coup d'oeil,* the Cardinal de Richelieu. In both the *ouverture* of the *salle* and the production of *Mirame,* Richelieu achieved what d'Aubignac calls "les moyens de reüssir dans l'estime des Spectateurs, qu'il a seulement lors en l'Esprit." [58] The Cardinal made successful use of the theater as a mirror of his political power. In fact, the political resonance of Richelieu's tableau was indicated by Campion:

Il s'intéresse plus en l'honneur de cette pièce qu'il n'a jamais fait à l'événement de toutes les campagnes passées.[59]

More than any military campaign, theater-in-the-round at the Palais Cardinal was capable of generating the *trompe-l'oeil* best significative of Richelieu's princely virtue. The Salle de la Comédie was built in order

56. Cited by Lacour, p. 115.
57. *Ibid.,* pp. 115–116.
58. d'Aubignac, p. 38.
59. Cited by Lacour, p. 116.

to bolster Richelieu's image as the nucleus of monarchical order and harmony.

But what was the position of Louis XIII in this spectacle? Why has the king not been shown to be the ultimate referent of monarchical order? After all, he and Anne of Austria joined Richelieu in the honor of sharing the *échafaud* and its perfect perspective. Still, Richelieu remained the sole creator of the playhouse, the spectacle, and the play within the play. In all cases, perfect mental unification depended on the Cardinal alone. But most important, Richelieu maintained a dominant position in his theater and society only because of Louis XIII's attitude toward theater in general. First, the king was not sensitive to the political power derived from the dramatic spectacle. For instance, on the opening night of Richelieu's theater, Louis "se retira aussitôt que la Comédie fut finie." [60] He did not stay for what will presently be shown to be the most symbolic spectacle of the evening: the royal ball. Lacour has suggested that the king's departure might be attributed to his favorite pastime, hunting. [61] His love for carefree activities placed Louis in an alternate world of *théâtre* which is suggested by Furetière in the following manner:

Le plaisir d'un Roi, est de l'être quelquefois moins; de sortir du *théâtre,* & de jouër un rôle plus familier. [62]

Louis's disdain for the theater of Richelieu and for its polite society allowed him to enjoy the more entertaining public theater at the Hôtel de Bourgogne. His penchant for comedy, farce, and the disorder accompanying them was mirrored by his political concerns and activities. And, in contrast to Richelieu who catered to the serious actors of tragedy at the Théâtre du Marais, Louis adopted the Bourgogne's "plus familier" players of farce to be his *comédiens du roi.* [63] Nor was the king himself lacking in theatrical talent. His inability to direct ordered events, not to mention his insensitivity to Richelieu's theatrical feigning of order, must have resulted in his being "un Roi de théâtre." Such a *Roi* was, as Furetière informs us,

60. Marolles, p. 237.
61. Lacour, p. 137.
62. Furetière, vol. IV; *s.v.* "théâtre."
63. Please refer to n. 9.

un Prince qui laisse gouverner absolument son Etat par ses Ministres; qui n'a la representation d'un Roi, & qui ne regne point par lui-même.[64]

Indeed, it was Richelieu who, with the aid of theatrical ruses, produced and directed Louis's histrionic appearances as king.

A striking tableau of the actual political structure of the French monarchy was presented as the final event of the OUVERTURE *de la Grande Salle.* The setting for the ball following *Mirame* was the most subtle piece of theatrical propaganda contrived by the Cardinal for his opening night. With the termination of *Mirame,* the proscenium-arch curtain was closed. Attention was given to Richelieu and the queen who were imbibing the pleasures of "vingt bassins de vermeil doré, chargés de citrons doux & de confitures."[65] Next, the sudden opening of the curtain revealed:

une grande salle en perspective, dorée et enrichie des plus magnifiques ornements, éclairée de *seize chandeliers* de cristal, au fond de laquelle étaient un trône pour la Reine . . . tout ce meuble de gris de lin et argent.[66]

The disclosure of this scene destroyed the architectonic unity that had previously connected the *salle* and the stage. All eyes now move from the main hall which "n'était éclairé que sobrement" to a higher, brightly illuminated area more rich in ornaments, linen, and gold.[67] Momentarily, the main hall of the theater-in-the-round would be abandoned for a more picturesque and more exclusive scene of grandeur.

On a gilded bridge, which extended from the stage to the *échafaud,* the queen and the Cardinal ceremoniously ascended, through the proscenium arch, to their distinctive, emblematically suggestive thrones. In a renewal of the royal entry tableau, the Cardinal was no longer viewed as the hero in the *center* of his court. By transcending his mundane seat of centrality, he had taken the position of a veritable god of power, the center of a universe. His audience must have been struck by the tableau described by Marolles:

64. Furetière, IV; s.v. "roi."
65. Marolles, p. 237.
66. Lacour, p. 114 (emphasis added).
67. Diderot suggested that a sudden change of illumination in one area was the perfect means for training the vision on one particular tableau. Refer to Fried.

Son Eminence, un pas derriere elle [la Reine], avoit un manteau long de tafetas couleur de feu, sur un cimarre de petite étoffe noire, aiant le colet & le rebord d'en-bas fourré d'hermine.[68]

The Cardinal's audience looked up from the *parterre* to view an image of a god, a self-proclaimed *deus ex machina* looking somewhat daemonic, who, knowing his power over sight and suggestion, symbolically maintained his subordinate position as the all-powerful counselor to the monarch. That the actual order and stability of France was mirrored by this dramatic tableau of Richelieu the demiurge is most fully validated by d'Aubignac's eulogy of the Cardinal:

Enfin la gloire et la grandeur des Spectacles ne pouvoit mieux venir que de celuy qui s'etoit rendu luy-mesme *le plus glorieux* et *le plus grand Spectacle du Monde*.[69]

By fashioning himself as the most spectacular *coup d'oeil* in this final event of the *ouverture,* Richelieu took advantage of the theater to portray the image of a leader best suited for the France of his dreams.

If Richelieu was the "plus grand spectacle" of the *ouverture,* he was also its greatest spectator. Nothing was more clear to him than his position of authority as signified by "ce bal si bien ordoné." For Armand Jean du Plessis, Cardinal de Richelieu, the opening night of his Salle de la Comédie was the supreme expression of theater as mirror. The mirror seen both by the royalty in attendance and by Richelieu himself was the same as that described by Mlle de Scudéri:

Je me suis vû en autrui, comme on se voit dans un miroir, & beaucoup mieux que je ne me voyois en moi-même.[70]

The Salle de la Comédie presented a mirror of interdependence through which the aristocracy could verify their position as Richelieu's subordinates in the French aristocratic hierarchy. Richelieu, in turn, was able to reify his role as the French surrogate monarch mirrored by his subjects, hierarchically ordered below him. Such was the political significance of the Cardinal's theater—the mirror of a prince.

68. Marolles, p. 237.
69. d'Aubignac, pp. 16–17 (emphasis added).
70. Furetière, vol. III.

Notes on Contributors

CEDRIC C. BROWN is Lecturer in English in the University of Reading, England. He has been at work for a number of years on a book on Milton's theatrical entertainments and is currently editing a new edition of the poems and masques of Aurelian Townshend.

JEFFREY FISCHER, who studied English at Yale, teaches remedial English and math at the Vocational Improvement Program at Hillhouse High School in New Haven.

PAULA JOHNSON teaches in the English Department of Yale University. She is the author of *Form and Transformation in Music and Poetry of the English Renaissance,* as well as of articles in the Renaissance field and on the teaching of writing.

GORDON KIPLING is an Associate Professor of English at UCLA. His book, *The Triumph of Honour: Burgundian Origins of the Elizabethan Renaissance,* has been published this fall by the University of Leiden Press. He is preparing a book-length study of the triumph as a dramatic form.

MICHAEL McCANLES is a Professor in the Department of English, Marquette University. He is presently writing a study of Machiavelli and Sidney, a sequel to his recently published *Dialectical Criticism and Renaissance Literature* (Berkeley, 1975).

ALICE MISKIMIN, who is Senior Lecturer in English at Yale, is the author of *The Renaissance Chaucer.*

LOUIS ADRIAN MONTROSE is an Assistant Professor in the Department of Literature of The University of California, San Diego. He has published articles and a monograph on *Love's Labour's Lost,* and is currently studying the strategies of Elizabethan court literature in their social context.

TIMOTHY C. MURRAY is a teaching fellow in Comparative Literature at The Johns Hopkins University. His essays have appeared in *MLN* and *Glyph.*

BRUCE R. SMITH is an Assistant Professor of English at Georgetown University, author of an essay on Ben Jonson's collected *Epigrammes* and an essay on sixteenth-century productions of Roman comedy in *Renaissance Drama,* New Series VI (1973). He is presently at work on a book-length study of productions of Greek and Roman comedy and tragedy in Renaissance England.

JUDITH DOOLIN SPIKES is teaching English composition and building a learning-skills center at Iona College in New Rochelle, New York, raising a family in Larchmont, and working on a book-length study of the Spanish history play in the interstices.

MARY C. WILLIAMS is Professor of English at North Carolina State University, specializing in Renaissance drama and Arthurian legend. She is the author of *Unity in Ben Jonson's Early Comedies* and the editor with Guy Owen of *New Southern Poets.*